W9-BMS-188

THE JUDICIAL RECORD OF JUSTICE WILLIAM O. DOUGLAS

THE JUDICIAL RECORD OF
JUSTICE WILLIAM O. DOUGLAS

VERN COUNTRYMAN

Harvard University Press, Cambridge, Massachusetts, 1974

Library of Congress Catalog Card Number 74-76655

ISBN 0-674-48876-8

Printed in the United States of America

PREFACE

In April 1970, House minority Leader Gerald R. Ford, now Vice President by default, and Congressman Louis C. Wyman, whose only other claim on history is as a one-man Un-American Activities Committee in the state of New Hampshire while serving as its Attorney General, proposed to the House of Representatives that Justice William O. Douglas should be impeached.

Their proposal did not come as a surprise. In November 1969, while President Nixon's nomination of Clement F. Haynsworth, Jr., for appointment to the Supreme Court was encountering heavy going, and shortly before it was rejected by the Senate, Ford had publicly stated that if Haynsworth was not confirmed, Douglas should be impeached. His proposal to the House came just one week after Nixon's second nominee, G. Harrold Carswell, was also rejected.

The sorry list of charges tendered by Ford and Wyman was baseless, as a subcommittee of the House Judiciary Committee later concluded. Their real objection to Douglas, it seemed to me as it did to such others as the *Washington Post*, the *New York Times*, and the *Wall Street Journal*, was not included in their charges. They did not like his judicial record.

It seemed an appropriate time to present a comprehensive account of that record, as I have here undertaken to do. It was a formidable task. The time consumed in preparing this volume for publication was such that it covers the record only through the court term ending in June 1971. Douglas had by then served more than thirty-two years on the Court, and had contributed almost 1100 opinions to the ninety-seven volumes of the Court's reports covering that period. (On October 27, 1973, Justice Douglas surpassed Justice Stephen Field's prior record tenure of thirty-four years and 196 days.)

Obviously it is not possible in one volume to deal fully with what the Court has done in ninety-seven. Even after the cases dealing with the more technical aspects of the Court's work have been excluded, those remaining cannot receive the detailed analysis they would be given in a law school classroom or a lawyer's brief. Only an overview can be presented, but it is, I hope, an overview that will be enlightening to both the lawyer and the nonlawyer.

A *caveat* is in order. I served as law clerk to Justice Douglas thirty-one years ago and have admired him for a longer period that that. But, while my presentation of his record is sympathetic, it is also, I believe, honest.

I am indebted to Myra Karstadt, who diligently and cheerfully checked my manuscript for error, and to Gail Peto and Sally H. Littleton, who typed it.

Cambridge, Massachusetts
January 1974

CONTENTS

THE JUDICIAL RECORD OF JUSTICE WILLIAM O. DOUGLAS

INTRODUCTION

It is now more than thirty-five years since William O. Douglas was appointed to the Supreme Court of the United States to fill the vacancy created by the retirement of Mr. Justice Brandeis—an appointment which met with the latter's "supreme satisfaction."[1]

Justice Douglas brought to the bench a remarkable background.[2] The self-supporting son of an impoverished west coast family had become, as a professor of law at Columbia and Yale and later as a member and ultimately chairman of the Securities and Exchange Commission, a recognized expert on problems of business and finance. As a consequence of his boyhood in the Cascade range of Washington, he was also a devoted naturalist and conservationist. And, as a consequence of his exposure in the wheat fields of Washington to the revolutionary doctrines of the Industrial Workers of the World, he was not alarmed by inflamatory talk. Yet he was no radical. The men he most admired in public life were Gifford Pinchot, Hiram Johnson, William E. Borah—and Louis D. Brandeis, who taught that democracy works best when its

1. A. Mason, *Brandeis: A Free Man's Life* (New York: Viking, 1946), p. 635.

2. For biographical data, see W. Douglas, *Go East, Young Man: The Early Years* (New York: Random House, 1974); F. Rodell, "As Justice Bill Douglas Completes His First Thirty Years on the Court," 16 *UCLA L. Rev.* 704 (1969); J. Frank, "Justice William O. Douglas," in L. Freedman and F. Israel, *The Justices of the United States Supreme Court* (New York: Bowker, 1969), IV, 2447-2490; V. Countryman, *Douglas of the Supreme Court* (New York: Doubleday, 1959), ch. 1.

citizens are free to speak, that government exists to serve its constituents and serves them best if it is free to experiment with new ideas, and that in business those entrusted with other people's money occupy positions of trust and must be held to the highest standards of fiduciary responsibility.

For nearly a half century preceding Douglas' appointment to the Court, that body had—frequently over the dissents of Justice Holmes and later of Justices Brandeis and Cardozo—struck down as unconstitutional a broad variety of social legislation designed to regulate the economy. This it did primarily by three techniques. It gave a restrictive reading to the clause authorizing Congress to "regulate Commerce . . . among the several States"[3] so as not to permit Congress to regulate the production of goods for such commerce. At the same time it gave an expansive reading to the "negative implications" of the commerce clause so as to prevent state action even though Congress had not acted. Finally, it gave new meaning to the constitutional prohibitions against deprivation of "life, liberty, or property, without due process of law" imposed upon the national government by the Fifth Amendment and upon the states by the Fourteenth. These clauses had long been regarded as exacting only requirements of procedural fairness, but shortly after the turn of the century the Court began to find also a substantive requirement that state and federal legislation should be "reasonable."

Much of President Franklin D. Roosevelt's early New Deal legislation ran afoul of the existing constitutional interpretation, and he was inspired, early in 1937, to launch his plan to expand the size of, and thus to "pack," the Court. The effort failed, but it seemed to have effect on at least some members of the Court which, in 1937, began by close votes to find the Constitution less restrictive on both state and national governments. The margin of votes for the new constitutional interpretation increased as Justice Black replaced Justice Van Devanter and Justice Reed replaced Justice Sutherland in 1937. When Justice Frankfurter later replaced Justice Cardozo in 1938, the balance was maintained.

As Part III of this book will reveal, Justice Douglas joined the Court

3. U.S. Const., Art. I, §8, Cl. 3.

in time to contribute to the new reading of the commerce and due process clauses, and this was the aspect of the Court's work most noted at that time. But the Court that Douglas joined in 1939 had also taken another stance little remarked in the depression-laden thirties. In a series of decisions following World War I it had—again over the frequent dissents of Justices Holmes and Brandeis—sustained sedition prosecutions against antiwar and other dissidents in decisions which gave scant regard to the First Amendment's guarantees of freedom of speech and the press. During Justice Douglas' time on the Court these decisions have also undergone reexamination. And the Court's interpretation of the First Amendment and of other constitutional guarantees of political and civil liberty, the subject of Parts I and II of this book, has come to overshadow its interpretation of those constitutional provisions bearing on governmental power to regulate the economy.

It is now a commonplace that most of the dissents of Justices Holmes and Brandeis have become the law during the period of Justice Douglas' term on the Court. What is less well appreciated is that during the same period of time even more of the dissents of Justice Douglas have become the law. But all of the reversals of position have not come from other members of the Court. As Douglas has grown on the job, as experience and reflection persuade him that he himself has been in error, he has not hesitated to take a new position. This openness of mind, this capacity for growth, in addition to his remarkable ability, industry, and devotion to democratic principles, have made him one of the most effective justices on a Court that has had to deal with an increasing range of problems as our society grows more complex and the role of government increasingly more pervasive.

PART I DEMOCRATIC GOVERNMENT

1 THOSE WHO GOVERN

The Constitution allocates the powers of government among the legislative, executive, and judicial branches. And, to the end that powers conferred may be exercised effectively, it confers some protections for those who govern.

One protection for congressmen is the constitutional provision that "for any Speech or Debate in either House, they shall not be questioned in any other Place."[1] This provision was long ago held to protect members of Congress, though not the sergeant-at-arms of the House, from a damage action for false imprisonment by a witness whom the House had held in contempt for refusal to answer questions of a congressional committee, even though the Court held the committee's inquiry into the "private affairs" of a bankrupt company indebted to the United States to be invalid, as not for a proper legislative purpose.[2] Douglas has since concurred in a decision reversing the conviction of a former congressman for conspiracy to defraud the United States on the ground that part of the evidence upon which it was based consisted of a speech he had made, while in Congress, on the floor of the House.[3] He has agreed also that the speech or debate clause protects members of

1. U.S. Const., Art. I, §6, Cl. 1.
2. Kilbourn v. Thompson, 103 U.S. 168 (1880).
3. United States v. Johnson, 383 U.S. 169 (1966) (concurring and dissenting opinion).

Congress, though not congressional employees, from suits for damages based on their allegedly illegal seizure of evidence in connection with a committee hearing[4] and protects members of Congress, though not congressional employees, from declaratory judgment actions as to the legality of their conduct in excluding an elected member of the House.[5] But he dissented when the Court interpreted an 1871 federal Civil Rights Act not to authorize a damage action against a state legislative committee, whose members are not protected by the speech or debate clause in the federal Constitution, for alleged infringement of the constitutional guaranty of free speech. The plaintiff had recanted prior testimony that he had given before a California Un-American Activities Committee and publicly alleged that the committee had used him in a deliberate campaign to smear as a "Red" a candidate for public office. He had thereafter been summoned back before the committee, refused to testify, and was tried for contempt in a proceeding which ended when the jury refused to return a verdict. He then brought an action for damages against members of the committee, alleging that they had conspired to violate the Civil Rights Act, which prescribes liability for those who "under color of" law deprive others "of any rights, privileges, or immunities secured by the Constitution." The Court, assuming without deciding that Congress could impose such liability on state legislators "acting in a field where legislators traditionally have power to act," concluded that it had not intended to do so by the Civil Rights Act. "We cannot believe that Congress—itself a staunch advocate of legislative freedom—would impinge on a tradition [of similar freedom for members of the English Parliament, and for state legislators under Speech or Debate clauses in forty-one state constitutions, not including California's] so well grounded in history and reason by covert inclusion in the general language before us." It therefore approved of dismissal of plaintiff's complaint without trial. Douglas thought that the statute covered the case alleged and that the plaintiff should have been allowed to try to prove his allegations:[6]

4. Dombrowski v. Eastland, 387 U.S. 82 (1967).
5. Powell v. McCormack, 395 U.S. 486 (1969) (concurring opinion).
6. Tenney v. Brandhove, 341 U.S. 367 (1951) (dissenting opinion).

We are dealing here with a right protected by the Constitution—the right of free speech. The charge seems strained and difficult to sustain; but it is that a legislative committee brought the weight of its authority down on respondent for exercising his right of free speech. Reprisal for speaking is as much an abridgment as a prior restraint. If a committee departs so far from its domain to deprive a citizen of a right protected by the Constitution, I can think of no reason why it should be immune . . .

No other public official has complete immunity for his actions. Even a policeman who exacts a confession by force and violence can be held criminally liable under the Civil Rights Act . . . Yet now we hold that no matter the extremes to which a legislative committee may go it is not answerable to an injured party under the civil rights legislation. That result is the necessary consequence of our ruling since the test of the statute . . . is whether a constitutional right has been impaired, not whether the domain of the committee was traditional. It is one thing to give great leeway to the legislative right of speech, debate, and investigation. But when a committee perverts its power, brings down on an individual the whole weight of government for an illegal or corrupt purpose, the reason for the immunity ends. It was indeed the purpose of the civil rights legislation to secure federal rights against invasion by officers and agents of the states. I see no reason why any officer of government should be higher than the Constitution from which all rights and privileges of an office obtain.

The Constitution also provides that no person shall be a representative who is not twenty-five years old, seven years a citizen of the United States, and an inhabitant of the state in which he is elected. It further provides that each House "shall be the Judge of the Elections, Returns and Qualifications of its own Members," and that each House may "punish its Members for disorderly Behavior, and, with the Concurrence of two thirds, expel a Member."[7] When, in 1967, the House by a two-thirds vote refused to seat reelected Congressman Adam Clayton Powell, who met the age, citizenship, and residency requirements, on the ground that he had wrongfully used House funds and made false reports thereon and had acted improperly in some state court litigation, the Supreme Court declared the action invalid. This was not an instance

7. U.S. Const., Art. I, §2, Cl. 2; §5, Cls. 1 and 2.

of expelling a member, the Court held. The elected congressman had not yet been seated and the operative resolution had been framed as an "exclusion" rather than an "expulsion," the Speaker had ruled in advance of the vote on it that a majority vote would be sufficient, the conduct of Powell on which the resolution was based had occurred prior to the convening of the 90th Congress, which took the action, and the House had previously expressed doubt about its power to expel for such prior conduct. There could be no assurance, therefore, that there would have been a two-thirds vote on an expulsion resolution. Since there was no expulsion, this was simply a case of the House judging the qualifications of its own members and it was confined to those qualifications of age, citizenship, and residence specified in the Constitution. Justice Douglas concurred in this decision, adding that he would not consider the House's action subject to judicial review if it had voted either to expel or to exclude for failure to meet a qualification specified in the Constitution. But he regarded it as an infringement of the "integrity of the electoral process" to say that after his constituents had elected a congressman, the House could disenfranchise the electors by excluding him for any reason sufficient to a majority of the House.[8]

Douglas also voted with a unanimous court to hold that the Georgia House of Representatives could not exclude newly elected member Julian Bond because of statements critical of federal policy in Vietnam and of the Selective Service Law. While conceding that the state could require its legislators to take an oath to support the Constitution of the United States—which Bond was willing to take—the Court held that the state legislature could not "test the sincerity" of his oath on the basis of speech clearly protected by the First Amendment. The state's argument that it could exact a higher standard of loyalty from legislators than from other citizens was rejected: "The manifest function of the First Amendment in a representative government requires that legislators be given the widest latitude to express their views on issues of policy . . . The interest of the public in hearing all sides of a public issue is hardly advanced by extending more protection to citizen critics than to legislators. Legislators have an obligation to take positions on

8. Powell v. McCormack, note 5, *supra*.

controversial political questions so that their constituents can be fully informed by them, and be better able to assess their qualifications for office; also so they may be represented in governmental debates by the person they have elected to represent them."[9]

The Constitution provides in Article I that "All legislative Powers herein granted shall be vested in . . . Congress," that Congress shall have power to "declare War," to "raise and support Armies," to "provide and maintain a Navy," to make rules for the government and regulation "of the land and naval Forces," and to levy taxes "and provide for the common Defence."[10] It also provides in Article II that the president shall have the "executive Power," shall take "Care that the Laws be faithfully executed," shall inform Congress of the "State of the Union" and recommend legislative measures, "shall be the Commander in Chief of the Army and Navy," shall negotiate treaties and appoint ambassadors, subject to the advice and consent of the Senate, and shall receive ambassadors and other public ministers from other countries.[11] This heavy emphasis on foreign affairs has been read to mean that the president "is the sole organ of the nation in its external relations."[12]

During World War II, Congress, by the War Labor Disputes Act, authorized the president to seize production facilities necessary for the war effort whenever operation was threatened by labor disputes. Questions arising from the president's seizure of the coal mines under that act twice reached the Supreme Court without any challenge to the basic seizure authority.[13] But in 1952, during the Korean hostilities, President Truman without statutory authority seized the steel mills to avert a nationwide steel strike and indicated that if the union and the employees did not promptly settle the dispute the United States as substitute "employer" would grant a wage increase. His action was

9. Bond v. Floyd, 385 U.S. 116 (1966).

10. U.S. Const., Art. I, §1, §8, Cls. 1, 11, 12, 13, and 14.

11. *Id.*, Art. II, §1, Cl. 1; §2, Cls. 1 and 2; §3.

12. United States v. Curtiss-Wright Export Corp., 299 U.S. 304 (1936).

13. United States v. United Mine Workers, 330 U.S. 258 (1947), involving a contempt proceeding against a union for violating a restraining order against a strike in seized coal mines, and United States v. Pewee Coal Co., 341 U.S. 114 (1951), holding that the seizure constituted a taking of property under the Fifth Amendment which required compensation of the mine owners.

challenged and the Court held it illegal. Douglas concurred in that decision in an opinion which said in part:[14]

The President can act more quickly than the Congress . . . All executive power—from the reign of ancient kings to the rule of modern dictators—has the outward appearance of efficiency.

Legislative power, by contrast, is slower to exercise . . . Legislative action may indeed often be cumbersome, time-consuming, and apparently inefficient. But as Mr. Justice Brandeis stated . . . : "The doctrine of the separation of powers was adopted by the Convention of 1787 not to promote efficiency but to preclude the exercise of arbitrary power. The purpose was not to avoid friction, but, by means of the inevitable friction incident to the distribution of the governmental powers among three departments, to save the people from autocracy" . . .

If we sanctioned the present exercise of power by the President, we would be expanding Article II of the Constitution and rewriting it to suit the political conveniences of the present emergency. Article II which vests the "executive Power" in the President defines that power with particularity. [It] makes the Chief Executive the Commander in Chief of the Army and Navy. But our history and tradition rebel at the thought that the grant of military power carries with it authority over civilian affairs. [It] provides that the President shall "from time to time give to the Congress Information of the State of the Union, and recommend to their Consideration such Measures as he shall judge necessary and expedient." The power to recommend legislation, granted to the President, serves only to emphasize that it is his function to recommend and that it is the function of the Congress to legislate. Article II . . . also provides that the President "shall take Care that the Laws be faithfully executed." But . . . the power to execute the laws starts and ends with the laws Congress has enacted . . .

We pay a price for our system of checks and balances, for the distribution of power among the three branches of government. It is a price that today may seem exorbitant to many. Today a kindly President uses the seizure power to effect a wage increase and to keep the steel furnaces in production. Yet tomorrow another President might use the same power to prevent a wage increase, to curb trade-unionists, to regiment labor as oppressively as industry thinks it has been regimented by this seizure.

14. Youngstown Sheet & Tube Co., v. Sawyer, 343 U.S. 579 (1952) (concurring opinion).

During a time of declared war, Douglas voted with the Court to hold that "it was within the constitutional power of Congress and the executive arm of Government," acting together in the exercise of their war powers, to prescribe a curfew for persons of Japanese ancestry on the Pacific Coast,[15] and to exclude them from the coast,[16] although he later wrote for the Court to hold that the executive order under which the program operated did not authorize the continued incarceration of persons of conceded loyalty after their removal.[17]

During a time of declared war also, Douglas voted with the Court to hold that Congress and the president, acting jointly, could set up a military commission, subject to review in the courts in habeas corpus proceedings, to try enemy belligerents who entered this country surreptitiously for purposes of sabotage and in violation of the international law of war[18] and to try members of the enemy forces for violation of the law of war in combat zones.[19] The Court later held that it had no jurisdiction to review by habeas corpus the actions of a military tribunal set up after the termination of hostilities by the Allied powers in Japan to try Japanese government officials and military officers for alleged war crimes. Douglas disagreed on the jurisdictional point, since the defendants were in the custody of an American military officer, but concurred in the result on the ground that the president, acting in conjunction with the Allied powers and without congressional authorization, could, as the sole organ of the United States in the field of foreign relations, punish the enemy for violations of the law of war.[20] He dissented again on the jurisdictional point when the Court denied an application for habeas corpus by German nationals imprisoned by United States military officers in Germany after

15. Hirabayashi v. United States, 320 U.S. 81 (1943) (concurring opinion). Compare Douglas' dissent a quarter-century later in Stotland v. Pennsylvania, 398 U.S. 916 (1970), from the refusal of the Court to consider the constitutionality of joint action by a mayor and city council to impose a curfew as a means of riot prevention.

16. Korematsu v. United States, 323 U.S. 214 (1944).

17. *Ex parte* Endo, 323 U.S. 283 (1944).

18. *Ex parte* Quirin, 317 U.S. 1 (1942).

19. *In re* Yamashita, 327 U.S. 1 (1946); Homma v. Patterson, 327 U.S. 759 (1946).

20. Hirota v. MacArthur, 338 U.S. 197 (1948) (concurring opinion).

conviction of violations of the law of war in China by an American military tribunal set up after the end of hostilities solely by the executive branch.[21] And he voted with the Court to hold that a federal statute did not authorize the governor of the territory of Hawaii, even with presidential approval, to declare martial law during World War II and thus subject to military tribunals civilians charged with offenses which were not violations of the law of war.[22]

He voted with the Court again to invalidate a statute which would have subjected a former American serviceman, after his discharge, to trial by military court martial for crimes allegedly committed while in service in Korea—the combined military powers of the president and the Congress were not sufficient to deprive "civilian ex-soldiers who had severed all relationship with the military" of the independent federal judges, jury trials, and other procedural safeguards provided in civilian, but not in military courts.[23] But he voted with the Court to hold that the president could set up a tribunal in our postwar occupation forces in Germany which could try the wife of a member of those forces for the murder of her husband in that country.[24]

When a majority of the Court voted, however, that Congress and the president could subject wives who were overseas with husbands serving in postwar, nonoccupational military forces to trial by court martial for the murder of their husbands, he joined in dissents protesting this extension of military power at the expense of procedural safeguards.[25] One year later the Court reversed itself and adopted the dissenters' view. Even though treaties with the foreign nations concerned authorized such trials, treaties also are subject to the Constitution, which "cannot be nullified by the Executive or by the Executive and the Senate combined." And the power of Congress to make rules to govern those serving in the "land and naval Forces" could not extend to those who were not in such services. "Every extension of military

21. Johnson v. Eisentrager, 339 U.S. 763 (1950) (dissenting opinion).
22. Duncan v. Kahanamoku, 327 U.S. 304 (1946).
23. United States *ex rel.* Toth v. Quarles, 350 U.S. 11 (1955).
24. Madsen v. Kinsella, 343 U.S. 341 (1952).
25. Kinsella v. Krueger, 351 U.S. 470 (1956) (dissenting opinion); Reid v. Covert, 351 U.S. 487 (1956) (dissenting opinion).

jurisdiction is an encroachment on the jurisdiction of the civil courts, and more important, acts as a deprivation of the right to jury trial and of other treasured constitutional protections."[26]

In recent years Douglas has consistently dissented from the refusal of the Court to consider cases challenging the validity of our military operations in Vietnam and the validity of the use of the Selective Service Act to support those operations, both because Congress has not declared a state of war to exist and because of alleged violations of various treaties to which the United States is a party.[27]

The independence of the judges of the federal civil courts, to which the Court referred in deciding cases involving the jurisdiction of military courts martial, is prescribed by the Constitution. It provides that those judges "shall hold their Offices during good Behaviour," that their compensation shall not be diminished during their continuance in office,[28] and that they are subject, like other civil officers, to removal by "Impeachment for, and Conviction of, Treason, Bribery, or other high Crimes and Misdemeanors."[29] In 1966 and again in 1970, Douglas dissented from the refusal of the Court to intervene when a judicial council for one of the federal circuits, composed of the Circuit Court of Appeals judges, first took away all cases from, and later rescinded that action but barred assignment of any new cases to, a district judge whose

26. Reid v. Covert, 354 U.S. 1 (1957). A unanimous Court applied the same rule to noncapital offenses in Kinsella v. Singleton, 361 U.S. 234 (1960), and a majority, including Douglas, applied the same rule also to overseas civilian employees of the armed forces. McElroy v. United States, 361 U.S. 281 (1960); Grisham v. Hagan, 361 U.S. 278 (1960). The power of military tribunals over those in the military service, is dealt with in Chapter 5.

27. Massachusetts v. Laird, 400 U.S. 886 (1970) (dissenting opinion); McArthur v. Clifford, 393 U.S. 1002 (1968) (dissenting opinion); United States v. O'Brien, 391 U.S. 367 (1968) (dissenting opinion); Hart v. United States, 391 U.S. 956 (1968) (dissenting opinion); Mora v. McNamara, 389 U.S. 934 (1967) (dissenting opinion); Mitchell v. United States, 386 U.S. 972 (1967) (dissenting opinion). *See also* Scaggs v. Larsen, 396 U.S. 1206 (1969); Drifka v. Brainard, 89 S. Ct. 434 (1968); Morse v. Boswell, 393 U.S. 1052 (1969) (dissenting opinion); Johnson v. Powell, 393 U.S. 920 (1968) (concurring opinion); Hawthorne v. Hardaway, 393 U.S. 802 (1968) (dissenting opinion); Winters v. United States, 390 U.S. 993 (1968), on reconsideration, 391 U.S. 910 (1968).

28. U.S. Const., Art. III, §1.

29. *Id.*, Art. II, §4. Impeachment charges are filed by the House and tried by the Senate. *Id.*, Art. I, §2, Cl. 5, §3, Cl. 6.

performance the council considered unsatisfactory.[30] On the second occasion he explained his position as follows:

An independent judiciary is one of this Nation's outstanding characteristics. Once a federal judge is confirmed by the Senate and takes his oath, he is independent of every other judge. He commonly works with other federal judges who are likewise sovereign. But neither one alone nor any number banded together can act as censor and place sanctions on him. Under the Constitution the only leverage that can be asserted against him is impeachment, where pursuant to a resolution passed by the House, he is tried by the Senate, sitting as a jury . . .

What the Judicial Council did when it ordered petitioner to "take no action whatsoever in any case or proceeding now or hereafter pending" in his court was to do what only the Court of Impeachment can do. If the business of the federal courts needs administrative oversight, the flow of cases can be regulated. Some judges work more slowly than others; some cases may take months while others take hours or days. Matters of this kind may be regulated by the assignment procedure. But there is no power under our Constitution for one group of federal judges to censor or discipline any federal judge and no power to declare him inefficient and strip him of his power to act as a judge.

The mood of some federal judges is opposed to this view and they are active in attempting to make all federal judges walk in some uniform step. What has happened to petitioner is not a rare instance; it has happened to other federal judges who have had perhaps a more libertarian approach to the Bill of Rights than their brethren. The result is that the nonconformist has suffered greatly at the hands of his fellow judges.

The problem is not resolved by saying that only judicial administrative matters are involved. The power to keep a particular judge from sitting on a racial case, a church-and-state case, a free-press case, a search-and-seizure case, a railroad case, an antitrust case, or a union case may have profound consequences. Judges are not fungible; they cover the constitutional spectrum; and a particular judge's emphasis may make a world of difference when it comes to rulings on evidence, the temper of the courtroom, the tolerance for a proferred defense, and the like. Lawyers recognize this when they talk about "shopping" for a judge; Senators recognize this when they are asked to give their "advice and consent" to judicial appointments; laymen

30. Chandler v. Judicial Council, 398 U.S. 74 (1970) (dissenting opinion); Chandler v. Judicial Council, 382 U.S. 1003 (1966) (dissenting opinion).

recognize this when they appraise the quality and image of the judiciary in their own community.

These are subtle, imponderable factors which other judges should not be allowed to manipulate to further their own concept of the public good. That is the crucial issue at the heart of the present controversy.

But, while Douglas would preserve the independence of judges, he would not give them the same immunity congressmen enjoy under the speech and debate clause of the Constitution. The Constitution is silent as to judicial immunity, but at common law, judges enjoyed complete immunity. The Supreme Court in an early case adopted the common-law immunity as applicable to a judge of a District of Columbia court, explaining that it "is not for the protection or benefit of a malicious or corrupt judge, but for the benefit of the public, whose interest it is that the judges should be at liberty to exercise their functions with independence, and without fear of consequences."[31]

In 1967, the Court held that Congress had not abrogated the common-law absolute immunity by a Civil Rights Act prescribing liability for "every person" who under color of law deprives another of his constitutional rights. Hence, it approved dismissal of a suit against a state court judge who had convicted blacks for attempting to use segregated facilities in a Mississippi bus terminal under an unconstitutional state law. Douglas dissented:[32]

I do not think that all judges, under all circumstances, no matter how outrageous their conduct are immune from suit under [the Act] . . .

. . . To most, "every person" would mean *every person*, not every person *except* judges . . .

This is not to say that a judge who makes an honest mistake should be subjected to civil liability . . . The judicial function involves an informed exercise of judgment. It is often necessary to choose between differing versions of fact, to reconcile opposing interests, and to decide closely contested issues. Decisions must often be made in the heat of trial. A vigorous and independent mind is needed to perform such delicate tasks. It would be unfair to require a judge to exercise his independent judgment and then to punish him for having exercised it in a manner which, in retrospect, was erroneous. Imposing liability for

31. Bradley v. Fisher, 13 Wall. 335 (1872).
32. Pierson v. Ray, 386 U.S. 547 (1967) (dissenting opinion).

mistaken, though honest judicial acts, would curb the independent mind and spirit needed to perform judicial functions. Thus, a judge who sustains a conviction on what he forthrightly considers adequate evidence should not be subjected to liability when an appellate court decides that the evidence was not adequate. Nor should a judge who allows a conviction under what is later held an unconstitutional statute.

But that is far different from saying that a judge shall be immune from the consequences of any of his judicial actions, and that he shall not be liable for the knowing and intentional deprivation of a person's civil rights. What about the judge who conspires with local law enforcement officers to "railroad" a dissenter? What about the judge who knowing turns a trial into a "kangaroo" court? Or one who intentionally flouts the Constitution in order to obtain a conviction? Congress, I think, concluded that the evils of allowing intentional, knowing deprivations of civil rights to go unredressed far outweighed the speculative inhibiting effects which might attend an inquiry into a judicial deprivation of civil rights.

Douglas' insistence on judicial independence extends also to the performance of the Supreme Court. When that Court, solely in reliance upon the solicitor general's confession of error, reversed a conviction as having been based on evidence obtained by an illegal search, he dissented:[33]

I do not believe we should take our law from the Department of Justice or from any other litigant. The reasons why the Department of Justice confesses error in a case may be wholly honorable. For example, those in the Solicitor General's office may be honestly converted to the point of view which their colleagues opposed below. I assume that is true in the present case. But I also know that litigants usually have selfish purposes. What the motivation behind a particular confession of error may be will seldom be known. We cannot become a party to it without serving the unknown cause of the litigant . . .

. . . If the courts are to retain their independence, they must decide cases taken on the merits . . . Once we accept a confession of error at face value and make it the controlling and decisive factor in our decision, we no longer administer a system of justice under a government of laws.

Again, when the Court reversed a conviction for mailing obscene matter because the solicitor general confessed that the prosecution had been

33. Casey v. United States, 343 U.S. 808 (1952) (dissenting opinion).

contrary to a Department of Justice policy to prosecute only aggravated cases, Douglas concurred in the reversal of the conviction, "not because it violates the policy of the Justice Department, but because it violates the Constitution."[34]

With the great growth of administrative agencies, many functions formerly performed by judges are now performed by trial examiners, who conduct hearings, find facts, and make recommendations for agency decision. Because of a concern that these trial examiners, as employees of the agencies, might be subject to something akin to the "command influence" that has affected military tribunals, Congress enacted a requirement that they be given independence and tenure within the civil service system. When the Court approved rules adopted by the Civil Service Commission to implement this plan, Douglas joined dissenters, principally because the rules left the agencies with unlimited discretion in the assignment of examiners to cases, whereas the statute required that they be assigned "in rotation." This departure from the statute, the dissenters thought, went "a long way toward frustrating the purpose of Congress to give examiners independence."[35]

Included in the judicial power that the Constitution vests in the federal courts[36] and that state constitutions vest in state courts is the power to punish for contempt. It may be exercised through a civil contempt proceeding, which puts the contemnor under continuing incarceration, or increasing fines, or both, until the contempt ceases.[37] Or it may be exercised through a criminal contempt proceeding, which punishes the contemnor with a fixed sentence, or fine, or both, for prior contempts.[38] Douglas has consistently maintained the view that power to punish for criminal contempt should be exercised with great restraint.

Thus, he wrote for the Court to interpret a statute giving federal courts summary power to punish without jury trial criminal contempts committed in their presence "or so near thereto as to obstruct the

34. Redmond v. United States, 384 U.S. 264 (1966) (concurring opinion). *See also* Petite v. United States, 361 U.S. 529 (1960) (concurring opinion).

35. Ramspeck v. Federal Trial Examiners Conference, 345 U.S. 128 (1953) (dissenting opinion).

36. U.S. Const., Art. III, §1.

37. Gompers v. Bucks Stove & Range Co., 221 U.S. 418 (1911).

38. Michaelson v. United States, 266 U.S. 42 (1924).

administration of justice" as requiring a "geographical" rather than a "causal" connection between the contempt and the courtroom. Hence, the summary criminal contempt power did not extend to acts which took place one hundred miles away even though such acts had a "reasonable tendency" to "obstruct the administration of justice." An earlier decision adopting the reasonable tendency test, over the dissents of Holmes and Brandeis, was overruled.[39]

When the Court later read Federal Rules of Criminal Procedure to authorize a court to proceed summarily, without notice, time to prepare a defense, and a hearing, to punish a contempt that did not occur in the court's presence, Douglas joined a dissenting minority.[40] Seven years later he wrote for the Court to overrule the prior decision and to adopt the dissenters' view that the summary procedure was reserved for exceptional circumstances "such as acts threatening the judge or disrupting a hearing or obstructing court proceedings."[41]

Douglas also voted with the Court to hold that, even where summary federal contempt proceedings are proper, if they are not necessary to prevent the breakdown of trial proceedings but are postponed to the end of the trial and if the alleged contempt involves a conflict of personal feelings between the trial judge and the alleged contemnor, a different judge should try the contempt case.[42] He has recently written for the court to hold that the due process clause of the Fourteenth Amendment imposes the same requirement on state contempt proceedings, even though in this instance the trial judge was not "an activist seeking combat" but was the victim of outrageously insulting conduct by the contemnor.[43] And in a number of cases he has dissented when he thought the Court permitted a departure from that requirement.[44]

39. Nye v. United States, 313 U.S. (1941). Douglas has also voted with the Court to hold that an attorney trying a case in court is not an "officer" of the court within the meaning of another provision of the statute, which gives the court summary power to punish as criminal contempt "misbehavior of any of its officers, in their official transactions." Cammer v. United States, 350 U.S. (1956).

40. Brown v. United States, 359 U.S. 41 (1959) (dissenting opinion).

41. Harris v. United States, 382 U.S. 162 (1965).

42. Offutt v. United States, 348 U.S. 11 (1954) (concurring opinion).

43. Mayberry v. Pennsylvania, 400 U.S. 455 (1971). *See also* Johnson v. Mississippi, 400 U.S. 991 (1971).

44. Ungar v. Sarafite, 376 U.S. 575 (1964) (dissenting opinion); Nilva v. United States, 352 U.S. 385 (1957) (dissenting opinion); Sacher v. United States, 343 U.S.

Douglas agreed with the Court when it held that a state judge sitting as a "one-man grand jury" could not in the secret grand jury proceeding try and convict a witness of contempt and thus deprive him of his constitutional right to a public trial,[45] and that the judge could not, consistent with the requirements of due process, try the witness in a later public proceeding either, since the judge had become in his investigation as grand juror a part of the "accusatory process" directed at the very person he later tried for contempt.[46] But he again dissented when the Court refused to apply the public trial requirement to a witness held in contempt after refusal to answer a federal grand jury's questions although ordered to do so by the federal judge who then proceeded to hold him in contempt. He objected that "the contemptuous conduct, the adjudication of guilt, and the imposition of sentence all took place after the public had been excluded from the courtroom, in what began and was continued as 'a Grand Jury proceeding.' "[47]

Beginning in 1952, Douglas also joined with a minority to assert that defendants in criminal contempt proceedings were entitled to the jury trial guaranteed by the Sixth Amendment in "all criminal prosecutions."[48] The court finally adopted that view sixteen years later for cases where the punishment exceeds six months imprisonment, a line which it drew by reference to a federal statute declaring all federal misdemeanors for which the penalty does not exceed six months imprisonment or a fine of $500 to constitute "petty offenses."[49] Douglas rejects this "mechanical" definition of a "petty offense" and

1 (1952) (dissenting opinion). *See also In re* Isserman, 345 U.S. 286 (1953) (dissenting opinion); Isserman v. Ethics Committee, 345 U.S. 927 (1953) (dissenting opinion); Sacher v. Association of the Bar, 347 U.S. 388 (1954). *Cf. In re* Isserman, 348 U.S. 1 (1954).

45. *In re* Oliver, 333 U.S. 257 (1948).

46. *In re* Murchison, 349 U.S. 133 (1955).

47. Levine v. United States, 362 U.S. 610 (1960) (dissenting opinion).

48. Sacher v. United States, 343 U.S. 1 (1952) (dissenting opinion); Isserman v. Ethics Committee, 345 U.S. 927 (1953) (dissenting opinion); Offutt v. United States, 348 U.S. 11 (1954) (concurring opinion); Green v. United States, 356 U.S. 165 (1958) (dissenting opinions); Piemonte v. United States, 367 U.S. 556 (1961) (dissenting opinion); United States v. Barnett, 376 U.S. 681 (1964) (dissenting opinions).

49. Bloom v. Illinois, 391 U.S. 194 (1968). Jury trials are not required for civil contempt proceedings. Shillitani v. United States, 384 U.S. 364 (1966).

insists that, if an exception is to be made, it should be based on the nature and gravity of the offense itself and not on the length of the sentence authorized or imposed.[50]

In 1970, the Court sustained the action of a state court in excluding from the courtroom, as an alternative to holding in contempt, a defendant in an armed robbery case who persisted after repeated warnings in disrupting the proceedings by vile and abusive language and threats on the judge's life; it denied relief by way of habeas corpus. Douglas agreed with the result because of the inadequacy of the record for review, but he objected to the decision on the merits and to the majority opinion's going further to indicate that the trial judge might also properly do in some cases what was not involved in this case—order the defendant bound and gagged.[51]

> There is more than an intimation in the present record that the defendant was a mental case. [But the condition of the record] makes it . . . impossible to determine what the mental condition of the defendant was . . .
>
> Our real problems . . . lie not with this case but with other kinds of trials. *First* are the political trials . . .
>
> In Anglo-American law, great injustices have at times been done to unpopular minorities by judges, as well as by prosecutors . . .
>
> Problems of political indictments and of political judges raise profound questions going to the heart of the social compact. For that compact is two-sided: majorities undertake to press their grievances within limits of the Constitution and in accord with its procedures; minorities agree to abide by constitutional procedures in resisting those claims.
>
> Does the answer to that problem involve defining the procedure for conducting political trials or does it involve the designing of constitutional methods for putting an end to them? This record is singularly inadequate to answer those questions. It will be time enough to resolve those weighty problems when a political trial reaches this Court for review.

50. Cheff v. Schnackenberg, 384 U.S. 373 (1966) (dissenting opinion); Dyke v. Taylor Implement Mfg. Co., 391 U.S. 216 (1968) (dissenting opinion); Frank v. United States, 395 U.S. 147 (1969) (dissenting opinion). The concept of the "petty offense" as not subject to the constitutional guaranty of jury trial is further explored in Chapter 12.

51. Illinois v. Allen, 397 U.S. 337 (1970) (separate opinion). *See also* Bitter v. United States, 389 U.S. 15 (1967).

Second are trials used by minorities to destroy the existing constitutional system and bring on repressive measures. Radicals on the left historically have used those tactics to incite the extreme right with the calculated design of fostering a regime of repression from which the radicals on the left hope to emerge as the ultimate victor. The left in that role is the provocateur. The Constitution was not designed as an instrument for that form of rough-and-tumble contest. The social compact has room for tolerance, patience, and restraint, but not for sabotage and violence. Trials involving that spectacle strike at the very heart of constitutional government.

I would not try to provide in this case the guidelines for those two strikingly different types of cases.

Douglas has also maintained the view that, in contempt proceedings, the Court should never exercise more than "the least possible power adequate to the end proposed" so that, when civil contempt proceedings are adequate to compel obedience to a court order, criminal proceedings should not be invoked. He would also test the fines imposed in criminal contempt proceedings by the Eighth Amendment's prohibition against excessive fines.[52]

Douglas has invariably agreed with the Court when it has struck down state court criminal contempt convictions based on newspaper comments or other out-of-court statements about pending litigation. Finding in each case that the comments created no "clear and present danger" of an obstruction of justice, the Court concluded that the convictions violated the First Amendment guarantees of free speech and press.[53] The conclusion was not unrelated to the notion of judicial independence. As Douglas wrote for the Court in one of these cases, "the law of contempt is not made for the protection of judges who may be sensitive to the winds of public opinion. Judges are supposed to be men of fortitude, able to thrive in a hardy climate."[54]

In one other area, Douglas has come to believe that the Constitution imposes a limitation not recognized by the Court on the judicial

52. United States v. United Mine Workers, 330 U.S. 258 (1947).

53. Bridges v. California, 314 U.S. 252 (1941); Pennekamp v. Florida, 328 U.S. 331 (1946); Craig v. Harney, 331 U.S. 367 (1947). *See also* Fisher v. Pace, 336 U.S. 155 (1949) (dissenting opinion); *In re* Sawyer, 360 U.S. 622 (1959); *In re* McConnell, 370 U.S. 230 (1962). For Douglas' later views on the "clear and present danger test," see pp. 70-71, *infra.*

54. Craig v. Harney, 331 U.S. 367 (1947).

power. It has long been the practice of Congress to enact legislation authorizing the Supreme Court to promulgate rules of procedure for the lower federal courts—enactments currently in force require that the rules, and any amendments thereto, when approved by the Court shall be transmitted to Congress and shall take effect if Congress does not act within a specified time. In practice, the rules are not drafted by the Court but by committees of lawyers, law teachers, and judges selected by the Judicial Conference of the United States—a conference made up of lower federal court judges, presided over by the chief justice of the United States. For many years Douglas joined in the approval of these rules and of amendments thereto, dissenting only where he thought that particular rules infringed on substantive rights or that they embodied unwise procedure.[55] But in 1963 he and Justice Black joined in dissent from an order approving a series of amendments, many of which they regarded as determining "matters so substantially affecting the rights of litigants in lawsuits that in practical effect they are the equivalent of new legislation which, in our judgment, the Constitution requires to be initiated and enacted by the Congress and approved by the President."[56] They have since persisted in that view.[57]

55. 368 U.S. 1012 (1961).

56. 374 U.S. 865 (1963). They also suggested, as a better alternative than the present plan, that the rule-approving function be transferred to the Judicial Conference, both because the conference "can participate more actively in fashioning the rules and affirmatively contribute to their content and design better than we can" and because such a transfer "would relieve us of the embarrassment of having to sit in judgment on the constitutionality of rules which we have approved and which as applied in given situations might have to be declared invalid." *Id.*, 870.

57. 383 U.S. 1032, 1089 (1966); 398 U.S. 979 (1970); 400 U.S. 1031 (1971); 401 U.S. 1018-1019 (1971).

2 THE RIGHT TO VOTE

The Constitution provides that the president, the vice-president, and the Congress—categories which include those who nominate and confirm the judges—shall be elected. It provides that each state shall appoint, "in such Manner as the Legislature thereof may direct," electors for president and vice-president, and that the qualifications of voters for representatives and for senators shall be those "requisite for Electors of the most numerous Branch of the State Legislature."[1]

It provides also that the "Times, Places and Manner of holding Elections for Senators and Representatives shall be prescribed in each State by the Legislature thereof; but the Congress may at any time by Law make or alter such Regulations."[2] It provides further, in the Fifteenth and Nineteenth Amendments, that neither the United States nor any state shall deny or abridge the right to vote on account of race, color, previous condition of servitude, or sex. Finally, it forbids, in the Fourteenth Amendment, any state to deny any person within its jurisdiction the equal protection of the laws or to abridge the privileges or immunities of citizens of the United States.

These are limitations on governmental, not on private, action. Before Douglas came to the Court, it had held that a state denies equal

1. U.S. Const., Art. I, §2, Cl. 2; Art. II, §1, Cl. 1, 2; Seventeenth Amendment.
2. *Id.*, Art. I, §4, Cl. 1.

protection of the laws by enacting a statute forbidding blacks to vote in a party primary for the nomination of candidates for state and federal office,[3] or by giving the authority to determine party membership to a party committee which then excludes blacks from the primaries.[4] But no denial of equal protection was found where the racial discrimination in membership was mandated by the state convention of the party, which was held not to be an organ of the state.[5]

Douglas voted with the Court to overrule the last-mentioned holding on the ground that the state had so far embodied the state primary into its statutory electoral machinery as to render the discriminatory action of the party convention state action which violated the Fifteenth Amendment.[6] He voted with the Court again to hold that this decision could not be evaded through the device of the state's permitting an all-white "private" political organization to conduct its primary free of state regulation, where it was the dominant political group and the later state-operated primary served usually to ratify the results of the private primary.[7] He has also voted with a unanimous Court to strike down under the Fifteenth Amendment the gerrymandering of city boundaries on racial grounds,[8] and to invalidate a state law requiring the designation of a candidate's race on the ballot.[9]

But he dissented when the Court construed a criminal provision in an ancient Civil Rights Act, forbidding conspiracies to injure a citizen in the exercise "of any right or privilege secured to him by the Constitution or laws of the United States," to cover the alteration or miscounting of ballots in a primary election. He agreed that Congress

3. Nixon v. Herndon, 273 U.S. 536 (1927).
4. Nixon v. Condon, 286 U.S. 73 (1932).
5. Grovey v. Townsend, 295 U.S. 45 (1935).
6. Smith v. Allwright, 321 U.S. 649 (1944).
7. Terry v. Adams, 345 U.S. 461 (1953).
8. Gomillion v. Lightfoot, 364 U.S. 339 (1960). He dissented when he thought the Court failed to apply the same principle to a New York apportionment of adjoining congressional districts so that 86 percent of one district and only 5 percent of another were black and Puerto Rican. Wright v. Rockefeller, 376 U.S. 52 (1964) (dissenting opinion). *See also* Whitcomb v. Chavis, 403 U.S. 124 (1971) (dissenting in part and concurring in part); Ely v. Klahr, 403 U.S. 109 (1971) (concurring opinion).
9. Anderson v. Martin, 375 U.S. 399 (1964).

had the power to forbid such conduct, but thought that the statute was too vague and imprecise to support such an application in a criminal proceeding where the defendants were entitled to some advance notice of the conduct prohibited.[10]

Douglas also wrote for a unanimous Court to hold that a state literacy test for voters was not unconstitutional on its face where there was no showing that it was administered in a discriminatory manner,[11] and voted with the Court to invalidate those which were so administered.[12] He also agreed with the Court that Congress had authority under the Fourteenth Amendment to forbid, in the Voting Rights Act of 1965, a state literacy requirement that the would-be voter be literate in English as applied to those who were literate in another language.[13] And he later voted with a unanimous Court to hold that Congress could, under the authority conferred by both the Fourteenth and Fifteenth Amendments "to enforce this article by appropriate legislation," forbid literacy tests entirely in both federal and state elections.[14]

The Court in 1946 refused to grant relief in a suit challenging the failure of a state legislature so to revise the boundaries of congressional voting districts as to keep pace with population changes, and thus to ensure approximate equality of voting power, on the ground that this was a "political" question beyond the competence of the judiciary. Douglas joined in a dissent asserting that the state was denying equal protection of the law and that the issue was no more political than questions of racial discrimination involving voting rights.[15] Sixteen

10. United States v. Classic, 313 U.S. 299 (1941) (dissenting opinion).

11. Lassiter v. Northampton County Board of Elections, 360 U.S. 45 (1959).

12. Louisiana v. United States, 380 U.S. 145 (1965); Alabama v. United States, 371 U.S. 37 (1962); Schnell v. Davis, 336 U.S. 933 (1949). *See also* United States v. Mississippi, 380 U.S. 128 (1965); United States v. Alabama, 362 U.S. 602 (1960); United States v. Thomas, 362 U.S. 58 (1960).

13. Katzenbach v. Morgan, 384 U.S. 641 (1966) (separate opinion). *See also* his dissent in Cardona v. Power, 384 U.S. 672 (1966).

14. United States v. Arizona, 400 U.S. 112 (1970) (concurring and dissenting opinion). *See also* Perkins v. Matthews, 400 U.S. 379 (1971); Gaston County v. United States, 395 U.S. 285 (1969); South Carolina v. Katzenbach, 383 U.S. 301 (1966).

15. Colegrove v. Green, 328 U.S. 549 (1946) (dissenting opinion). *See also* South v. Peters, 339 U.S. 276 (1950) (dissenting opinion).

years later the Court adopted essentially that view in the first of a series of cases which have now established the "one man, one vote" rule for general elections to both houses of state legislatures,[16] for general elections for United States representatives,[17] for primary elections for United States senator and statewide offices,[18] and for general elections for county commissioners[19] and trustees of a junior college district.[20] Douglas also voted with the Court to hold that there is a denial of equal protection where a state limits the vote for elected school boards to property holders and parents of schoolchildren[21] or limits the vote on public bond issues to property holders.[22]

But he wrote for the Court to hold that these decisions do not forbid a state to have county school boards whose members are appointed rather than elected,[23] and that, where councilmen are elected by all voters of the city, it is permissible to elect some at large without regard to residence and others as residents of particular boroughs.[24] He voted with the Court also to hold that members of appointed county school boards cannot be appointed by a grand jury from which blacks are systematically excluded and that appointments to such boards cannot be limited to property owners.[25]

16. Baker v. Carr, 369 U.S. 186 (1962) (concurring opinion); Reynolds v. Sims, 377 U.S. 533 (1964); WMCA, Inc. v. Lomenzo, 377 U.S. 633 (1964); Maryland Committee v. Tawes, 377 U.S. 656 (1964); Davis v. Mann, 377 U.S. 678 (1964); Roman v. Sincock, 377 U.S. 695 (1964); Lucas v. Forty-Fourth General Assembly, 377 U.S. 713 (1964); Swann v. Adams, 385 U.S. 440 (1967); Fortson v. Dorsey, 379 U.S. 433 (1965) (dissenting opinion); Whitcomb v. Chavis, note 8, *supra* (dissenting opinion); Ely v. Klahr, note 8, *supra* (dissenting opinion).

17. Wesberry v. Sanders, 376 U.S. 1 (1964); Kirkpatrick v. Preisler, 394 U.S. 526 (1969); Wells v. Rockefeller, 394 U.S. 542 (1969).

18. Gray v. Sanders, 372 U.S. 368 (1963).

19. Avery v. Midland County, 390 U.S. 474 (1968). *See also* Abate v. Mundt, 403 U.S. 182 (1971) (dissenting opinion).

20. Hadley v. Junior College District, 397 U.S. 50 (1970).

21. Kramer v. Oregon Free School District No. 15, 395 U.S. 621 (1969).

22. Parish School Board v. Stewart, 400 U.S. 884 (1970); Phoenix v. Kolodziejski, 399 U.S. 204 (1970); Cipriano v. City of Houara, 395 U.S. 701 (1969). But he agreed with the Court that there was no denial of equal protection where a state required a 60 percent vote of the electorate to approve all public bond issues, since "We can discern no independently identifiable group or category that favors bonded indebtedness over other forms of financing." Gordon v. Lance, 403 U.S. 1 (1971).

23. Sailors v. Board of Education, 387 U.S. 105 (1967).

24. Dusch v. Davis, 387 U.S. 112 (1967).

25. Turner v. Fouche, 396 U.S. 346 (1970).

Douglas dissented, however, from a decision sustaining a state procedure whereby, when no candidate for governor receives a majority vote in a general election, the selection of a governor is committed to the legislature. He did not agree with the Court that the question was whether a state could select a governor by legislative action. It was, rather, "whether the legislature may make the final choice when the election has been entrusted to the people and no candidate has received a majority of the votes"—whether the legislative choice could be treated as a second stage in the popular election. Such treatment, he thought, violated the one man, one vote requirement applicable to popular elections:[26]

A legislator when voting for governor has only a single vote. Even if he followed the majority vote of his constituency, he would necessarily disregard the votes of those who voted for the other candidate, whether their votes almost carried the day or were way in the minority. He would not be under a mandate to follow the majority or plurality votes in his constituency, but might cast his single vote on the side of the minority in his district. Even if he voted for the candidate receiving a plurality of votes cast in his district and even if each Senator and Representative followed the same course, a candidate who received a minority of the popular vote might receive a clear majority of the votes cast in the legislature.

Douglas also dissented when, in 1948, the Court found no denial of equal protection in a state requirement that a petition to form and nominate candidates for a new political party must have signatures of at least two hundred voters of at least fifty counties, contending that this requirement was unconstitutional because it gave the less populous counties a disproportionate vote on the matter.[27] In 1969 he wrote for the Court to overrule that decision and adopt his earlier dissenting view.[28]

Douglas has also voted with the Court to invalidate under the equal protection clause state laws which would disfranchise members of the armed services despite their residence in the state,[29] and which

26. Fortson v. Morris, 385 U.S. 231 (1966) (dissenting opinion).
27. McDougall v. Green, 335 U.S. 281 (1948) (dissenting opinion).
28. Moore v. Ogilvie, 394 U.S. 814 (1969). *See also* Williams v. Rhodes, 393 U.S. 23 (1968) (concurring opinion). *Cf.* Jenness v. Fortson, 403 U.S. 431 (1971).
29. Carrington v. Rash, 380 U.S. 89 (1965).

similarly disfranchised residents of federally owned property within a state who were subjected to other state laws.[30]

The Court has had little to say about the Electoral College, which formally votes for president and vice-president and whose members are to be selected in each state "in such Manner as the Legislature thereof may direct."[31] But it has held that the Constitution does not prevent Alabama from enforcing a requirement of its state Democratic Executive Committee that each candidate for elector pledge to support the nominees of the Democratic National Convention. Douglas disagreed and joined in a dissenting opinion, which recognized that the required pledge "does no more than to make a legal obligation of what has been a voluntary general practice" and that the Electoral College idea has "suffered atrophy almost indistinguishable from *rigor mortis.*" But he insisted nonetheless that the Constitution contemplated that the electors "would be free agents, to exercise an independent and nonpartisan judgment as to the men best qualified for the Nation's highest offices" and that the Constitution could not be amended by custom.[32]

Douglas dissented again when the Court sustained a state poll tax.[33] Fifteen years later he wrote for the Court to hold that the poll tax, as applied to state elections, was a denial of equal protection.[34] Meanwhile, the Twenty-Fourth Amendment had been adopted, forbidding the use of the poll tax in federal elections, and Douglas voted with the Court to hold invalid under that amendment a state law requiring those who did not pay a poll tax to file, six months before the election, a witnessed or notarized certificate of residence, where no such proof of residence was required of those who paid the poll tax.[35]

By a 1970 statute Congress conferred the right to vote in federal and

30. Evans v. Cornman, 398 U.S. 419 (1970).

31. U.S. Const., Art. II, §1, Cl. 2. The Twelfth Amendment also provides that the electors shall meet in their respective states "and vote by ballot for President and Vice-President, one of whom, at least, shall not be an inhabitant of the same state with themselves."

32. Ray v. Blair, 343 U.S. 214 (1952) (dissenting opinion).

33. Butler v. Thompson, 34 U.S. 937 (1951) (dissent).

34. Harper v. Virginia Board of Elections, 383 U.S. 663 (1966).

35. Harman v. Forssenius, 380 U.S. 528 (1965).

state elections on all citizens eighteen years of age. When the Court upheld this statute as applied to national elections but invalidated it as applied to state elections, Douglas dissented in part, contending that it could validly apply to all elections as an exercise of the power given Congress to enforce the equal protection clause of the Fourteenth Amendment:[36]

> Congress might well conclude that a reduction in voting age from 21 to 18 was needed in the interests of equal protection. The Act itself brands the denial of the franchise to 18-year-olds as "a particularly unfair treatment of such citizens in view of the national defense responsibilities imposed" on them . . . The fact that only males are drafted while the vote extends to females as well is not relevant, for the female component of these families or prospective families is also caught up in war and hit hardest by it. Congress might well believe that men and women alike should share the fateful decision.
>
> It is said, why draw the line at 18? Why not 17? Congress can draw lines and I see no reason why it cannot conclude that 18-year-olds have that degree of maturity which entitles them to the franchise. They are "generally considered by American law to be mature enough to contract, to marry, to drive an automobile, to own a gun, and to be responsible for criminal behavior as an adult." Moreover . . . under state laws, mandatory school attendance does not, as a matter of practice, extend beyond the age of 18 . . . Much is made of the fact that Article I . . . of the Constitution gave Congress only the power to regulate the "Manner of holding Elections," not the power to fix qualifications for voting in elections. But the Civil War Amendments—the Thirteenth, Fourteenth and Fifteenth made vast inroads on the power of the States. Equal protection became a standard for state action and Congress was given authority to "enforce" it.

In the same case Douglas voted with the Court to sustain other provisions of the act, confined to presidential elections, which eliminate all durational residential requirements and provide uniform national rules for absentee voting. The right to vote in presidential elections, he concluded, was one of the "privileges and immunities" of national citizenship which the Fourteenth Amendment forbids the states to abridge and authorizes the Congress to enforce.

36. United States v. Arizona, 400 U.S. 112 (1970) (concurring and dissenting opinion).

Three months after this decision Congress submitted to the state legislatures for ratification a proposed amendment to the Constitution giving the right to vote in all federal and state elections to those eighteen years of age or older. It took slightly more than another three months for the requisite three-fourths of the states to ratify the Twenty-Sixth Amendment.

3 CITIZENSHIP

The Constitution authorizes Congress to enact a uniform law on naturalization[1] and the Fourteenth Amendment provides that "All persons born or naturalized in the United States, and subject to the jurisdiction thereof, are citizens of the United States and of the State wherein they reside."

Problems of naturalized citizens, involving withholding and revocation of citizenship, have long plagued the Court. In 1943 Douglas concurred in a decision holding that the government could not revoke naturalized citizenship, as illegally procured in 1927, under a naturalization law requiring that for five years prior to naturalization the applicant must have "behaved as a man of good moral character attached to the principles of the Constitution of the United States, and well disposed to the good order and happiness of the same." The government did not establish that the applicant was disqualified in 1927, the Court held, by showing that he was then, and for five years prior thereto had been, a member of the Communist party of the United States. A right so precious as United States citizenship should not be revoked except on "clear, unequivocal, and convincing" evidence. And where the naturalized citizen testified that he did not advocate forcible overthrow of the government during the critical

1. U.S. Const., Art. I, §8, Cl. 4.

period, that evidence was not overcome by proof of Communist party membership. There were two major defects in the government's case: first, it had not established with certainty that the Communist party of the United States advocated forcible overthrow of the government or, if it did, that the defendant so understood its program, and second, it relied on the doctrine of guilt by association, whereas "under our traditions beliefs are personal and not a matter of mere association"—"men in adhering to a political party or other organization notoriously do not subscribe unqualifiedly to all of its platforms or asserted principles."[2]

In the following year Douglas concurred in another decision finding that the government had failed to meet its burden of proof in an action to revoke the naturalized citizenship of one of German ancestry, who had at the time of and before naturalization expressed sympathy for Hitler.[3] But he wrote for the Court a few years later to sustain a revocation where the government was found to have proved by "solid, convincing evidence that [the naturalized citizen] before the date of his naturalization, at that time, and subsequently was a thoroughgoing Nazi and a faithful follower of Adolph Hitler" so that he swore falsely, and was guilty of fraud, when he foreswore allegiance to the German Reich.[4] In the course of his opinion Douglas explained why the heavy burden of proof was placed upon the government:

> Citizenship obtained through naturalization is not a second-class citizenship . . . [I]t carries with it the privilege of full participation in the affairs of our society, including the right to speak freely, to criticize officials and administrators, and to promote changes in our laws including the very Charter of our Government. Great tolerance and caution are necessary lest good faith exercise of the rights of citizenship be turned against the naturalized citizen and be used to deprive him of the cherished status. Ill-tempered expressions, extreme views, even the promotion of ideas which run counter to our American ideals, are not to be given disloyal connotations in absence of solid, convincing evidence that that is their significance. Any other course would run

2. Schneiderman v. United States, 320 U.S. 118 (1943) (concurring opinion). *See also* Nowak v. United States, 356 U.S. 660 (1958).

3. Baumgartner v. United States, 322 U.S. 665 (1944) (separate opinion).

4. Knauer v. United States, 328 U.S. 654 (1946).

counter to our traditions and make denaturalization proceedings the ready instrument for political persecutions.

In subsequent cases Douglas wrote for the Court to hold that the government failed to meet its burden when it sought to revoke naturalized citizenship because of alleged concealment of a record of arrests for minor offenses[5] and dissented where the Court held the burden met on the issue whether the naturalized citizen had concealed his occupation as a bootlegger.[6]

In a series of cases decided before Douglas' appointment to the Court, that body had dealt with a statutory requirement that a naturalized citizen must take an oath "that he will support and defend the Constitution and laws of the United States against all enemies, foreign and domestic, and bear true faith and allegiance to the same," and the further requirement that the naturalized citizen be "attached to the principles of the Constitution of the United States, and well disposed to the good order and happiness of the same." Although the applicants for citizenship were willing to take the oath, the Court concluded, over the dissents of Holmes, Brandeis, and Hughes, that these statutory requirements disqualified a fifty-two-year-old woman pacifist who was personally unwilling to bear arms,[7] a male applicant aged at least forty-seven who was willing to bear arms if he was free to judge the necessity of the war,[8] and another woman applicant of undisclosed age who had served as a nurse in France in World War I and who was likewise unwilling to bear arms personally.[9]

In 1946 Douglas wrote for the Court to overrule these cases and to admit to citizenship a male Seventh Day Adventist who for religious reasons was unwilling to bear arms but was willing to render noncombatant military service:[10]

5. Chaunt v. United States, 364 U.S. 350 (1960).
6. Costello v. United States, 365 U.S. 265 (1961) (dissenting opinion).
7. United States v. Schwimmer, 279 U.S. 644 (1929).
8. United States v. Macintosh, 283 U.S. 605 (1931).
9. United States v. Bland, 283 U.S. 636 (1931).
10. Girouard v. United States, 328 U.S. 61 (1946). Douglas had previously dissented when the Court held, with considerable reliance on the earlier naturalization cases, that a state could refuse a license to practice law to one who refused to bear arms. *In re* Summers, 325 U.S. 561 (1945) (dissenting opinion).

The oath required . . . does not in terms require [a] promise to bear arms . . . [W]e could not assume that Congress intended to make such an abrupt and radical departure from our traditions unless it spoke in unequivocal terms.

The bearing of arms . . . is not the only way in which our institutions may be supported and defended, even in times of great peril . . . The nuclear physicists who developed the atomic bomb, the worker at his lathe, the seamen on cargo vessels, construction battalions, nurses, engineers, litter bearers, doctors, chaplains—these, too, made essential contributions . . . One may serve his country faithfully and devotedly, though his religious scruples make it impossible for him to shoulder a rifle . . .

Petitioner's religious scruples would not disqualify him from becoming a member of Congress or holding other public offices. While . . . the Constitution provides that such officials, both of the United States and the several states, "shall be bound by Oath or Affirmation, to support this Constitution," it significantly adds that "no religious Test shall ever be required as a Qualification to any Office or public Trust under the United States" . . .

. . . Religious scruples against bearing arms have been recognized by Congress in the various draft laws . . .

Mr. Justice Holmes stated [in his dissent in one of the prior cases]: "if there is any principle of the Constitution that more imperatively calls for attachment than any other it is the principle of free thought—not free thought for those who agree with us but freedom for the thought that we hate. I think that we should adhere to that principle with regard to admission into, as well as to life within this country" . . . The victory for freedom of thought recorded in our Bill of Rights recognizes that in the domain of conscience there is a moral power higher than the State . . . The test oath is abhorrent to our tradition. Over the years Congress has meticulously respected that tradition and even in time of war has sought to accommodate the military requirements to the religious scruples of the individual. We do not believe that Congress intended to reverse that policy when it came to draft the naturalization oath.

Congress has from time to time enacted laws providing for forfeiture of citizenship—whether acquired by birth or naturalization—on the commission of certain proscribed acts. Beginning in 1940, it greatly expanded these expatriation laws and a variety of cases involving these laws came before the Court thereafter.

Prior to 1940 there were only three decisions of the Court which seemed to bear closely on the problem. An 1898 decision held that a child born in the United States of parents of Chinese descent residing in the United States acquired citizenship at birth even though his parents were not eligible for citizenship under the then naturalization laws. Since the Fourteenth Amendment provides that "All persons born or naturalized in the United States . . . are citizens of the United States and of the State wherein they reside," the Court concluded that "citizenship by birth is established by the mere fact of birth under the circumstances defined in the Constitution." And it added that the "Fourteenth Amendment . . . has conferred no authority upon Congress to restrict the effect of birth, declared by the Constitution to constitute a sufficient and complete right to citizenship." Moreover, the "power of naturalization, vested in Congress by the Constitution, is a power to confer citizenship, not a power to take it away."[11]

A second decision in 1915 upheld a statute providing that an American woman who married a foreigner would take the nationality of her husband. This statute, as applied to a woman citizen by birth, was held valid even if it be conceded "that a change of citizenship cannot be . . . imposed without the concurrence of the citizen," since it dealt "with a condition voluntarily entered into."[12]

The third decision, in 1939, held that a citizen by birth of naturalized parents who returned to Sweden with the child and there renounced their American citizenship did not lose her American citizenship, even though by Swedish law she had also acquired the Swedish citizenship of her parents, if she returned to the United States on reaching majority and elected to retain her American citizenship without voluntarily having done anything to relinquish it.[13]

The first of the new cases to challenge the expatriation laws was the *Perez* case, involving a provision for forfeiture of citizenship by voting in an election in a foreign state. The Court upheld the statute as applied to a citizen by birth who had voted in elections in Mexico, explaining

11. United States v. Wong Kim Ark, 169 U.S. 649 (1898).
12. Mackenzie v. Hare, 239 U.S. 299 (1915).
13. Perkins v. Elg, 307 U.S. 325 (1939).

that, while "Congress can attach loss of citizenship only as a consequence of conduct engaged in voluntarily," the voluntary conduct which had that consequence need not indicate an intent on the part of the citizen to renounce his citizenship. Douglas joined in a dissent which conceded that a citizen could voluntarily relinquish his citizenship, but denied all power in Congress to take it away:[14]

> [Under the Fourteenth Amendment] United States citizenship is . . . the constitutional birthright of every person born in this country . . . The Constitution also provides that citizenship can be bestowed under a "uniform Rule of Naturalization," but there is no corresponding provision authorizing divestment. Of course, naturalization unlawfully procured can be set aside. But apart from this circumstance, the status of the naturalized citizen is secure . . . Under our form of government, as established by the Constitution, the citizenship of the lawfully naturalized and the native-born cannot be taken from them.

At the same time this case was decided, the Court also considered another expatriation law forfeiting citizenship for service in the armed forces of a foreign state by one who acquires citizenship in such foreign state. This law, the Court held, could not be invoked against one who held American citizenship by birth and, under Japanese law, also held Japanese citizenship because of the nationality of his parents, and who was inducted into Japanese military service while in Japan, because the government had failed to prove that his military service in Japan was voluntary. Douglas concurred in the decision, but added that the result should have been the same even though the military service was voluntary, since otherwise "a citizen could be transformed into a stateless outcast for evading his taxes, for fraud upon the Government, for counterfeiting its currency, for violating its voting laws and on and on *ad infinitum.*"[15]

At the same time the Court also held that another statutory provision for forfeiture of citizenship on conviction by a court martial of desertion from the military forces could not validly be applied to a citizen by birth whose court martial conviction was based on one day's

14. Perez v. Brownell, 356 U.S. 44 (1958) (dissenting opinions).
15. Nishikawa v. Dulles, 356 U.S. 129 (1958) (concurring opinion).

absence from base. A plurality opinion concluded that, since the action here, unlike that in *Perez*, did not involve "those international problems that were thought to arise by reason of a citizen's having voted in a foreign election," its sole purpose was to punish for desertion and punishment of such magnitude was "cruel and unusual" within the ban of the Eighth Amendment. Douglas concurred in that opinion, but added that even if citizenship could be involuntarily forfeited, guilt should not be determined by a military tribunal, but "in a civilian court of justice where all the protections of the Bill of Rights guard the fairness of the outcome."[16]

Six years later, the Court also held invalid a provision for forfeiture of citizenship by one who departed from or remained outside the United States during time of war or national emergency for the purpose of evading military service. Again the Court found that the sole purpose was to impose punishment, and this was done without the procedural safeguards required by the Fifth and Sixth Amendments for criminal trials. Again Douglas concurred on the ground that Congress had exceeded its powers.[17]

Douglas later wrote for the Court to invalidate another provision which would forfeit the naturalized citizenship of one who returned to and resided for three years in the country of his birth—this discrimination between naturalized and natural born citizens was held to be so arbitrary as to violate the due process clause of the Fifth Amendment.[18]

In 1967, in the *Afroyim* case, the Court reconsidered the *Perez* decision and overruled it, holding that Congress could not constitutionally forfeit the naturalized citizenship of one who voted in an Israeli election. The Court now asserted, as Douglas had for the past nine years, that "the Fourteenth Amendment was designed to, and does, protect every citizen of this Nation against a congressional forcible destruction of his citizenship . . . Our holding does no more than to give to this citizen that which is his own, a constitutional right

16. Trop v. Dulles, 356 U.S. 86 (1958) (concurring opinion).
17. Kennedy v. Mendoza-Martinez, 372 U.S. 144 (1963) (separate opinion). *Cf.* Ceballos v. Shaughnessy, 352 U.S. 599 (1957).
18. Schneider v. Rusk, 377 U.S. 163 (1967).

to remain a citizen in a free country unless he voluntarily relinquishes that citizenship."[19]

Four years later in the *Bellei* case, however, the Court upheld another statute which provides that persons born abroad, of one alien and one citizen parent who has resided in the United States for a specified time, are "citizens of the United States at birth" but will lose their citizenship unless they spend five continuous years in the United States between the ages of fourteen and twenty-eight. Conceding the power of Congress to grant citizenship at birth to plaintiff, who was born in Italy of an Italian father and an American mother, the Court found the first sentence of the Fourteenth Amendment,[20] on which it had relied four years earlier, inapplicable to him. Since he was neither born in the United States nor naturalized in the United States, he was "simply . . . not a Fourteenth-Amendment-first-sentence citizen." And, since the action of Congress was not "arbitrary," there was no other constitutional obstacle to termination of his citizenship. Douglas joined in a dissent which said in part:[21]

> Less than four years ago [in the *Afroyim* case] this Court held that "the Fourteenth Amendment was designed to, and does, protect every citizen of this Nation against a congressional forcible destruction of his citizenship . . ."
>
> The Court today holds that Congress can indeed rob a citizen of his citizenship just so long as five members of this Court can satisfy themselves that the congressional action was not . . . "arbitrary" . . .
>
> Under the view adopted by the majority today, all children born to Americans while abroad would be excluded from the protections of the Citizenship Clause and would instead be relegated to the permanent status of second-class citizenship, subject to revocation at the will of Congress . . . Bellei was not "born . . . in the United States," but he was, constitutionally speaking, "naturalized in the United States." Although those Americans who acquire their citizenship under statutes conferring citizenship on the foreign-born children of citizens are not popularly thought of as naturalized citizens, the use of the word "naturalize" in this way has a considerable constitutional history.

19. Afroyim v. Rusk, 387 U.S. 253 (1967).
20. See text following note 1, *supra*.
21. Rogers v. Bellei, 401 U.S. 815 (1970) (dissenting opinion).

Congress is empowered by the Constitution to "establish an uniform Rule of Naturalization" . . . The first congressional exercise of this power, entitled "An Act to establish an uniform Rule of Naturalization," was passed in 1790 . . . It provided in part: "And the children of citizens of the United States, that may be born . . . out of the limits of the United States, shall be considered as natural born citizens: *Provided*, That the right of citizenship shall not descend to persons whose fathers have never been resident in the United States" . . . This provision is the earliest form of the statute under which Bellei acquired his citizenship . . .

The majority opinion appears at times to rely on the argument that Bellei, while he concededly might have been a naturalized citizen, was not naturalized "in the United States" . . . I cannot accept [this] narrow and extraordinarily technical reading of the Fourteenth Amentment . . . If, for example, Congress should decide to vest the authority to naturalize aliens in American embassy officials abroad rather than having the ceremony performed in this country, I have no doubt that those so naturalized would be just as fully protected by the Fourteenth Amendment as are those who go through our present naturalization procedures. Rather than the technical reading adopted by the majority, it is my view that the word "in" as it appears in the phrase "in the United States" was surely meant to be understood in two somewhat different senses: one can become a citizen of this country by being born *within* it or by being naturalized *into* it.

4 POLITICAL AND RELIGIOUS FREEDOM

It is not likely that a democratic government would function well if its citizens' role was confined to registering their views at periodic intervals in elections. That is the theory of the First Amendment, made applicable to the states by the Fourteenth, providing that "Congress shall make no law respecting an establishment of religion, or prohibiting the free exercise thereof; or abridging the freedom of speech, or of the press; or the right of the people peaceably to assemble, and to petition the Government for a redress of grievances."

In a famous footnote to a 1937 opinion, Justice Stone suggested that, unlike legislation regulating economic activity, "legislation which restricts those political processes which can ordinarily be expected to bring about repeal of undesirable legislation" may be "subjected to more exacting judicial scrutiny."[1] Later, he reformulated the idea to say that the freedoms guaranteed by the First Amendment, being vital to the democratic process, are "in a preferred position" among the guarantees of the Bill of Rights.[2] Douglas has long adhered to that view.[3]

1. United States v. Carolene Products Co., 304 U.S. 144, n. 4 (1938).
2. Jones v. Opelika, 316 U.S. 584 (1942) (dissenting opinion).
3. Murdock v. Pennsylvania, 319 U.S. 105 (1943); United States v. CIO, 335 U.S. 106 (1948) (dissenting opinion); Breard v. Alexandria, 341 U.S. 622 (1951)

RELIGION

Apart from cases discussed in Chapter One finding protection in the First Amendment against contempt convictions, most of the cases arising under that amendment in the first decade of Douglas' service on the Court involved Jehovah's Witnesses who go about distributing literature, proselytizing, and soliciting contributions, thus exercising rights of free speech, press, and religion. With Douglas concurring, statutes requiring licenses for such activity and leaving discretion with the licensing authority to grant or deny were struck down. They constituted prior restraints on the exercise of First Amendment freedoms even though the licensing authority's action was subject to judicial review.[4] A fortiori, the absolute prohibition of the distribution of religious literature on the public streets was invalid, even though that literature also solicited contributions.[5]

When the Court originally held, in *Jones v. Opelika*,[6] that the sale of religious literature or the solicitation of contributions in connection with its distribution rendered the activity sufficiently commercial to justify a state license tax, Douglas joined in dissent. The following year the Court reversed itself and adopted the dissenters' view.[7] Douglas wrote for the Court in a companion case:[8]

(dissenting opinion); Beauharnais v. Illinois, 343 U.S. 250 (1952) (dissenting opinion); Poulos v. New Hampshire, 345 U.S. 395 (1953) (dissenting opinion).

4. Cantwell v. Connecticut, 310 U.S. 296 (1940); Largent v. Texas, 318 U.S. 418 (1943). *See also* Kunz v. New York, 340 U.S. 290 (1951); Saia v. New York, 334 U.S. 558 (1943); Poulos v. New Hampshire, 345 U.S. 395 (1953) (dissenting opinion).

5. Jamison v. Texas, 318 U.S. 413 (1943). Douglas also agreed when the Court earlier reached the same conclusion with respect to the distribution of political and labor union literature, suggesting that if the concern was about littering of the streets the state could punish those who dropped on the streets the literature they received from the defendants. Schneider v. State, 308 U.S. 147 (1939). But he also voted with the Court to sustain a prohibition of street distribution of commercial handbills, even though the defendant "with the intent, and for the purpose, of evading the prohibition" had placed on the reverse side of the handbills a protest against the action of the city in refusing him wharfage facilities at a city pier. Valentine v. Chrestensen, 316 U.S. 52 (1942). *Cf.* NAACP v. Alabama, 377 U.S. 288 (1964).

6. 316 U.S. 584 (1942).

7. Jones v. Opelika, 319 U.S. 103 (1943).

8. Murdock v. Pennsylvania, 319 U.S. 105 (1943). *See also* Douglas v. City of Jeannette, 319 U.S. 157 (1943).

Spreading one's religious beliefs or preaching the Gospel through distribution of religious literature and through personal visitations is an age-old type of evangelism with as high a claim to constitutional protection as the more orthodox types . . .

The alleged justification for the exaction of this license tax is the fact that the religious literature is distributed with a solicitation of funds . . . Situations will arise where it will be difficult to determine whether a particular activity is religious or purely commercial . . . But the mere fact that the religious literature is "sold" by itinerant preachers rather than "donated" does not transform evangelism into a commercial enterprise. If it did, then the passing of the collection plate in church would make the church service a commercial project. The constitutional rights of those spreading their religious beliefs through the spoken and printed word are not to be gauged by standards governing retailers or wholesalers of books. The right to use the press for expressing one's views is not to be measured by the protection afforded commerical handbills. It should be remembered that the pamphlets of Thomas Paine were not distributed free of charge. It is plain that a religious organization needs funds to remain a going concern. But an itinerant evangelist, however misguided or intolerant he may be, does not become a mere book agent by selling the Bible or religious tracts to help defray his expenses or to sustain him. Freedom of speech, freedom of the press, freedom of religion are available to all, not merely to those who can pay their own way . . .

We do not mean to say that religious groups and the press are free from all financial burdens of government . . . We have here something quite different, for example, from a tax on the income of one who engages in religious activities or a tax on property used or employed in connection with those activities. It is one thing to impose a tax on the income or property of a preacher. It is quite another thing to exact a tax from him for the privilege of delivering a sermon. The tax imposed [here] is a flat license tax, the payment of which is a condition of the exercise of . . . constitutional privileges.

In other cases Douglas voted with the Court to invalidate, as applied to Jehovah's Witnesses, an ordinance forbidding knocking on doors or ringing doorbells for the purpose of distributing literature,[9] and to hold that the facts that a town was company-owned and the prohibiton against distribution of religious literature was company-imposed would

9. Martin v. City of Struthers, 319 U.S. 141 (1943) (concurring opinion).

not justify the state's imposition of criminal sanctions for violation of the prohibition.[10]

Jehovah's Witnesses did not always prevail, however. Douglas voted with the Court to hold that they were subject to reasonable state regulation of the use of streets for parades[11] and that the state could prevent their minor children from distributing literature on the streets.[12] He voted with the Court again to hold that the state could prosecute a Witness for calling a town marshal, in a face-to-face encounter, "A God damned racketeer" and "a damned Fascist"—such "fighting words," which "by their very utterance . . . tend to incite an immediate breach of the peace," were thought to be "of such slight social value" as to find no protection in the First Amendment.[13]

The Witnesses suffered another setback in a 1940 decision, in which Douglas joined, holding that a state's compulsory flag salute in the public schools, as applied to their children, did not violate their religious freedom.[14] But in their dissenting opinion in *Jones v. Opelika* in 1942[15] Justices Black, Douglas, and Murphy took the occasion to state that they had concluded that they were wrong in the flag salute case. The following year they joined with the Court to overrule that decision and to declare: "if there is any fixed star in our constitutional constellation, it is that no official, high or petty, can prescribe what shall be orthodox in politics, nationalism, religion, or other matters of opinion or force citizens to confess by word or act their faith therein."[16]

Another religion was involved a few years later when Douglas wrote for the Court to sustain the Mann Act prosecution of members of a fundamentalist Mormon sect who were still practicing polygamy,[17] but

10. Marsh v. Alabama, 326 U.S. 501 (1946).

11. Cox v. New Hampshire, 312 U.S. 569 (1941). *Cf.* Shuttlesworth v. City of Birmingham, 394 U.S. 147 (1969).

12. Prince v. Massachusetts, 321 U.S. 158 (1944).

13. Chaplinsky v. New Hampshire, 315 U.S. 568 (1942).

14. Minersville School District v. Gobitis, 310 U.S. 586 (1940).

15. 316 U.S. 584 (1942).

16. West Virginia State Board of Education v. Barnette 319 U.S. 624 (1943) (concurring opinion). *See also* Torcaso v. Watkins, 367 U.S. 488 (1961), where Douglas voted with the Court to hold that a state cannot require notaries public to proclaim a belief in God as a test of office.

17. Cleveland v. United States, 329 U.S. 14 (1946).

the case involved only an interpretation of the act—the claim that the practice of polygamy was protected as a "free exercise" of religion under the First Amendment was rejected long ago.[18] When, however, the Court remanded a state prosecution for conspiracy to advocate the practice of polygamy to the state courts for further proceedings, Douglas joined in a dissent which urged that the convictions should be reversed because the jury was not instructed on the distinction between permissible advocacy and impermissible incitement:[19]

> It is axiomatic that a democratic state may not deny its citizens the right to criticize existing laws and to urge that they be changed. And yet, in order to succeed in an effort to legalize polygamy it is obviously necessary to convince a substantial number of people that such conduct is desirable. But conviction that the practice is desirable has a natural tendency to induce the practice itself. Thus, depending on where the circular reasoning is started, the advocacy of polygamy may either be unlawful as inducing a violation of law, or be constitutionally protected as essential to the proper functioning of the democratic process.
>
> In the abstract the problem could be solved in various ways. At one extreme it could be said that society can best protect itself by prohibiting only the substantive evil and relying on a completely free interchange of ideas as the best safeguard against demoralizing propaganda. Or we might permit advocacy of lawbreaking, but only so long as the advocacy falls short of incitement. But the other extreme position, that the state may prevent any conduct which induces people to violate the law, or any advocacy of unlawful activity, cannot be squared with the First Amendment. At the very least . . . under the clear-and-present-danger rule, the second alternative stated marks the limit of the state's power as restricted by the Amendment.

These cases all involved freedom of speech, or the "free exercise" of religion, or both. The meaning of the First Amendment's prohibition of

18. Reynolds v. United States, 98 U.S. 145 (1878). *See also* Mormon Church v. United States, 136 U.S. 1 (1890).

19. Musser v. Utah, 333 U.S. 95 (1948) (dissenting opinion). *See also* United States v. Ballard, 322 U.S. 78 (1944), where Douglas wrote for the Court to hold that, in a prosecution for using the mails to defraud by soliciting funds for a religious movement, the First Amendment precluded submission to the jury of the question of the "truth" of defendants' religious doctrines, as distinguished from their good faith belief in them.

any law "respecting an establishment of religion" was involved in the decision in the *Everson* case,[20] in which Douglas joined, holding that provision not infringed where a state provided bus transportation for parochial school pupils as part of a general program of providing such transportation for students in the public schools. While the Court was clear that the establishment clause forbade the use of state funds "to support any religious activities or institutions" and that the clause was intended to erect "a wall of separation between church and state," it was equally clear that the free exercise clause would forbid the exclusion of persons from the benefits of public welfare legislation "because of their faith, or lack of it.[21] And here it thought the state was merely "extending its general state law benefits to all its citizens without regard to their religious belief," just as it did when it provided traffic policemen at both public and parochial schools. The First Amendment "requires the state to be a neutral in its relations with groups of religious believers and non-believers; it does not require the state to be their adversary."

Thereafter, Douglas voted with the Court to invalidate a system of religious instruction by religious teachers in the public schools during school hours, with students who did not wish such instruction being required to leave their classrooms and go elsewhere in the building to pursue their secular studies. This was held "beyond all question a utilization of the tax-established and tax-supported public school system to aid religious groups" in violation of the establishment clause.[22] Douglas also wrote for the Court to uphold a "released time" program under which public school pupils were given the option to leave the public school to take religious instruction elsewhere. Since this program involved "neither religious instruction in public school classrooms nor the expenditure of public funds," it was held not to breach the wall of separation between church and state:[23]

20. Everson v. Board of Education, 330 U.S. 1 (1947).

21. The Court later held, with Douglas concurring, that a state could not deny unemployment compensation to a Seventh Day Adventist because of her refusal on religious grounds to accept employment involving work on Saturday. Sherbert v. Verner, 374 U.S. 398 (1963) (concurring opinion).

22. Illinois *ex rel.* McCollum v. Board of Education, 333 U.S. 203 (1948).

23. Zorach v. Clauson, 343 U.S. 306 (1952).

So far as interference with the "free exercise" of religion and an "establishment" of religion are concerned, the separation must be complete and unequivocal. The First Amendment within the scope of its coverage permits no exception; the prohibition is absolute. The First Amendment, however, does not say that in every and all respects there shall be a separation of Church and State. Rather, it studiously defines the manner, the specific ways, in which there shall be no concert or union or dependency one on the other. That is the common sense of the matter. Otherwise the state and religion would be aliens to each other—hostile, suspicious, and even unfriendly. Churches could not be required to pay property taxes. Municipalities would not be permitted to render police or fire protection to religious groups.

Douglas wrote for the Court again to hold that a Jehovah's Witness could not be convicted for violation of an ordinance forbidding religious meetings in a public park, where it was conceded that the ordinance was not enforced against Catholics and Protestants. Such discriminatory enforcement amounted to "the state preferring some religious groups over this one."[24]

In another group of cases sustaining state Sunday Closing Laws, Douglas has dissented—contending that they violate both the free exercise and the establishment clauses of the First Amendment.[25]

He has concurred in decisions holding that the use in New York of a state-prescribed prayer in the public schools violates the First Amendment, even though no student was required to participate in the recitation of the prayer.[26] He took the occasion to say, however, that he had been wrong to accept state-supported school bussing for parochial schools as constitutional in the *Everson* case,[27] and that he was now persuaded that the state "oversteps the bounds when it finances a religious exercise," even though there was no coercion, "no effort at indoctrination and no attempt at exposition." True, the time

24. Fowler v. Rhode Island, 345 U.S. 67 (1953). *See also* Niemotko v. Maryland, 340 U.S. 268 (1951).

25. Braunfeld v. Brown, 366 U.S. 599 (1961) (dissenting opinion); Gallagher v. Crown Kosher Super Market, 366 U.S. 617 (1961) (dissenting opinion); McGowan v. Maryland, 366 U.S. 420 (1961) (dissenting opinion); Arlan's Department Store v. Kentucky, 371 U.S. 218 (1962) (dissenting opinion).

26. Engel v. Vitale, 370 U.S. 421 (1962) (concurring opinion).

27. Everson v. Board of Education, 330 U.S. 1 (1947).

devoted by the teacher who lead the prayer was "minuscule," but "the person praying is a public official on the public payroll, performing a religious exercise in a governmental institution":

> At the same time I cannot say that to authorize this prayer is to establish a religion in the strictly historic meaning of those words. A religion is not established in the usual sense merely by letting those who choose to do so say the prayer that the public school teacher leads. Yet once government finances a religious exercise it inserts a divisive influence into our communities. The New York Court said that the prayer given does not conform to all of the tenets of the Jewish, Unitarian, and Ethical Culture groups. One of the petitioners is an agnostic.

When the Court later invalidated, on the protest of Unitarians and atheists, a state practice of reading passages from the Bible in the public schools, Douglas again concurred and elaborated on his views:[28]

> These regimes violate the Establishment Clause in two different ways. In each case the State is conducting a religious exercise; and, as the Court holds, that cannot be done without violating the "neutrality" required of the State by the balance of power between individual, church and state that has been struck by the First Amendment. But the Establishment Clause is not limited to precluding the State itself from conducting religious exercises. It also forbids the State to employ its facilities or funds in a way that gives any church, or all churches, greater strength in our society than it would have by relying on its members alone. Thus, the present regimes must fall under that clause for the additional reason that public funds, though small in amount, are being used to promote a religious exercise. Through the mechanism of the State, all of the people are being required to finance a religious exercise that only some of the people want and that violates the sensibilities of others . . .
>
> . . . It is not the amount of public funds expended; as this case illustrates, it is the use to which public funds are put that is controlling. For the First Amendment does not say that some forms of extablishment are allowed; it says that "no law respecting an establishment of religion" shall be made.

28. Abbington School District v. Schempp, 374 U.S. 203 (1963) (concurring opinion).

Given this analysis, it was not surprising that Douglas should dissent when the Court followed its decision approving bussing for parochial schools in the *Everson* case to hold in 1968 that the state might also provide textbooks for parochial schools. As he put it:[29]

The statutory system provides that the parochial school will ask for the books that it wants. Can there be the slightest doubt that the head of the parochial school will select the book or books that best promote its sectarian creed?

If the board of education supinely submits by approving and supplying the sectarian or sectarian-oriented textbooks, the struggle to keep church and state separate has been lost. If the board resists, then the battle line between church and state will have been drawn and the contest will be on to keep the school board independent or to put it under Church domination and control.

Whatever may be said of *Everson*, there is nothing ideological about a bus . . . [But a] parochial school textbook may contain many, many more seeds of creed and dogma than a prayer.

Douglas agreed with the Court in another case that prior decisions "inevitably determine" that a state law prohibiting the teaching of the theory of evolution in the public schools violated the First Amendment's requirement of state neutrality, where it was "clear that fundamentalist sectarian conviction was and is the law's reason for existence."[30] But he dissented again when, in 1970, the Court held that a state's granting of property tax exemptions for property used solely for religious worship was a sufficiently neutral act to satisfy the First Amendment:[31]

My Brother Harlan [in his concurring opinion] says he "would suppose" that the tax exemption extends to "groups whose avowed tenets may be antitheological, atheistic, or agnostic" . . . If it does, then the line between believers and nonbelievers has not been drawn. But, with all respect, there is not even a suggestion in the present record that the statute covers property used exclusively by organizations for "antitheological purposes," "atheistic purposes" or "agnostic purposes" . . .

29. Board of Education v. Allen, 392 U.S. 236 (1968) (dissenting opinion).
30. Epperson v. Arkansas, 393 U.S. 97 (1968).
31. Walz v. Tax Commission, 397 U.S. 664 (1970) (dissenting opinion).

There is a line between what a State may do in encouraging "religious" activity [as exemplified by the decision upholding the "released time" program], and what a State may not do by using its resources to promote "religious" activities . . . Yet that line may not always be clear. Closing public schools on Sunday is in the former category; subsidizing churches, in my view, is in the latter. Indeed I would suppose that in common understanding one of the best ways to "establish" one or more religions is to subsidize them, which a tax exemption does . . .

[The Court first held that the Fourteenth Amendment made the First Amendment applicable to the States in 1931 in *Stromberg* v. *California.*[32]] It was . . . not until 1962 that state-sponsored sectarian prayers were held to violate the Establishment Clause [in *Engel* v. *Vitale*][33] . . .

Engel was as disruptive of traditional state practices as was *Stromberg* . . .

Hence the question in the present case makes irrelevant the "two centuries of uninterrupted freedom from taxation" referred to by the Court . . . If history be our guide, then tax exemption of church property in this country is indeed highly suspect, as it arose in the early days when the church was an agency of the state.

Later the Court invalidated a Rhode Island plan under which the state would supplement 15 percent of the annual salaries of teachers of secular subjects in private schools, including church-related schools, and a Pennsylvania plan under which the state would reimburse private schools for teachers salaries and textbooks for secular subjects. All of the teachers receiving the Rhode Island supplement were employed by Roman Catholic schools, and nearly all of the schools receiving reimbursement from Pennsylvania were Roman Catholic schools. These plans, the Court concluded, violated the establishment clause because they involved "excessive entanglement between government and religion . . . Teachers have a substantially different ideological character than books." Douglas concurred in the decision:[34]

The surveillance or supervision of the states needed to police grants involved in these . . . cases, if performed, puts a public investigator in

32. 283 U.S. 359 (1931).
33. 370 U.S. 421 (1962).
34. Lemon v. Kurtzman, 403 U.S. 602 (1971) (concurring opinion).

every classroom and entails a pervasive monitoring of these church agencies by the secular authorities. Yet if that surveillance or supervision is not done the zeal of religious proselytizers promises to carry the day and make a shambles of the Establishment Clause. Moreover, when taxpayers of many faiths are required to contribute money for the propagation of one faith, the Free Exercise Clause is infringed.

The analysis of the constitutional objections to these two state systems . . . must start with the admitted and obvious fact that the *raison d'être* of parochial schools is the propagation of religious faith. They also teach secular subjects; but they came into existence in this country because Protestant groups were perverting the public schools by using them to propagate their faith. The Catholics naturally rebelled. If schools were to be used to propagate a particular creed or religion, then Catholic ideals should also be served. Hence the advent of parochial schools . . .

The story of conflict and dissension is long and well-known. The result was a state of so-called equilibrium where religious instruction was eliminated from public schools and the use of public funds to support religious schools was banned.

But the hydraulic pressures created by political forces and by economic stress were great and they began to change the situation. Laws were passed—state and federal—that dispensed public funds to sustain religious schools and the plea was always in the educational frame of reference: education in all sectors was needed from languages to calculus to nuclear physics. And it was forcefully argued that a linguist or mathematician or physicist trained in a religious school was equally competent with those trained in secular schools.

And so we have gradually edged into a situation where vast amounts of public funds are supplied each year to sectarian schools. [In 1970, $2.1 billion in federal funds and $100 million in state aid went to private colleges and universities.]

And the argument is made that the private parochial school system takes about $9 billion a year off the back of the government—as if that were enough to justify violating the Establishment Clause . . .

The Rhode Island Act allows a supplementary salary to a teacher in a sectarian school if he or she "does not teach a course in religion."

The Pennsylvania Act provides for state financing of instruction in mathematics, modern foreign languages, physical science, and physical education provided that the instruction in those courses "shall not include any subject matter expressing religious teaching, or the morals or forms of worship of any sect" . . .

Under these laws there will be vast governmental suppression, surveillance, or meddling in church affairs . . . The constitutional mandate can in part be carried out by censoring the curricula . . . But the problem only starts there. Sectarian instruction, in which of course a state may not indulge, can take place in a course on Shakespeare or in one on mathematics. No matter what the curriculum offers, the question is, what is *taught?* We deal not with evil teachers but with zealous ones who may use any opportunity to indoctrinate a class . . .

One can imagine what a religious zealot, as contrasted to a civil libertarian, can do with the Reformation or with the Inquisition. Much history can be given the gloss of a particular religion. I would think that policing these grants to detect sectarian instruction would be insufferable to religious partisans and would breed division between church and state.

At the same time, however, the Court upheld federal grants to church-sponsored colleges and universities to aid in the construction of buildings. The federal law under which the grants were made provided that the buildings could not be used "for sectarian instruction or as a place of religious worship" for a period of twenty years and that, if they were so used within that time, a proportion of the federal grant must be returned to the United States. The Court invalidated so much of the law as would permit sectarian use of the buildings after the first twenty years without liability to the United States, but in other respects found no violation of the free exercise clause or the establishment clause. Douglas dissented:[35]

The public purpose in secular education is, to be sure, furthered by the program. Yet the sectarian purpose is aided by making the parochial school system viable. The purpose is to increase "student enrollment" and the students obviously aimed at are those of the particular faith now financed by taxpayer's money. Parochial schools are not beamed at agnostics, atheists, or those of a competing sect. The more sophisticated institutions may admit minorites; but the dominant religious character is not changed . . . The Federal Government is giving religious schools a block grant to build certain facilities. The fact that money is given once at the beginning of a program rather than apportioned annually as in *Lemon*[36] . . . is without constitutional signifi-

35. Tilton v. Richardson, 403 U.S. 672 (1971) (dissenting in part).
36. Lemon v. Kurtzman, note 34, *supra*.

cance . . . The majority's distinction is in effect that small violations over a period of years are unconstitutional . . . while a huge violation occurring only once is *de minimus.* I cannot agree with such sophistry.

. . . The facilities financed by taxpayers' funds are not to be used "for sectarian" purposes. Religious teaching and secular teaching are so enmeshed in parochial schools that only the strictist supervision and surveillance would insure compliance with the condition. Parochial schools may require religious exercises, even in the classroom. A parochial school operates on one budget. Money not spent for one purpose becomes available for other purposes. Thus the fact that there are no religious observances in federally financed facilities is not controlling because required religious observances will take place in other buildings. Our decision in *Engel* v. *Vitale*[37] . . . held that a requirement of a prayer in public schools violated the Establishment Clause. Once those schools become federally funded they became bound by federal standards . . . and accordingly adherence to *Engel* would require an end to required religious exercises. That kind of surveillance and control will certainly be obnoxious to church authorities and if done will radically change the character of the parochial school. Yet if that surveillance is not searching and continuous, this federal financing is obnoxious under the Establishment and Free Exercise Clauses all for the reasons stated in [*Lemon*] . . .

I dissent not because of any lack of respect for parochial schools, but out of a feeling of despair that the respect which through history has been accorded the First Amendment is this day lost.[38]

SPEECH AND PRESS

The numerous other First Amendment problems that have come to the Court without involvement of religious issues arose in a variety of contexts. Some arose from legislative efforts to purge the political process of coercion and corruption. One such effort is the federal Hatch Act, which seeks to immunize federal executive employees from

37. 370 U.S. 421 (1962).

38. Douglas' views on the treatment of conscientious objectors under the Selective Service Act are discussed in Chapter 5. For other accounts of Douglas' views on religious issues, see H. Linde, "Justice Douglas on Freedom in the Welfare State," 39 *Wash. L. Rev.* 4 (1964), 40 *Wash. L. Rev.* 10 (1965); L. Manning, "The Douglas Concept of God in Government," 39 *Wash. L. Rev.* 47 (1964); D. Louisell, "The Man and the Mountain: Douglas on Religious Freedom," 73 *Yale L.J.* 975 (1964).

political pressure by forbidding them to take "any active part in political management or political campaigns," even during their off-duty hours. When the Court upheld this act, as applied to a roller in the federal mint, as a "reasonable" restriction of First Amendment rights, Douglas dissented. He thought that, at least as to industrial workers as distinguished from administrative personnel, the statute went too far by its "partial political sterilization," particularly since a law could be drawn which would focus on the real source of the evil—those who would use coercion on government employees for political purposes.[39]

Other instances are provided by corrupt practices acts. Douglas concurred in a reversal of a conviction of a newspaper publisher, under a state act, for publishing an editorial on election day urging electors to vote for a mayor-council form of government—"a blatant violation of freedom of the press."[40] When the Court, in order to avoid constitutional questions, construed a provision of the federal act forbidding corporations and labor unions to make "expenditures" in connection with primary and general elections for federal office as not applying to the cost of a union newspaper distributed to union workers, he did not agree that the act could be so construed. But he concurred in dismissal of the prosecution on the ground that the act, as applied, violated the First Amendment's guarantees of freedom of speech, press, and assembly. Assuming that valid regulation of expenditures might be imposed to protect against corruption, or against "undue influence" of unions and corporations in the electoral process, he thought that outright prohibition of all expenditures went too far.[41] When, in a later case, the Court held the act applicable to the expenditure of union funds for television broadcasts designed to influence a federal election and remanded the case for trial without passing on the constitutional issues, he dissented on the ground that the act was unconstitutional.[42]

39. United Public Workers of America v. Mitchell, 330 U.S. 75 (1947) (dissenting in part).

40. Mills v. Alabama, 384 U.S. 214 (1966) (concurring opinion).

41. United States v. CIO, 335 U.S. 106 (1948) (concurring opinion).

42. United States v. United Automobile Workers, 352 U.S. 567 (1957) (dissenting opinion).

A third source of such instances is the federal Regulation of Lobbying Act, which requires reports to Congress from any person who "solicits, collects, or receives" contributions "to be used principally to aid, or the principal purpose of which person is to aid," in the passage or defeat of federal legislation. When that act was challenged under the First Amendment, the Court in 1954 first construed it to be limited to "lobbying in its commonly accepted sense," to "direct communication with members of Congress," and found it, as so construed, constitutional. Douglas dissented:[43]

> [If Congress can] impose registration requirements on the exercise of First Amendment rights, saving to the courts the salvage of the good from the bad, and meanwhile causing all who might possibly be covered to act at their peril, the law would in practical effect be a deterrent to the exercise of First Amendment rights. The Court seeks to avoid that consequence by construing the law narrowly as applying only to those who are paid to "buttonhole" Congressmen or who collect and expend moneys to get others to do so . . .
>
> The language of the Act is so broad that one who writes a letter or makes a speech or publishes an article or distributes literature . . . has no fair notice when he is close to the prohibited line. No construction we give it today will make clear retroactively the vague standards that confronted appellees when they did the acts now charged against them as criminal . . . Since the Act touches on the exercise of First Amendment rights, and is not narrowly drawn to meet precise evils, its vagueness has some of the evils of a continuous and effective restraint.

Other First Amendment cases arose under laws which, at least in their inception, were designed to protect one person from annoyance, offense, or more serious injury by the act of another. Some of these laws were aimed directly at speech and press. Others would cover also activity not protected by the First Amendment.

A clear example of the former is a city ordinance aimed at the use of sound trucks. Douglas wrote for the Court to invalidate an ordinance which forbade their use without a permit and which gave the licensing authority complete discretion to grant or deny the permit. Like the statutes requiring licenses for the distribution of literature, this

43. United States v. Harriss, 347 U.S. 612 (1954) (dissenting opinion). *See also* United States v. Rumely, 345 U.S. 41 (1953) (concurring opinion).

ordinance constituted a prior restraint on the exercise of First Amendment rights. "Any abuses which loud-speakers create can be controlled by narrowly drawn statutes."[44] But when the Court sustained the conviction of a sound-truck user under an ordinance forbidding the use on the streets of any such truck "which emits . . . loud and raucous noises," he dissented on the ground that neither the charge against the defendant nor the instructions to the jury included the "loud and raucous noises" element, so that the effect was to apply the ordinance to forbid all use of sound trucks—an even more flagrant violation of the First Amendment than the licensing ordinance struck down in the previous case.[45]

Another example was provided in the *Terminiello* case, which involved the disorderly conduct conviction of one who had made a speech. According to the evidence, it could have been found by the jury that his speech was anti-Semitic and had provoked the throwing of rocks, bricks, bottles, and stink-bombs and the breaking of windows and doors of the auditorium in which he spoke by those outside, whom he characterized as "slimy scum," "snakes" and "bedbugs." But the jury had been instructed that the crime was committed if the speech "stirs the public to anger, invites dispute, brings about a condition of unrest, or creates a disturbance, or if it molests the inhabitants in the enjoyment of peace and quiet by arousing alarm." Douglas wrote for the Court to invalidate this conviction without reaching the question whether the speech consisted of "fighting words" not entitled to First Amendment protection: "[I]t is said that throughout the appellate proceedings the [state] courts assumed that the only conduct punishable and punished under the ordinance was conduct constituting 'fighting words' . . . Petitioner was not convicted under a statute so narrowly construed. For all anyone knows he was convicted under the parts of the ordinance [as construed by the trial court] which, for example, make it an offense merely to invite dispute or to bring about a condition of unrest."[46]

44. Saia v. New York, 334 U.S. 558 (1943).
45. Kovacs v. Cooper, 336 U.S. 77 (1949) (dissenting opinion).
46. Terminiello v. Chicago, 337 U.S. 1 (1949). *See also* Carroll v. President & Commissioners of Princess Anne, 393 U.S. 175 (1968) (separate opinion).

But when, in a later case, the Court sustained the disorderly conduct conviction of a speaker who had characterized two city mayors and the president of the United States as "bums" and the American Legion as "a Nazi Gestapo" and who had ignored a police officer's order to stop speaking (an order delivered after one man in the audience told the officer he would remove the speaker from the platform if the officer did not), Douglas dissented:[47]

> One high function of the police is to protect these lawful gatherings so that the speakers may exercise their constitutional rights. When unpopular causes are sponsored from the public platform, there will commonly be mutterings and unrest and heckling from the crowd. When a speaker mounts a platform it is not unusual to find him resorting to exaggeration, to vilification of ideas and men, to the making of false charges. But those extravagances . . . do not justify penalizing the speaker by depriving him of the platform or by punishing him for his conduct.
>
> A speaker may not, of course, incite a riot any more than he may incite a breach of the peace by the use of "fighting words" . . . But this record shows no such extremes. It shows an unsympathetic audience and the threat of one man to haul the speaker from the stage. It is against that kind of threat that speakers need police protection. If they do not receive it and instead the police throw their weight on the side of those who would break up the meetings, the police become the new censors of speech.

In other cases Douglas has voted with the Court to upset breach of the peace convictions based on peaceful demonstrations before courthouses,[48] state capitols,[49] and city halls[50] and inside segregated

47. Feiner v. New York, 340 U.S. 315 (1951) (dissenting opinion). *See also* Street v. New York, 394 U.S. 576 (1969). In Cohen v. California, 403 U.S. 14 (1971), Douglas voted with the Court to hold that a state could not punish one who appeared in a courthouse wearing a jacket bearing the words "Fuck the Draft" for the crime of "offensive conduct" which "has a tendency to provoke others to acts of violence."

48. Cox v. Louisiana, 379 U.S. 536 (1965); Cox v. Louisiana, 379 U.S. 559 (1965). *See also* Cameron v. Johnson, 390 U.S. 611 (1968) (dissenting opinion). The protection given labor union picketing under the First Amendment is discussed in Chapter 22.

49. Edwards v. South Carolina, 372 U.S. 229 (1963).

50. Henry v. City of Rock Hill, 376 U.S. 776 (1964).

county libraries[51] to protest racial discrimination. But when the Court sustained a trespass conviction based on a peaceful demonstration before a county jail to protest racial segregation and the jailing of earlier protesters because jails are "built for security purposes" and not "open to the public," he dissented:[52]

> The jailhouse, like an executive mansion, a legislative chamber, a courthouse, or the statehouse itself ... is one of the seats of government, whether it be the Tower of London, the Bastille, or a small county jail. And when it houses political prisoners or those who many think are unjustly held, it is an obvious center for protest. The right to petition for the redress of grievances has an ancient history and is not limited to writing a letter or sending a telegram to a congressman; it is not confined to appearing before the local city council, or writing letters to the President or Governor or Mayor ... Conventional methods of petitioning may be, and often have been, shut off to large groups of our citizens. Legislators may turn deaf ears; formal complaints may be routed endlessly through a bureaucratic maze; courts may let the wheels of justice grind very slowly. Those who do not control television and radio, those who cannot afford to advertise in a newspapers or circulate elaborate pamphlets may have only a more limited type of access to public officials. Their methods should not be condemned as tactics of obstruction and harassment as long as the assembly and petition are peaceable, as these were.

When the Court later reversed the disorderly conduct conviction of peaceful demonstrators against segregation in public schools in Chicago, who had marched from city hall to the mayor's residence, Douglas joined in a concurring opinion which suggested some limits:[53]

> Our Federal Constitution does not render the States powerless to regulate the conduct of demonstrators and picketers, conduct which is more than "speech," more than "press," more than "assembly," and more than "petition," as those terms are used in the First Amendment. Narrowly drawn statutes regulating the conduct of demonstrators and picketers are not impossible to draft. And narrowly drawn statutes regulating these activities are not impossible to pass if the people who elect their legislators want them passed. Passage of such laws, however,

51. Brown v. Louisiana, 383 U.S. 131 (1966).
52. Adderley v. Florida, 385 U.S. 39 (1966) (dissenting opinion).
53. Gregory v. Chicago, 394 U.S. 111 (1969) (concurring opinion).

like the passage of all other laws, constitutes in the final analysis a choice of policies by the elected representatives of the people.

I, of course, do not mean to say or even to intimate that freedom of speech, press, assembly, or petition can be abridged so long as the First Amendment remains unchanged in our Constitution. But to say that the First Amendment grants those broad rights free from any exercise of governmental power to regulate conduct, as distinguished from speech, press, assembly, or petition, would subject all the people of the Nation to the uncontrollable whim and arrogance of speakers, and writers, and protesters, and grievance bearers . . . Were the authority of government so trifling as to permit anyone with a complaint to have the vast power to do anything he pleased, wherever he pleased, and whenever he pleased, our customs and our habits of conduct, social, political, economic, ethical, and religious, would all be wiped out, and become no more than relics of a gone but not forgotten past. Churches would be compelled to welcome into their buildings invaders who came but to scoff and jeer; streets and highways and public buildings would cease to be available for the purposes for which they were constructed and dedicated whenever demonstrators and picketers wanted to use them for their own purposes. And perhaps worse than all other changes, homes, the sacred retreat to which families repair for their privacy and their daily way of living, would have to have their doors thrown open to all who desired to convert the occupants to new views, new morals, and a new way of life. Men and women who hold public office would be compelled, simply because they did hold public office, to lose the comforts and privacy of an unpicketed home. I believe that our Constitution, written for the ages, to endure except as changed in the manner it provides, did not create a government with such monumental weaknesses. Speech and press are, of course, to be free, so that public matters can be discussed with impunity. But picketing and demonstrating can be regulated like other conduct of men. I believe that the homes of men, sometimes the last citadel of the tired, the weary, and the sick, can be protected by government from noisy, marching, tramping, threatening picketers and demonstrators bent on filling the minds of men, women and children with fears of the unknown.

Douglas voted with the Court also to invalidate an ordinance forbidding the distribution of literature which did not disclose the identity of the distributor, as applied to one who distributed handbills urging a boycott of merchants practicing racial discrimination in employment. The state sought to justify the ordinance as a protection against fraud, false advertising and libel. But the ordinance was not so "limited to prevent these or any other supposed evils," and "identification and fear of reprisal" of the distributor would tend "to restrict freedom to distribute information and thereby freedom of expression."[54]

The states have long had laws forbidding attorneys to solicit business, either directly or through intermediaries, and laws forbidding the stirring up of litigation. The Court invalidated the application of such laws to the NAACP, a national organization devoted to combatting racial discrimination, in part by instigating test lawsuits and providing counsel therefore. Such application was viewed as infringing on freedom of association and expression exercised in an effort to seek legal redress for violation of other constitutional rights. Douglas agreed that the First Amendment was violated, but added that since the state's enforcement effort was confined exclusively to this organization, it also was an unconstitutional discrimination in violation of the equal protection clause.[55] He also voted with the Court to hold that the First Amendment similarly forbade the application of such laws to labor union "legal aid" schemes, designed to provide lawyers for injured members in order to protect their rights under federal and state compensation laws.[56]

Libel laws, providing for damages to persons injured by untrue defamatory statements, are older than the Constitution. But a few years ago some states added to their traditional libel laws, which protected only individuals specifically defamed, "group" libel laws. One such law came before the Court in the *Beauharnais* case in 1952. It provided criminal penalties for anyone who falsely portrayed "depravity, criminality, unchastity, or lack of virtue of a class of citizens, of any

54. Talley v. California, 362 U.S. 60 (1960).

55. NAACP v. Button, 371 U.S. 415 (1963) (concurring opinion). *See also* Harrison v. NAACP, 360 U.S. 167 (1959) (dissenting opinion); NAACP v. Bennett, 360 U.S. 471 (1959) (dissenting opinion).

56. Brotherhood of Railroad Trainmen v. Virginia *ex rel.* Virginia State Bar, 377 U.S. 1 (1964); United Mine Workers of America v. Illinois State Bar Association, 389 U.S. 217 (1967); United Transportation Union v. State Bar of Michigan, 401 U.S. 576 (1971).

race, color, creed or religion" and had been employed to convict one who had defamed blacks in petitions which he had circulated seeking to persuade the city mayor and council to pass segregation laws. The Court concluded that the law did not violate the First Amendment. Although no clear and present danger of disorder was shown, certain classes of speech—"the lewd and obscene, the profane, the libelous, and insulting or 'fighting' words"—were considered to be "of such slight social value as a step to truth that any benefit that may be derived from them is clearly outweighed by the social interest in order and morality." Douglas dissented:[57]

The First Amendment is couched in absolute terms—freedom of speech shall not be abridged. Speech has therefore a preferred position as contrasted to some other civil rights. For example, privacy, equally sacred to some, is protected by the Fourth Amendment only against unreasonable searches and seizures. There is room for regulation of the ways and means of invading privacy. No such leeway is granted the invasion of the right of free speech guaranteed by the First Amendment. Until recent years that had been the course and direction of constitutional law. Yet recently the Court in this and in other cases has engrafted the right of regulation onto the First Amendment by placing in the hands of the legislative branch the right to regulate "within reasonable limits" the right of free speech . . . Today a white man stands convicted for protesting in unseemly language against our decisions invalidating restrictive covenants.[58] Tomorrow a Negro will be haled before a court for denouncing lynch law in heated terms. Farm laborers in the West who compete with field hands drifting up from Mexico; whites who feel the pressure of orientals; a minority which finds employment going to members of the dominant religious group—all of these are caught in the mesh of today's decision. Debate and argument even in the courtroom are not always calm and dispassionate. Emotions sway speakers and audience alike. Intemperate speech is a

57. Beauharnais v. Illinois, 343 U.S. 250 (1952). The majority opinion's assumption in this case that the First Amendment makes an exception for profane speech remains to be tested. A state statute authorizing censorship of "sacreligious" films was invalidated in a decision in which Douglas joined in Joseph Burstyn, Inc. v. Wilson, 343 U.S. 495 (1952), as a prior restraint on freedom of speech and press, but the term "sacreligious" was held unconstitutionally vague. The exception for obscenity is considered below.

58. See p. 135, *infra*.

distinctive characteristic of man. Hotheads blow off and release destructive energy in the process. They shout and rave, exaggerating weakness, magnifying error, viewing with alarm. So it has been from the beginning; and so it will be throughout time. The Framers of the Constitution knew human nature as well as we do. They too had lived in dangerous days; they too knew the suffocating influence of orthodoxy and standardized thought. They weighed the compulsions for restrained speech and thought against the abuses of liberty. They chose liberty. That should be our choice today no matter how distasteful to us the pamphlet of Beauharnais may be.

Other cases in recent years have involved the permissible reach of the traditional libel laws. In 1964, in *New York Times v. Sullivan*, the Court read the First Amendment to mean that the state could not award damages for libel against the defamatory criticism of a "public official" (a county commissioner) unless the statement was made with "actual malice—that is, with knowledge that it was false or with reckless disregard of whether it was false or not." Such a reading was necessary, the Court thought, because otherwise "would-be critics of official conduct may be deterred from voicing their criticism, even though it is believed to be true and even though it is in fact true, because of doubt whether it can be proved in Court or fear of the expense of having to do so," and the result would be to "dampen the vigor and limit the variety of public debate." Douglas concurred, but thought that there should be an absolute immunity for such criticism. The Court's rule, he thought, would still leave the would-be critic subject to the dampening effect of possible libel actions.[59] He has persisted in that view as subsequent decisions have held that public officials include judges,[60] county attorneys and police chiefs,[61] a deputy chief of city detectives,[62] elected court clerks,[63] deputy sheriffs,[64] a mayor who was a candidate for county tax assessor,[65] and a county supervisor of

59. New York Times Co. v. Sullivan, 376 U.S. 254 (1964) (concurring opinion).
60. Garrison v. Louisiana, 379 U.S. 64 (1964) (concurring opinions).
61. Henry v. Collins, 380 U.S. 356 (1965) (concurring opinion).
62. Time, Inc. v. Pape, 401 U.S. 279 (1971) (separate opinion).
63. Beckley Newspapers Corp. v. Hanks, 389 U.S. 81 (1967) (concurring opinion).
64. St. Amant v. Thompson, 390 U.S. 727 (1968) (dissenting opinion).
65. Oscala Star-Banner Co. v. Damron, 401 U.S. 295 (1971) (separate opinion).

recreation appointed by the county commissioners, at least where the criticism is directed at the county commissioner also.[66] And in the case last mentioned he suggested that "public issues" rather than "public officials" would provide the better test for application of the doctrine. He has persisted in his argument for absolute immunity also when the Court extended the doctrine to embrace "public figures," such as a private citizen seeking nomination in a primary election to become a candidate for the United States Senate,[67] university football coaches, and retired generals who inject themselves into public affairs.[68] He has persisted too as the Court has read the doctrine to limit the power of a school board to discharge a public school teacher for criticism of the board,[69] and to limit the power of the states to award damages for invasion of privacy to private citizens whose private lives had been brought into the news by events over which they had no control.[70]

A great number of First Amendment issues have arisen out of federal and state efforts to purge the government and, in some instances, the body politic, of persons variously described as "disloyal," "security risks," and "subversives." These efforts to some extent seek to protect

66. Rosenblatt v. Baer, 383 U.S. 75 (1966). *See also* Ginzburg v. Goldwater, 396 U.S. 1049 (1970) (dissenting opinion).

67. Monitor Patriot Co. v. Roy, 401 U.S. 265 (1971) (separate opinion).

68. Curtis Publishing Co. v. Butts, 388 U.S. 130 (1967) (concurring and dissenting opinion). *See also* Greenbolt Cooperative Publishing Ass'n. v. Bresler, 398 U.S. 6 (1970) (concurring opinion); Time, Inc. v. Bon Air Hotel, Inc., 393 U.S. 859 (1968) (dissenting opinion).

69. Pickering v. Board of Education, 391 U.S. 563 (1968) (concurring opinion). Douglas dissented when the Court refused to consider whether college students can be expelled for distributing a leaflet, "ill tempered and in bad taste," criticizing the college administration. Jones v. State Board of Education, 397 U.S. 31 (1970) (dissenting opinion).

70. Time, Inc. v. Hill, 385 U.S. 374 (1967) (concurring opinions). *See also* Ashton v. Kentucky, 384 U.S. 195 (1966), where Douglas wrote for the Court to hold a state's common law crime of libel unconstitutionally vague under the First Amendment. In Rosenbloom v. Metromedia, Inc., 403 U.S. 29 (1971), a 5–3 decision in which Douglas did not participate, the Court held the *Sullivan* doctrine applicable in the libel action of a private citizen who had been charged with but acquitted of selling obscene literature, when he sued a radio broadcaster for pretrial reports of the charges. Three justices based their decision on the "public issues" test, one on the ground that the issue involved public officials although the plaintiff was not one, and Justice Black adhered to the view he shared with Justice Douglas that the news media should be absolutely immune from libel judgments.

against "seditious" speech and to some extent are intended to be prophylactic—to go beyond laws defining such hostile acts as treason, sabotage, and espionage and to identify, isolate, and in some instances incarcerate those thought likely to commit hostile acts in the future. In the enforcement of laws directed at hostile acts, Douglas consistently voted to sustain convictions in the several treason prosecutions which reached the Court after World War II.[71] In the only other case during his tenure involving guilt or innocence of an act hostile to the state, he voted to affirm an espionage conviction.[72] But in the cases in this area involving governmental action against belief, expression, and association, he has frequently found obstacles in the First Amendment,[73] as well as in certain procedural guarantees to be mentioned later.

One method frequently pursued by the government is to exact a loyalty oath from government officials and employees, and for a time under a federal law now repealed, from labor union officials. Douglas has voted with the Court to sustain an oath requiring candidates for political office to swear that they are not engaged in an attempt to overthrow the government by force and are not knowingly members of organization engaged in such an attempt.[74] He has voted with the Court also to invalidate, as overly broad under the First Amendment, oaths which go further and require state employees to swear that they do not belong to designated organizations without regard to their knowledge of the organizations' purposes,[75] or require all teachers in public schools and state colleges to list annually every organization to

71. Cramer v. United States, 325 U.S. 1 (1945) (dissenting opinion); Haupt v. United States, 330 U.S. 631 (1947) (separate opinion); Kawakita v. United States, 343 U.S. 717 (1952).

72. Gorin v. United States, 312 U.S. 19 (1941).

73. But in his first two such cases, involving convictions for making speeches and distributing literature which obstructed recruiting and attempted to cause disloyalty in the armed services, where no constitutional questions were raised, he dissented from decisions that the evidence was insufficient to support the convictions. Hartzel v. United States, 322 U.S. 680 (1944) (dissenting opinion); Keegan v. United States, 325 U.S. 478 (1945) (dissenting opinion). He also dissented, in another case where no constitutional questions were raised, from reversal of a conviction for failure to register as the agent of a foreign principal. Viereck v. United States, 318 U.S. 236 (1943) (dissenting opinion).

74. Gerende v. Board of Supervisors, 341 U.S. 56 (1951).

75. Wieman v. Updegraff, 344 U.S. 183 (1952) (concurring opinions).

which they have belonged or regularly contributed during the past five years,[76] or require all state employees to swear that they have never lent their "aid, support, advice, counsel or influence to the Communist Party,"[77] or require all teachers to swear that they are not "subversive persons" and "will by precept and example promote respect for the flag and the institutions of the United States . . . and the State . . . reverence for law and order and undivided allegiance to the government of the United States,"[78] and an oath which does not make clear that the teacher taking it does not disavow attempts to alter the form of government by peaceful means as well as by force.[79] And in 1966 he wrote for the Court to invalidate a state employees' oath which disavowed knowing membership in any organization having as "one of its purposes" the forceful overthrow of the government, without regard to whether the employee shared that purpose:[80]

> One who subscribes to this . . . oath and who is, or thereafter becomes, a knowing member of an organization which has as "one of its purposes" the violent overthrow of the government, is subject to immediate discharge and criminal penalties [for perjury] . . . The "hazard of being prosecuted for knowing but guiltless behavior" . . . is a reality. People often label as "communist" ideas which they oppose; and they often make up our juries. "[P]rosecutors too are human . . . " Would a teacher be safe and secure in going to a Pugwash Conference? Would it be legal to join a seminar group predominantly Communist and therefore subject to control by those who are said to believe in overthrow of the Government by force and violence? Juries might convict though the teacher did not subscribe to the wrongful aims of the organization . . .
>
> Those who join an organization but do not share its unlawful purposes and who do not participate in its unlawful activities surely pose no threat, either as citizens or as public employees. Laws such as this which are not restricted in scope to those who join with the "specific intent" to further illegal actions impose, in effect, a conclusive

76. Shelton v. Tucker, 364 U.S. 479 (1960).
77. Cramp v. Board of Public Instruction, 368 U.S. 278 (1961) (separate opinion).
78. Baggett v. Bullitt, 377 U.S. 360 (1964).
79. Whitehall v. Elkins, 389 U.S. 54 (1967).
80. Elfbrandt v. Russell, 384 U.S. 11 (1966).

presumtpion that the member shares the unlawful aims of the organization.

. . . A statute touching [First Amendment] rights must be "narrowly drawn to define and punish specific conduct as constituting a clear and present danger to a substantial interest of the State" . . . A law which applies to membership without the "specific intent" to further the illegal aims of the organization infringes unnecessarily on protected freedoms. It rests on the doctrine of "guilt by association" which has no place here.

In an earlier case, in which the Court was evenly divided, Douglas would have invalidated the requirement of the former federal oath for union officials, which required them to swear that they did "not believe in" and were not members of and did not support "any organization that believes in" overthrow of the government "by force or by any illegal or unconstitutional methods."[81]

In 1971 the Court held that a Florida oath for teachers was constitutional insofar as it required them to swear to support the constitutions of the state and the United States but that it violated procedural due process insofar as it would bar from public employment, without hearing, any who would not also swear that they did not believe in forcible overthrow of the government. Douglas concurred in the decision, but on different grounds with respect to the latter feature of the oath.[82]

I agree that Florida may require state employees to affirm that they "will support the Constitution of the United States and of the State of Florida." Such a forward-looking, promissory oath . . . does not in my view offend the First Amendment's command that the grant or denial of governmental benefits cannot be made to turn on the political viewpoints or affiliations of a would-be beneficiary. I also agree that Florida may not base its employment decisions, as to state teachers, or any other hiring category, on an applicant's willingness *vel non* to affirm "that I do not believe in the overthrow of the government of the United States or of the State of Florida by force or violence."

However, in striking down the latter oath, the Court has left the clear implication that its objection runs, not against Florida's determination

81. Osman v. Douds, 339 U.S. 846 (1950) (dissenting opinion).
82. Connell v. Higginbotham, 403 U.S. 207 (1971) (concurring opinion).

to exclude those who "believe in the overthrow," but only against the State's decision to regard unwillingness to take the oath as conclusive, irrebuttable proof of the proscribed belief. Due process may rightly be invoked to condemn Florida's mechanistic approach to the question of proof. But in my view it simply does not matter what kind of evidence a state can muster to show that a job applicant "believes in the overthrow." For state action injurious to an individual cannot be justified on account of the nature of the individual's beliefs, whether he "believes in the overthrow" or has any other sort of belief . . .

I would strike down Florida's "overthrow" oath plainly and simply on the ground that belief as such cannot be the predicate of governmental action.

A second method employed by government to protect against subversion is the sedition law, which forbids advocacy thought to be dangerous. It was in cases involving such laws, in prosecutions during and after World War I, that Justices Holmes and Brandeis formulated the "clear and present danger" test in an effort to give the First Amendment more effect than the Court was then disposed to give it.

Similar cases arose after World War II, in prosecutions under the federal Smith Act for conspiracy to advocate forcible overthrow of the government, and first reached the Court in 1951 in *Dennis v. United States*, which involved national officers of the Communist party of the United States. When the Court found the clear and present danger test satisfied, Douglas dissented:[83]

Communism in the world scene is no bogeyman; but Communism as a political faction or party in this country plainly is. Communism has been so thoroughly exposed in this country that it has been crippled as a political force. Free speech has destroyed it as an effective political party . . . In days of trouble and confusion, when bread lines were long, when the unemployed walked the streets, when people were starving, the advocates of a short-cut by revolution might have a chance to gain adherents. But today there are no such conditions. The country is not in despair; the people know Soviet Communism; the doctrine of Soviet revolution is exposed in all of its ugliness and the American people want none of it.

How it can be said that there is a clear and present danger that this

83. Dennis v. United States, 341 U.S. 494 (1951) (dissenting opinion).

advocacy will succeed is, therefore, a mystery. Some nations less resilient than the United States, where illiteracy is high and where democratic traditions are only budding, might have to take drastic steps and jail these men for merely speaking their creed. But in America they are miserable merchants of unwanted ideas; their wares remain unsold. The fact that their ideas are abhorrent does not make them powerful.

... To believe that petitioners and their following are placed in such critical positions as to endanger the Nation is to believe the incredible ... Only those held by fear and panic could think otherwise.

He persisted in this view in a subsequent Smith Act case, in which the Court reversed the conviction for failure to give proper instructions to the jury on the necessity for proof that defendants had used inciting language.[84] And when, under another provision of the same act, the Court once affirmed a conviction for knowing membership in the Communist party as an organization advocating forcible overthrow[85] and once reversed for insufficiency of evidence,[86] he dissented in the first case and concurred in the second on the ground that both convictions violated the First Amendment. As he put it in the first of those cases:

We legalize today guilt by association, sending a man to prison when he committed no unlawful act. Today's break with tradition is a serious one. It borrows from the totalitarian philosophy ...

The case is not saved by showing that petitioner was an active member. None of the activity constitutes a crime ...

Not one single illegal act is charged to petitioner. That is why the essence of the crime covered by the indictment is merely belief—belief in the proletarian revolution, belief in Communist creed ...

... The creed truer to our faith was stated by the Bar Committee headed by Charles E. Hughes which in 1920 protested the refusal of the New York Assembly to seat five members of the Socialist Party: "... it is of the essence of the institutions of liberty that it be recognized that guilt is personal and cannot be attributed to the holding of opinion or to mere intent in the absence of overt acts ..."

Of course, government can move against those who take up arms

84. Yates v. United States, 354 U.S. 298 (1957) (concurring and dissenting). *Cf.* Mesarosh v. United States, 352 U.S. 1 (1956).

85. Scales v. United States, 367 U.S. 203 (1961) (dissenting opinion).

86. Noto v. United States, 367 U.S. 290 (1961) (concurring opinion).

against it. Of course, the constituted authority has the right of self-preservation. But we deal in this prosecution . . . only with the legality of ideas and beliefs, not with overt acts. The Court speaks of the prevention of "dangerous behavior" by punishing those "who work to bring about that behavior." That formula returns man to the dark days when government determined what behavior was "dangerous" and then policed the dissidents for tell-tale signs of advocacy.

In 1969, when the Court invalidated a state conviction of a Ku Klux Klan leader for advocating force, Douglas concurred because the state law made no distinction between advocacy and incitement. But he was by then convinced that some ancient doctrine was outmoded:[87]

The "clear and present danger" test was adumbrated by Mr. Justice Holmes in a case arising during World War I—a war "declared" by the Congress, not by the Chief Executive—[and elaborated by Holmes and Brandeis in subsequent cases] . . .

The dissents [of Holmes and Brandeis in later cases] show how easily "clear and present danger" is manipulated to crush what Brandeis called "[t]he fundamental right of free men to strive for better conditions through new legislation and new institutions" by argument and discourse . . . even in time of war. Though I doubt if the "clear and present danger" test is congenial to the First Amendment in time of a declared war, I am certain it is not reconcilable with the First Amendment in days of peace . . . In *Dennis* v. *United States*[88] . . . we opened wide the door, distorting the "clear and present danger" test beyond recognition.

In that case the prosecution dubbed an agreement to teach the Marxist creed a "conspiracy." The case was submitted to a jury on a charge that the jury could not convict unless it found that the defendants "intended to overthrow the Government 'as speedily as circumstances would permit' " . . . The Court sustained convictions under that charge, construing it to mean a determination of "whether the gravity of the evil, discounted by its improbability, justifies such invasion of free speech as is necessary to avoid the danger" . . .

My own view is quite different. I see no place in the regime of the First Amendment for any "clear and present danger" test, whether strict and tight as some would make it, or free-wheeling as the Court in *Dennis* rephrased it.

87. Brandenburg v. Ohio, 395 U.S. 444 (1969) (concurring opinion).
88. 341 U.S. 494 (1951).

When one reads the opinions closely and sees when and how the "clear and present danger" test has been applied, great misgivings are aroused. First, the threats were often loud but always puny and made serious only by judges so wedded to the *status quo* that critical analysis made them nervous. Second, the test was so twisted and perverted in *Dennis* as to make the trial of those teachers of Marxism an all-out political trial which was part and parcel of the cold war that has eroded substantial parts of the First Amendment.

Congress in 1962 sought in another way to protect at least some of our citizens from at least some dangerous ideas. It enacted a statute forbidding the Post Office Department to deliver mail originating abroad which contained "communist political propaganda" unless the addressee, after notification, requested its delivery. Douglas wrote for the Court to invalidate this statute in a decision indicating that the First Amendment protects the right to hear as well as to speak:[89]

The Act . . . is unconstitutional because it requires an official act (*viz.*, returning the reply card) as a limitation on the unfettered exercise of the addressee's First Amendment rights. As stated by Mr. Justice Holmes . . . : "The United States may give up the Post Office when it sees fit, but while it carries it on the use of the mails is almost as much a part of free speech as the right to use our tongues . . . "

Here the Congress—expressly restrained by the First Amendment from "abridging" freedom of speech and of the press—is the actor. The Act sets administrative officials astride the flow of mail to inspect it, appraise it, write the addressee about it, and await a response before dispatching the mail . . . The addressee carries an affirmative obligation which we do not think the Government may impose on him. This requirement is almost certain to have a deterrent effect, especially as respects those who have sensitive positions. Their livelihood may be dependent on a security clearance. Public officials, like school teachers who have no tenure, might think they would invite disaster if they read what the Federal Government says contains the seeds of treason. Apart from them, any addressee is likely to feel some inhibition in sending for literature which federal officials have condemned as "communist political propaganda."

As the concern of at least some of those who govern has tended in recent years to identify threats from dissidents other than the

89. Lamont v. Postmaster General, 381 U.S. 301 (1965).

Communists, Douglas has voted with the Court to hold that public school children may not be disciplined for wearing black armbands to protest hostilities in Vietnam,[90] that a man cannot be convicted of a crime for saying "we don't need no damn flag" under circumstances which created no threat of disturbance[91] or for picketing with anti-Vietnam placards which bear no "fighting words,"[92] and that an actor who wears an army uniform in an antiwar skit cannot be punished under the federal statute which permits the wearing of the uniform of any armed force in theatrical productions only "if the portrayal does not tend to discredit that armed force."[93] But the Court upheld a conviction for burning a selective service registration certificate as a protest "against the war and against the draft" on the ground that a provision in the Selective Service Act forbidding destruction of such certificates was a reasonable requirement in the administration of the Selective Service System. Douglas dissented because the Court refused to consider whether that act was valid in the absence of a congressional declaration of war.[94] He dissented also when the Court refused to consider whether a man can be convicted for wearing a vest fashioned out of a cut-up American flag.[95]

Another of the prophylactic programs much in vogue since World War II is the "loyalty" or "security risk" program, designed to detect and exclude or remove from the public service potential traitors, spies, and saboteurs. Typically, these programs involve probing into the beliefs, expressions, and associations of their subjects and hence raise grave questions under the First Amendment. They involve also serious questions of constitutional procedure, which will be considered later.

When questions as to the constitutionality of the federal loyalty

90. Tinker v. Des Moines Independent Community School District, 393 U.S. 503 (1969).

91. Street v. New York, 394 U.S. 576 (1969). In this case the defendant had also burned an American flag, but his conviction for unlawfully defiling, burning, and casting contempt upon the flag was reversed because it could have been based solely on the language he used. Hence, the Court did not reach the question whether the conviction could have been sustained if based solely on the burning of the flag.

92. Bachellar v. Maryland, 397 U.S. 564 (1970).

93. Schacht v. United States, 398 U.S. 58 (1970).

94. United States v. O'Brien, 391 U.S. 367 (1968) (dissenting opinion).

95. Cowgill v. California, 396 U.S. 371 (1970).

program first reached it, the Court was equally divided and hence affirmed a decision of a lower court sustaining the program.[96] But Douglas, in a concurring opinion in another case involving only procedural issues, made clear that he was one of the four who would have reversed.[97] Subsequent cases involving the federal program have also been disposed of on procedural or statutory issues, but Douglas has voted with the Court to contain its operation within statutory bounds[98] and to invalidate action taken when those administering the loyalty program did not follow their own rules.[99] And in dissenting opinions dealing with related questions, he has made clear his view that "our initial error in all this business [of sedition laws and loyalty programs] was our disregard [in the first Smith Act case][100] of the basic principle that government can concern itself only with the actions of men, not with their opinions or beliefs,"[101] and that this is "the deep-seated fault in the infamous loyalty-security hearings which, since 1947 when President Truman launched them, have processed 20,000,000 men and women. Those hearings were primarily concerned with one's thoughts, ideas, beliefs and convictions. They were the most blatant violations of the First Amendment we have ever known."[102]

The Court did sustain a New York loyalty program against First Amendment challenge in the *Adler* case in 1952. Under the Feinberg Law of that state, the board of regents compiled a list of "subversive organizations" and issued regulations providing that present membership in a listed organization should constitute prima facie evidence of disqualification for employment as a public school teacher and that past membership should be presumptive evidence of present

96. Bailey v. Richardson, 341 U.S. 918 (1951).

97. Joint Anti-Fascist Refugee Committee v. McGrath, 341 U.S. 123 (1951) (concurring opinion).

98. Cole v. Young, 351 U.S. 536 (1956); Greene v. McElroy, 360 U.S. 474 (1959). *Cf.* Cafeteria & Restaurant Workers Union v. McElroy, 367 U.S. 886 (1961) (dissenting opinion). *See also* Greene v. United States, 376 U.S. 149 (1964).

99. Service v. Dulles, 354 U.S. 363 (1957); Vitarelli v. Seaton, 359 U.S. 535 (1959); Peters v. Hobby, 349 U.S. 331 (1955) (concurring opinion).

100. Dennis v. United States, 341 U.S. 494 (1951).

101. Beilan v. Board of Public Education, 357 U.S. 399 (1958) (dissenting opinion).

102. Brandenburg v. Ohio, 395 U.S. 444 (1969) (concurring opinion).

membership. The Court held that this program did not violate the First Amendment, since the teachers were left with a free choice—they could work for the school system on its terms or "retain their beliefs and associations and go elsewhere." Douglas dissented:[103]

> I have not been able to accept the recent doctrine that a citizen who enters the public service can be forced to sacrifice his civil rights. I cannot for example find in our constitutional scheme the power of a state to place its employees in the category of second-class citizens by denying them freedom of thought and expression. The Constitution guarantees freedom of thought and expression to everyone in our society. All are entitled to it; and none needs it more than the teacher . . .
>
> The present law proceeds on a principle repugnant to our society—guilt by association. A teacher is disqualified because of her membership in an organization found to be "subversive" . . . The mere fact of membership in the organization raises a prima facie case of her own guilt. She may, it is said, show her innocence. But innocence in this case turns on knowledge; and when the witch hunt is on, one who must rely on ignorance leans on a feeble reed.
>
> The very threat of such a procedure is certain to raise havoc with academic freedom . . . Any organization committed to a liberal cause, any group organized to revolt against an hysterical trend, any committee launched to sponsor an unpopular program becomes suspect. These are the organizations into which Communists often infiltrate. Their presence infects the whole, even though the project was not conceived in sin. A teacher caught in that mesh is almost certain to stand condemned. Fearing condemnation, she will tend to shrink from any association that stirs controversy. In that manner freedom of expression will be stifled.
>
> But that is only part of it. Once a teacher's connection with a listed organization is shown, her views become subject to scrutiny to determine whether her membership in the organization is innocent or, if she was formerly a member, whether she has *bona fide* abandoned her membership.
>
> The law inevitably turns the school system into a spying project. Regular loyalty reports on the teachers must be made out. The principals become detectives; the students, the parents, the community become informers. Ears are cocked for tell-tale signs of disloyalty . . .

103. Adler v. Board of Education, 342 U.S. 485 (1952) (dissenting opinion).

What was the significance of the reference of the art teacher to socialism? Why was the history teacher so openly hostile to Franco Spain? Who heard overtones of revolution in the English teacher's discussion of the Grapes of Wrath? What was behind the praise of Soviet progress in metallurgy in the chemistry class? . . .

. . . There can be no real academic freedom in that environment. Where suspicion fills the air and holds scholars in line for fear of their jobs, there can be no exercise of the free intellect. Supineness and dogmatism take the place of inquiry. A "party line"—as dangerous as the "party line" of the Communists—lays hold. It is the "party line" of the orthodox view, of the conventional thought, of the accepted approach.

. . . It produces standardized thought, not the pursuit of truth. Yet it was the pursuit of truth which the First Amendment was designed to protect.

Fifteen years later the Court again considered the constitutionality of the New York program and invalidated it, both because the standards employed for disqualification of teachers were unconstitutionally vague, and because, as Justice Douglas had recently written for the Court in a case involving loyalty oaths,[104] "those who join an organization but do not share its unlawful purposes and who do not participate in its unlawful activities surely pose no threat, either as citizens or as public employees." Constitutional doctrine "which has emerged" since the *Adler* decision was said to have "rejected its major premise."[105]

Douglas has also read the First Amendment to forbid extension of state loyalty programs to those not in public employment. He concurred in decisions invalidating requirements that taxpayers seeking exemptions as war veterans or for church property must first take an oath that they did not advocate forcible overthrow of the government.[106] And, as the Court has pursued a torturous course in its

104. Elfbrandt v. Russell, 384 U.S. 11 (1966).

105. Keyishian v. Board of Regents, 385 U.S. 589 (1967). Douglas' views on the problems of public employees are dealt with more fully in W. Van Alstyne, "The Constitutional Rights of Public Employees," 16 *UCLA L. Rev.* 751 (1969), and H. Linde, "Justice Douglas on Freedom in the Welfare State," 40 *Wash. L. Rev.* 10 (1965).

106. Speiser v. Randall, 357 U.S. 513 (1958) (concurring opinions); First Unitarian Church v. Los Angeles, 357 U.S. 545 (1958) (concurring opinions).

attempt to deal with state action refusing to license applicants for the practice of law because of their beliefs and associations,[107] he has consistently adhered to the view that "beliefs are immune from bar association inquisitions designed to lay a foundation for barring an applicant from the practice of law"[108] and that a state cannot exclude an applicant from practice "because he has belonged to organizations that advocate violent overthrow of the Government even if his membership was 'knowing' and he shared the organization's aims."[109]

Closely related to government programs concerned with the loyalty of individuals is the Internal Security Act of 1950, which, as later amended, set up the Subversive Activities Control Board, authorized it to conduct hearings and to label organizations as "Communist action," "Communist front," and "Communist infiltrated," required such organizations to register with the attorney general, giving information as to finances, officers, members, and printing presses, and to use the Board's label on all mail and in all radio and television broadcasts, barred the members of such labeled organizations from defense plant employment or labor union office, and made them ineligible for passports.

When the Board's first order—finding the Communist party of the United States to be a "Communist action" organization—reached the Court in 1956, Douglas joined in sending the case back to the Board to resolve a contention that three of the witnesses on whose testimony the Board relied had perjured themselves in other proceedings.[110] When the case returned to the Court five years later with the testimony of the

107. See *In re* Summers, 325 U.S. 561 (1945) (dissenting opinion); Schware v. Board of Bar Examiners, 353 U.S. 232 (1957); Konigsberg v. State Bar, 353 U.S. 252 (1957); Konigsberg v. State Bar, 366 U.S. 36 (1961) (dissenting opinion); *In re* Anastaplo, 366 U.S. 82 (1961) (dissenting opinion); Baird v. State Bar, 401 U.S. 1 (1971) (plurality opinion); Law Students Civil Rights Research Council, Inc. v. Wadmond, 401 U.S. 154 (1971) (dissenting opinion). *See also* Barsky v. Board of Regents, 347 U.S. 442 (1954) (dissenting opinions); Black v. Cutter Laboratories, 351 U.S. 292 (1956) (dissenting opinion).

108. Baird v. State Bar, 401 U.S. 1 (1971) (plurality opinion).

109. Law Students Civil Rights Research Council, Inc. v. Wadmond, 401 U.S. 154 (1971) (dissenting opinion).

110. Communist Party v. Subversive Activities Control Board, 351 U.S. 115 (1956). *Cf.* Mesarosh v. United States, 352 U.S. 1 (1956), where a Smith Act conviction was reversed for the same reason.

three witnesses expunged and the Board's order reaffirmed without it, the Court upheld the order over First Amendment objections. Douglas agreed as to the First Amendment, since he accepted the findings of Congress and of the Board that the Communist party, unlike other groups which might be labeled by the Board, was an agent of the Soviet Union. But he dissented from the Court's refusal to consider at this point whether the registration requirements of the act did not violate the Fifth Amendment's privilege against self-incrimination.[111] (As indicated in Chapter 10, the registration provisions were later to founder on this point.) Thereafter, the Court remanded two cases involving Board findings that organizations were "Communist front" organizations, largely due to their connections with the "Communist action" Communist party. Proceedings on appeal had been delayed until the order as to the Communist party had been finally approved and the records made before the Board were stale. Douglas again dissented from the Court's refusal to decide the constitutional issues at that point.[112] And, in a later opinion dissenting from the Court's approval of a refusal to enjoin the initiation of proceedings before the Board against another alleged Communist front group, he made clear that he considered the "Communist front" provisions of the act invalid under the First Amendment:[113]

> A Communist-front organization, as defined [in the Act], is not a group engaged in *action* but *advocacy* . . .
>
> I see no constitutional method whereby the Government can punish or penalize one for "being a Communist" or "supporting Communists" or "promoting communism" . . . If government can investigate ideas, beliefs, and advocacy at the left end of the spectrum, I see no reason why it may not investigate at any other part of the spectrum. Yet as I read the Constitution, one of its essential purposes was to take government off the backs of people and keep it off. There is the line between

111. Communist Party v. Subversive Activities Control Board, 367 U.S. 1 (1961) (dissenting opinion).

112. American Committee for Protection of Foreign Born v. Subversive Activities Control Board, 380 U.S. 503 (1965) (dissenting opinion); Veterans of Abraham Lincoln Brigade v. Subversive Activities Control Board, 380 U.S. 513 (1965) (dissenting opinion).

113. W.E.B. Du Bois Clubs of America v. Clark, 389 U.S. 309 (1967) (dissenting opinion).

action on the one hand and ideas, beliefs, and advocacy on the other. The former is a legitimate sphere for legislation. Ideas, beliefs and advocacy are beyond the reach of committees, agencies, Congress, and the courts.

Meanwhile, as will be elaborated below, the provision of the act which would have denied passports to Communist party members had been held unconstitutional. And in 1967, Douglas voted with the Court to hold that the provision of the act barring all Communist party members from defense plant employment was overly broad under the First Amendment, since it lumped knowing with innocent membership.[114]

Still another reaction of some of those who govern to political ideas considered dangerous is the legislative investigating committee—most often set up by the sole action of one house of the legislature.

The Court on which Douglas sits first considered the relation of the First Amendment to such a committee in a different context than is common today. The United States House of Representatives had, by resolution, established a committee to investigate "all lobbying activities," and the secretary of a right-wing organization "engaged in the sale of books of a particular political tendentiousness" had been convicted of contempt for refusal to disclose to the committee the names of those who made bulk purchases of books for further distribution. The Court reversed the conviction, but, in order to avoid First Amendment questions, construed the authorizing resolution as confining the committee to "lobbying in its commonly accepted sense," that is "representations made directly to the Congress, its members, or its committees." Douglas did not agree that the resolution would bear this interpretation, but concurred on the ground that the inquiry violated the First Amendment:[115]

A requirement that a publisher disclose the identity of those who buy his books, pamphlets, or papers is indeed the beginning of surveillance

114. United States v. Robel, 389 U.S. 258 (1967). *See also* Schneider v. Smith, 390 U.S. 17 (1968).

115. United States v. Rumely, 345 U.S. 41 (1953) (concurring opinion). *See also* United States v. Harriss, 347 U.S. 612 (1954) (dissenting opinion).

of the press. True, no legal sanction is involved here. Congress has imposed no tax, established no board of censors, instituted no licensing system. But the potential restraint is equally severe. The finger of government leveled against the press is ominous . . . The purchase of a book or pamphlet today may result in a subpoena tomorrow. Fear of criticism goes with every person into the bookstall . . . Some will fear to read what is unpopular, what the powers-that-be dislike . . . Through the harassment of hearings, investigations, reports, and subpoenas government will hold a club over speech and over the press. Congress could not do this by law. The power of investigation is also limited.

The Court next considered this question in 1959, in a case involving the House Un-American Activities Committee (now the House Internal Security Committee), which had then for twenty years been operating under a House resolution authorizing it to investigate "un-American propaganda." A witness who had refused on First Amendment grounds to answer questions about past and present membership in the Communist party had been convicted of contempt of the committee, and the Court affirmed the conviction. After finding that the House, by acquiescence in the committee's activities, had clothed it with "pervasive authority to investigate Communist activities in this country," the Court concluded that there was no violation of the First Amendment because the "public interest" in learning of Communist activity "outweighed" the witness' "private interest" in First Amendment freedoms, although it intimated that the constitutional question might be answered differently if the Communist party were "an ordinary political party." Douglas joined in a dissent that objected to this "judicial balancing process," pointing out that even as employed it erroneously classified as a "private interest" the "interest of the people as a whole in being able to join organizations, advocate causes and make political 'mistakes' without later being subjected to governmental penalties" of "exposure, obloquy and public scorn" for "having dared to think for themselves," and rejecting the implication "that the ordinary . . . requirements of the Constitution do not apply because the Committee is merely after Communists and they do not constitute a political party but only a criminal gang." "No matter how often or how quickly we repeat the claim that the Communist Party is not a political party, we cannot outlaw it, as a group, without endangering the liberty of all of us."[116] Douglas has persisted in his dissent on this issue with respect to this committee[117] and has made it clear that he takes the same view of similar inquiries by the Senate Subcommittee on Internal Security.[118]

He has also voted with the Court to reverse contempt convictions of witnesses called before the House committee, and occasionally of those called before the Senate subcommittee, for a variety of reasons which precluded reaching First Amendment questions. The statute on which these convictions were based makes it a crime for a witness summoned before a committee to refuse to answer any question "pertinent to the question under inquiry." Convictions have been reversed because the committee had not made clear to the witness the nature of the subject under inquiry, so that a conviction would violate the due process requirement that criminal statutes must provide an ascertainable standard of guilt,[119] because the questions the witness refused to answer were not pertinent to the subject under inquiry,[120] because the government failed to prove in the contempt proceeding the nature of the subject under inquiry,[121] and because the indictments for contempt did not identify the subject under inquiry.[122] Contempt convictions have also been reversed because of the failure of the committee clearly to direct the witness to answer the question put to him,[123] because the witness had properly invoked his privilege against

116. Barenblatt v. United States, 360 U.S. 109 (1959) (dissenting opinion).

117. Wilkinson v. United States, 365 U.S. 399 (1961) (dissenting opinions); Braden v. United States, 365 U.S. 431 (1961) (dissenting opinions).

118. Russell v. United States, 369 U.S. 749 (1962) (concurring opinion).

119. Watkins v. United States, 354 U.S. 178 (1957).

120. Sacher v. United States, 356 U.S. 576 (1958).

121. Deutch v. United States, 367 U.S. 456 (1961). Douglas dissented in McPhaul v. United States, 364 U.S. 372 (1960), from affirmance of a conviction for failure to produce subpoenaed records where there was no proof that the witness had custody of or control over the records.

122. Russell v. United States, 369 U.S. 749 (1962) (concurring opinion); Silber v. United States, 370 U.S. 717 (1962); Gojack v. United States, 384 U.S. 702 (1966). *See also* Morford v. United States, 339 U.S. 258 (1950).

123. Quinn v. United States, 349 U.S. 155 (1955); Emspak v. United States, 349 U.S. 190 (1955). *See also* Flaxer v. United States, 358 U.S. 147 (1958).

self-incrimination before the committee,[124] and because the committee had violated its own rules.[125]

The Court has also had several occasions to consider the proceedings of state legislative investigations of "subversive" or "un-American" activities. Douglas voted with the Court to reverse a contempt conviction of a witness who refused to answer questions about a lecture he had delivered at a state university and about his knowledge of the participation of others in a left-wing political organization, where the witness was summoned by the New Hampshire attorney general acting as a "one-man legislative committee" under a joint resolution of the state legislature, and where it was not clear from the resolution that the attorney general was authorized to ask such questions. A conviction in such circumstances was held to deny due process of law.[126] The Court also reversed another contempt proceeding where a witness summoned before the same one-man committee in 1963 testified that he had not been involved with the Communist party since 1957 and had no knowledge of its activities since that time but refused to answer questions concerning earlier periods. Douglas wrote for a Court then committed to the "balancing" of First Amendment rights against internal security:[127]

> Investigation is a part of lawmaking and the First Amendment, as well as the Fifth, stands as a barrier to state intrusion on privacy. No attack is made on the truthfulness of the questions answered by appellant stating that he does not serve in a subversive role and lacks knowledge of any current subversion. There is no showing of "overriding and compelling state interest" . . . that would warrant intrusion into the realm of political and associational privacy protected by the First Amendment. The information being sought was historical, not current.

124. Quinn v. United States, 349 U.S. 155 (1955); Emspak v. United States, 349 U.S. 190 (1955).

125. Yellin v. United States, 374 U.S. 109 (1963); Gojack v. United States, 384 U.S. 702 (1966). *See also* Christoffel v. United States, 338 U.S. 846 (1949), where Douglas voted with the Court to reverse a perjury conviction because a quorum of the committee was not present at the time of the alleged perjury. In two other cases, in which Douglas did not participate, the absence of a quorum of the committee was held to be no defense to prosecutions for contempt. United States v. Bryan, 339 U.S. 323 (1950); United States v. Fleischman, 339 U.S. 349 (1950).

126. Sweezy v. New Hampshire, 354 U.S. 234 (1957).

127. DeGregory v. Attorney General, 383 U.S. 825 (1966).

Lawmaking at the investigatory stage may properly probe historic events for any light that may be thrown on present conditions and problems. But the First Amendment prevents use of the power . . . to probe at will and without relation to existing need . . . The present record is devoid of any evidence that there is any Communist movement in New Hampshire. The 1955 Report [of the Attorney General on Subversive Activities in New Hampshire] deals primarily with "world-wide Communism" and the Federal Government. There is no showing whatsoever of present danger of sedition against the State itself, the only area to which the authority of the State extends.

In an earlier case arising in the same state, *Uphaus v. Wyman*, the Court had sustained the contempt conviction of an operator of a summer camp in New Hampshire who refused to produce the names of all persons attending the camp, because there was some evidence that the witness had participated in "Communist front" activities and that some of the speakers had either been members of the Communist party "or had connections with or affiliations with it" or with other "subversive" organizations. Hence, the Court concluded, "the governmental interest in self-preservation is sufficiently compelling to subordinate the interest in associational privacy." Douglas joined in a dissent which denied that any state interest was revealed by a record which showed that the sole purpose of the attorney general was "exposure for exposure's sake" and not any legitimate legislative purpose. The attorney general already had a list of those who had made speeches at the camp and had in his 1955 report published the names of those on whom he had some evidence of "subversive activity" as well as the names of thirty-six others concerning whom "it is not possible for this office to guarantee that [they] do not have such activity in their backgrounds." Douglas also dissented separately to indicate his continuing disagreement with the "balancing" test of First Amendment rights.[128] He dissented in three later cases where the Court once summarily affirmed[129] and twice declined to review[130] contempt convictions arising out of the New Hampshire investigations.

In other cases involving state investigations, Douglas has voted with

128. Uphaus v. Wyman, 360 U.S. 72 (1959) (dissenting opinions).

129. DeGregory v. Attorney General, 368 U.S. 19 (1961).

130. DeGregory v. Wyman, 360 U.S. 717 (1959) (dissenting opinion); Uphaus v. Wyman, 364 U.S. 388 (1960) (dissenting opinions).

the Court to reverse contempt convictions under the due process clause because the committee had not made clear to the witness the subject under inquiry,[131] had not clearly directed him to answer the question,[132] or had first advised the witnesses that they could invoke their privilege against self-incrimination and then, when they did so, had them convicted for contempt because a statute conferring immunity from prosecution for matters covered by the questions put to them rendered the privilege unavailable.[133] When the Court also reversed a contempt conviction of one who refused a state committee's request for NAACP membership records because there was "no suggestion" that the NAACP was a "subversive organization," so that there was no showing of an "overriding and compelling state interest," Douglas concurred. But he again registered his objection to the use of the "balancing" test:[134]

> In my view, government is not only powerless to legislate with respect to membership in a lawful organization; it is also precluded from probing the intimacies of spiritual and intellectual relationships in the myriad of such societies and groups that exist in this country, regardless of the legislative purpose sought to be served . . . If that is not true, I see no barrier to investigation of newspapers, churches, political parties, clubs, societies, unions, and any other association for their political, economic, social, philosophical, or religious views. If, in its quest to determine whether existing laws are being enforced or new laws are needed, an investigating committee can ascertain whether known Communists or criminals are members of an organization not shown to be engaged in conduct properly subject to regulation, it is but a short and inexorable step to the conclusion that it may also probe to ascertain what effect they have had on the other members.

In a dissenting opinion in a case involving a related matter, Douglas summed up many of his concerns about legislative investigations:

> We have repeatedly said that a congressional investigation which exposes for exposure's sake or which is "conducted solely for the

131. Scull v. Virginia, 359 U.S. 344 (1959).

132. Slagle v. Ohio, 366 U.S. 259 (1961).

133. Raley v. Ohio, 360 U.S. 423 (1959). *See also* Black Unity League v. Miller, 394 U.S. 100 (1969).

134. Gibson v. Florida Legislative Investigation Committee, 372 U.S. 539 (1963) (concurring opinion).

personal aggrandizement of the investigators or to 'punish' those investigated is indefensible" ... Congress is not a law enforcement agency; that power is entrusted to the Executive. Congress is not a trial agency; that power is entrusted to the Judiciary ... By reason of the First Amendment Congress, being unable to abridge freedom of speech or freedom of the press, may not probe into what a witness reads ... or why a publisher chose one editorial policy rather than another. Since by reason of the First Amendment Congress may make no law "prohibiting the free exercise" of religion, it may not enter the field through investigation and probe the minds of witnesses as to whether they go to church or to the confessional regularly, why they chose this church rather than that one, etc. By reason of the Self-Incrimination Clause of the Fifth Amendment, witnesses may refuse to answer certain questions ...

In these and other related ways, congressional committees are fenced in. Yet in the view of some of us the tendency has been to trench on First Amendment rights ... There was a time when a committee, knowing that a witness would not answer a question by reason of the Fifth Amendment, would not put the question to him. Today, witnesses who invoke the Fifth Amendment at the threshold have been minutely examined, apparently to see how many times they can be forced to invoke it. Hearings have indeed often become a spectacle.[135]

Douglas dissented when the Court declined to review, as presenting no federal question, the action of a state court in dismissing a complaint filed by motion picture writers and actors alleging that they had been damaged by a conspiracy of motion picture producers and distributors and members of the House Un-American Activities Committee to have them blacklisted for employment because they invoked the Fifth Amendment when questioned by the committee about their political beliefs and associations. He thought that the state court had, in violation of the equal protection clause, fashioned a different rule for this case than for other cases involving interference with the right of work.[136] But when one served with a House committee subpoena attempted to sue a committee investigator on the theory the investigator himself had issued the subpoena without

135. United States v. Welden, 377 U.S. 95 (1964) (dissenting (opinion).

136. Wilson v. Loew's Inc., 355 U.S. 597 (1958) (dissenting opinion). *See also* Tenney v. Brandhove, 341 U.S. 367 (1951).

committee authority, and that the mere service of the subpoena on him had caused loss of his job, Douglas wrote for the Court to hold that neither the Constitution nor any federal law provided a remedy.[137]

In 1931 Chief Justice Hughes wrote for the Court in *Near v. Minnesota*,[138] to hold that the state could not enjoin the publication of a newspaper on the ground that it published "malicious, scandalous and defamatory" matter about public officials, private citizens, and Jews. The injunction, which would have subjected the owner to contempt if he had resumed publication of his paper, was held to violate the guaranty of a free press by imposing a "previous restraint" on publication. That guaranty was said to require, "principally although not exclusively, immunity from previous restraints or censorship." The fact that the state law recognized a defense for a publisher who could convince the court that what he had published was true and was published with good motives was held not to save it. If such a law was valid, "it would be equally permissible for the legislature to provide that at any time the publisher of any newspaper could be brought before a court . . . and required to produce proof of the truth of his publication, or of what he intended to publish, and of his motives, or stand enjoined. If this can be done, the legislature may provide machinery for determining in the complete exercise of its discretion what are justifiable ends and restrain publication accordingly. And it would be but a step to a complete system of censorship."

June 12–14, 1971, the *New York Times* published summaries and extracts from a forty-seven-volume, "top secret" government document entitled "History of U.S. Decision-Making Process on Vietnam Policy," covering the period 1945 to 1967. On June 15, the United States obtained a temporary restraining order from a federal district court in New York, but, after an *in camera* hearing, the court on June 19 concluded that the United States had not shown that publication of these historical documents would seriously jeopardize national security, though it might cause some embarrassment. But the stay was continued while an appeal was taken and the federal court of appeals in New York

137. Wheeldin v. Wheeler, 373 U.S. 647 (1963).
138. 283 U.S. 697 (1931).

reversed and remanded to the district court for further hearings, again continuing the stay.[139]

Meanwhile, the *Washington Post* began publication of other material from these "Pentagon papers" on June 17. The United States filed affidavits with and sought a temporary restraining order from a federal district court in the District of Columbia that was denied. The federal court of appeals reversed and remanded for a hearing, granting a stay in the meanwhile. After an *in camera* hearing the district court again denied a stay, and this time the court of appeals on June 23 affirmed, agreeing that the government had not shown a sufficient risk of harm to national security to override First Amendment interests. But it granted a stay pending submission of the case to the Supreme Court.[140]

With further *Washington Post* publications of the material stayed, the *Boston Globe* began publishing the material. The government obtained a stay pending hearing from a federal district court in Boston. But when newspapers in the midwest and on the Pacific coast began publications from the materials, the government abandoned further applications for stays and concentrated its efforts on the argument of the *New York Times* and *Washington Post* cases in the Supreme Court on June 26.

That Court had on June 25 agreed to hear the cases and had continued the stays in both cases pending decision. This action was taken over the dissents of Justices Black, Douglas, Brennan, and Marshall, who would have vacated the order of the court of appeals in New York, vacated the stays, and declined to hear arguments on the cases.[141]

The Supreme Court decided the cases on June 30, agreeing by a 6-3 vote with both district courts and with the court of appeals for the District of Columbia that the government had not met its "heavy burden of showing justification of such a restraint." The decision was announced in a brief per curiam order. But each Justice filed a separate

139. See United States v. New York Times Co., 328 F. Supp. 324 (S.D. N.Y. 1971), reversed 444 F.2d 544 (2d Cir. 1971).

140. See United States v. Washington Post Company, 446 F.2d 1323, 1327 (D.C. Cir. 1971).

141. New York Times Co. v. United States, 403 U.S. 942 (1971); United States v. Washington Post Co., 403 U.S. 943 (1971). *See also* New York Times Co. v. United States, 403 U.S. 944 (1971).

opinion, and, in addition, some concurred in the opinions of others. Those in the majority expressed different opinions. Justice Brennan thought all restraining orders issued in the cases had been erroneously issued on the facts shown but preserved for the future the question whether there might be a "narrow class of cases in which the First Amendment's ban on prior restraints may be overridden," such as news of troop movements in time of war. Justices Stewart and White agreed that the government had not met "the very heavy burden which it must meet . . . at least in the absence of express and appropriately limited congressional authorization for prior restraints in circumstances such as these." Justice Marshall thought that the executive branch had no authority to seek an injunction in these cases without express congressional authorization. Justice Black, in an opinion in which Douglas joined, took the position that the First Amendment forbade all three branches of government to restrain freedom of press in the name of "national security." Douglas also wrote an opinion in which Black joined:[142]

It should be noted at the outset that the First Amendment provides that "Congress shall make no law . . . abridging the freedom of speech or of the press." That leaves, in my view, no room for governmental restraint on the press.

There is, moreover, no statute barring the publication by the press of the material which the Times and Post seek to use . . .

. . . Thus Congress has been faithful to the command of the First Amendment in this area.

So any power that the Government possesses must come from its "inherent power."

The power to wage war is "the power to wage war successfully" . . . But the war power stems from a declaration of war. The Constitution . . . gives Congress, not the President, power "to declare war." Nowhere are Presidential wars authorized. We need not decide therefore what leveling effect the war power of Congress might have.

These disclosures may have a serious impact. But that is no basis for sanctioning a previous restraint on the press . . .

The Government says that it has inherent powers to go into court

142. New York Times Co. v. United States, 403 U.S. 713 (1971) (separate opinion).

and obtain an injunction to protect that national interest, which in this case is alleged to be national security.

Near v. *Minnesota*[143] . . . repudiated that expansive doctrine in no uncertain terms.

The dominant purpose of the First Amendment was to prohibit the widespread practice of governmental suppression of embarrassing information. It is common knowledge that the First Amendment was adopted against the widespread use of the common law of seditious libel to punish the dissemination of material that is embarrassing to the powers-that-be . . . The present cases will, I think, go down in history as the most dramatic illustration of that principle. A debate of large proportions goes on in the Nation over our posture in Vietnam. That debate antedated the disclosure of the contents of the present documents. The latter are highly relevant to the debate in progress.

Secrecy in government is fundamentally anti-democratic, perpetuating bureaucratic errors. Open debate and discussion of public issues are vital to our national health. On public questions there should be "open and robust debate." *New York Times Co.* v. *Sullivan* . . . [144]

The stays in these cases that have been in effect for more than a week constitute a flouting of the principles of the First Amendment as interpreted in *Near* v. *Minnesota.*

FREEDOM OF ASSOCIATION

A number of the above cases have referred to a right of "association" as well as to rights of belief, expression and assembly. Douglas joined in an opinion of the Court in 1958 which clearly recognized that there was a right under the First Amendment to "engage in association for the advancement of beliefs and ideas," since effective advocacy "is undeniably enhanced by group association." Hence, Alabama was held not entitled to compel the NAACP to produce its entire state membership list, at least where the state made no real showing of need for it in pending litigation over the question whether the NAACP was a "corporation" "doing business" in the state, which must qualify to do business as a foreign corporation. "Compelled disclosure of affiliation with groups engaged in advocacy may constitute [an] effective . . .

143. 283 U.S. 697 (1931).
144. 376 U.S. 254 (1964).

restraint on freedom of association" and "privacy in group association may . . . be indispensable to preservation of freedom of association, particularly where a group espouses dissident beliefs."[145] In later cases he concurred in a decision that invalidated, as a violation of freedom of association, an ordinance applied to the NAACP requiring all organizations operating within the city to supply membership lists for public recording,[146] and he joined in the unanimous decision which finally held that the First Amendment right of free association prevented Alabama from forbidding the NAACP to operate in that state because of its failure to qualify to do business as a foreign corporation. "This case . . . involves not the privilege of a corporation to do business in a State, but rather the freedom of individuals to associate for the collective advocacy of ideas."[147]

Freedom of expression and association and the use of the products of legislative investigation in a criminal proceeding were all involved in *Dombrowski v. Pfister.* Officials of a civil rights organization brought an action in federal court to enjoin threatened prosecutions under a state Subversive Activities and Communist Control Law, which required all members of "Communist front" organizations to register and provided that the fact that an organization had been identified as such by any congressional committee should be presumptive evidence that it was such an organization. By the time the case reached the Supreme Court the plaintiffs had in fact been indicted for failure to register as members of organizations cited by the House Un-American Activities Committee as Communist fronts. Plaintiffs alleged that the prosecutions were not brought in good faith, but for purposes of harrassment, and that the statute on which they were based was unconstitutional on its face. Douglas joined with the Court to hold that the court below had erred in dismissing the complaint. Since it relied upon the citation of organizations by a committee which did not employ procedural

145. NAACP v. Alabama, 357 U.S. 449 (1958). *See also* NAACP v. Alabama, 360 U.S. 240 (1959); NAACP v. Gallion, 368 U.S. 16 (1961). *Cf.* Talley v. California, 362 U.S. 60 (1960); Gibson v. Florida Legislative Investigation Committee, 372 U.S. 539 (1963).

146. Bates v. Little Rock, 361 U.S. 516 (1960) (concurring opinion). *See also* Louisiana *ex rel.* Gremillion v. NAACP, 366 U.S. 293 (1961).

147. NAACP v. Alabama, 377 U.S. 288 (1964).

safeguards that would impose "a minimum requirement to insure . . . rationality," the statute was invalid on its face. And, so long as this invalid statute "remains available to the State the threat of prosecutions of protected expression is a real and substantial one. Even the prospect of ultimate failure of such prosecutions by no means dispels their chilling effect on protected expression."[148] The usual rule that a federal court should not enjoin state prosecutions but should leave the defendant to raise his constitutional defenses in the state proceeding would not apply where "statutes are justifiably attacked on their face as abridging free expression, or as applied for the purpose of discouraging protected activities."

In subsequent cases Douglas has dissented from the failure of the Court to apply the *Dombrowski* rule to allow injunctions against proceedings by the Subversive Activities Control Board where he considered the Subversive Activities Control Act void on its face, [149] and injunctions against a state law forbidding picketing, which he considered void as applied for the purpose of discouraging a peaceful demonstration in front of the county courthouse to protest racial discrimination.[150] He dissented again in 1971 when the Court in two cases drastically limited the effect of *Dombrowski* and denied injunctive relief to one being prosecuted by the state for "criminal syndicalism" because he distributed leaflets advocating change from capitalism to socialism through peaceful political action,[151] and to blacks in Chicago who had been arrested and anticipated prosecution under a statute prescribing "intimidation."[152] It was not enough, the Court held, despite what was said in *Dombrowski*, that a statute might be void on its face. No federal injunction should issue unless the complaints also alleged and proved that the prosecutions were in bad faith or for the purpose of harassment. Douglas protested this retrenchment:[153]

148. Dombrowski v. Pfister, 380 U.S. 479 (1965).

149. W.E.B. Du Bois Club of America v. Clark, 389 U.S. 309 (1967) (dissenting opinion). *See also* Black Unity League v. Miller, 394 U.S. 100 (1969).

150. Cameron v. Johnson, 390 U.S. 611 (1968) (dissenting opinion).

151. Younger v. Harris, 401 U.S. 37 (1971).

152. Boyle v. Landry, 401 U.S. 77 (1971).

153. Younger v. Harris, 401 U.S. 37 (1971) (dissenting opinion).

Dombrowski governs statutes which are a blunderbuss by themselves or when used *en masse*—those that have an "overbroad" sweep. [As was said in *Dombrowski*,] "If the rule were otherwise, the contours of regulation would have to be hammered out case by case—and tested only by those hardy enough to risk criminal prosecution to determine the proper scope of regulation" . . .

The special circumstances when federal intervention in a state criminal proceeding is permissible are not restricted to bad faith on the part of state officials or the threat of multiple prosecutions. They also exist where for any reason the state statute being enforced is unconstitutional on its face . . .

As the standards of certainty in statutes containing criminal sanctions are higher than those in statutes containing civil sanctions, so are the standards of certainty touching on freedom of expression higher than those in other areas . . .

The eternal temptation, of course, has been to arrest the speaker rather than to correct the conditions about which he complains. I see no reason why these appellees should be made to walk the treacherous ground of these statutes. They, like other citizens, need the umbrella of the First Amendment as they study, analyze, discuss, and debate the troubles of these days. When criminal prosecutions can be leveled against them because they express unpopular views, the society of the dialogue is in danger.

But Douglas concurred in the denial of injunctive relief in a third case to complainants charged with criminal anarchy where the statute was not, as applied to them, "palpably unconstitutional," since there were charges of the acquisition of weapons and gunpowder and the storage of gasoline to start fires, which, if proved in the state prosecution, would be entitled to no First Amendment protection.[154]

OBSCENITY

There is another large area of First Amendment problems which may seem to have little to do with political freedom: the problems of obscenity.

During the first twenty years of his tenure, Douglas wrote for the Court to hold that under a statute giving second-class mailing privileges to periodicals publishing "information of a public character" or

154. Samuels v. Mackell, 401 U.S. 66 (1971) (concurring opinion).

devoted to "literature" or to "arts," the postmaster general had no authority to revoke such mailing privileges for *Esquire* magazine because he concluded that it contained items which were "indecent, vulgar, and risque."[155] He also voted with the Court to hold that a statute forbidding sale of literature principally made up of "news or stories of criminal deeds of bloodshed or lust so massed as to become vehicles for inciting violent and depraved crimes" was unconstitutionally vague,[156] and that a statute forbidding the sale of literature containing obscene matter "tending to the corruption of the morals of youth" was unconstitutional since its effect was "to reduce the adult population . . . to reading only what is fit for children."[157] And when the Court struck down state systems for advance screening of motion pictures to eliminate obscenity because the standards employed were unconstitutionally vague, he concurred on the ground that the prior restraint was itself unconstitutional: "The First and the Fourteenth Amendments say that Congress and the States shall make 'no law' which abridges freedom of speech or of the press. In order to sanction a system of censorship I would have to say that 'no law' does not mean what it says, that 'no law' is qualified to mean 'some' laws. I cannot take that step."[158]

But when, in 1957, the Court upheld convictions for selling literature which "has a tendency" to "excite lustful" or "lascivious" thoughts or offends "the common conscience of the community by present-day standards" and announced that obscenity, which it defined as that "which deals with sex in a manner appealing to prurient interest" and which was "utterly without redeeming social importance," was "not within the area of constitutionally protected speech or press," he dissented:[159]

I can understand (and at times even sympathize) with programs of civic groups and church groups to protect and defend the existing moral

155. Hannegan v. Esquire, Inc., 327 U.S. 146 (1946).
156. Winters v. New York, 333 U.S. 507 (1948).
157. Butler v. Michigan, 352 U.S. 380 (1957).
158. Superior Films, Inc. v. Department of Education, 346 U.S. 587 (1954) (concurring opinion).
159. Roth v. United States, 354 U.S. 476 (1957) (dissenting opinion).

standards of the community. I can understand the motives of the Anthony Comstocks who would impose Victorian standards on the community. When speech alone is involved, I do not think that government, consistently with the First Amendment, can become the sponsor of any of these movements. I do not think that government, consistently with the First Amendment, can throw its weight behind one school or another. Government should be concerned with antisocial conduct, not with utterances. Thus, if the First Amendment guarantee of freedom of speech and press is to mean anything in this field, it must allow protests even against the moral code that the standard of the day sets for the community. In other words, literature should not be suppressed merely because it offends the moral code of the censor.

The legality of a publication in this country should never be allowed to turn either on the purity of thought which it instills in the mind of the reader or on the degree to which it offends the community conscience. By either test the role of censor is exalted, and society's values in literary freedom are sacrificed.

Douglas has persisted in that view as the Court has tested literature and motion pictures against the original and revised definitions of obscenity to conclude that a film version of *Lady Chatterley's Lover* may not be banned because it "alluringly portrays adultery as proper behavior";[160] that a bookseller cannot be punished for having in his possession an obscene book when its contents were unknown to him;[161] that a publisher may be punished for mailing literature not in itself obscene if he resorts to "pandering" in his advertising and methods of distribution;[162] that publishers of obscene books may be punished if their publications appeal to the prurient interest of a "clearly defined deviant sexual group" for which it is designed, though not to the prurient interest of the "average person";[163] that *Fanny Hill*

160. Kingsley International Pictures Corp. v. Regents, 360 U.S. 684 (1959) (concurring opinion). *See also* One, Inc. v. Olesen, 355 U.S. 371 (1958).

161. Smith v. California, 361 U.S. 147 (1959) (concurring opinion).

162. Ginzburg v. United States, 383 U.S. 463 (1966) (dissenting opinion).

163. Mishkin v. New York, 383 U.S. 502 (1966) (dissenting opinion). *See also* Manual Enterprises v. Day, 370 U.S. 478 (1962), where two justices concluded that, since pictures of male nudes were not "obnoxiously debasing portrayals of sex," they were not "patently offensive" and could not be excluded from the mails even if they did appeal to the prurient interest of homosexuals. Douglas and two others concurred on the ground that the Comstock Act, which provided only

could not be suppressed because it is not "utterly without redeeming social value" (three justices), or not "hard core pornography" (one justice);[164] and that a state may prohibit the sale of material to children under seventeen on the basis of its prurient appeal to them.[165]

And as the Court has given its approval or disapproval to procedures for advance state screening of allegedly obscene matter, depending on the time involved to complete the process, he has maintained that all such devices constitute unconstitutional prior restraints on speech and press.[166] His positions on an exception to the First Amendment for obscenity and on the invalidity of prior restraints are not unrelated. As he put it in one dissenting opinion:[167]

It is one thing for parents and the religious organizations to be active and involved. It is quite a different matter for the state to become implicated as a censor. As I read the First Amendment, it was designed to keep the state and the hands of all state officials off the printing presses of America and off the distribution systems for all printed literature. Anthony Comstock wanted it the other way; he indeed put the police and the prosecutor in the middle of this publishing business . . .

---

criminal penalties for sending obscene matter through the mails, did not authorize the postmaster general to censor the mail in advance.

164. A Book Named "John Cleland's Memoirs of a Woman of Pleasure" v. Attorney General, 383 U.S. 413 (1966) (concurring opinion). *See also* Jacobellis v. Ohio, 378 U.S. 184 (1964) (concurring opinion); Byrne v. Karalexis, 396 U.S. 976 (1969) (dissenting opinion). The view of the various justices on the proper constitutional test, as they then were, are summarized in Redrup v. New York, 386 U.S. 767 (1967), which found the literature there involved to be protected by the First Amendment under any test. *See also* Redmond v. United States, 384 U.S. 264 (1966) (concurring opinion); Lee Art Theatre, Inc. v. Virginia, 392 U.S. 636 (1968) (concurring opinion).

165. Ginsberg v. New York, 390 U.S. 629 (1968) (dissenting opinion). *See also* Rabeck v. New York, 391 U.S. 462 (1968) (concurring opinion).

166. Kingsley Books, Inc. v. Brown, 354 U.S. 436 (1957) (dissenting opinion); Times Film Corp. v. Chicago, 365 U.S. 43 (1961) (dissenting opinions); Bantam Books, Inc. v. Sullivan, 372 U.S. 58 (1963) (concurring opinion); Freedman v. Maryland, 380 U.S. 51 (1965) (concurring opinion); Teitel Film Corp. v. Cusack, 390 U.S. 139 (1968) (concurring opinion); *See also* Marcus v. Search Warrant, 367 U.S. 717 (1961) (concurring opinion); A Quantity of Copies of Books v. Kansas, 378 U.S. 205 (1964) (concurring opinion). *Cf.* Blount v. Rizzi, 400 U.S. 410 (1971).

167. Ginsberg v. New York, 390 U.S. 629 (1968) (dissenting opinion).

Today this Court sits as the Nation's board of censors. With all respect, I not know of any group in the country less qualified first, to know what obscenity is when they see it, and second, to have any considered judgment as to what the deleterious or beneficial impact of a particular publication may be on minds either young or old.

When the Court in 1971 completed its evisceration of the doctrine of *Dombrowski v. Pfister*[168] by refusing federal relief against pending state prosecutions of booksellers and a publisher of a bimonthly newspaper for sale or possession of obscene materials, all of which the state authorities had seized under allegedly unconstitutional statutes, Douglas again dissented.[169] He expressed his views in the case involving the newspaper publisher:[170]

The raids in this case were search-and-destroy missions in the Vietnamese sense of the phrase. In each case the police came at night . . . [In the first raid, the] seizures included: two tons of [the] newspaper . . . one photograph enlarger, two portable typewriters, two electric typewriters, one camera, "numerous obscene photographs," and $5.43 in money. [The second raid was] in response to a claim that marihuana was concealed on the premises . . . Not finding any marihuana . . . the sergeant asked instructions from his lieutenant. He was told to seize pornographic literature and any equipment used to make it. He "didn't know what to seize and what not to seize so [he] just took everything." "Everything" included a Polaroid camera, a Kodak Brownie, a Flocon camera, a Kodak lamp, a floating fixture lamp, a three-drawer desk containing printer's supplies, a drafting square, a drafting table, two drawing boards, a mailing tube, two telephones, a stapler, five cardboard boxes containing documents, one electric typewriter, and one typewriter desk. A poster of Mao Tse-Tung, credit cards, costume jewelry, cans of spices, a brown sweater, and a statute of a man and woman in an embrace were also seized. Thus the newspaper . . . was effectively put out of business.

. . . If this search-and-destroy technique can be employed against this . . . newspaper, then it can be done to the New York Times, the Washington Post, the Seattle Post-Intelligencer, the Yakima Herald-Republic, the Sacramento Bee, and all the rest of our newspapers. For . . . the Texas statute governing "obscenity" is plainly unconstitutional.

168. See text at notes 149-153, *supra*.
169. Perez v. Ledesma, 401 U.S. 82 (1971); Dyson v. Stein, 401 U.S. 200 (1971).
170. Dyson v. Stein, 401 U.S. 200 (1971) (dissenting opinion).

Government certainly has no power to close down newspapers. Even censorship—whether for obscenity, for irresponsible reporting or editorials, or otherwise—is taboo . . . Vicious, irresponsible, and depraved as the press often is, the constitutional remedy is not censorship. The antidote is education, pinning our faith to the Jeffersonian creed that by education we may in time become a mature people . . .

If a publication deemed "obscene" is not under the umbrella of the First Amendment, then I do not see how it enjoys many constitutional safeguards . . . The Constitution contains no standards or suggestions of standards respecting the vast array of subjects that various vocal groups would like to have suppressed—obscenity, sacrilege, un-Americanism, anti-clerical ideas, atheistic or anti-ecclesiastical ideas, Communism, racism, and so on. Under the Constitution as written there are no standards of "good" or "bad" for the press . . . Absent a controlling constitutional standard, I would think that a legislature could treat literature as it treats sewage effluent or infectious disease. That is not a happy prospect, for some would put even *The Song of Solomon* under the ban.

Another dissenting opinion elaborates on Douglas' reasons for considering the obscenity matter so important:[171]

When our rewards go to people for thinking alike, it is no surprise that we become frightened at those who take exception to the current consensus. Then the hue and cry goes up for censors; and that is the start of an ominous trend. What can be done to literature under the banner of "obscenity" can be done to other parts of the spectrum of ideas when party or majoritarian demands mount and propagandists start declaiming the law . . .

If "obscenity" can be carved out of the First Amendment, what other like exceptions can be created? Is "sacrilege" also beyond the pale? Are utterances or publications made with "malice" unprotected? How about "seditious" speech or articles? False, scandalous and malicious writings or utterances against the Congress or the President "with intent to defame" or to bring them "into contempt or disrepute" or to "excite" against them "the hatred of the good people" or "to stir up sedition," or to "excite" people to "resist, oppose or defeat" any law were once made a crime [under the Alien and Sedition Acts of 1798].

We forget today that under our constitutional system neither

171. Byrne v. Karalexis, 396 U.S. 976 (1969) (dissenting opinion).

Congress nor the States have any power to pass on the value, the propriety, the Americanism, the soundness of any idea or expression. It is that insulation from party or majoritarian control provided by the First Amendment—not our gross national product or mass production or pesticides or space ships or nuclear arsenal—that distinguishes our society from the other planetary regimes.

The Court concluded in 1969 in *Stanley v. Georgia* that the First Amendment forbade a state to punish a man for having obscene films in his possession in his own home. Douglas joined in an opinion which said in part:[172]

It is now well established that the Constitution protects the right to receive information and ideas . . . Also fundamental is the right to be free, except in a very limited circumstances, from unwanted governmental intrusions into one's privacy.

. . . Whatever may be the justifications for other statutes regulating obscenity, we do not think they reach into the privacy of one's own home. If the First Amendment means anything, it means that a State has no business telling a man, sitting alone in his own house, what books he may read or what films he may watch. Our whole constitutional heritage rebels at the thought of giving government the power to control men's minds.

Two years later the Court rejected the apparently logical implications of this decision to hold that the First Amendment gave no protection against customs agents who seized obscene materials which a traveler sought to bring in for private use nor against criminal prosecution of booksellers who mail obscene materials to adults for their private use.[173] Douglas joined in a dissent which said in part:[174]

Wholly aside from my own views of what the First Amendment demands, I do not see how the reasoning of [the plurality] opinion . . . can be reconciled with [*Stanley v. Georgia*] . . . It would seem to me that if a citizen had a right to possess "obscene" material in the privacy of his home he should have the right to receive it voluntarily through

172. Stanley v. Georgia, 394 U.S. 557 (1969).

173. United States v. Thirty-Seven (37) Photographs, 402 U.S. 363 (1971); United States v. Reidel, 402 U.S. 351 (1971).

174. United States v. Thirty-Seven (37) Photographs, 402 U.S. 363 (1971) (dissenting opinion).

the mail. Certainly when a man legally purchases such material abroad he should be able to bring it with him through customs to read later in his home. The mere act of importation for private use can hardly be more offensive to others than is private perusal in one's home. The right to read and review any literature and pictures at home is hollow indeed if it does not include a right to carry that material privately in one's luggage when entering the country.

In another recent case, the Court upheld under the First Amendment and in the interest of privacy a federal statute authorizing any person who receives in the mails any "pandering advertisements," which the addressee "in his sole discretion believes to be erotically arousing or sexually provocative," to request the postmaster general to order the sender to refrain from any further mailings to him. The postmaster general is required to issue such order, which is enforceable in the courts. Douglas concurred in the decision but noted that there might be constitutional difficulties if a case arose under a further provision in the statute that authorized the addressee to request the postmaster general to include in the prohibitory order the names of any of the addressee's children under age nineteen.[175]

PRIVACY

The concept of privacy is not confined to obscenity cases, nor to cases arising under the First Amendment. In 1943 the Court concluded that the failure of a municipal utilities commission to prohibit a street railway and bus company from broadcasting radio programs (complete with commercials) in its cars and buses constituted governmental action subject to constitutional limitations, but that the "liberty" guaranteed under the due process clause of the Fifth Amendment did not include a right of privacy on a public vehicle. Douglas dissented:[176]

The right to be let alone is indeed the beginning of all freedom. Part of our claim to privacy is in the prohibition of the Fourth Amendment against unreasonable searches and seizures. It gives the guarantee that a

175. Rowan v. United States Post Office Department, 397 U.S. 728 (1970) (concurring opinion).

176. Public Utilities Commission v. Pollak, 343 U.S. 451 (1952) (dissenting opinion).

man's home is his castle beyond invasion either by inquisitive or by officious people. A man loses that privacy of course when he goes upon the streets or enters public places. But even in his activities outside the home he has immunities from controls bearing on privacy. He may not be compelled against his will to attend a religious service; he may not be forced to make an affirmation or observe a ritual that violates his scruples; he may not be made to accept one religious, political, or philosophical creed as against another. Freedom of religion and freedom of speech guaranteed by the First Amendment give more than the privilege to worship, to write, to speak as one chooses; they give freedom not to do nor to act as the government chooses . . . To think as one chooses, to believe what one wishes are important aspects of the constitutional right to be let alone.

If we remembered this lesson taught by the First Amendment, I do not believe we would construe "liberty" within the meaning of [the due process clause] as narrowly as the Court does. The present case involves a form of coercion to make people listen. The listeners are of course in a public place . . . In one sense it can be said that those who ride the streetcars do so voluntarily. Yet in a practical sense they are forced to ride, since this mode of transportation is today essential for many thousands. Compulsion which comes from circumstances can be as real as compulsion which comes from a command . . .

The government may use the radio (or television) on public vehicles for many purposes. Today it may use it for a cultural end. Tomorrow it may use it for political purposes. So far as the right of privacy is concerned the purpose makes no difference. The music selected by one bureaucrat may be as offensive to some as it is soothing to others. The news commentator chosen to report on the events of the day may give overtones to the news that please the bureau head but which rile the streetcar captive audience. The political philosophy which one radio speaker exudes may be thought by the official who makes up the streetcar programs to be best for the welfare of the people. But the man who listens to it on his way to work in the morning and on his way home at night may think it marks the destruction of the Republic.

More than a decade later Douglas wrote for the Court to invalidate a state law forbidding dissemination of birth control information and devices to married persons. This result the law achieved by forbidding use and by making it a crime to aid and abet in use. After reviewing the cases finding that freedom of belief, freedom to hear, and freedom of association, though not expressly included in the First Amendment, had been held protected by that amendment because their existence was "necessary in making the express guarantees fully meaningful," he continued:[177]

> The foregoing cases suggest that specific guarantees in the Bill of Rights have penumbras, formed by emanations from those guarantees, that help give them life and substance . . . Various guarantees create zones of privacy. The right of association contained in the penumbra of the First Amendment [which entitles organizations to protect the secrecy of their membership lists] is one . . . The Third Amendment in its prohibition against the quartering of soldiers "in any house" in time of peace without the consent of the owner is another facet of that privacy. The Fourth Amendment explicitly affirms the "right of the people to be secure in their persons, houses, papers, and effects, against unreasonable searches and seizures." The Fifth Amendment in its Self-Incrimination Clause enables the citizen to create a zone of privacy which government may not force him to surrender to his detriment. The Ninth Amendment provides: "The enumeration in the Constitution, of certain rights, shall not be construed to deny or disparage others retained by the people" . . .
>
> The present case, then, concerns a relationship lying within the zone of privacy created by several fundamental constitutional guarantees. And it concerns a law which, in forbidding the *use* of contraceptives rather than regulating their manufacture or sale, seeks to achieve its goals by means having a maximum destructive impact upon that relationship. Such a law cannot stand in light of the familiar principle . . . that a "governmental purpose to control or prevent activities constitutionally subject to state regulation may not be achieved by means which sweep unnecessarily broadly and thereby invade the area of protected freedoms" . . . Would we allow the police to search the sacred precincts of marital bedrooms for telltale signs of the use of contraceptives? The very idea is repulsive to the notions of privacy surrounding the marriage relationship.

FREEDOM TO TRAVEL

Another developing right not expressly recognized in the Constitution is the right to travel. Shortly after Douglas joined the

177. Griswold v. Connecticut, 381 U.S. 479 (1965). *See also* Poe v. Ullman, 367 U.S. 497 (1961) (dissenting opinion).

Court, it held unconstitutional, as a burden on interstate commerce, a state statute making it a crime to bring an indigent person into the state. Douglas concurred in the decision, but on the ground that the "right to move freely from State to State is an incident of *national* citizenship" protected from state interference by the Fourteenth Amendment's provision that "No State shall make or enforce any law which shall abridge the privileges or immunities of citizens of the United States."[178] The Court has since agreed that such a right exists without ascribing "the source of this right to travel interstate to a particular constitutional provision."[179]

Attempts by Congress and the State Department in recent years to assert control over the movement of citizens through denial of, or restrictions on, passports have led to the recognition also of a right to travel abroad.

In 1958 Douglas wrote for the Court to hold that federal statutes requiring passports for travel abroad did not authorize the secretary of state to deny a passport to a citizen, either on the ground that he was a Communist,[180] or on the ground that because of his association with Communists and suspected spies his travel abroad would be "contrary to the best interest of the United States."[181] His opinion in the first of these cases asserted that, as the solicitor general had conceded, "The right to travel is a part of the 'liberty' of which the citizen cannot be deprived without due process of law under the Fifth Amendment." But, because of the Court's interpretation of the statutes, it was not necessary to decide "the extent to which it can be curtailed."

Thereafter the Subversive Activities Control Board found the Communist party to be a "Communist action" group, thus bringing into operation a provision of the Internal Security Act forbidding the issuance of passports to a member of such a group. Douglas joined with the Court to hold this provision unconstitutional on its face as an overly broad restriction of the liberty guaranteed by the due process

178. Edwards v. California, 314 U.S. 160 (1941).

179. Shapiro v. Thompson, 394 U.S. 618 (1969). *See also* United States v. Guest, 383 U.S. 745 (1966); Graham v. Richardson, 403 U.S. 365 (1971).

180. Kent v. Dulles, 357 U.S. 116 (1958).

181. Dayton v. Dulles, 357 U.S. 144 (1958).

clause, since it applied to all members of the party whether or not they knew of the party's proscribed purposes, whether or not they knew the party had been found to be a "Communist action" group, regardless of the purposes of their trips, and regardless of the sensitivity of the areas in which they wished to travel.[182]

The Court thereafter held that a statute providing that the "Secretary of State may grant and issue passports" authorized the secretary to adopt a policy of refusing to validate passports for travel to Cuba except to "persons whose travel may be regarded as being in the best interests of the United States, such as newsmen or businessmen with previously established business interests." And, since "Cuba is the only area in the Western Hemisphere controlled by a Communist government," this restriction was held to be a permissible limitation on the right to travel guaranteed by the due process clause, because "travel to Cuba by American citizens might involve the Nation in dangerous international incidents." The applicant's further contention that the First Amendment guaranteed a right to travel so that he might acquaint himself "at first hand with the effects abroad of our Government's policies, foreign and domestic, and with conditions abroad which might affect such policies" was rejected because what was involved was an "inhibition of action," and there were "few restrictions on action which could not be clothed by ingenious argument in the garb of decreased data flow." Douglas dissented:[183]

[The earlier decision that the right to travel overseas was guaranteed by the due process clause] reflected a judgment as to the peripheral rights of the citizen under the First Amendment. The right to know, to converse with others, to consult with them, to observe social, physical, political and other phenomena abroad as well as at home gives meaning and substance to freedom of expression and freedom of the press. Without those contacts First Amendment rights suffer . . .

Since we deal with rights peripheral to the enjoyment of First Amendment guarantees, restrictive legislation must be "narrowly drawn" . . . to meet a precise evil. Only last Term . . . we reaffirmed

182. Aptheker v. Secretary of State, 378 U.S. 500 (1964) (concurring opinion).
183. Zemel v. Rusk, 381 U.S. 1 (1965) (dissenting opinion).

that when we struck down a provision of the Subversive Activities Control Act . . . because it "too broadly and indiscriminately" restricted the right to travel . . . We should do the same here.

I agree that there are areas to which Congress can restrict or bar travel. Pestilences may rage in a region making it necessary to protect not only the traveler but those he might infect on his return. A theatre of war may be too dangerous for travel . . . But the only so-called danger present here is the Communist regime in Cuba. The world, however, is filled with Communist thought; and Communist regimes are on more than one continent. They are part of the world spectrum; and if we are to know them and understand them, we must mingle with them . . . Keeping alive intellectual intercourse between opposing groups has always been important and perhaps was never more important than now.

Thereafter Douglas voted with a unanimous Court to hold that a statute providing criminal penalties for citizens who "depart from" the United States without "a valid passport" was not applicable to one who departed for Cuba with a valid passport, although it had not been specifically validated for travel to Cuba, as required by the secretary of state's policy. Criminal statutes are to be narrowly construed; this statute was enacted long before the secretary announced that passports would not "be valid for travel to . . . Cuba unless specifically endorsed for such travel" and should not be construed to apply to area restrictions on otherwise valid passports.[184]

184. United States v. Laub, 385 U.S. 475 (1967); Travis v. United States, 385 U.S. 491 (1967).

5 MILITARY SERVICE

As previously indicated, Douglas has been unable to persuade the Court to consider the validity of the use of the Selective Service Act to conscript men for military service abroad in a conflict that has not been sanctioned by a congressional declaration of war and which has been challenged as in violation of treaties to which the United States is a party.[1] But in a number of cases in recent years the Court has considered other aspects of the Selective Service Act.

Many of those cases have involved the exemption for conscientious objectors. The act exempted one who, "by reason of religious training and belief, is conscientiously opposed to war in any form" and defined "religious training and belief" to mean "an individual's belief in relation to a Supreme Being involving duties superior to those arising from any human relation," though not to include "essentially political, sociological, or philosophical views or a merely personal moral code." In *Sicurella v. United States*,[2] Douglas voted with the Court to reverse the conviction, for refusal to submit to induction, of a Jehovah's Witness whose claim of conscientious objector status had been rejected because he conceded his willingness to engage in a "theocratic war" if Jehovah so commanded and to fight at Armageddon, but without the

1. See Chapter 1.
2. 348 U.S. 385 (1955).

use of "carnal weapons" of warfare. A selective service appeal board had acted on advice of the Department of Justice that Sicurella could not qualify as one opposed by religious belief "to war in any form." But the Court concluded that his belief had "neither the bark nor the bite of war as we know it today."

Later, in the *Seeger* case, the Court read the statute to include "all sincere religious beliefs which are based upon a power or being, or upon a faith, to which all else is subordinate or upon which all else is ultimately dependent," but not to require a belief in "the orthodox God." It was enough to show a "sincere and meaningful belief which occupies in the life of its possessor a place parallel to that filled by the God of those admittedly qualifying for the exemption." The Court rejected the notion that a distinction should be made between "externally and internally derived beliefs" and held the definition satisfied by persons who were not members of any religious sect, whose beliefs were apparently the product primarily of personal study and reflection, and who were inclined to attribute a supreme "power" or a "creative intelligence" to the cosmic order rather than to an anthropomorphic entity and hence were unwilling to affirm a belief in a "Supreme Being" as they understood that term. Douglas concurred in that interpretation, stating that otherwise he would have difficulties, under the free exercise of religion clause of the First Amendment and under the due process prohibition of invidious discrimination, with a statute which preferred some religions over others.[3]

Five years later, in the *Welsh* case, Douglas voted with the Court to hold that the *Seeger* interpretation applied to one whose opposition to all war stemmed from his "moral, ethical, or religious beliefs about what is right and wrong" if "these beliefs be held with the strength of traditional religious convictions." And the exclusion of "essentially political, sociological, or philosophical views or a merely personal moral code" was said not to exclude "those who hold strong beliefs about our domestic or foreign affairs or even those whose conscientious objection to participation in all wars is founded to a substantial extent upon considerations of public policy. The two groups of registrants that

3. United States v. Seeger, 380 U.S. 163 (1965) (concurring opinion).

obviously do not fall within these exclusions from the exemption are those whose beliefs are not deeply held and those whose objection to war does not rest at all upon moral, ethical, or religious principle but instead rest solely upon considerations of policy, pragmatism, or expediency."[4] (In 1967, after the decision in *Seeger*, and after the *Welsh* case arose but before it was decided, Congress amended the act to delete the reference to a "Supreme Being.")

In 1971 in the *Gillette* case, the Court held that the exemption for one who, "by reason of religious training and belief, is conscientiously opposed to participation in war in any form" was not available to "selective objectors" who did not oppose participation in all wars but only in "unjust" wars and who viewed the military operation in Vietnam as unjust. The decision involved two persons—Negre, a devout Catholic, and Gillette, an asserted Humanist. There was no question of the sincerity of their beliefs, and the Court did not inquire into whether Gillette's beliefs were religious. Neither did it determine that the beliefs involved were excluded from protection under the statute, as "essentially political, sociological, or philosophical views, or a merely personal moral code." It was enough to take both men out of the statutory exemption that they were not conscientiously opposed to "participating personally in any war and all war." And the statute, as construed, was held neither to amount to an establishment of religion nor to interfere with the free exercise of religion within the meaning of the First Amendment. Douglas did not disagree with the interpretation of the statute but dissented on the ground that it was unconstitutional, not only as applied to Negre, the Catholic, but also as applied to Gillette, the Humanist, whose views he apparently did not consider religious:[5]

> The question, can a conscientious objector, whether his objection be rooted in "religion" or in moral values, be required to kill? has never been answered . . . It is true that the First Amendment speaks of the free exercise of religion and not of the free exercise of conscience or belief, yet conscience and belief are the main ingredients of First

4. Welsh v. United States, 398 U.S. 333 (1970) (dissenting opinion).
5. Gillette v. United States, 401 U.S. 437 (1971).

> Amendment rights. They are the bedrock of free speech as well as religion. The implied First Amendment right of "conscience" is certainly as high as the "right of association" which we [have] recognized . . .
>
> The law as written is a species of those which show an invidious discrimination in favor of religious persons and against others with like scruples. Mr. Justice Black once said: "The First Amendment has lost much if the religious follower and the atheist are no longer to be judicially regarded as entitled to equal justice under law" . . .
>
> While there is no Equal Protection Clause in the Fifth Amendment, our decisions are clear that invidious classifications violate due process . . . A classification of "conscience" based on a "religion" and a "conscience" based on more generalized, philosophical grounds is . . . invidious by reason of our First Amendment standards.

In 1971 also the Court invalidated the denial of conscientious objector status to Cassius Clay on the ground that a selective service appeal board had acted on erroneous advice from the Department of Justice as to Clay's Muslim religion qualifying as a "religion" and as to the sincerity of his beliefs. Hence, it reversed his conviction for refusal to submit to induction without reaching the question whether he was conscientiously opposed to war in any form. Clay had testified that it was a tenet of his faith that "we do not take part . . . in any part of war unless declared by Allah himself, or unless it's an Islamic world war or a Holy war." Douglas, concurring, would have disposed of the case somewhat differently:[6]

> In the present case there is no line between "carnal" war and "spiritual" or symbolic wars [as in *Sicurella v. United States*].[7] Those who know the history of the Mediterranean littoral know that the *jihad* of the Moslem was a bloody war . . .
>
> The *jihad* is the counterpart of the "just" war as it has been known in the West. Neither Clay nor Negre [in the *Gillette* case][8] should be subject to punishment because they will not renounce the "truth" of the teaching of their respective churches that wars indeed may exist which are just wars in which a Moslem or Catholic has a respective duty to participate.

6. Clay v. United States, 403 U.S. 698 (1971) (concurring opinion).
7. Note 2, *supra*.
8. Note 5, *supra*.

What Clay's testimony adds up to is that he believes only in war as sanctioned by the Koran, that is to say, a religious war against nonbelievers. All other wars are unjust.

That is a matter of belief, of conscience, of religious principle. Both Clay and Negre were "by reason of religious training and belief" conscientiously opposed to participation in war of the character proscribed by their respective religions. That belief is a matter of conscience protected by the First Amendment which Congress has no power to qualify or dilute as it did . . . when it restricted the exemption to those "conscientiously opposed to participation in war in any form".

Other Selective Service Act cases have dealt with the procedures for claiming exemption from service. Douglas voted with the Court in *Falbo v. United States*[9] when it read the act to mean that one who was denied conscientious objector status by his local board, who failed to appeal that action within the selective service system as authorized by presidential regulations, and who failed to comply with the board's order to report for induction, could not reopen his conscientious objector claim when he was prosecuted for failure to report. But he wrote for the Court in another case construing the act to mean that one denied CO status who did report for induction but then refused to take the induction oath could not be forcibly inducted and tried by court martial for refusal to obey military orders. While his refusal to submit to induction was an offense for which he could be charged, he must be tried in a civil court.[10]

Douglas wrote for the Court again in *Estep v. United States*,[11] to hold that Jehovah's Witnesses whose claims to exemption as ministers were denied by their local boards, who exhausted their appeals within the selective service system, and who reported for but refused to submit to induction, could challenge the denial of ministerial exemption when prosecuted for refusal to submit. The act gave the local boards power "within their respective jurisdictions" to rule on exemption claims and provided that "decisions of . . . local boards shall be final except where an appeal is authorized in accordance with such rules and regulations as

9. 320 U.S. 549 (1944).
10. Billings v. Truesdell, 321 U.S. 542 (1944).
11. 327 U.S. 119 (1946).

the President may prescribe." The act also provided for prosecution in civil courts of those who knowingly fail to perform any duty imposed upon them by the act or regulations, but said nothing of defenses to such actions:

> Thus we start with a statute which makes no provision for judicial review of the actions of the local boards or the appeal agencies. That alone, of course, is not decisive.
>
> . . . It is only orders [of local boards] "within their respective jurisdictions" that are made final. It would seem therefore, that if a Pennsylvania board ordered a citizen and resident of Oregon to report for induction, the defense that it acted beyond its jurisdiction could be interposed in a prosecution under [the act] . . .
>
> Any other case where a local board acts so contrary to its granted authority as to exceed its jurisdiction does not stand on a different footing . . .
>
> We cannot read [the act] as requiring the courts to inflict punishment on registrants for violating whatever orders the local boards might issue. We cannot believe that Congress intended that criminal sanctions were to be applied to orders issued by local boards no matter how flagrantly they violated the rules and regulations which define their jurisdiction. We are dealing here with a question of personal liberty . . . We cannot readily infer that Congress departed so far from the traditional concepts of a fair trial when it made the actions of the local boards "final" as to provide that a citizen of this country should go to jail for not obeying an unlawful order of an administrative agency . . . The provision making the decisions of the local board "final" means to us that Congress chose not to give administrative action under this Act the customary scope of judicial review which obtains under other statutes. It means that the courts are not to weigh the evidence to determine whether the classifications made by the local boards made in conformity with the regulations are final even though they may be erroneous. The question of jurisdiction of the local board is reached only if there is no basis in fact for the classification which it gave the registrant . . .
>
> *Falbo* v. *United States*[12] . . . does not preclude such a defense in the present cases. In the *Falbo* case the defendant challenged the order of his local board before he had exhausted his administrative remedies. Here these registrants had pursued their administrative remedies to the

12. Note 9, *supra*.

end. All had been done that could be done. Submission to induction would be satisfaction of the orders of the local boards, not a further step to obtain relief from them.

If [the act] were not construed to permit the accused to defend on the ground that his local board acted beyond its jurisdiction, a curious result would follow. [Under the federal Judicial Code] the remedy of *habeas corpus* extends to a case where a person "is in custody in violation of the Constitution or of a law . . . of the United States . . . " It has been assumed that *habeas corpus* is available only after a registrant has been inducted into the armed services. But if we now hold that a registrant could not defend at his trial on the ground that the local board had no jurisdiction in the premises, it would seem that the way would then be open to him to challenge the jurisdiction of the local board after conviction by *habeas corpus.* The court would then be sending men to jail today when it was apparent that they would have had to be released tomorrow.[13]

At one time the Selective Service Act provided that if a claim for conscientious objector status was denied by a local board and an appeal to an appeal board was taken, the case should be referred to the Department of Justice for "inquiry and hearing," after which the department should make recommendations to the appeal board for disposition of the appeal. The department used the FBI to make the "inquiry" preceding the hearing, and at the hearing it advised the appellant of the "general nature and character" of any "unfavorable" evidence developed by the FBI but did not permit him to see the FBI report or to learn the names of those interviewed by the FBI. When the Court held that this procedure satisfied the statute, Douglas dissented on the ground that the statute contemplated a fair hearing, which could not be had unless the appellant could see the FBI report and confront his accusers:[14]

The use of statements by informers who need not confront the person under investigation or accusation has such an infamous history that it

13. Douglas later voted with the Court to find that a local board had no basis in fact for denying ministerial exemption to a Jehovah's Witness, Dickinson v. United States, 346 U.S. 359 (1953), and dissented where the Court found that a board had a basis in fact for denying conscientious objector status to another member of the same sect. Witmer v. United States, 348 U.S. 375 (1955).

14. United States v. Nugent, 346 U.S. 1 (1953) (dissenting opinion).

should be rooted out from our procedure. A hearing at which these faceless people are allowed to present their whispered rumors and yet escape the test and torture of cross-examination is not a hearing in the Anglo-American sense. We should be done with the practice—whether the life of a man is at stake, or his reputation, or any matter touching upon his status or his rights. If FBI reports are disclosed in administrative or judicial proceedings, it may be that valuable underground sources will dry up. But that is not the choice. If the aim is to protect the underground of informers, the FBI report need not be used. If it is used, then fairness requires that the names of the accusers be disclosed. Without the identity of the informer the person investigated or accused stands helpless. The prejudices, the credibility, the passions, the perjury of the informer are never known. If they were exposed, the whole charge might wither under cross-examination.

In other cases Douglas has voted with the Court to hold that the appellant does not receive a fair hearing under the act where he is not given a fair résumé of the FBI report,[15] and to upset a conviction for refusing to submit for induction where the registrant was not given a copy of the Justice Department's recommendation to the appeal board.[16] And, as previously indicated, he has also voted with the Court to upset convictions where the department's recommendations to the board contained erroneous advice.[17]

The claim for conscientious objector status may be made at any time before an order to report for induction is mailed and must be ruled on by the registrant's local selective service board. The claim may also be made after induction, in which event it will be ruled on by military authorities. In 1971 the Court interpreted a selective service regulation providing that the classification of a registrant shall not be reopened before the local board after the board has mailed an order to report for induction unless there has been a change in status "resulting from circumstances over which the registrant had no control." This regulation was held to justify a local board in refusing to consider a claim filed by a registrant in the interval between his receipt of the order to report for induction and the date set for induction, despite his contention that his conscientious objection had crystallized after

15. Simmons v. United States, 348 U.S. 397 (1955).
16. Gonzales v. United States, 348 U.S. 407 (1955).
17. Sicurella v. United States, note 2, *supra;* Clay v. United States, note 6, *supra.*

receipt of the induction notice. The Court agreed with the board that the regulation should be construed to permit exceptions only for "objectively identifiable" and "extraneous" circumstances relating to other exemptions from service, such as physical injury or the death of a brother which left the registrant exempt as the only surviving son. Douglas dissented:[18]

> The rather stuffy judicial notion that an inductee's realization that he has a "conscientious" objection to war is not a circumstance over which he has "no control" within the meaning of the Regulation is belied from experience . . .
>
> The stories of sudden conversion are legion in religious history; and there is no reason why the Selective Service boards should not recognize them, deal with them, and, if sincere, act on them even though they come after notice of induction has been received . . .
>
> [The Court's] conclusion is not required by the Regulation . . .
>
> It is therefore a *tour de force* for the Court to say that in-service processing by the military is required. Certainly that result is not mandated by the Act. Since it is not, we have a choice in construction which really involves a choice of policy. Faced with that choice we should not hesitate to leave these matters to civilian authorities . . .
>
> The mind of the military has reacted more violently to the conscientious objector than the mind of the priest or other civilian. [Accounts of the treatment by the military of conscientious objectors in World Wars I and II and in the present day reveal many instances of cruelty.] [I do not] suggest that every conscientious objector is treated as cruelly . . . I do suggest however that in my time[19] every conscientious objector was "fair game" to most top sergeants who considered that he had a "yellow streak" and therefore was a coward or was un-American. The conscientious objector never had an easy time asserting First Amendment rights in the Armed Services.
>
> What might happen to him in the barracks or in the detention center is, of course, not the measure of what would transpire at the hearings [on his exemption claim]. But the military mind is educated to other values; it does not reflect the humanistic, philosophical values most germane to ferreting out First Amendment claims that are genuine.

A number of other cases have also arisen from the manner in which the selective service system is administered. Douglas wrote for the

18. Ehlert v. United States, 402 U.S. 99 (1971).
19. Douglas served as a sergeant in the Army in World War I.

Court in the *Oestereich* case to invalidate the action of a draft board in revoking the exemption of a theological student because he had turned in his registration certificate in protest against our policy in Vietnam. Since the Selective Service Act provides that "students preparing for the ministry" in qualified schools "shall be exempt," and the board had deprived him of the exemption "because of conduct or activities unrelated to the merits of granting or continuing the exemption," the board's action was "basically lawless." And a provision added to the act in 1967 forbidding judicial review in civil courts of "classification or processing of any registrant by local boards," save in prosecutions for refusal to report for induction, was held not to forbid a suit to enjoin induction in this instance, since it was construed not to apply to a case involving "a clear departure by the Board from its statutory mandate."[20]

The Court later held that this restriction on judicial review was applicable where the only question was whether a board had properly concluded, on the evidence before it, that a registrant was not entitled to classification as a conscientious objector, Douglas agreed but added:[21]

> I would take a different view if this were a case where a registrant was moved from a CO . . . classification to I-A because he made a speech, unpopular with the Board.
>
> This would also be a different case if the registrant were a member of an institutionalized group, such as the Quakers, whose opposition to war was well known and the registrant, though perhaps unpopular with the Board, was a bona fide member of the group. Then, too, a Board would act in a lawless way if it moved a registrant from a CO classification to I-A and disregarding all the evidence denied him a CO classification.

Douglas later wrote for the Court to reverse a conviction for refusal to report for induction of one who was classified I-A, but whose induction was accelerated by his board because of his "delinquency" in turning in his registration certificate in protest against our Vietnam policy and who did not therefore have it in his personal possession, as

20. Oestereich v. Selective Service Local Board, 393 U.S. 233 (1968).
21. Clark v. Gabriel, 393 U.S. 256 (1968) (concurring opinion).

required by selective service regulations. Douglas noted that the act prescribes criminal penalties for violation of valid regulations, such as the one requiring a registrant to keep his certificate in his possession, but concluded that both the board's action in accelerating induction and the "delinquency" regulations which purported to authorize such action were not authorized by the act:[22]

> The power under the regulations to declare a registrant "delinquent" has no statutory standard or even guidelines. The power is exercised entirely at the discretion of the local board. It is a broad, roving authority, a type of administrative absolutism not congenial to our law-making traditions. In *Kent* v. *Dulles*[23] . . . we refused to impute to Congress the grant of "unbridled discretion" to the Secretary of State to issue or withhold a passport from a citizen "for any substantive reason he may choose" . . . Where the liberties of the citizen are involved, we said that "we will construe narrowly all delegated powers that curtail or dilute them" . . . We search the Act in vain for any clues that Congress desired the Act to have punitive sanctions apart from the criminal prosecutions specifically authorized. Nor do we read it as granting personal privileges that may be forfeited for transgressions that affront the local board. If federal or state laws are violated by registrants, they can be prosecuted. If induction is to be substituted for these prosecutions, a vast rewriting of the Act is needed. Standards would be needed by which the legality of a declaration of "delinquency" could be judged. And the regulations, when written, would be subject to the customary inquiries as to infirmities on their face or in their application, including the question whether they were used to penalize or punish the free exercise of constitutional rights.

Thereafter, Douglas voted with the Court to hold that a draft board should be enjoined from using the delinquency regulations to revoke the student deferment of a registrant who had also turned in his draft card as a protest against Vietnam policy. Not only were the action and the delinquency regulations on which it was based illegal, as previously held, but they were such a "clear departure" from the statutory mandate that, as held in *Oestereich*, the provision forbidding judicial review in advance of induction was inapplicable. The fact that the act

22. Gutknecht v. United States, 396 U.S. 295 (1970).
23. 357 U.S. 116 (1958).

gave religious students "exemption," while providing "deferments" to other students, was held to make no difference, since the "effect of either type of classification is that the registrant cannot be inducted as long as he remains so classified.[24]

Another recent selective service case involved a black who sought to enjoin his induction on the ground that blacks had been systematically excluded from his draft board in violation of the Selective Service Act and the Constitution. The trial court denied relief and by the time the registrant's case reached the court of appeals he had been ordered to report for induction, had refused, and had been convicted for his refusal and given a five-year sentence. An appeal from that conviction was pending. The court of appeals held that the conviction did not render the case moot since, if the induction was illegal, the registrant would be entitled to relief from his sentence. But it also held that exclusion of blacks from the draft board, even if proved, would not deprive the board of jurisdiction to induct the registrant into the armed forces. When the Court declined to review the case, Douglas dissented:[25]

> [The act] provides for the selection of members of Selective Service Boards "in an impartial manner" under rules and regulations prescribed by the President, "Provided, That in the selection of persons for training and service under this title . . . and *in the interpretation and execution of* the provisions of this title . . . there shall be no discrimination against any person on account of race or color . . . " [Emphasis supplied.]
>
> If we assume that Sellers has a statutory right to a bi-racial Board, he would be entitled to pre-induction judicial review, if *Oestereich* is to have any life or meaning.
>
> If that is true, a Board compounds the injury by bulldozing the man into the Army. I cannot believe we would ever hold that lawless Board action can render a case moot.
>
> What the facts of this case on the issue of racial discrimination are we do not know . . .
>
> . . . [T]he presence of an all-white Board in a racially prejudiced community may well result in blacks carrying more than their fair share

24. Breen v. Selective Service Local Board, 396 U.S. 460 (1970).
25. Sellers v. Laird, 395 U.S. 950 (1969) (dissenting opinion).

of the Vietnam burden . . . I assume that is what [the Act] is designed to prevent.

Except for one case previously discussed involving the right to vote,[26] the Court's consideration of other military service cases has been limited to a review of some aspects of court martial proceedings.[27]

Of the various constitutional guarantees, only the Fifth Amendment's provision for indictment by grand jury contains an express exception for "cases arising in the land or naval forces." Nonetheless, the military tribunals have never provided jury trials, and the Court has held that none are required.[28]

In several cases decided during Douglas' tenure, however, the Court has considered the application of other constitutional or statutory requirements. (Civil courts review these military proceedings only by writs of habeas corpus, and Douglas wrote for the Court to hold that the writ is not available until the defendant has exhausted all avenues for review within the military system.[29])

Douglas wrote for the Court when it held that, since review on habeas corpus is confined to questions which go to the jurisdiction of the military tribunal, including the denial of constitutional rights, the civil courts may not by that means review alleged error by a court martial in evaluating the evidence on the question of a defendant's insanity defense in a rape case.[30] The same decision held that there was no constitutional right to have enlisted men sitting on the court martial—a right which Congress later conferred by statute.[31]

But Douglas joined the dissenters when the Court held that failure to comply with a statutory requirement that "no charge will be referred to a general court martial for trial until after a thorough and imparital

26. See text at note 29, p. 29, *supra*.

27. Cases dealing with limitations on the jurisdiction of courts martial and other military tribunals to try persons not in military service are discussed in Chapter 1.

28. Kahn v. Anderson, 255 U.S. 1 (1921). *See also Ex parte* Quirin, 317 U.S. 1 (1942).

29. Whelchel v. McDonald, 340 U.S. 122 (1950).

30. Gusik v. Schilder, 340 U.S. 128 (1950). *See also* Noyd v. Bond, 395 U.S. 683 (1969). *Cf.* United States v. Augenblick, 393 U.S. 348 (1969).

31. 10 USC §825.

investigation thereof shall have been made" did not deprive the court martial of jurisdiction so as to entitle the defendant to relief by habeas corpus. The dissenters thought that the requirement served two purposes—saving the Army's time by eliminating frivolous cases, and protecting an accused from court martial on groundless charges:[32]

> If the [requirement] is ignored, and the court martial finds the defendant innocent, the error can never be corrected—the [court's] time has been wasted and the defendant's record is forever besmirched by the words "general court martial." Yet if the prisoner is found guilty, there is still no sanction. For military authorities will not set aside a conviction unless the . . . accused . . . has been prejudiced. And if the trial has been fair, and resulted in conviction, who will say that the defendant has been prejudiced because preliminary investigation was wanting?
>
> Unless a civilian court is able to enforce the requirement, then it is not a requirement at all, but only a suggestion which should be observed. Today the Court adopts the latter alternative . . . It makes [the requirement] a virtual dead letter.

Douglas joined the dissenters also when the Court held that the Fifth Amendment's guarantee against double jeopardy was not violated when the defendant was brought to trial for rape before a court martial in Germany during World War II, the proceeding was terminated for "tactical" reasons after some witnesses had been heard, and the defendant was thereafter tried and convicted before another court martial. Assuming that the defendant had been put in "jeopardy" when the first court martial began taking evidence, the Court concluded that the double jeopardy guarantee should not apply when the purpose of terminating the first trial was "the tactical situation brought about by a rapidly advancing army," so that presumably the first court martial's officers were "needed to perform their military functions." The dissenters disagreed with this reading of the double jeopardy guarantee:[33] "The harassment to the defendant from being repeatedly tried is not less because the army is advancing. The guarantee of the Constitution against double jeopardy is not to be eroded away by a tide

32. Humphrey v. Smith, 336 U.S. 695 (1949) (dissenting opinion).
33. Wade v. Hunter, 336 U.S. 684 (1949) (dissenting opinion).

of plausible-appearing exceptions . . . Adaptations of military justice to the expediencies of tactical situations is the prerogative of the commander in the field, but the price of such expediency is compliance with the Constitution."

Douglas dissented again when the Court sustained a denial of a hearing in habeas corpus proceedings on a petition alleging that death sentences for murder were based, for one defendant, on a confession obtained during a five-day period of interrogation while he was held incommunicado, and, for a second defendant, on the testimony of a third defendant who had testified against him and who now swore that he was beaten and forced to confess and that his testimony was false. The Court concluded that the court martial and the military reviewing tribunals had fully considered the question whether the confession was voluntary and whether the testimony of the third defendant was false, and that it was "not the duty of the civil courts simply to repeat the process." Their function, rather, was "to determine whether the military have given fair consideration to each of these claims." While agreeing that, as he had previously written for the Court, the civil courts do not "sit in review of the weight of the evidence before the military tribunal,"[34] Douglas thought that there should be a hearing granted in the habeas corpus proceeding:[35]

If a prisoner is coerced by torture or other methods to give the evidence against him, if he is beaten or slowly "broken" by third-degree methods, then the "trial" before the military tribunal becomes an empty ritual. The real trial takes place in secret where the accused without benefit of counsel succumbs to physical or psychological pressures. A soldier or sailor convicted in that manner has been denied due process of law; and, like the accused in criminal cases . . . he should have relief by way of habeas corpus . . .

If the military agency has fairly and conscientiously applied the standards of due process formulated by this Court, I would agree that a rehash of the same facts by a federal court would not advance the cause

34. See text at note 30, *supra*.

35. Burns v. Wilson, 346 U.S. 137 (1953) (dissenting opinion). See also Jackson v. Taylor, 353 U.S. 569 (1957), and Fowler v. Wilkinson, 353 U.S. 583 (1957), where Douglas, dissenting, thought the Army boards of review had exceeded their statutory authority in modifying court martial sentences.

of justice. But where the military reviewing agency has not done that, a court should entertain the petition for habeas corpus [and hold a hearing on the issues raised] . . .

The *undisputed* facts in this case make a prima facie case that our rule on coerced confessions . . . was violated here. No court has considered the question whether repetitious questioning over a period of 5 days while the accused was held incommunicado without benefit of counsel violated [the due process clause of] the Fifth Amendment . . .

There has been at no time any considered appraisal of the facts surrounding these confessions . . . Before these men go to their death, such an appraisal should be made.

Douglas wrote for the Court in interpreting a statute, since repealed, providing that "no person shall be tried by court-martial for murder or rape committed within the geographical limits of the States of the Union . . . in time of peace." Involved was a charge of conspiracy to commit murder, allegedly committed by a serviceman in California in June 1949, after the 1945 cessation of hostilities in World War II but before official termination of the war with Germany and Japan by Congressional Resolution and Presidential Proclamations in 1951 and 1952. The Court concluded that the alleged crime occurred "in time of peace," so that a court martial did not have jurisdiction:[36]

We do not write on a clean slate. The attitude of a free society toward the jurisdiction of military tribunals—our reluctance to give them authority to try people for nonmilitary offenses—has a long history . . .

The power to try soldiers for the capital crimes of murder and rape was long withheld [from military tribunals]. Not until 1863 was authority granted . . . And then it was restricted to times of "war, insurrection, or rebellion." The theory was that the civil courts, being open, were wholly qualified to handle these cases . . . Civil courts were, indeed, thought to be better qualified than military tribunals to try nonmilitary offenses. They have a more deeply engrained judicial attitude, a more thorough indoctrination in the procedural safeguards necessary for a fair trial. Moreover, important constitutional guarantees come into play once the citizen—whether soldier or civilian—is charged

36. Lee v. Madigan, 358 U.S. 228 (1959).

with a capital crime such as murder or rape. The most significant of these is the right to trial by jury, one of the most important safeguards against tyranny which our law has designed. We must assume that the Congress ... was alive to the importance of those constitutional guarantees when it gave [the statute in question] its particular phrasing ... [The] Judge Advocate General, in testifying in favor of the forerunner of the present [statute], spoke of the protection it extended the officer and the soldier by securing them "a trial by their peers." We think the [statute] should be read generously to achieve that end.

Douglas wrote for the Court again in the *O'Callahan* case holding that a court martial had no jurisdiction to try a serviceman stationed in Hawaii in peacetime for the crimes of housebreaking, attempted rape, and assault with intent to commit rape, all committed on a single victim in a hotel in Honolulu while the serviceman was off base on an evening pass. The Court held that court martial jurisdiction over persons on active military duty was confined to "service connected" crimes:[37]

The Fifth Amendment specifically exempts "cases arising *in the land or naval forces* ... " from the requirement of prosecution by indictment and inferentially, from the right of trial by jury ...

If the case does not arise "*in the land and naval forces*," then the accused gets *first*, the benefit of an indictment by a grand jury and *second*, a trial by a jury before a civilian court ...

A court martial is tried, not by a jury of the defendant's peers which must decide unanimously, but by a panel of officers [or, if an accused enlisted man requests it, a panel including at least one-third enlisted men] empowered to act by a two-thirds vote. The presiding officer at a court-martial is not a judge whose objectivity and independence are protected by tenure and undiminishable salary and nurtured by the judicial tradition, but is a military law officer. Substantially different rules of evidence and procedure apply in military trials. Apart from those differences, the suggestion of the possibility of influence on the actions of the court martial by the officer who convenes it, selects its members and the counsel on both sides, and who usually has direct

37. O'Callahan v. Parker, 395 U.S. 258 (1969). Douglas did not participate in the decision in Wilson v. Girard, 354 U.S. 524 (1957), finding no constitutional objection to a 1952 treaty with Japan whereby the United States consented to the trial in Japanese courts of American servicemen stationed in Japan for offenses committed there.

command authority over its members is a pervasive one in military law, despite strenuous efforts to eliminate the danger.

A court martial is not yet an independent instrument of justice but remains to a significant degree a specialized part of the overall mechanism by which military discipline is preserved.

Article 134 of the Code of Military Justice provides that, "[t]hough not specifically mentioned in this chapter, all disorders and neglects to the prejudice of good order and discipline in the armed forces, all conduct of a nature to bring discredit upon the armed forces, and crimes and offenses not capital, of which persons subject to this chapter may be guilty, shall be taken cognizance of by a . . . court martial." The Code also contains its own definition of a number of crimes, including the capital offenses of premeditated murder and forcible rape. But the Court concluded:

that the crime to be under military jurisdiction must be service connected, lest "cases arising in the land and naval forces . . . be expanded to deprive every member of the armed services of the benefits of an indictment by a grand jury and a trial by a jury of his peers . . . We were advised on oral argument that Art. 134 is construed by the military to give it power to try a member of the armed services for income tax evasion. This article has been called "a catch-all" that "incorporates almost every Federal penal statute into the . . . Code" . . . The catalogue of cases put within reach of the military is indeed long; and we see no way of saving to servicemen and servicewomen in any case the benefits of indictment and of trial by jury, if we conclude that this petitioner was properly tried by court-martial.

In the present case petitioner was properly absent from his military base when he committed the crimes with which he is charged. There was no connection—not even the remotest one—between his military duties and the crimes in question. The crimes were not committed on a military post or enclave; nor was the person whom he attacked performing any duties relating to the military. Moreover, Hawaii, the situs of the crime, is not an armed camp under military control, as are some of our far-flung outposts.

Finally, we deal with peacetime offenses, not with authority stemming from the war power. Civil courts were open. The offenses were committed within our territorial limits, not in the occupied zone of a foreign country. The offenses did not involve any question of the flouting of military authority, the security of a military post, or the integrity of military property.

Douglas later joined with a unanimous Court to hold that the ruling in *O'Callahan* did not apply to a serviceman charged with rape, of the sister of one fellow serviceman and the wife of another, committed on his military base in New Jersey in 1961.[38]

38. Relford v. Commandant, U.S. Disciplinary Barracks, 401 U.S. 355 (1971).

6 EQUAL TREATMENT

The Fourteenth Amendment provides that "No State . . . shall . . . deprive any person of life, liberty, or property, without due process of the law; nor deny to any person within its jurisdiction the equal protection of the laws." The Fifth Amendment, applicable to the federal government, contains a due process clause but no equal protection clause.

The Court's interpretation of the equal protection clause of the Fourteenth Amendment to require of the states substantive equality in voting rights and its reading of the due process clause of the Fifth Amendment to forbid arbitrary discrimination by the federal government in the treatment of naturalized and natural-born citizens have been earlier described.[1] Its treatment of cases involving discrimination in the treatment of the poor is described in Chapter 28. In a variety of other contexts the Court has also dealt with constitutional requirements that the government act with an even hand.

In one area the Court finds this constitutional requirement where Douglas believes it should not. The Court has consistently read the word "person" in the Fourteenth Amendment's due process and equal protection clauses to include corporations. Before Douglas came to the Court, Justice Black challenged that interpretation, contending (1) that

1. See Chapters 2 and 3.

as a matter of history the purpose of this post–Civil War Amendment was to give citizenship to and provide fair and equal treatment for blacks, and (2) that as a matter of language the Fourteenth Amendment also used the word "person" in conferring citizenship, in apportioning representatives among the states and in imposing limitations on who could serve as senators and representatives—a use of the term which clearly did not include corporations.[2] When the Court in 1949 allowed a corporation to invoke the equal protection clause to invalidate a state tax, Douglas dissented, indorsing Black's view:[3]

> The purpose of the Amendment was to protect human rights—primarily the rights of a race which had just won its freedom . . . [This] was apparently plain to the people who voted to make the Fourteenth Amendment a part of our Constitution. For as Mr. Justice Black pointed out . . . the submission of the Amendment to the people was on the basis that it protected human beings. There was no suggestion in its submission that it was designed to put negroes and corporations into one class and so dilute the police power of the States over corporate affairs . . .
>
> It requires distortion to read "person" as meaning one thing, then another, within the same clause and from clause to clause . . .
>
> . . . It may be most desirable to give corporations this protection from the operation of the legislative process. But that question is not for us. It is for the people. If they want corporations to be treated as humans are treated, if they want to grant corporations this large degree of emancipation from state regulation, they should say so. The Constitution provides a method by which they may do so. We should not do it for them through the guise of interpretation.

Douglas wrote for the Court to hold that a state violates the equal protection clause by providing for compulsory sterilization of those twice convicted of robbery or larceny, but excepting those convicted of embezzlement.[4] In 1968 he wrote for the Court again to find a similar violation where the state denied a recovery to illegitimate children for the wrongful death of their mother while allowing such recovery by

2. Connecticut General Life Insurance Co. v. Johnson, 303 U.S. 77 (1938) (dissenting opinion).

3. Wheeling Steel Corp. v. Glander, 337 U.S. 562 (1949) (dissenting opinion).

4. Skinner v. Oklahoma, 316 U.S. 535 (1942).

legitimate children,[5] or denied to the mother a recovery for the wrongful death of illegitimate children while allowing such recovery for legitimate children.[6] But in 1971 the Court found no constitutional infirmity in a state law which provided that illegitimate children could not inherit from their father if he died without a will so long as other relatives survived him, although, if he had executed a document publicly acknowledging them, he could leave them property by will. This law, as applied to a publicly acknowledged child whose father died without a will, while it did discriminate against illegitimate children, just as it did against concubines, was said to be a constitutionally permitted discrimination because the "social difference between a wife and a concubine is analagous to the difference between a legitimate and an illegitimate child" and the state was entitled to distinguish between licit and illicit relationships. Douglas joined in a dissenting opinion which protested that the Court was allowing the state to punish "illegitimate children for the misdeeds of their parents" and that "only a moral prejudice, prevelant in 1825 when the . . . statutes under consideration were adopted, can support" such discrimination.[7]

When the court sustained a state statute exempting women from jury service unless they voluntarily registered for it, holding both that the distinction between men and women was a reasonable one since "woman is still regarded as the center of home and family life" and that there was no showing that the state had "arbitrarily undertaken to exclude women from jury service," Douglas joined in a cryptic concurrence on the second ground only.[8] He also wrote for the Court to reverse, as not satisfying federal statutory requirements, the federal fraud conviction of a mother and son who were indicted by a grand jury and convicted by a petit jury from which women were systematically excluded,[9] and voted with it to invalidate the use in federal courts in civil cases of juries from which wage earners had been

5. Levy v. Louisiana, 391 U.S. 68 (1968). See also King v. Smith, 392 U.S. 309 (1968) (concurring opinion).

6. Glona v. American Guarantee & Liability Insurance Co., 391 U.S. 23 (1968).

7. Labine v. Vincent, 401 U.S. 532 (1971) (dissenting opinion).

8. Hoyt v. Florida, 368 U.S. 57 (1961).

9. Ballard v. United States, 329 U.S. 187 (1946).

systematically excluded.[10] And he dissented when the Court sanctioned the use, in state criminal prosecutions, of "blue ribbon" juries, which he thought deprived the defendant of his right to a jury "fairly drawn from a cross-section of the community."[11]

Douglas dissented again when the Court held that a state did not violate the equal protection clause by denying a woman a license to work as a bartender unless she was the "wife or daughter of a male owner" of a licensed liquor establishment.[12] And he has recently dissented from the Court's refusal to consider whether the state may exclude male students from public schools because of the length of their hair.[13]

But most of the Court's decisions in this area in recent years have involved racial discrimination. During World War II, Douglas joined with the Court to hold that persons of Japanese ancestry on the Pacific coast could, without violation of the due process clause, be subjected by the federal government to a curfew order and then excluded from the area altogether. Although conceding that discrimination based solely on race was always suspect, the Court concluded that, in view of "threatened air raids and invasion by the Japanese forces" and the "danger of sabotage and espionage," the government could rationally act on the basis of race alone, particularly since the only alternatives seemed to be for the government to impose the same restrictions "on all citizens within the military area, or on none."[14]

At a time when persons of Japanese ancestry were not eligible for naturalization (although their children born in the United States

10. Thiel v. Southern Pacific Co., 328 U.S. 217 (1946).

11. Fay v. New York, 332 U.S. 261 (1947) (dissenting opinion); Moore v. New York, 333 U.S. 565 (1948) (dissenting opinion).

12. Goesaert v. Cleary, 335 U.S. 464 (1943) (dissenting opinion). Douglas also voted with the Court to find a violation of a provision in the Civil Rights Act of 1964 forbidding discrimination in employment on grounds of sex where an employer refused to hire the mothers of preschool children but imposed no similar ban on the employment of fathers of such children. Phillips v. Martin Marietta Corp. 400 U.S. 542 (1971).

13. Ferrell v. Dallas Independent School District, 393 U.S. 856 (1968) (dissenting opinion).

14. Hirabayashi v. United States, 320 U.S. 81 (1943) (concurring opinion); Korematsu v. United States, 323 U.S. 214 (1944), both discussed in another connection in Chapter 1.

became citizens by birth under the Fourteenth Amendment[15]), the Court invalidated under the equal protection clause a state's alien land law that forbade aliens ineligible for citizenship to acquire agricultural land and provided that if any alien paid for such land, it should be presumed that he acquired it. Since for all other minor children the state's law presumed that where a parent pays for land taken in the name of his child, a gift to the child is intended, the Court held the alien land law unconstitutionally discriminated against a minor United States citizen whose Japanese father bought land in his name. Douglas concurred, but on the ground that the law unconstitutionally discriminated against the parent.[16] He also voted with the Court to invalidate another law of the same state that forbade persons ineligible for citizenship to acquire commercial fishing licenses.[17] And he dissented when the Court declined to decide whether a state had denied equal protection when, in a suit by the survivors of an American Indian for breach of an internment contract, the state courts sustained as a defense to the action a restrictive covenant in the contract limiting burials to members of the Caucasian race.[18]

Douglas also voted with the Court to reverse the murder conviction and dismiss the indictment of a defendant of Mexican descent because other persons of Mexican descent were systematically excluded from the grand jury that indicted and the petit jury that convicted him.[19] And he dissented when the Court declined to review a case involving alleged discrimination in the public schools against persons of mixed Indian and Spanish ancestry.[20]

The other equal protection cases to come before the Court have involved discrimination against the black race. In 1896, in *Plessy v. Ferguson*,[21] the Court sustained a state law providing for segregation of white and black races in railroad coaches, finding the equal protection

15. See p. 37, *supra*.
16. Oyama v. California, 332 U.S. 633 (1948) (concurring opinion).
17. Takahashi v. Fish and Game Commission, 334 U.S. 410 (1948).
18. Rice v. Sioux City Memorial Park Cemetary, Inc., 349 U.S. 70 (1955) (dissenting opinion).
19. Hernandez v. Texas, 347 U.S. 475 (1954).
20. Tijerina v. Henry, 398 U.S. 922 (1970) (dissenting opinion).
21. 163 U.S. 537 (1896).

clause satisfied by "separate but equal" facilities. That concept was thereafter used to justify similar segregation in public schools and in state universities. But in a series of decisions beginning in 1938, before Douglas was appointed to it, the Court began to insist that, where the state provided no separate graduate and professional schools for blacks,[22] or separate facilities that were not equal to those provided for whites,[23] it must admit blacks to its white facilities on a nonsegregated basis,[24] and it could not meet its constitutional obligation by providing tuition fees for them to go out of state.[25]

Douglas was on the Court in time to join in all but the first of these decisions, and he dissented when, in 1952, the Court declined to consider whether the "separate but equal" concept, as applied to public schools, was consistent with the equal protection clause.[26] Two years later he joined a unanimous Court in *Brown v. Board of Education*[27] to hold that separate was not equal in public schools and to order the states to end segregation in those schools with "all deliberate speed."[28] He also voted with a unanimous Court to hold that racial segregation in the public schools of the District of Columbia, a federal enclave, violated the due process clause of the Fifth Amendment.[29] Thereafter, he voted with the Court to forbid segregation in state universities[30] and professional schools.[31]

In a number of subsequent cases he has voted with the Court also to

22. Missouri *ex rel.* Gaines v. Canada, 305 U.S. 337 (1938) (law school); Sipuel v. Board of Regents, 332 U.S. 631 (1948) (law school); Fisher v. Hurst, 333 U.S. 147 (1948) (law school).

23. Sweatt v. Painter, 339 U.S. 629 (1950) (law school).

24. McLaurin v. Oklahoma State Regents, 339 U.S. 637 (1950) (graduate school).

25. Missouri *ex rel.* Gaines v. Canada, note 22, *supra.*

26. Briggs v. Elliott, 342 U.S. 350 (1952) (dissenting opinion).

27. 347 U.S. 483 (1954). *See also* his vote with the Court in Pennsylvania v. Board of Directors of City Trusts, 353 U.S. 230 (1957), to hold that a school created by and funded under the will of a private citizen for "poor white male orphans" must be desegregated where a city served as trustee under the will. *Cf.* Evans v. Abney, note 46, *infra.*

28. Brown v. Board of Education, 349 U.S. 294 (1955).

29. Bolling v. Sharpe, 347 U.S. 497 (1954).

30. Adams v. Lucy, 351 U.S. 931 (1956).

31. Florida *ex rel.* Hawkins v. Board of Control, 350 U.S. 413 (1956).

require desegregation of faculty and staff as well as student body,[32] to invalidate delaying tactics in desegregating public schools,[33] to hold that a county could not close its public schools and give tuition grants to white children attending private schools,[34] and to hold that a variety of transfer and "free choice" plans would not satisfy constitutional requirements.[35] He joined the Court also in 1964, ten years after *Brown v. Board of Education*, to rule that "the time for mere 'deliberate speed' has run out"[36] and in subsequent cases to insist that dual school systems must be terminated "at once."[37] Finally, in 1971, he voted with the Court to approve a county's compulsory bussing program to eliminate its dual school system,[38] to approve the action of a federal district court in requiring a school district to resort to compulsory bussing, at least to the extent that its dual school system was the product of discriminatory action by school officials rather than of the "*de facto* segregation" in housing patterns,[39] and to invalidate a state law forbidding such compulsory bussing plans.[40] And he dissented in 1971 when the Court declined to review a case in which the lower Court had refused to attempt to redress the de facto segregation in schools resulting from alleged racial discrimination in public and private housing markets.[41]

32. Bradley v. School Board, 382 U.S. 103 (1965); Rogers v. Paul, 382 U.S. 198 (1965); United States v. Montgomery County Board of Education, 395 U.S. 225 (1969).

33. Cooper v. Aaron, 358 U.S. 1 (1958); Rogers v. Paul, note 32, *supra*. *See also* McNeese v. Board of Education, 373 U.S. 668 (1963).

34. Griffin v. County School Board, 377 U.S. 218 (1964).

35. Goss v. Board of Education, 373 U.S. 683 (1963); Green v. County School Board, 391 U.S. 430 (1968); Raney v. Board of Education, 391 U.S. 443 (1968); Monroe v. Board of Commissioners, 391 U.S. 450 (1968). *See also* Calhoun v. Latimer, 377 U.S. 263 (1964).

36. Griffin v. County School Board, note 34, *supra*.

37. Alexander v. Holmes County Board of Education, 396 U.S. 19 (1969); Carter v. West Feliciana Parish School Board, 396 U.S. 290 (1970); Northcross v. Board of Education, 397 U.S. 232 (1970).

38. McDaniel v. Barresi, 402 U.S. 39 (1971).

39. Swann v. Charlotte-Mecklenburg Board of Education, 402 U.S. (1971). *See also* Davis v. Board of School Commissioners, 402 U.S. 33 (1971).

40. North Carolina State Board of Education v. Swann, 402 U.S. 43 (1971).

41. Deal v. Cincinnati Board of Education, 402 U.S. 962 (1971).

Prior to the *Brown* decision, Douglas had voted with the Court to hold that a state statute requiring racial segregation of bus passengers within the state was an unconstitutional burden on interstate commerce as applied to an interstate passenger[42] and had joined in a decision that an interstate railway's segregation of passengers violated the Interstate Commerce Act.[43] After *Brown*, he voted with the Court to hold that the equal protection clause forbids government-imposed segregated seating on city buses or on privately owned transportation facilities.[44] He voted with the Court also when it extended the constitutional prohibition against segregation to public auditoriums,[45] public parks,[46] public golf courses,[47] public beaches,[48] courtrooms,[49] and prison systems.[50]

But in 1971 the Court held that a city could close its public swimming pools after a federal court had ruled that their prior operation on a segregated basis was unconstitutional. To the argument that the decision to close was motivated by a desire to avoid integration, the Court replied that "no case in this Court has held that a

42. Morgan v. Virginia, 328 U.S. 373 (1946).

43. Mitchell v. United States, 313 U.S. 80 (1941). *See also* Henderson v. United States, 339 U.S. 816 (1950).

44. Gayle v. Browder, 352 U.S. 903 (1956); Bailey v. Patterson, 369 U.S. 31 (1962). *See also* Taylor v. Louisiana, 370 U.S. 154 (1962).

45. Schiro v. Bynum, 373 U.S. 395 (1964).

46. Holmes v. Atlanta, 350 U.S. 879 (1955); New Orleans City Park Improvement Ass'n. v. Detiege, 358 U.S. 54 (1958); Wright v. Georgia, 373 U.S. 284 (1963); Watson v. Memphis, 373 U.S. 526 (1963). Douglas also voted with the Court to hold that where a private citizen's will left a tract of land to a city in trust for a park for white people only, the park could not be operated as a segregated facility even after the city had resigned as trustee and private trustees were appointed, since the park still retained its "public character." Evans v. Newton, 382 U.S. 296 (1966). When the state court then ruled that the property reverted to the donor's heirs and the Supreme Court found no constitutional objection to that ruling, Douglas dissented, contending that the state court decision was "only a gesture toward a state-sanctioned segregated way of life, now *passe.*" Evans v. Abney, 396 U.S. 450 (1970) (dissenting opinion). *Cf.* Pennsylvania v. Board of Directors of City Trusts, note 27, *supra.*

47. Holmes v. Atlanta, note 46, *supra.*

48. Mayor & City Council v. Dawson, 350 U.S. 877 (1955).

49. Johnson v. Virginia, 373 U.S. 61 (1963).

50. Lee v. Washington, 390 U.S. 333 (1968).

legislative act may violate equal protection solely because of the motivations of the men who voted for it." Douglas dissented:[51]

Our cases condemn the creation of state laws and regulations which foster racial discrimination—segregated schools, segregated parks, and the like. The present case, to be sure, is only an analogy. The State enacts no law saying that the races may not swim together, yet it eliminated all its swimming pools so that the races will not have an opportunity to swim together. While racially motivated state action is involved, it is of an entirely negative character. Yet it is in the penumbra of the policies of the Thirteenth, Fourteenth, and Fifteenth Amendments and as a matter of Constitutional policy should be in the category of those enumerated rights protected by the Ninth Amendment. If not included, those rights become narrow legislative concepts which turn on the formalism of laws not on their spirit.

I conclude that though a State may discontinue any of its municipal services—such as schools, parks, pools, athletic fields, and the like—it may not do so for the purpose of perpetuation or installing *apartheid* or because it finds life in a multi-racial community difficult or unpleasant. If that is its reason, then abolition of a designated public service becomes a device for perpetuating a segregated way of life that a State may not do.[52]

Douglas wrote for the Court to sustain the power of the Congress to forbid segregation in privately owned restaurants in the District of Columbia, in terms which recognized a similar power in the states,[53] and voted with the Court to uphold state laws forbidding racial discrimination in employment by an interstate air carrier[54] and racial discrimination in membership by a labor union representing federal postal employees.[55]

He has also voted with the Court to find the state sufficiently involved in the racial discrimination of private restaurant operators to render the discrimination "state action," forbidden by the equal protec-

51. Palmer v. Thompson, 403 U.S. 217 (1971).
52. *Cf.* Evans v. Abney, note 46, *supra.*
53. District of Columbia v. John R. Thompson Co., 346 U.S. 100 (1953).
54. Colorado Anti-Discrimination Commission v. Continental Air Lines, 373 U.S. 714 (1963).
55. Railway Mail Association v. Corsi, 326 U.S. 88 (1945).

tion clause, where the state has leased space to the private operator in a public parking facility,[56] or a public airport,[57] or where the state requires the discrimination by legislative[58] or executive[59] action. He concurred in the decision last referred to and suggested other bases for decision: (1) Use of the state police, state prosecutors and state courts to prosecute blacks who refused to leave a restaurant when they were denied service is "state action" forbidden by the equal protection clause, and (2) "State licensing and surveillance of a business serving the public" converts it into "an instrumentality of the State since the State charges it with duties to the public and supervises its performance."[60]

When the Court thereafter reversed state convictions based on "sit-ins" at privately owned amusement parks and restaurants because of state administrative action discouraging service to blacks,[61] because the owner employed a deputy sheriff to enforce his discriminatory policy,[62] for lack of evidence,[63] because of repeal of the state law on which the conviction was based,[64] or because that law was unconstitutionally vague,[65] Douglas concurred on different grounds:[66]

> The issue in this case, according to [the dissenting opinion], is whether a person's "personal prejudices" may dictate the way in which he uses his property and whether he can enlist the aid of the State to enforce those "personal prejudices." With all respect, that is not the real issue. The corporation that owns this restaurant did not refuse service to these Negroes because "it" did not like Negroes. The reason

56. Burton v. Wilmington Parking Authority, 365 U.S. 715 (1961).

57. Turner v. Memphis, 369 U.S. 350 (1962). Douglas voted with the Court also to hold that where an interstate bus line leases space in its terminal to a private restaurant operator, the latter becomes subject to the Interstate Commerce Act's prohibition against racial discrimination. Boynton v. Virginia, 364 U.S. 454 (1960).

58. Peterson v. Greenville, 373 U.S. 244 (1963); Gober v. Birmingham, 373 U.S. 373 (1963). *See also* Shuttlesworth v. Birmingham, 373 U.S. 263 (1963).

59. Lombard v. Louisiana, 373 U.S. 157 (1961) (concurring opinion).

60. *See also* Garner v. Louisiana, 368 U.S. 157 (1961) (concurring opinion).

61. Robinson v. Florida, 378 U.S. 153 (1964) (concurring opinion).

62. Griffin v. Maryland, 378 U.S. 130 (1964) (concurring opinion).

63. Barr v. Columbia, 378 U.S. 146 (1964) (concurring opinion).

64. Bell v. Maryland, 378 U.S. 226 (1964) (separate opinion).

65. Bouie v. Columbia, 378 U.S. 347 (1964) (concurring opinion).

66. Bell v. Maryland, note 64, *supra.* (concurring opinion).

"it" refused service was because "it" thought "it" could make more money by running a segregated restaurant . . .

Here, as in most of the sit-in cases before us, the refusal of service did not reflect "personal prejudices" but business reasons. Were we today to hold that segregated restaurants, whose racial policies were enforced by a State, violated the Equal Protection Clause, all restaurants would be on an equal footing and the reasons given in this and most of the companion cases for refusing service to Negroes would evaporate . . .

. . . [Even if it be assumed that the issue is as stated by the dissent, the] case in that posture deals with a relic of slavery—an institution that has cast a long shadow across the land, resulting today in a second-class citizenship in this area of public accommodations.

The Thirteenth, Fourteenth, and Fifteenth Amendments had [as the Court said in an 1873 decision] "one pervading purpose . . . we mean the freedom of the slave race, the security and firm establishment of that freedom, and the protection of the newly-made freeman and citizen from the oppressions of those who had formerly exercised unlimited dominion over him" . . .

Prior to those Amendments, Negroes were segregated and disallowed the use of public accommodations except and unless the owners chose to serve them. To affirm these judgments would remit those Negroes to their old status and allow the States to keep them there by the force of their police and their judiciary . . .

The Fourteenth Amendment says "No State shall make or enforce any law which shall abridge the privileges or immunities of citizens of the United States." The Fourteenth Amendment also makes every person who is born here a citizen; and there is no second or third or fourth class of citizenship . . .

We deal here with incidents of national citizenship . . .

When one citizen because of his race, creed, or color is denied the privilege of being treated as any other citizen in places of public accommodation, we have classes of citizenship, one being more degrading than the other. That is at war with the one class of citizenship created by the Thirteenth, Fourteenth, and Fifteenth Amendments . . .

The problem in this case, and in the other sit-in cases before us, is presented as though it involved the situation of "a private operator conducting his own business on his own premises and exercising his own judgment" as to whom he will admit to the premises.

The property involved is not, however, a man's home or his yard or even his fields. Private property is involved, but it is property that is serving the public . . . Here it is a restaurant refusing service to a Negro.

But so far as principle and law are concerned it might just as well be a hospital refusing admission to a sick or injured Negro . . . or a drugstore refusing antibiotics to a Negro, or a bus denying transportation to a Negro, or a telephone company refusing to install a telephone in a Negro's home.

The problem with which we deal has no relation to opening or closing the door of one's home. The home, of course, is the essence of privacy, in no way dedicated to public use, in no way extending an invitation to the public . . . But such is not this case. The facts of these sit-in cases have little resemblance to any institution of property which we customarily associate with privacy . . .

Apartheid . . . is barred by the common law as respects innkeepers and common carriers. There were, to be sure, criminal statutes that regulated the common callings. But the civil remedies were made by judges who had no written constitution. We, on the other hand, live under a constitution that proclaims equal protection under the law. Why then, even in the absence of a statute, should *apartheid* be given constitutional sanction in the restaurant field? . . . Constitutionally speaking, why should Hooper Food Co., Inc., or Peoples Drug Stores—or any other establishment that dispenses food or medicines—stand on a higher, more sanctified level than Greyhound Bus when it comes to a constitutional right to pick and choose its customers? . . .

. . . Is the right of a person to eat less basic than his right to travel, which we protected in *Edwards* v. *California* . . . ?[67] Does not a right to travel in modern times shrink in value materially when there is no accompanying right to eat in public places?

The right of any person to travel *interstate* irrespective of race, creed, or color is protected by the Constitution. *Edwards* v. *California*, *supra.* Certainly his right to travel *intrastate* is as basic. Certainly his right to eat at public restaurants is as important in the modern setting as the right of mobility. In these times that right is, indeed, practically indispensable to travel either interstate or intrastate . . .

Segregation of Negroes in the restaurants and lunch counters of parts of America is a relic of slavery. It is a badge of second-class citizenship. It is a denial of a privilege and immunity of national citizenship and of the equal protection guaranteed by the Fourteenth Amendment against abridgment by the States. When the state police, the state prosecutor, and the state courts unite to convict Negroes for renouncing that relic of slavery, the "State" violates the Fourteenth Amendment.

67. See text at note 178, p. 101, *supra.*

The Court long ago struck down state efforts to segregate residential housing as in conflict with both the due process clause of the Fourteenth Amendment and with an 1866 Civil Rights Act giving all citizens the same right as white citizens to own property.[68] But, in 1926, in *Corrigan v. Buckley*[69] it allowed the enforcement by injunction of a restrictive covenant in a deed which forbade the property owner to sell to a Negro.

Douglas voted with the Court to change the latter rule and to hold that the equal protection clause forbids state courts either to enforce such covenants by injunction or to award damages for their breach,[70] and that the 1866 Civil Rights Act likewise forbids federal courts in the District of Columbia to enforce such covenants.[71] He also concurred when the Court held that the 1866 act "bars *all* racial discrimination, private as well as public, in the sale or rental of property" and that, as construed, the act is authorized by provisions of the Thirteenth Amendment prohibiting slavery and involuntary servitude and authorizing Congress to enforce that prohibition by "appropriate legislation." "Congress has the power under the Thirteenth Amendment rationally to determine what are the badges and incidents of slavery, and the authority to translate that determination into effective legislation."[72] When the Court invalidated, under the equal protection clause, a state constitutional amendment which overturned existing laws forbidding racial discrimination in residential housing, and deprived the state of power to enact such laws in the future, Douglas concurred:[73]

Real estate brokers and mortgage lenders are largely dedicated to the maintenance of segregated communities. Realtors commonly believe it is unethical to sell or rent to a Negro in a predominantly white or all-white neighborhood, and mortgage lenders throw their weight along-

68. Buchanan v. Warley, 245 U.S. 60 (1917); Harmon v. Tyler, 273 U.S. 668 (1927); Richmond v. Deans, 281 U.S. 704 (1930).

69. 271 U.S. 323 (1926).

70. Shelley v. Kraemer, 334 U.S. 1 (1948); Barrows v. Jackson, 346 U.S. 249 (1953).

71. Hurd v. Hodge, 334 U.S. 24 (1948).

72. Jones v. Mayer Co., 392 U.S. 409 (1968) (concurring opinion). *See also* his opinion for the Court in Sullivan v. Little Hunting Park, 396 U.S. 229 (1969).

73. Reitman v. Mulkey, 387 U.S. 369 (1967) (concurring opinion).

side segregated communities, rejecting applications by members of a minority group who try to break the white phalanx save and unless the neighborhood is in process of conversion into a mixed or a Negro community . . . The builders join in the same scheme . . .

[The state constitutional amendment] is a form of sophisticated discrimination whereby the people of California harness the energies of private groups to do indirectly what they cannot under our decisions allow their government to do . . .

If we were in a domain exclusively private, we would have different problems. But urban housing is in the public domain as evidenced not only by the zoning problems presented but by the vast schemes of public financing with which the States and the Nation have been extensively involved in recent years. Urban housing is clearly marked with the public interest. Urban housing, like restaurants, inns, and carriers . . . or like telephone companies, drugstores, or hospitals, is affected with a public interest in the historic and classical sense . . .

Since the real estate brokerage business is one that can be and is state-regulated and since it is state-licensed, it must be dedicated, like the telephone companies and the carriers and the hotels and motels, to the requirements of service to all without discrimination—a standard that in its modern setting is conditioned by the demands of the Equal Protection Clause of the Fourteenth Amendment.

Douglas also joined in another decision invalidating on the same ground an amendment to a city charter which would require any ordinance adopted by the city council dealing with racial, religious or ancestral discrimination in housing to have the approval of a majority of the voters, since a similar burden was not imposed on housing ordinances devoted to other purposes.[74]

When the Court sustained those provisions of the 1964 Civil Rights Act forbidding discrimination in public accommodations as a valid exercise of the interstate commerce power, Douglas concurred but preferred to base his position on that provision of the Fourteenth Amendment which authorized Congress to enforce its provisions by "appropriate legislation."[75] "A decision based on the Fourteenth

74. Hunter v. Erickson, 393 U.S. 385 (1969).

75. Heart of Atlanta Motel, Inc. v. United States, 379 U.S. 241 (1964) (concurring opinion). *See also* Katzenbach v. McClung, 379 U.S. 294 (1964) (concurring opinion); Hamm v. Rock Hill, 379 U.S. 306 (1964) (concurring opinion) Daniel v. Paul, 395, U.S. 298 (1969) (concurring opinion).

Amendment would have a more settling effect, making unnecessary litigation over whether a particular restaurant or inn is within the commerce definitions of the Act or whether a particular customer is an interstate traveler. Under my construction, the Act would apply to all customers in all the enumerated places of public accommodation. And that construction would put an end to all obstructionist strategies and finally close one door on a bitter chapter in American history."

Consistently with that view, he was one of six justices who asserted in *United States v. Guest*[76] that an 1870 Civil Rights Act penalizing conspiracies by "two or more persons . . . to injure, oppress, threaten, or intimidate any citizen in the free exercise . . . of any right . . . secured to him by the Constitution or laws of the United States" would reach to a private conspiracy to interfere with the right guaranteed by the Fourteenth Amendment to use public facilities without discrimination as to race. He has also written for the Court to hold that the penal provision of the 1870 Act will reach to "conspiracies by outside hoodlums to assault Negroes for exercising their right to equality in public accommodation under . . . the Civil Rights Act of 1964"[77] and has voted with the Court to hold that those provisions also reach a conspiracy of police officials and private citizens to murder civil rights workers and thus to deprive them of their lives without due process of law.[78]

Earlier, in *Collins v. Handyman*, the Court had held that a provision in the Ku Klux Act of 1871 imposing civil liability in damages on those who conspire to deprive others "of equal protection of the laws or of equal privileges and immunities under the laws" was not violated by American Legionnaires who broke up a public meeting on the Marshall Plan. The basis for decision was that a private group could not deprive others of legal rights unless the group had taken over the machinery of state government, but this narrow interpretation was placed on the act in order to avoid "constitutional problems of great magnitude." Douglas joined in a dissent which maintained that the plaintiffs had been

76. 383 U.S. 745 (1966) (concurring opinion). *See also* Douglas' dissenting opinion in United States v. Williams, 341 U.S. 70 (1951).

77. United States v. Johnson, 390 U.S. 563 (1968).

78. United States v. Price, 383 U.S. 787 (1966).

deprived of their First Amendment right to petition the federal government for a redress of grievances, that the language of the act was clearly applicable to private conduct, and that Congress was constitutionally empowered to create such a remedy against private individuals.[79] Twenty years later, in a decision in which Douglas did not participate, the Court held the same statute applicable to a private conspiracy to interfere with black plaintiffs rights of interstate travel, noting that "in the light of the evolution of decisional law in the years that have passed" since *Collins v. Hardyman* was decided, "many of the constitutional problems there perceived simply do not exist."[80]

Douglas also wrote the plurality opinion construing a provision of an 1866 Civil Rights Act penalizing any person who, "under color of any law, statute, ordinance, regulation, or custom, willfully subjects . . . any inhabitant of any State . . . to the deprivation of any rights secured or protected by the Constitution and laws of the United States," to reach the action of police officers who murder a prisoner and thus deprive him of his life without due process of law.[81] He later wrote for the Court to hold this provision violated by a police officer who used physical force to obtain a confession and thus deprived his prisoner of the right to be tried by due process of law.[82]

He wrote for the Court again to hold that a section of the Ku Klux Act of 1871, providing for recovery of damages from "every person who, under color of any statute, ordinance, regulation, custom, or usage of any State . . . subjects any citizen of the United States or other person . . . to the deprivations of any rights . . . secured by the Constitution and laws" of the United States, reaches the action of police officers in making a search and an arrest in violation of the Fourth Amendment.[83] And he dissented when the Court held that the Ku Klux Act would not reach a restaurant owner in Mississippi who refused service to a white person because she was accompanied by blacks even though the owner acted "under color of [a] . . . custom . . . of [the]

79. Collins v. Hardyman, 341 U.S. 651 (1951) (dissenting opinion).
80. Griffin v. Breckenridge, 403 U.S. 88 (1971).
81. Screws v. United States, 325 U.S. 91 (1945). *Cf.* his dissent in United States v. Classic, note 10, p. 27, *supra*.
82. Williams v. United States, 341 U.S. 97 (1951).
83. Monroe v. Pape, 365 U.S. 167 (1961).

state" because the custom did not have "the force of law" in that it was not "state enforced." Just as the provision forbidding discrimination in the sale of property in the 1866 Civil Rights Act was not confined to state action because based on the Thirteenth Amendment,[84] so the Ku Klux Act of 1871 was based on the Thirteenth Amendment and required no state action. Hence, he would have read "custom" to include "dominant communal sentiment," whether or not enforced by state officials.[85]

Long before Douglas came to the Court it had recognized that the equal protection clause forbids the states systematically to exclude blacks from grand and petit juries.[86] Douglas has consistently voted to enforce those prohibitions at the behest of black defendants in criminal cases,[87] and he dissented when the Court concluded that the defendant had not proved such systematic exclusion through the prosecutor's use of peremptory challenges.[88] He recently agreed with the Court that the

84. See text at note 78, *supra*.

85. Adickes v. S. H. Kress & Co., 398 U.S. 144 (1970) (dissenting in part). Douglas voted with the Court to hold that an employer violated provisions against racial discrimination in employment under the Civil Right Act of 1964 where he imposed educational job requirements which bore no demonstrable relationship to successful performance but which operated to disqualify blacks at a substantially higher rate than whites. Griggs v. Duke Power Co., 401 U.S. 424 (1971).

86. Strauder v. West Virginia, 100 U.S. 303 (1879); Neal v. Delaware, 103 U.S. 370 (1880).

87. Smith v. Texas, 311 U.S. 128 (1940); Hill v. Texas, 316 U.S. 400 (1942); Patton v. Mississippi, 332 U.S. 463 (1947); Avery v. Georgia, 345 U.S. 559 (1953); Williams v. Georgia, 349 U.S. 375 (1955); Eubanks v. Louisiana, 356 U.S. 584 (1958); Arnold v. North Carolina, 376 U.S. 773 (1964); Coleman v. Alabama, 377 U.S. 129 (1964); Whitus v. Georgia, 385 U.S. 545 (1967); Coleman v. Alabama, 389 U.S. 22 (1967); Jones v. Georgia, 389 U.S. 24 (1967); Sims v. Georgia, 389 U.S. 404 (1967). *Cf.* Akins v. Texas, 325 U.S. 398 (1945). He also dissented from a decision that, where state law required all challenges to the grand jury to be filed within three days of the expiration of the grand jury's term, that limitation could be invoked against a black defendant who fled the state shortly after the crime was committed and remained outside the state until after the time for challenge had expired. "His flight was a wrong that could be punished. But it is dangerous doctrine to deprive a man of his constitutional rights in one case for his wrongful conduct in another." Michel v. Louisiana, 350 U.S. 91 (1955) (dissenting opinion).

88. Swain v. Alabama, 380 U.S. 202 (1965) (dissenting opinion). *See also* his dissent from the refusal of the Court to consider whether systematic exclusion of blacks from Selective Service boards violates the Selective Service Act. Sellers v. Laird, note 25, p. 115, *supra*. *See also* Brown v. Allen, 344 U.S. 443 (1953) (dissenting opinions).

constitutional point can be raised not only by black defendants but also by blacks who wish to serve as jurors, but he dissented from the Court's refusal to invalidate the use of the state's jury system because it did not provide for proportional representation of the two races on the commission which selected jurors.[89] As previously noted, he also joined in another decision holding that the state could not allow its county board of education to be appointed by a grand jury from which blacks had been systematically excluded.[90]

Finally, Douglas voted with the Court to invalidate an antimiscegenation law which forbade marriages between "white persons" and "colored persons and Indians." It was not enough, the Court said, that the law was applied equally to the white and colored parties to such marriages. Classifications based on race alone, "if they are ever to be upheld . . . must be shown to be necessary to the accomplishment of some permissible state objective." And the only conceivable objective here was "to maintain White Supremacy," which was not a permissible state objective under the Fourteenth Amendment.[91]

89. Carter v. Jury Commission, 396 U.S. 320 (1970) (dissenting in part).
90. Turner v. Fouche, note 25, p. 28, *supra*.
91. Loving v. Virginia, 388 U.S. 1 (1967). *See also* McLaughlin v. Florida, 379 U.S. 184 (1964) (concurring opinion). For another treatment of Douglas' views in this area, see Karst, "Invidious Discrimination: Justice Douglas and the Return of the Natural-Law-Due Process Formula," 16 *UCLA L. Rev.* 716 (1969).

PART II FAIR GOVERNMENTAL PROCEDURES

It is important, for a variety of reasons, that the procedure by which government acts against the individual be fair. Fairness, and the appearance of fairness, in the operation of government are desirable ends in themselves. Moreover, many of the requirements of fairness—such as the opportunity to present a defense in a criminal case—can be justified in terms of efficient law enforcement. An unfair proceeding may result in an erroneous application of the law. Beyond this, some of the requirements of fairness are imposed because they preserve some value thought to be more important than efficient law enforcement. Thus, the protection afforded by the Fourth Amendment against unreasonable searches and seizures, however burdensome to crime detection, is justified in terms of preserving individual privacy.

7 DUE PROCESS OF LAW

Although Douglas has rejected the notion that the due process clauses of the Fifth and Fourteenth Amendments impose substantive limits on the powers of the federal and state governments to enact economic regulations, he has consistently voted with the Court to hold that these clauses impose requirements of procedural fairness when government acts against a person's life, liberty, or property and has not infrequently dissented when he thought the Court had failed to observe those requirements.[1] Thus, at a minimum, due process requires notice of the basis for proposed action and a fair opportunity to be heard, not only in criminal prosecutions,[2] and in criminal contempt proceedings,[3] but also in proceedings for the deportation of aliens,[4] in proceedings for

1. For cases involving the fairness of trials by military court martial, see Chapter 5.

2. Smith v. Baldi, 344 U.S. 561 (1953) (dissenting opinion); Darcy v. Handy, 351 U.S. 454 (1956) (dissenting opinion); Roviaro v. United States, 353 U.S. 53 (1957).

3. *In re* Oliver, 333 U.S. 257 (1948); Sacher v. United States, 343 U.S. 1 (1952) (dissenting opinion); Offutt v. United States, 348 U.S. 11 (1954) (concurring opinion); Nilva v. United States, 352 U.S. 385 (1957) (dissenting opinion); *In re* Green, 369 U.S. 689 (1962).

4. Ludecke v. Watkins, 335 U.S. 160 (1948) (dissenting opinions); Kwong Hai Chew v. Colding, 344 U.S. 590 (1953); Shaughnessy v. Mezei, 345 U.S. 206 (1953) (dissenting opinion); Accardi v. Shaughnessy, 347 U.S. 260 (1954); Jay v. Boyd, 351 U.S. 345 (1956) (dissenting opinion).

lawyers' admission to practice or for their disbarment,[5] and in post office fraud order proceedings.[6]

Douglas found that the federal employees' loyalty program failed to meet these basic due process requirements. Under that program the attorney general compiled lists of "subversive" organizations. "Membership in, affiliation with or sympathetic association with" such organizations was then taken as evidence against any employee subjected to loyalty proceedings. When the Court held, on complaint of some listed organizations, that the attorney general could not proceed to compile his lists without notice or hearing to the organizations concerned, Douglas concurred:[7]

> It is not enough to know that the men applying the standard are honorable and devoted men. This is a government of *laws*, not of *men*. The powers being used are the powers of government over the reputations and fortunes of citizens. In situations far less severe or important than these a party is told the nature of the charge against him. Thus when a defendant is summoned before a federal court to answer a claim for damages or to a demand for an injunction against him, there must be [under the federal rules of civil procedure] a "plain statement of the claim showing that the pleader is entitled to relief." If that is necessary for even the most minor claim asserted against a defendant, we should require no less when it comes to determinations that may well destroy the group against whom the charge of being "subversive" is directed. When the Government becomes the moving party and levels its great powers against the citizen, it should be held to the same standards of fair dealing as we prescribe for other legal contests. To let the Government adopt such lesser ones as suits the convenience of its officers is to start down the totalitarian path . . .
>
> Notice and opportunity to be heard are fundamental to due process of law . . . The gravity of the present charges is proof enough of the need for notice and hearing before the United States officially brands these organizations as "subversive." No more critical governmental ruling can be made against an organization these days. It condemns

5. Isserman v. Ethics Committee, 345 U.S. 927 (1953) (dissenting opinion); Willner v. Committee on Character and Fitness, 373 U.S. 96 (1963); *In re* Ruffalo, 390 U.S. 544 (1968).

6. Reilly v. Pinkus, 338 U.S. 269 (1949).

7. Joint Anti-Fascist Refugee Committee v. McGrath, 341 U.S. 123 (1951) (concurring opinion).

without trial. It destroys without opportunity to be heard. The condemnation may in each case be wholly justified. But government in this country cannot by edict condemn or place beyond the pale. The rudiments of justice, as we know it, call for notice and hearing—an opportunity to appear and to rebut the charge.

In the same opinion he indicated his views on the loyalty procedures as applied to individual employees—procedures which the Court sustained by an evenly divided vote in the *Bailey* case.[8]

The system used to condemn these organizations is bad enough. The evil is only compounded when a government employee is charged with being disloyal. Association with or membership in an organization found to be "subversive" weighs heavily against the accused. He is not allowed to prove that the charge against the organization is false. That case is closed; that line of defense is taken away. The technique is one of guilt by association—one of the most odious institutions of history . . . Guilt under our system of government is personal. When we make guilt vicarious we borrow from systems alien to ours and ape our enemies . . .

It is not without significance that most of the provisions of the Bill of Rights are procedural. It is procedure that spells much of the difference between rule by law and rule by whim or caprice. Steadfast adherence to strict procedural safeguards is our main assurance that there will be equal justice under law. The case of Dorothy Bailey is an excellent illustration of how dangerous a departure from our constitutional standards can be. She was charged with being a Communist and with being active in a Communist "front organization." The Review Board stated that the case against her was based on reports, some of which came from "informants certified to us by the Federal Bureau of Investigation as experienced and entirely reliable."

Counsel for Dorothy Bailey asked that their names be disclosed. That was refused.[9]

Counsel for Dorothy Bailey asked if these informants had been active

8. Bailey v. Richardson, 341 U.S. 918 (1951).

9. Douglas later voted with the Court to hold that an alien could not be deported without hearing even though the attorney general had determined that the deportation order was "based on information of a confidential nature, the disclosure of which would be prejudicial to the public interest." Kwong Hai Chew v. Colding, note 4, *supra*. And in Roviaro v. United States, note 2, *supra*, he voted with the Court to reverse a conviction for sale of narcotics to "John Doe" because the identity of "John Doe," an informer, was not disclosed to the defendant.

in a certain union. The Chairman replied, "I haven't the slightest knowledge as to who they were or how active they have been in anything."

Counsel for Dorothy Bailey asked if these statements of the informants were under oath. The Chairman answered, "I don't think so."

The Loyalty Board convicts on evidence which it cannot even appraise. The critical evidence may be the word of an unknown witness who is "a paragon of veracity, a knave, or the village idiot." His name, his reputation, his prejudices, his animosities, his trustworthiness are unknown both to the judge and to the accused. The accused has no opportunity to show that the witness lied or was prejudiced or venal. Without knowing who her accusers are she has no way of defending. She has nothing to offer except her own word and the character testimony of her friends.

Dorothy Bailey was not, to be sure, faced with a criminal charge . . . But she was on trial for her reputation, her job, her professional standing. A disloyalty trial is the most crucial event in the life of a public servant. If condemned, he is branded for life as a person unworthy of trust or confidence. To make that condemnation without meticulous regard for the decencies of a fair trial is abhorrent to fundamental justice.[10]

In a later case where the Court reversed the action of the Loyalty Review Board because of the board's violation of its own rules, Douglas again concurred on due process grounds:[11]

Dr. Peters was condemned by faceless informers, some of whom were not known even to the Board that condemned him. Some of these informers were not even under oath. None of them had to submit to cross-examination. None had to face Dr. Peters. So far as we or the Board know, they may be psychopaths or venal people, like Titus Oates, who revel in being informers. They may bear old grudges. Under cross-examination their stories might disappear like bubbles. Their whispered confidences might turn out to be yarns conceived by twisted minds or by people who, though sincere, have poor faculties of observation and memory.

10. Douglas had similar objections to the New York loyalty program for teachers which was first sustained over his dissent in Adler v. Board of Education, 342 U.S. 485 (1952), and later invalidated in Keyishian v. Board of Regents, 385 U.S. 589 (1967). See discussion in Chapter 4.

11. Peters v. Hobby, 349 U.S. 331 (1955) (concurring opinion). *See also* Cafeteria & Restaurant Workers Union v. McElroy, 367 U.S. 886 (1961) (dissenting opinion).

. . . We have here a system where government with all its power and authority condemns a man to a suspect class and the outer darkness, without the rudiments of a fair trial. The practice of using faceless informers has apparently spread through a vast domain. It is used not only to get rid of employees in the Government, but also employees who work for private firms having contracts with the Government. It has touched countless hundreds of men and women and ruined many. It deprives men of "liberty" within the meaning of the Fifth Amendment, for one of man's most precious liberties is his right to work. When a man is deprived of that "liberty" without a fair trial, he is denied due process.

When in a later case the Court upheld procedures by which the federal Civil Rights Commission, investigating alleged black voting rights deprivations, summoned state registrars of voters to testify, without disclosing to them the identities of those who had filed complaints against them or allowing them to cross examine others who had testified, Douglas dissented:[12]

At the bottom of this controversy is the right to vote protected by the Fifteenth Amendment . . .

Yet important as these civil rights are, it will not do to sacrifice other civil rights in order to protect them. We live and work under a Constitution. The temptation of many men of goodwill is to cut corners, take short cuts, and reach the desired end regardless of the means. Worthy as I think the ends are which the Civil Rights Commission advances in these cases, I think the particular means used are unconstitutional . . .

Complaints have been filed with the Commission charging respondents, who are registrars of voters . . . , with depriving persons of their voting rights by reason of their color. If these . . . charges are true and if the registrars acted willfully . . . the registrars are criminally responsible under [the 1866 Civil Rights Act] . . . The investigation and hearing by the Commission are therefore necessarily aimed at determining if this criminal law has been violated.

. . . The procedure seems to me patently unconstitutional, whether the hearing is public or secret. Under the Commission's rules the accused is deprived of the right to notice of the charges against him and the opportunity of cross-examination. This statutory provision, fash-

12. Hannah v. Larche, 363 U.S. 420 (1960) (dissenting opinion).

ioned to protect witnesses as such rather than a prospective defendant, permits the Commission to exclude the accused entirely from the hearing and deny him the opportunity even to observe the testimony of his accusers. And even if the Commission were inclined in a particular case to protect the accused from the opprobrium likely to flow from the testimony of individual witnesses against him by holding secret sessions, this would be little comfort after the Commission's findings, based on such untested evidence, were publicized across the Nation . . .

The Civil Rights Commission, it is true, returns no indictment. Yet in a real sense the hearings on charges that a registrar has committed a federal offense are a trial. Moreover, these hearings before the Commission may be televised or broadcast on the radio . . . This is in reality a trial in which the whole Nation sits as a jury. Their verdict does not send men to prison. But it often condemns men or produces evidence to convict and even saturates the Nation with prejudice against an accused so that a fair trial may be impossible . . .

What we do today is to allow under the head of due process a fragmentation of proceedings against accused people that seems to me to be foreign to our system. No indictment is returned, no commitment to jail is made, no formal criminal charges are made. Hence the procedure is condoned as violating no constitutional guarantee. Yet what is done is another short cut used more and more these days to "try" men in ways not envisaged by the Constitution. The result is as damaging as summoning before [legislative] committees men who it is known will invoke the Fifth Amendment and pillorying them for asserting their constitutional rights. This case—like the others—is a device to expose people as suspects or criminals. The concept of due process which permits the invention and use of prosecutorial devices not included in the Constitution makes due process reflect the subjective or even whimsical notions of a majority of this Court as from time to time constituted. Due process under the prevailing doctrine is what the judges say it is; and it differs from judge to judge, from court to court. This notion of due process makes it a tool of the activists who respond to their own visceral reactions in deciding what is fair, decent, or reasonable.

Even where constitutional issues are not raised, Douglas is reluctant to find authority in the government to act against a citizen without hearing. A provision in a standard government construction contract provided that in "all disputes concerning questions of fact arising under this contract" the decision of the secretary of interior or his designated representative should be "final and conclusive." When the Court construed this as forbidding the Court of Claims to review the departmental decision save for fraud, he dissented:[13]

> Law has reached its finest moments when it has freed man from the unlimited discretion of some ruler, some civil or military official, some bureaucrat. Where discretion is absolute, man has always suffered. At times it has been his property that has been invaded; at times, his privacy; at times, his liberty of movement; at times, his freedom of thought; at times, his life. Absolute discretion is a ruthless master. It is more destructive of freedom than any of man's other inventions.
>
> . . . The result reached by the Court can be rationalized or made plausible by casting it in terms of contract law: the parties need not have made this contract; those who contract with the Government must turn square corners; the parties will be left where their engagement brought them. And it may be that in this case [involving compensation for extra work] the equities are with the Government, not with the contractor. But the rule we announce has wide application and a devastating effect. It makes a tyrant out of every contracting officer. He is granted the power of a tyrant even though he is stubborn, perverse or captious. He is allowed the power of a tyrant though he is incompetent or negligent. He has the power of life and death over a private business even though his decision is grossly erroneous. Power granted is seldom neglected.
>
> . . . We should allow the Court of Claims, the agency close to these disputes, to reverse an official whose conduct is plainly out of bounds whether he is fraudulent, perverse, captious, incompetent, or just palpably wrong.

Congressional reaction to the Court's decision in this case was to enact a statute providing that the finality clause in government contracts will not prevent judicial review of the agency or departmental decision to determine whether it is "fraudulent or capricious or arbitrary or so

13. United States v. Wunderlich, 342 U.S. 98 (1951) (dissenting opinion). *See also* United States v. Holpuch Co., 328 U.S. 234 (1946), where Douglas dissented in part in protest of a "harsh and unfair" interpretation of a government contract against the contractor, and Lichter v. United States, 334 U.S. 742 (1948), where he voted with the Court to sustain the constitutionality of the Renegotiation Act, under which the United States recovers excess profits realized by contractors on defense contracts.

grossly erroneous as necessarily to imply bad faith, or is not supported by substantial evidence."[14]

Douglas is similarly reluctant to tolerate unfair procedures by private persons or organizations with power to affect the liberty or property of others. Thus, when the Court recently ruled that a labor union member had received a "full and fair hearing" before being expelled from his union, as required by the Labor-Management Reporting and Disclosure Act, he dissented. The evidence taken before the union's trial committee showed that the member had assaulted a union official in charge of the union hiring hall in a dispute over work assignments. He was charged with attempting "to create dissension among the [union] members" in violation of the union's constitution and with attempting to prevent the official "from properly discharging the duties of his office" in violation of a union bylaw. The trial committee simply found him "guilty as charged." Douglas thought the evidence insufficient to support the first charge and the committee's findings, therefore, insufficient to support the expulsion:[15]

> Even if every conceivable procedural guarantee is provided, a hearing is not "fair" when all substantive rights are stripped away to reach a pre-ordained result. If there is to be a "fair hearing" there must, I submit, be some evidence directed to the charges to support the conclusion.
>
> Membership in a union may be the key to livelihood itself . . . It is unthinkable to me that Congress . . . gave unions the authority to expel members for such reasons as they chose . . .
>
> For respondent to use force against [the official] may well have been an attempt "to prevent him from properly discharging the duties of his office" . . . But how an isolated fist fight could "create dissension" among union members . . . remains a mystery.
>
> The finding of the union was the general one "guilty as charged." Under which provision—constitution or by-law—it suspended him indefinitely is not made clear. Perhaps it was under only one or perhaps under both provisions.
>
> . . . It is as much a denial of due process to sustain [the action] merely

14. 41 U.S.C. §321.

15. International Brotherhood of Boiler Makers v. Hardeman, 401 U.S. 233 (1971) (dissenting opinion).

because a verdict of guilty *might* have been rendered on a valid ground as it is to send an accused to prison following conviction of a charge on which he was never tried.

In another recent case, Douglas wrote for the Court to invalidate a state statute which authorized certain governmental officials, or the spouse of the subject, to post a notice in liquor establishments that the subject was guilty of "excessive drinking," after which posting it was illegal to sell or give liquor to the subject. The case involved an adult woman "posted" by the chief of police:[16]

Where a person's good name, reputation, honor, or integrity is at stake because of what the government is doing to him, notice and an opportunity to be heard are essential. "Posting" under the [statute] may to some be merely the mark of illness, to others it is a stigma, an official branding of a person. The label is a degrading one. Under the [statute, the subject] is given no process at all. This appellee was not afforded a chance to defend herself. She may have been the victim of the official's caprice. Only when the whole proceedings leading to the pinning of an unsavory label on a person are aired can oppressive results be prevented.

Quite apart from the requirement that laws impinging on First Amendment rights must be narrowly and precisely drawn,[17] the due process clause has long been interpreted to require that all criminal laws be drawn with sufficient clarity to provide a reasonably ascertainable standard of guilt,[18] and the same test has been applied to a statute that does not impose criminal penalties but seeks to exact obedience by making contracts found to be in violation of the law unenforceable.[19] Douglas has found occasion to apply that test to statutes imposing criminal penalties and forfeiting goods illegally used.[20]

16. Wisconsin v. Constantineau, 400 U.S. 433 (1971).
17. See pp. 57, 67, *supra*.
18. See, *e.g.*, International Harvester Co. v. Kentucky, 234 U.S. 216 (1914); Connally v. General Construction Co., 269 U.S. 385 (1926); Lanzetta v. New Jersey, 306 U.S. 451 (1939).
19. Small Co. v. American Sugar Refining Co., 267 U.S. 233 (1925).
20. United States v. Classic, 313 U.S. 299 (1941) (dissenting opinion), discussed in text at note 10, p. 27, *supra;* United States v. Five Gambling Devices, 346 U.S. 441 (1953) (concurring opinion).

When the Court held that a homosexual alien who had been in the country for eight years was deportable under a statute applicable to one "afflicted with a psychopathic personality," and that there was no need for an ascertainable standard "so that one may avoid the applicability of the law," because the alien was already a homosexual when he presented himself for entry, Douglas dissented:[21]

> The term "psychopathic personality" is a treacherous one like "communist" or in an earlier day "Bolshevik." A label of this kind when freely used may mean only an unpopular person. It is much too vague by constitutional standards for the imposition of penalties or punishment . . .
>
> Many experts think that it is a meaningless designation . . .
>
> It is common knowledge that in this century homosexuals have risen high in our own public service—both in Congress and in the Executive Branch—and have served with distinction. It is therefore not credible that Congress wanted to deport everyone and anyone who was a sexual deviate, no matter how blameless his social conduct had been nor how creative his work nor how valuable his contribution to society . . . The legislative history [of the statute] should not be read as imputing to Congress a purpose to classify under the heading "psychopathic personality" every person who has ever had a homosexual experience . . .
>
> If we are to hold, as the Court apparently does, that any acts of homosexuality suffice to deport the alien, whether or not they are part of a fabric of antisocial behavior, then we face a serious question of due process. By that construction a person is judged by a standard that is almost incapable of definition . . .
>
> We deal here . . . with an aspect of "liberty" and the requirements of due process. They demand that the standard be sufficiently clear as to forewarn those who may otherwise be entrapped and to provide full opportunity to conform. "Psychopathic personality" is so broad and vague as to be little more than an epithet. The Court seeks to avoid this question by saying that the standard being applied relates only to what petitioner had done prior to his entry, not to his postentry conduct. *But at least half of the questioning of this petitioner [in the deportation proceedings] related to his postentry conduct.*

He later voted with the Court to hold invalid on its face a city ordinance making it a crime for "three or more persons to assemble on

21. Boutilier v. Immigration Service, 387 U.S. 118 (1967) (dissenting opinion).

any of the sidewalks . . . and there conduct themselves in a manner annoying to persons passing by."[22] The Court also invalidated another "suspicious person ordinance" making criminal "any person who wanders about the streets . . . or who is found abroad at late or unusual hours in the night without any visible or lawful business and who does not give a satisfactory account of himself," as applied to one whom police observed letting a girl out of his car late at night in a parking lot and then using a two-way radio in his car and who, after his arrest, gave three different addresses for himself and said he did not know the girl's name or where she was going when she left him. The Court thought that, while the defendant could reasonably be charged with knowing that he was out at a late or unusual hour and that his explanation was not satisfactory, the ordinance gave insufficient notice that such conduct was enough to show that defendant was "without visible or lawful business." Douglas concurred, but on the ground that the ordinance was unconstitutionally vague on its face, regardless of the application in the particular case.[23] "A policeman has a duty to investigate suspicious circumstances, and the circumstances of a person wandering the streets late at night without apparent lawful business may often present the occasion for police inquiry. But in my view government does not have constitutional power to make that circumstance, without more, a criminal offense." And he dissented when the Court upheld a District of Columbia statute making it a felony for a doctor to perform an abortion "unless the same were done as necessary for the preservation of the mother's life or health." He thought the law was void on its face.[24]

I agree with the Court that a physician—within the limits of his own expertise—would be able to say that an abortion at a particular time performed on a designated patient would or would not be necessary for the "preservation" of her "life or health." That judgment, however, is highly subjective, dependent on the training and insight of the particular physician and his standard as to what is "necessary" for the "preservation" of the mother's "life or health."

22. Coates v. City of Cincinnati, 402 U.S. 611 (1971).
23. Palmer v. City of Euclid, 402 U.S. 544 (1971).
24. United States v. Vuitch, 402 U.S. 62 (1971).

The answers may well differ, physician to physician. Those trained in conventional obstetrics may have one answer; those with deeper psychiatric insight may have another. Each answer is clear to the particular physician. If we could read the Act as making that determination conclusive, not subject to review by judge and by jury, the case would be simple . . . But that does such violence to the statutory scheme that I believe it beyond the range of judicial interpretation so to read the Act. If it is to be revised in that manner, Congress should do it.

Hence, I read the Act . . . as requiring submission to the court and jury of the physician's decision. What will the jury say? The prejudices of jurors are customarily taken care of by challenges for cause and by peremptory challenges. But vagueness of criminal statutes introduces another element that is uncontrollable. Are the concepts so vague that possible offenders have no safe guidelines for their own action? Are the concepts so vague that jurors can give them a gloss and meaning drawn from their own predelictions and prejudices? Is the statutory standard so easy to manipulate that although physicians can make good-faith decisions based on the standard, juries can nonetheless make felons out of them? . . .

A doctor may well remove an appendix far in advance of rupture in order to prevent a risk that may never materialize. May he act in a similar way under this abortion statute?

May he perform abortions on unmarried women who want to avoid the "stigma" of having an illegitimate child? Is bearing a "stigma" a "health" factor? Only in isolated cases? Or is it such whenever the woman is unmarried?

Is any unwanted pregnancy a "health" factor because it is a source of anxiety?

Is an abortion "necessary" in the statutory sense if the doctor thought that an additional child in a family would unduly tax the mother's physical well-being by reason of the additional work which would be forced upon her?

Would a doctor be violating the law if he performed an abortion because the added expense of another child in the family would drain its resources, leaving an anxious mother with an insufficient budget to buy nutritious food?

Is the fate of an unwanted child or the plight of the family into which it is born relevant to the factor of the mother's "health"? . . .

Abortion statutes deal with conduct which is heavily weighted with religious teachings and ethical concepts. Mr. Justice Jackson once spoke of the "treacherous grounds we tread when we undertake to translate ethical concepts into legal ones, case by case" . . . The difficulty and danger are compounded when religion adds another layer of prejudice. The end result is that juries condemn what they personally disapprove . . .

I would affirm the [trial judge's] dismissal of these indictments and leave to the experts the drafting of abortion laws that protect good-faith medical practitioners from the treacheries of the present law.

Another case involving interpretation of criminal statutes presented no constitutional question but merely a question of the even-handed administration of federal criminal justice. Julius and Ethel Rosenberg had been convicted under the federal Espionage Act of 1917 of conspiring between 1944 and 1950 to transmit military secrets, including some relating to the atom bomb, to Russia. They had been sentenced to death, their convictions and sentences had been affirmed on appeal, and the Supreme Court had declined to review the case. A few hours after the Court had adjourned for the summer and three days before the Rosenbergs were scheduled for execution, an application for relief was presented to Justice Douglas which raised a new point in the case. The Atomic Energy Act of 1946 made it a crime to transmit atomic information to other nations, but it, unlike the older Espionage Act, authorized the death sentence only on recommendation of the jury (which had not considered the question of penalty in the Rosenbergs' case) and only if the offense was committed with intent to injure the United States (which was not charged in the indictment or considered by the jury in the Rosenbergs' case). The question was, therefore, whether the Rosenbergs, whose offense began before but continued after the effective date of the Atomic Energy Act, were entitled to the benefit of its more lenient penalty provisions. Douglas concluded that the question was a substantial one which should be considered, and that "before we allow human lives to be snuffed out we be sure—emphatically sure—that we act within the law." Accordingly, he granted a stay of execution.

A special term of Court was then convened one day before the scheduled execution to review his stay order. On the day of execution the Court vacated the stay order, President Eisenhower denied executive clemency, and the Rosenbergs were executed on schedule. Douglas dissented:[25]

When the motion for a stay was before me, I was deeply troubled by the legal question tendered. After twelve hours of research and study I concluded . . . that the question was a substantial one, never presented to this Court and never decided by any court. So I issued the stay order.

Now I have had the benefit of an additional argument and additional study and reflection. Now I know I am right on the law . . .

The crime . . . took place in substantial part *after* the new Act became effective, *after* Congress had written new penalties for conspiracies to disclose atomic secrets. One of the new requirements is that the death penalty for that kind of espionage can be imposed *only* if the jury recommends it. And here there was no such recommendation. To be sure, this espionage included more than atomic secrets. But there can be no doubt that the death penalty was imposed because of the Rosenbergs' disclosure of atomic secrets. The trial judge, in sentencing the Rosenbergs to death, emphasized that the heinous character of their crime was trafficking in atomic secrets . . .

But the Congress in 1946 adopted new criminal sanctions for such crimes. Whether Congress was wise or unwise in doing so is no question for us. The cold truth is that the death sentence may not be imposed for what the Rosenbergs did unless the jury so recommends.

Some say, however, that since a *part* of the Rosenbergs' crime was committed under the old law, the penalties of the old law apply. But it is law too elemental for citation of authority that where two penal statutes may apply—one carrying death, the other imprisonment—the court has no choice but to impose the less harsh sentence.

A suggestion is made that the question comes too late, that since the Rosenbergs did not raise this question on appeal, they are barred from raising it now. But the question of an unlawful sentence is never barred. No man or woman should go to death under an unlawful sentence merely because his lawyer failed to raise the point . . .

Before the present argument I knew only that the question was serious and substantial. Now I am sure of the answer. I know deep in my heart that I am right on the law. Knowing that, my duty is clear.

Douglas has voted with the Court to hold that it is a denial of due process of law for a state to convict a defendant at trial on one charge

25. Rosenberg v. United States, 346 U.S. 273 (1953) (dissenting opinion).

and to affirm the conviction on appeal on the ground that defendant is guilty of a different charge,[26] or to convict a defendant on a record which is devoid of any evidence to support the charge,[27] or to trick him into entering a guilty plea by misrepresenting the nature of the charge against him.[28]

The Court has long been concerned with the fairness of the circumstances under which pleas of guilty are entered in criminal cases. In 1927 it held that where the defendant in a criminal prosecution contended that he had been induced to plead guilty by the prosecutor's misrepresentation that a light sentence would be imposed, and the trial court allowed him to withdraw the plea, it was error to permit the prosecutor then to introduce the plea in evidence even though the trial judge instructed the jury to disregard it if they believed defendant's testimony about the prosecutor's misrepresentation.[29]

Many years later Douglas concurred in a decision that, where a defendant who has been convicted in state or federal court later makes detailed factual allegations—which are denied by the prosecutor—that his guilty plea had been induced by misrepresentations of the prosecutor as to the length of sentence to be imposed, or by threats of prosecutor or police, he is entitled to a hearing. A guilty plea, "if induced by promises or threats which deprive it of the character of a voluntary act, is void."[30] He also voted with the Court to hold that in federal criminal trials a federal rule of criminal procedure requires the trial court, before accepting a guilty plea, not only to satisfy itself "that there is a factual basis for the plea," but also to interrogate the defendant personally to determine that the plea is made voluntarily with understanding of the nature of the charge and the consequences of the plea, and that where the judge fails to make the necessary interroga-

26. Cole v. Arkansas, 333 U.S. 196 (1948). *See also* Paterno v. Lyons, 334 U.S. 314 (1948) (dissent); Turner v. New York, 386 U.S. 773 (1967) (dissenting opinion).

27. Thompson v. Louisville, 362 U.S. 199 (1960); Shuttlesworth v. Birmingham, 382 U.S. 87 (1965) (concurring opinion); Johnson v. Florida, 391 U.S. 596 (1968); Gregory v. Chicago, 394 U.S. 111 (1969) (concurring opinion). *See also* Turner v. United States, 396 U.S. 398 (1970) (dissenting opinion).

28. Smith v. O'Grady, 312 U.S. 329 (1941).

29. Kercheval v. United States, 274 U.S. 220 (1927).

30. Machibroda v. United States, 368 U.S. 487 (1962) (concurring opinion).

tion the guilty plea must be set aside and the defendant permitted to plead anew. The rule was said to be "designed to assist the . . . judge in making the constitutionally required determination that a defendant's guilty plea is truly voluntary" and to produce a record that the proper inquiry had been made.[31]

Later in the same year Douglas wrote for the Court to hold, in a state case where the defendant had been convicted on a guilty plea to each of five robbery counts and had received the death sentence on each count, that the convictions could not stand where the record did not show that the trial judge had made any effort to determine that the guilty pleas were voluntarily and knowingly entered:[32]

> A plea of guilty is more than a confession which admits that the accused did various acts; it is itself a conviction; nothing remains but to give judgment and determine punishment . . .
>
> . . . Ignorance, incomprehension, coercion, terror, inducements, subtle or blatant threats might be a perfect cover-up of unconstitutionality . . .
>
> Several federal constitutional rights are involved in a waiver that takes place when a plea of guilty is entered in a state criminal trial. First, is the privilege against compulsory self-incrimination . . . Second, is the right to trial by jury . . . Third, is the right to confront one's accusers . . . We cannot presume a waiver of these three important federal rights from a silent record.
>
> What is at stake for an accused facing death or imprisonment demands the utmost solicitude of which courts are capable in canvassing the matter with the accused to make sure he has a full understanding of what the plea connotes and of its consequence. When the judge discharges that function, he leaves a record adequate for any review that may later be sought . . . and forestalls the spin-off of collateral proceedings that seek to probe murky memories.

Douglas also joined with the Court in the *Jackson* case to invalidate that provision of the Federal Kidnaping Act which provides that if the victim was not released unharmed the defendant shall be punished by death "if the verdict of the jury shall so recommend," otherwise by

31. McCarthy v. United States, 394 U.S. 459 (1969). *Cf.* Lynch v. Overholser, 369 U.S. 705 (1962).

32. Boykin v. Alabama, 395 U.S. 238 (1969).

imprisonment for a term of years or life. Since the death penalty was authorized only for the defendant who pleaded not guilty and demanded a jury trial, it was held impermissably "to discourage the assertion of the Fifth Amendment right not to plead guilty and to deter exercise of the Sixth Amendment right to demand a jury trial.[33] He concurred also in a subsequent decision in the *Brady* case, finding that one who had plead guilty under the Kidnaping Act had not done so because of the coercion of the unconstitutional provision of the statute, but because he learned that his co-defendant had confessed, entered a guilty plea, and would be available to testify against him.[34] But he joined the dissent in another case where the Court sustained conviction on a guilty plea under a state statute which provided that the penalty for first degree burglary should be death unless the jury recommended a life sentence, but that if the defendant pleaded guilty the punishment should be life imprisonment. While the Court thought that here, as in *Brady*, "an otherwise valid plea is not involuntary because induced by the defendant's desire to limit the possible maximum penalty to less than that authorized if there is a jury trial," the dissenters contended that defendant should have an opportunity to demonstrate that the state's "unconstitutional capital punishment scheme was a significant factor in his decision to plead guilty."[35] In 1971 the Court sustained another conviction from the same state on a guilty plea to second degree murder where the state's statute applicable to first degree murder, like its statute applicable to first degree burglary, provided for the death penalty unless the jury recommended life, but provided also that the maximum sentence if a guilty plea was entered should be life. In this case, after the plea was entered, the prosecution had summarized a strong circumstantial case, though it had no eyewitnesses to the shooting of the victim. The defendant had also testified that he shot no one, but that he was pleading guilty to the lesser charge to avoid the

33. United States v. Jackson, 390 U.S. 570 (1965). See also Pope v. United States, 329 U.S. 651 (1968). Special due process problems in connection with jury trials are discussed in Chapter 12.

34. Brady v. United States, 397 U.S. 742 (1970) (concurring opinion).

35. Parker v. North Carolina, 397 U.S. 790 (1970) (dissenting opinion). *See also* McMann v. Richardson, 397 U.S. 759 (1970) (dissenting opinion).

threat of the death penalty. The dissenters, "without reaching the question whether due process permits the entry of judgment upon a plea of guilty accompanied by a contemporaneous denial of acts constituting the crime," thought that the denial of guilt coupled with the threat of the unconstitutional statute was enough to show that the guilty plea was not voluntary.[36]

In *Chambers v. Florida*[37] Douglas voted with the Court to invalidate convictions which were based on confessions found to have been obtained from the defendants by coercion. Three of the four defendants involved had also entered guilty pleas, but the Court made no distinction between them and the fourth, who pleaded not guilty and was convicted after a trial in which his confession was introduced against him. Later, in *Herman v. Claudy*[38] the Court unanimously held that an imprisoned defendant was entitled to a hearing on a petition for habeas corpus which alleged that he had entered a guilty plea without the assistance of counsel, following a confession coerced from him by the police. Petitioner was entitled to an opportunity to prove his allegations, the Court said, both because "a conviction . . . on a plea of guilty based on a confession extorted by violence or by mental coercion is invalid under the Federal Due Process Clause," and because, "the number and complexity of the charges against petitioner, as well as their seriousness, create a strong conviction that no laymen could have understood the accusations," so that due process also required representation by counsel. But in a 1970 case the Court reversed a lower federal court which had ordered hearings on petitions for habeas corpus alleging that defendants had been convicted on guilty pleas motivated by earlier coerced confessions. All defendants had been represented by counsel when they entered their pleas, the Court noted, so that it must have been counsels' judgments that, if they pleaded not guilty and went to trial, they would not be successful in their efforts to challenge the confessions as the product of coercion. Hence, the issue to be determined on the petitions for habeas corpus was whether counsel was

36. North Carolina v. Alford, 400 U.S. 25 (1971).
37. 309 U.S. 227 (1940).
38. 350 U.S. 116 (1956).

"reasonably competent." And the fact that "this Court might hold a defendant's confession inadmissible in evidence, possibly by a divided vote, hardly justifies a conclusion that the defendant's attorney was incompetent or ineffective when he thought the admissibility of the confession sufficiently probable to advise a plea of guilty." Prior cases were distinguished. In *Herman v. Claudy*, defendant had no counsel. And in *Chambers* v. *Florida*, where defendants did have counsel, "the circumstances that coerced the confession" had "abiding impact and also taint[ed] the plea"—although that fact was not noted in the *Chambers* opinion. Douglas joined dissenters who maintained that defendants were entitled to an opportunity to try to prove that their confessions were coerced and that they induced the guilty pleas. While the presence of counsel would be of some relevance on the latter issue, the dissenters asserted that "it cannot be blandly assumed" that counsel at the time of entry of the pleas "will be able to render effective assistance to the defendant in freeing him from the burdens of his unconstitutionally extorted confession."[39]

Before Douglas came to the Court it was established that a conviction after trial on a not guilty plea was invalid under the due process clause if the state introduced at the trial a confession obtained from the defendant by physical torture.[40] Douglas has since joined with the Court, in a constant grist of cases, to invalidate the use of confessions which were not voluntary because obtained by the use of coercion which fell short of resort to severe physical abuse,[41] as where the defendant was held incommunicado and subjected to protracted questioning,[42] or where "an already physically and emotionally exhausted

39. McMann v. Richardson, 397 U.S. 759 (1970) (dissenting opinion).

40. Brown v. Mississippi, 297 U.S. 278 (1936).

41. Chambers v. Florida, 309 U.S. 227 (1940); Canty v. Alabama, 309 U.S. 629 (1940); White v. Texas, 310 U.S. 530 (1940); Lomax v. Texas, 313 U.S. 544 (1941); Vernon v. Alabama, 313 U.S. 547 (1941); Ward v. Texas, 316 U.S. 547 (1942); Malinski v. New York, 324 U.S. 401 (1945); Beecher v. Alabama, 389 U.S. 35 (1967) (concurring opinion); Sims v. Georgia, 389 U.S. 404 (1967).

42. Ashcraft v. Tennessee, 322 U.S. 143 (1944); Ashcraft v. Tennessee, 327 U.S. 274 (1946); Watts v. Indiana, 338 U.S. 49 (1949) (concurring opinion); Turner v. Pennsylvania, 338 U.S. 62 (1949) (concurring opinion); Harris v. South Carolina, 338 U.S. 68 (1949) (concurring opinion); Fikes v. Alabama, 352 U.S. 191 (1957); Payne v. Arkansas, 356 U.S. 560 (1958); Spano v. New York, 360 U.S. 315 (1959)

suspect's ability to resist interrogation was broken to almost trance-like submission by use of the arts of a highly skilled psychiatrist,"[43] or where the evidence indicates "the strongest probability" that the defendant was insane during an eight or nine hour period of interrogation which led to the confession,[44] or where the widowed defendant questioned on a marijuana charge was threatened with loss of custody of her children,[45] or where the confession followed fourteen days' confinement in a "windowless sweatbox."[46] And he has dissented where he thought due process requirements were not properly applied.[47]

One case, in which Douglas wrote for the Court to invalidate the conviction of a fifteen-year-old black for murder in the course of a robbery of a confectionery, illustrates the difficulties and the subtleties of this matter. The boy had been arrested and taken to the police station at midnight. Thereafter he was questioned for five hours by the police, acting in relays of one or two each. Around 5 A.M., after being shown alleged confessions of two other boys also arrested for the crime (whose subsequent fates do not appear), he confessed. After the confession was signed, a newspaper photographer was allowed to see him and take his picture. Thereafter he was held incommunicado in jail for three days. A lawyer retained by his mother was twice denied permission to see him. He was not taken before a magistrate and charged with the crime until three days after the confession. His mother was not allowed to see him until two days after that. Defendant testified that he was beaten by the police; his mother testified that he was bruised and skinned when she saw him and that his clothes were torn and blood-

(concurring opinion); Reck v. Pate, 367 U.S. 433 (1961) (concurring opinion); Culombe v. Connecticut, 367 U.S. 568 (1961) (concurring opinion); Haynes v. Washington, 373 U.S. 503 (1963); Davis v. North Carolina, 384 U.S. 737 (1966); Clewis v. Texas, 386 U.S. 707 (1967).

43. Leyra v. Denno, 347 U.S. 556 (1954).

44. Blackburn v. Alabama, 361 U.S. 199 (1960).

45. Lynumn v. Illinois, 372 U.S. 528 (1963).

46. Brooks v. Florida, 389 U.S. 413 (1967).

47. Lisenba v. California, 314 U.S. 219 (1941) (dissenting opinion); Gallegos v. Nebraska, 342 U.S. 55 (1951) (dissenting opinion); Stroble v. California, 343 U.S. 181 (1952) (dissenting opinion); Stein v. New York, 346 U.S. 156 (1953) (dissenting opinion); Thomas v. Arizona, 356 U.S. 390 (1958) (dissent); Ashdown v. Utah, 357 U.S. 426 (1958) (dissenting opinion).

stained. The police denied that he had been beaten. Putting aside the disputed testimony as to the beating, Douglas ruled that the confession was not voluntary and was therefore inadmissible:[48]

What transpired would make us pause for careful inquiry if a mature man were involved. And when, as here, a mere child—an easy victim of the law—is before us, special care in scrutinizing the record must be used. Age 15 is a tender and difficult age for a boy of any race. He cannot be judged by the more exacting standards of maturity. That which would leave a man cold and unimpressed can overawe and overwhelm a lad in his early teens. This is the period of great instability which the crisis of adolescence produces. A 15-year-old lad, questioned through the dead of night by relays of police, is a ready victim of the inquisition. Mature men possibly might stand the ordeal from midnight to 5 a.m. But we cannot believe that a lad of tender years is a match for the police in such a contest. He needs counsel and support if he is not to become the victim first of fear, then of panic. He needs someone on whom to lean lest the overpowering presence of the law, as he knows it, crush him. No friend stood at the side of this 15-year-old boy as the police, working in relays, questioned him hour after hour, from midnight until dawn. No lawyer stood guard to make sure that the police went so far and no farther, to see to it that they stopped short of the point where he became the victim of coercion. No counsel or friend was called during the critical hours of questioning. A photographer was admitted once this lad broke and confessed. But not even a gesture towards getting a lawyer for him was ever made.

This disregard of the standards of decency is underlined by the fact that he was kept for over three days during which the lawyer retained to represent him twice tried to see him and twice was refused admission. A photographer was admitted at once; but his closest friend—his mother—was not allowed to see him for over five days after his arrest. It is said that these events are not germane to the present problem because they happened after the confession was made. But they show such a callous attitude of the police towards the safeguards which respect for ordinary standards of human relationships compels that we take with a grain of salt their present apologia that the five-hour grilling of this boy was conducted in a fair and dispassionate manner. When the police are so unmindful of these basic standards of conduct in their public

48. Haley v. Ohio, 332 U.S. 596 (1948).

dealings, their secret treatment of a 15-year-old boy behind closed doors in the dead of night becomes darkly suspicious.

Long before the Supreme Court reviewed a state conviction involving an alleged coerced confession, it had held that use of such a confession in a federal prosecution violated the Fifth Amendment's privilege against self-incrimination.[49] Since 1964, when that privilege was held applicable to the States under the Fourteenth Amendment,[50] state-used confessions have been tested by the same standards.[51]

In reviewing federal criminal prosecutions, the Supreme Court does not confine itself to constitutional requirements but exercises a general supervisory authority over federal criminal justice. Hence, in *McNabb v. United States*,[52] in a decision in which Douglas joined, it ruled inadmissible in federal courts a confession, even though voluntary, where obtained during a period of time when the arresting officers were holding the defendant in disregard of federal statutes and rules requiring that he be brought promptly before a committing magistrate for arraignment:

> Legislation such as [the arraignment statutes], requiring that the police must with reasonable promptness show legal cause for detaining arrested persons, constitutes an important safeguard—not only in assuring protection for the innocent but also in securing conviction of the guilty by methods that commend themselves to a progressive and self-confident society. For this procedural requirement checks resort to those reprehensible practices known as the "third degree" which, though universally rejected as indefensible, still find their way into use. It aims to avoid all the evil implications of secret interrogation of persons accused of crime. It reflects not a sentimental but a sturdy view of law enforcement. It outlaws easy but self-defeating ways in which brutality is substituted for brains as an instrument of crime detection. A statute carrying such purposes is expressive of a general legislative policy to which courts should not be heedless when appropriate situations call for its application.

49. Bram v. United States, 168 U.S. 532 (1897).
50. Malloy v. Hogan, 378 U.S. 1 (1964).
51. See pp. 230-231, *infra*.
52. 318 U.S. 332 (1943).

Douglas has also joined in subsequent decisions applying this rule,[53] and in a decision holding it inapplicable where the confession was not obtained during a period of illegal detention—where the defendant confessed promptly and spontaneously after his arrest and thereafter was held for eight days before arraignment.[54] But he disagreed when the Court refused to extend the *McNabb* rule in a case where defendant was arrested on an assault charge, held without arraignment for five hours, during which time he was interrogated about the assault and an unrelated murder and confessed to the assault, then was arraigned and committed for assault, and three days later, after further interrogation, confessed to the murder also. Douglas thought it improper to use the second confession to convict the defendant of murder:[55]

There are time-honored police methods for obtaining confessions from an accused. One is detention without arraignment, the problem we dealt with in *McNabb* v. *United States* . . . Then the accused is under the exclusive control of the police, subject to their mercy, and beyond the reach of counsel or of friends. What happens behind doors that are opened and closed at the sole discretion of the police is a black chapter in every country—the free as well as the despotic, the modern as well as the ancient. In the *McNabb* case we tried to rid the federal system of those breeding grounds for coerced confessions.

Another time-honored police method for obtaining confessions is to arrest a man on one charge (often a minor one) and use his detention for investigating a wholly different crime. This is an easy short cut for the police . . . Then the police can have access to the prisoner day and night. Arraignment for one crime gives some protection. But when it is a pretense or used as the device for breaking the will of the prisoner on long, relentless, or repeated questionings, it is abhorent. We should free the federal system of that disreputable practice which has honeycombed the municipal police system in this country. We should make illegal such a perversion of a "legal" detention.

The rule I propose would, of course, reduce the "efficiency" of the police. But so do the requirements for arraignment, the prohibition against coerced confessions, the right to bail, the jury trial, and most of

53. Upshaw v. United States, 335 U.S. 410 (1948); Mallory v. United States, 354 U.S. 449 (1957).

54. United States v. Mitchell, 322 U.S. 65 (1944) (concurring).

55. United States v. Carignan, 342 U.S. 36 (1951) (concurring opinion).

our other procedural safeguards. We in this country, however, early made the choice—that the dignity and privacy of the individual were worth more to society than an all-powerful police.

Douglas voted with the Court also to apply the *McNabb* rule to exclude in federal prosecutions confessions obtained by the federal agents who, pursuant to "working arrangements" with local police, interrogated defendants while they were held in custody by the local police pursuant to illegal arrests and without arraignment as required by state law.[56] But when the Court declined to apply the same rule to another case where the only apparent differences were that the arrests were made on tips supplied by the federal agents, the arrests may have been legal, and the local police may not have prolonged the period of illegal detention to enable the federal agents to complete their interrogation, he dissented:[57]

There has been much attention focused, in the progress of this case, on whether the Buffalo police and the F.B.I. had a "working arrangement" . . . by which petitioner's detention was effected. In my view, the activity of the federal agents in this case is proscribed without regard to whether there was, or was not, a pre-existing "working arrangement."

The confessions would be inadmissible . . . if the original arrest in this case had been made by federal officers. For the duty of a federal officer making an arrest is to take the arrested person "without unnecessary delay" before a judicial officer . . . in compliance with [the federal rules of criminal procedure] . . .

Arrest, and the resulting detention, serves, under the Federal Rules, the purpose of assuring that a person, accused on probable grounds of a crime, will be amenable to the orders of a competent court, which include by the terms of Rule 5(b) the right to counsel and to bail. It is not an administrative step preliminary to a secret interrogation. In *Mallory* v. *United States*[58] . . . this Court said that an accused "is not to be taken to police headquarters in order to carry out a process of inquiry . . . "

The only reason put forward for a different result in this case is that the "police headquarters" in which federal agents carried out the

56. Anderson v. United States, 318 U.S. 350 (1943).
57. Coppola v. United States, 365 U.S. 762 (1961).
58. 354 U.S. 449 (1957).

wrongful "process of inquiry" belonged to Buffalo police rather than the Federal Government. The Government contends here, as it did in *Anderson* v. *United States*[59] . . . that it is not "formally guilty of illegal conduct." The device is too transparent. I do not think that federal agents can avoid the impact of federal rules by taking advantage of an illegal detention arranged by state officers . . . In this case the federal agents used an illegal detention as the occasion to carry on a secret interrogation. What the federal agents cannot do in federal precincts they cannot do in a state jail. What we do today is to permit federal agents to flout the federal law so long as they let the accused stay in a state jail and interrogate him there to their heart's content.

As the state convictions coming before the Court have revealed increasingly sophisticated methods of coercive police interrogation,[60] Douglas has since 1949 unsuccessfully urged the Court to read the constitutional standard applicable to the states to exclude any confession obtained during a period of detention by state officers which is illegal by applicable state arraignment law. As he put his argument in a case where defendent was detained and extensively interrogated but not arraigned until six days after his arrest and shortly after his confession:[61] "It would be naive to think that this . . . custody was less than the inquisition. The man was held until he broke. Then and only then was he arraigned and given the protection which the law provides all accused . . . The procedure breeds coerced confessions. It is the root of the evil. It is the procedure without which the inquisition could not flourish in the country." As he put it in another case,[62] three years before the Court adopted his view that the Fifth Amendment's privilege against self-incrimination was applicable to the states:[63]

People arrested by the police may produce confessions that come gushing forth and carry all the earmarks of reliability. But detention *incommunicado* for days on end is so fraught with evil that we should

59. 318 U.S. 350 (1943).

60. See text at notes 41-46, *supra*.

61. Watts v. Indiana, note 42, *supra* (concurring opinion). *See also* Turner v. Pennsylvania, note 42, *supra* (concurring opinion); Harris v. South Carolina, note 42, *supra* (concurring opinion); Stroble v. California, note 47, *supra* (dissenting opinion).

62. Reck v. Pate, note 42, *supra* (concurring opinion).

63. *See* Malloy v. Hogan, note 50, *supra*.

hold it to be inconsistent with the requirements of that free society which is reflected in the Bill of Rights. It is the means whereby the commands of the Fifth Amendment (which I deem to be applicable to the States) are circumvented. It is true that the police have to interrogate to arrest; it is not true that they may arrest to interrogate . . .

In ordinary circumstances, the police, under law, are to conduct investigations of crime by interview, and not by interrogation. Typically, it is the Grand Jury or a Court, not the police, which has the power to compel testimony . . . To allow the police to use their power to arrest as a substitute for the power of subpoena is, I think, to strip the Fifth Amendment of its meaning.

Douglas has in several cases joined with the Court to hold that news coverage of a crime and of the defendant's subsequent prosecution so prejudiced the atmosphere of the locality in which the trial occurred as to deprive defendant of the fair trial which due process requires.[64] And he also voted with the Court when it held unconstitutional a state statute forbidding a change of venue for jury trials in misdemeanor cases regardless of the extent of local prejudice.[65] When the Court also held that the televising of the trial of Billie Sol Estes for swindling created such possibilities of unfairness as to violate due process, he agreed but joined in a concurring opinion which identified objections in addition to the possible impact on the judge, jurors, witnesses, and the defendant, with which the majority opinion was concerned:[66]

Should the television industry become an integral part of our system of criminal justice, it would not be unnatural for the public to attribute the shortcomings of the industry to the trial process itself. The public is aware of the television industry's consuming interest in ratings, and it is also aware of the steps that have been taken in the past to maintain viewer interest in television programs. Memories still recall vividly the scandal caused by the disclosure that quiz programs had been corrupted in order to heighten their dramatic appeal. Can we be sure that similar efforts would not be made to heighten the dramatic appeal of televised trials? Can we be sure that the public would not inherently distrust our

64. Irvin v. Dowd, 366 U.S. 717 (1961); Rideau v. Louisiana, 373 U.S. 723 (1963); Sheppard v. Maxwell, 384 U.S. 333 (1966).

65. Groppi v. Wisconsin, 400 U.S. 505 (1971).

66. Estes v. Texas, 381 U.S. 532 (1965) (concurring opinion).

system of justice because of its intimate association with a commercial enterprise?

Broadcasting in the courtroom would give the television industry an awesome power to condition the public mind either for or against an accused. By showing only those parts of its films or tapes which depict the defendant or his witnesses in an awkward or unattractive position, television directors could give the community, state or country a false and unfavorable impression of the man on trial. Moreover, if the case should end in a mistrial, the showing of selected portions of the trial, or even of the whole trial, would make it almost impossible to select an impartial jury for a second trial . . . To permit this powerful medium to use the trial process itself to influence the opinions of vast numbers of people, before a verdict of guilt or innocence has been rendered, would be entirely foreign to our system of justice.

The sense of fairness, dignity and integrity that all associate with the courtroom would become lost with its commercialization. Thus, the televising of trials would not only have an effect on those participating in the trials that are being televised, but also on those who observe the trials and later become trial participants.

It is argued that television not only entertains but also educates the public. But the function of a trial is not to provide an educational experience; and there is serious danger that any attempt to use a trial as an educational tool will both divert it from its proper purpose and lead to suspicions concerning the integrity of the trial process . . .

Finally, if the televising of criminal proceedings were approved, trials would be selected for television coverage for reasons having nothing to do with the purpose of trial. A trial might be televised because a particular judge has gained the fancy of the public by his unorthodox approach; or because the district attorney has decided to run for another office and it is believed his appearance would attract a large audience; or simply because a particular courtroom has a layout that best accommodates television coverage. For the most part, however, the most important factor that would draw television to the courtroom would be the nature of the case. The alleged perpetrator of the sensational murder, the fallen idol, or some other person who, like petitioner, has attracted the public interest would find his trial turned into a vehicle for television. Yet, these are the very persons who encounter the greatest difficulty in securing an impartial trial, even without the presence of television . . .

Nor does the exclusion of television cameras from the courtroom in any way impinge upon the freedoms of speech and the press. Court proceedings, as well as other public matters, are proper subjects for press coverage . . . So long as the television industry, like the other communications media, is free to send representatives to trials and to report on those trials to its viewers, there is no abridgement of the freedom of press. The right of the communications media to comment on court proceedings does not bring with it the right to inject themselves into the fabric of the trial process to alter the purpose of that process.

When the Court in another case found that a defendant had failed to show that preindictment publicity had prejudiced the grand jury which indicted him, Douglas disagreed on that finding of fact and urged that, although the state was not required to use a grand jury, due process required that when it did so it use an impartial one.[67]

Before Douglas came to the Court it had held that a defendant was denied due process where his conviction was obtained by the prosecutor's knowing use of perjured testimony.[68] Douglas has in later cases joined with the Court in the enforcement of that rule,[69] and he wrote for the Court to extend it to a case where the prosecutor suppressed evidence favorable to the defendant.[70]

The laws of many states forbid the execution of any person while he is insane. Long ago the Court held that the due process clause of the Fourteenth Amendment did not require that, once a defendant had been determined to be insane, a subsequent determination of sanity which would allow the execution to go forward must involve a jury trial.[71] In a more recent case in which Douglas did not participate, the Court also held that due process did not require the subsequent sanity determination to be made by a judicial officer rather than the governor.[72] But when the Court later held that the state could leave to the prison warden the absolute discretion to determine whether there was "good reason to believe" that a condemned man had become insane

67. Beck v. Washington, 369 U.S. 541 (1962) (dissenting opinion).

68. Mooney v. Holohan, 294 U.S. 103 (1935).

69. Pyle v. Kansas, 317 U.S. 213 (1942); Alcorta v. Texas, 355 U.S. 28 (1957); Napue v. Illinois, 360 U.S. 264 (1959).

70. Brady v. Maryland, 323 U.S. 83 (1963).

71. Nobles v. Georgia, 168 U.S. 398 (1897).

72. Solesbee v. Balkcom, 339 U.S. 9 (1950). *See also* Phyle v. Duffy, 334 U.S. 431 (1948) (concurring opinion).

and to initiate judicial proceedings to determine the issue, with no right on the part of the condemned man to put his case to the warden, he joined in a dissenting opinion:[73]

> Surely the right of an insane man not to be executed, a right based on moral principles deeply embedded in the traditions and feelings of our people and itself protected by the Due Process Clause of the Fourteenth Amendment,[74] merits the procedural protection that that Amendment safeguards. What kind of a constitutional right is it, especially if life is at stake, the vindication of which rests wholly in the hands of an administrative official whose actions cannot be inquired into, and who need not consider the claims of the person most vitally affected . . . ?
>
> *Audi alteram partem*—hear the other side!—a demand made insistently through the centuries, is now a command, spoken with the voice of the Due Process Clause of the Fourteenth Amendment, against state governments, and every branch of them—executive, legislative, and judicial—whenever any individual, however lowly and unfortunate, asserts a legal claim. It is beside the point that the claim may turn out not to be meritorious. It is beside the point that delay in the enforcement of the law may be entailed . . . The right to be heard somehow by someone before a claim is denied, particularly if life hangs in the balance, is far greater in importance to society, in the light of the sad history of its denial, than inconvenience in the execution of the law.

When in 1967 the Court for the first time tested juvenile court procedures by the due process clause it found them wanting due to failure to give the juvenile or his parents notice of the charges against him, an opportunity to be represented by counsel (including the appointment of counsel for indigent juveniles), the privilege against self-incrimination, and an opportunity to confront and cross-examine adverse witnesses. The case involved a fifteen-year-old boy who had been committed to a state industrial school as a "delinquent child"

73. Caritativo v. California 357 U.S. 549 (1958) (dissenting opinion).

74. This assumption has not yet been tested. In Solesbee v. Balkcom, note 72, *supra*, the Court found it unnecessary to decide whether "execution of an insane person is a type of 'cruel and unusual punishment' forbidden by the Fourteenth Amendment" because "the controlling Georgia statutes neither approve the practice of executing insane persons, nor is this petitioner about to be executed on such a premise."

until he reached age twenty-one for the offense of making a lewd telephone call (for which the maximum penalty for those over eighteen was $50 or two months' imprisonment) to a complaining witness who never appeared in the proceedings against him. Douglas joined in an opinion which said, in part:[75]

> It is of no constitutional consequence—and of limited practical meaning—that the institution to which he is committed is called an Industrial School. The fact of the matter is that, however euphemistic the title, a "receiving home" or an "industrial school" for juveniles is an institution of confinement in which the child is incarcerated for a greater or lesser time . . . Instead of mother and father and sisters and brothers and friends and classmates, his world is peopled by guards, custodians, state employees, and "delinquents" confined with him for anything from waywardness to rape and homicide.
>
> In view of this, it would be extraordinary if our Constitution did not require the procedural regularity and the exercise of care implied in the phrase "due process." Under our Constitution, the condition of being a boy does not justify a kangaroo court.

Douglas joined again, two years later, in a decision holding that the due process clause of the Fourteenth Amendment requires proof of a criminal charge beyond a reasonable doubt, and that this requirement—applicable by the law of all states in criminal prosecutions of adults—applies to a juvenile charged with an act of "delinquency" which would constitute the crime of larceny if committed by an adult:[76]

> The reasonable-doubt standard plays a vital role in the American scheme of criminal procedure. It is a prime instrument for reducing the risk of convictions resting on factual error . . .
>
> . . . The accused during a criminal prosecution has at stake interests of immense importance, both because of the possibility that he may lose his liberty upon conviction and because of the certainty that he would be stigmatized by the conviction. Accordingly, a society that values the good name and freedom of every individual should not condemn a man for commission of a crime when there is reasonable doubt about his guilt . . .
>
> Moreover, use of the reasonable-doubt standard is indispensable to

75. *In re* Gault, 387 U.S. 1 (1967).
76. *In re* Winship, 397 U.S. 358.

command the respect and confidence of the community in application of the criminal law. It is critical that the moral force of the criminal law not be diluted by a standard of proof that leaves people in doubt whether innocent men are being condemned. It is also important in our free society that every individual going about his ordinary affairs have confidence that his government cannot adjudge him guilty of a criminal offense without convincing a proper factfinder of his guilt with utmost certainty.

. . . The same considerations that demand extreme caution in factfinding to protect the innocent adult apply as well to the innocent child . . .

. . . It is true, of course, that the juvenile may be engaging in a general course of conduct inimical to his welfare that calls for judicial intervention. But that intervention cannot take the form of subjecting the child to the stigma of a finding that he violated a criminal law and to the possibility of institutional confinement on proof insufficient to convict him were he an adult.

In 1971, however, the Court held that due process does not require a jury trial in state juvenile delinquency proceedings although it does require a jury trial in corresponding state criminal proceedings.[77] The case involved a sixteen-year-old adjudged delinquent and placed on probation for participating with others in taking twenty-five cents from three teenagers, a fifteen-year-old adjudged delinquent and committed for an indefinite period for assault on a police officer who broke up a boys' fight, and some forty-five black children from eleven to fifteen years of age adjudged delinquent and placed on probation for engaging in a demonstration against school assignments which interfered with traffic. The Court concluded that a jury trial was not an essential of "fundamental fairness" in juvenile proceedings. Douglas dissented:[78]

Where a State uses its juvenile court proceedings to prosecute a juvenile for a criminal act and to order "confinement" until the child reaches 21 years of age, or where the child at the threshold of the proceedings faces that prospect, then he is entitled to the same procedural protection as an adult . . .

77. *See* Duncan v. Louisiana, 391 U.S. 145 (1968), discussed in Chapter 12.

78. McKeiver v. Pennsylvania, 403 U.S. 528 (1971). *See also* DeBacker v. Brainard, 396 U.S. 28 (1969) (dissenting opinion).

. . . No adult could be denied a jury trial in these circumstances . . . The Fourteenth Amendment . . . speaks of denial of rights to "any person," not denial of rights to "any adult person."

As previously noted,[79] the requirements of due process are not confined to criminal or quasi-criminal proceedings. In 1969 Douglas wrote for the Court to invalidate a garnishment procedure, long and commonly used in most of the states, which enabled a plaintiff—in this case a small loan company—to bring suit to collect an alleged debt, garnish one-half of the defendants wages (the amount exempted from garnishment varies from state to state), and require the employer to hold them pending the outcome of the suit:[80]

What happens in Wisconsin is that the clerk of court issues the summons at the request of the creditor's lawyer; and it is the latter who by serving the [employer] sets in motion the machinery whereby the wages are frozen. They may, it is true, be unfrozen if the trial of the . . . suit is ever had and the wage earner wins on the merits. But in the interim the wage earner is deprived of his enjoyment of earned wages without any opportunity to be heard and to tender any defense he may have, whether it be fraud or otherwise . . .

A procedural rule that may satisfy due process for [prejudgment] attachments [of property] in general . . . does not necessarily satisfy procedural due process in every case. The fact that a procedure would pass muster under a feudal regime does not mean it gives necessary protection to all property in its modern forms. We deal here with wages—a specialized type of property presenting distinct problems in our economic system . . .

A prejudgment garnishment of the Wisconsin type is a taking which may impose tremendous hardship on wage earners with families to support. Until [the federal Consumer Credit Protection Act of 1968] which forbids discharge of employees on the ground that their wages have been garnished, garnishment often meant the loss of a job. Over and beyond that was the great drain on family income.

The result is that a prejudgment garnishment . . . may as a practical matter drive a wage-earning family to the wall. Where the taking of one's property is so obvious, it needs no extended argument to conclude that absent notice and a prior hearing . . . this . . . procedure violates the fundamental principles of due process.

79. See text at notes 4-6, *supra*.
80. Sniadach v. Family Finance Corp., 395 U.S. 337 (1969).

Two years later Douglas voted with the Court to invalidate, on similar grounds, a state Motor Vehicle Safety Responsibility Act. Under the act an uninsured motorist involved in an accident would have his driver's license suspended unless he posted security to cover the amount of damages claimed by any other parties involved in the accident. There were exceptions from, and provisions for releases of, suspensions for cases in which such parties executed releases of their claims, or in which a court had decided that the driver was not liable, but unless or until either of these events occurred the license was to be suspended without any inquiry into the fault or liability of the driver. Due process required, the Court held, that before a license was suspended there be an official inquiry to determine "whether there is a reasonable possibility of judgments in the amounts claimed being rendered against the licensee."[81]

The Constitution, as submitted to the states for ratification, contained no express protection against arbitrary acts of government except provisions that neither Congress nor the states should pass any bill of attainder or ex post facto law,[82] a guaranty of jury trial in all federal criminal cases,[83] a provision that the writ of habeas corpus should not be suspended "unless when in Cases of Rebellion or Invasion the public Safety may require it,"[84] and a definition of the crime of treason, together with the requirement that no person be convicted of that crime "unless on the Testimony of two Witnesses to the same overt Act, or on Confession in open Court."[85]

The omission of a Bill of Rights was widely criticized and many of the states accompanied their ratifications with proposed amendments designed to add one. The first Congress submitted twelve of these proposals to the state legislatures and ten of them were ratified. In 1833 the Supreme Court held that the Fifth Amendment's prohibition against the taking of private property for public use without just compensation was not applicable to the states because the first ten

81. Bell v. Burson, 402 U.S. 535 (1971).
82. U.S. Const. Art. I, §9, Cl. 3, §10, Cl. 1.
83. *Id.*, Art. III, §2, Cl. 3.
84. *Id.*, Art. I, §9, Cl. 2.
85. *Id.*, Art. III, §3, Cl. 1.

amendments were designed for "security against the apprehended encroachments of the general government—not against those of the local governments."[86]

After the adoption of the Fourteenth Amendment, however, its due process clause was held in 1897 to incorporate and make applicable to the states the Fifth Amendment's restrictions on the taking of private property,[87] and in 1931 to incorporate the First Amendment's guarantees of freedom of speech and press.[88] But in 1875 it was held that neither the due process clause of the Fourteenth Amendment nor its guaranty of the privileges and immunities of national citizenship incorporated the Seventh Amendment's guaranty of trial by jury in civil suits at common law,[89] in 1884 that the Fourteenth Amendment did not incorporate the Fifth Amendment's guaranty of indictment by grand jury,[90] in 1890 that it did not incorporate the Eighth Amendment's prohibition against cruel and unusual punishment,[91] in 1900 that it did not incorporate the Sixth Amendment's guaranty of jury trial in criminal cases,[92] in 1904 that it did not incorporate the Sixth Amendment's right to confront adverse witnesses in criminal prosecutions,[93] and in 1908 that it did not incorporate the Fifth Amendment's privilege against self-incrimination.[94] In the last-mentioned case the test for incorporation was said to be, "Is it a fundamental principle of liberty and justice which inheres in the very idea of free government and in the inalienable right of a citizen of such a government?"—a test which the privilege against self-incrimination was held not to meet. By that test, it was held in 1914 that the Fourth Amendment's prohibition against unreasonable searches and seizures was likewise not incorporated.[95]

86. Barron v. Baltimore, 7 Pet. 243 (1833).

87. Chicago, Burlington & Quincy Railroad v. Chicago, 166 U.S. 226 (1897).

88. Stromberg v. California, 283 U.S. 359 (1931). *See also* Fiske v. Kansas, 274 U.S. 380 (1927).

89. Walker v. Sauvinet, 92 U.S. 90 (1875).

90. Hurtado v. California, 110 U.S. 516 (1884). *See also* Gaines v. Washington, 277 U.S. 81 (1928).

91. *In re* Kemmler, 136 U.S. 436 (1890).

92. Maxwell v. Dow, 176 U.S. 581 (1900).

93. West v. Louisiana, 194 U.S. 258 (1904).

94. Twining v. New Jersey, 211 U.S. 78 (1908).

95. Weeks v. United States, 232 U.S. 383 (1914).

When in 1937 the Court concluded also that the Fourteenth Amendment did not incorporate the Fifth Amendment's prohibition against being twice put in jeopardy for the same offense, it was explained that only those guarantees of the Bill of Rights that were "implicit in the concept of ordered liberty" were made applicable to the states by the Fourteenth Amendment.[96] When in 1947 the Court reaffirmed its prior decision that a defendant in a state prosecution was not denied a fair trial within the meaning of the due process clause because the privilege against self-incrimination was not observed, Douglas joined in a dissenting opinion which said in part:[97]

> This decision reasserts a constitutional theory spelled out in *Twining* v. *New Jersey*[98] . . . that this Court is endowed by the Constitution with boundless power under "natural law" periodically to expand and contract constitutional standards to conform to the Court's conception of what at a particular time constitutes "civilized decency" and "fundamental liberty and justice" . . .
>
> My study of the historical events that culminated in the Fourteenth Amendment, and the expressions of those who sponsored and favored, as well as those who opposed its submission and passage, persuades me that one of the chief objects that the provisions of the Amendment's first section, separately, and as a whole, were intended to accomplish was to make the Bill of Rights applicable to the states. With a full knowledge of the import of the *Barron* decision,[99] the framers and backers of the Fourteenth Amendment proclaimed its purpose to be to overturn the constitutional rule that case had announced. This historical purpose has never received full consideration or exposition in any opinion of this Court interpreting the Amendment . . .
>
> I cannot consider the Bill of Rights to be an outworn 18th Century "strait jacket" . . . Its provisions may be thought out-dated abstractions by some. And it is true that they were designed to meet ancient evils. But they are the same kind of human evils that have emerged from century to century wherever excessive power is sought by the few at the expense of the many. In my judgment the people of no nation can lose their liberty so long as a Bill of Rights like ours survives and its

96. Palko v. Connecticut, 302 U.S. 319 (1937). *See also* Brantley v. Georgia, 217 U.S. 284 (1910).
97. Adamson v. California, 332 U.S. 46 (1947) (dissenting opinion).
98. Note 94, *supra.*
99. Note 86, *supra.*

basic purposes are conscientiously interpreted, enforced and respected so as to afford continuous protection against old, as well as new, devices and practices which might thwart those purposes. I fear to see the consequences of the Court's practice of substituting its own concepts of decency and fundamental justice for the language of the Bill of Rights as its point of departure in interpreting and enforcing that Bill of Rights. If the choice must be between the selective process . . . applying some of the Bill of Rights to the States, or [a] rule applying none of them, I would choose the . . . selective process. But rather than accept either of these choices, I would follow what I believe was the original purpose of the Fourteenth Amendment—to extend to all the people of the nation the complete protection of the Bill of Rights.

The Court has never accepted that view. But the application of its doctrine of "selective incorporation" in the ensuing years has resulted, as will be indicated below, in most of the specific guarantees of the Bill of Rights being held applicable to the states as well as to the federal government.

8 SPEEDY AND PUBLIC TRIAL

The Sixth Amendment provides that, "In all criminal prosecutions, the accused shall enjoy the right to a speedy and public trial." In 1948 Douglas joined in a decision in the *Oliver* case which held that the guaranty of "public" trial was made applicable to the states by the Fourteenth Amendment and that it was violated where a state judge, operating as a "one-man grand jury" in his chambers from which the public had been excluded, held a witness in criminal contempt and sentenced him to sixty days in jail:[1]

Here we are concerned, not with petitioner's rights as a witness in a secret grand jury session, but with his rights as a defendant in a contempt proceeding. The power of the judge-grand jury who tried and convicted him in secret and sentenced him to jail . . . must likewise be measured, not by the limitations applicable to grand jury proceedings, but by the constitutional standards applicable to court proceedings in which an accused may be sentenced to a fine or imprisonment or both . . .

. . . Counsel have not cited and we have been unable to find a single instance of a secret criminal trial conducted in any federal, state, or municipal court during the history of this country. Nor have we found any record of even one such secret criminal trial in England since abolition of the Court of Star Chamber in 1641 . . .

1. *In re* Oliver, 333 U.S. 257 (1948). *Cf.* Gaines v. Washington, 277 U.S. 81 (1928).

The traditional Anglo-American distrust for secret trials has been variously ascribed to the notorious use of this practice by the Spanish Inquisition, to the excesses of the English Court of Star Chamber, and to the French monarchy's abuse of the *lettre de cachet.* All of these institutions obviously symbolized a menace to liberty. In the hands of despotic groups each of them had become an instrument for the suppression of political and religious heresies in ruthless disregard of the right of an accused to a fair trial. Whatever other benefits the guarantee to an accused that his trial be conducted in public may confer upon our society, the guarantee has always been recognized as a safeguard against any attempt to employ our courts as instruments of persecution. The knowledge that every criminal trial is subject to contemporaneous review in the forum of public opinion is an effective restraint on possible abuse of judicial power.

In a later case involving a witness before a federal judge and a grand jury in a courtroom from which the public had been excluded, where the judge convicted a witness for criminal contempt and sentenced him to one year's imprisonment, the Court sustained the conviction, stating that a criminal contempt proceeding was not a "criminal prosecution" within the meaning of the Sixth Amendement and that, since the witness' counsel was present and the witness did not request a public hearing when the proceedings switched from interrogation before the grand jury to prosecution before the judge for contempt, there was no denial of due process of law under the Fifth Amendment. Douglas joined in a dissenting opinion which argued that the decision could not be reconciled with *Oliver.*[2] Despite this decision, the Court has subsequently cited the *Oliver* case for the proposition that the due process clause of the Fourteenth Amendment "protects . . . the Sixth Amendment right to . . . public trial."[3]

The other requirement of this constitutional guaranty, that the trial be "speedy," has been held not violated by the federal government where defendant is indicted on a narcotics charge, his first conviction is vacated on his motion sixteen months later because of defects in the

2. Levine v. United States, 362 U.S. 610 (1960) (dissenting opinion). *See also In re* Groban, 352 U.S. 330 (1957) (dissenting opinion); Anonymous v. Baker, 360 U.S. 287 (1959) (dissenting opinion).

3. Duncan v. Louisiana, 391 U.S. 145 (1968).

indictment, he is reindicted two months later, and he moves to dismiss the second indictment one month thereafter. Recognizing that the guaranty "is an important safeguard to prevent undue and oppressive incarceration prior to trail, to minimize anxiety and concern accompanying public accusation and to limit the possibilities that long delay will impair the ability of an accused to defend himself," the Court pointed out that "in large measure because of the many procedural safeguards provided an accused, the ordinary procedures for criminal prosecution are designed to move at a deliberate pace" and concluded that the delay was neither unreasonable nor oppressive to the defendant.[4]

But this aspect of the guaranty has also been held applicable to the states and violated in a case where a civil rights demonstrator had been indicted for trespass, a misdemeanor; his first trial ended in a hung jury; and, seventeen months after the indictment, the state court had approved the prosecutor's motion to postpone prosecution indefinitely. Douglas joined in an opinion of the Court written nearly three years after the indictment:[5]

> The petitioner [who was not in custody] is not relieved of the limitations placed upon his liberty by this prosecution merely because its suspension permits him to go "whithersoever he will." The pendency of the indictment may subject him to public scorn and deprive him of employment, and almost certainly will force curtailment of his speech, associations and participation in unpopular causes. By indefinitely prolonging this oppression, as well as the "anxiety and concern accompanying public accusation," the criminal procedure condoned in this case . . . clearly denies the petitioner the right to a speedy trial.

Douglas also voted with the Court to hold that a state violates this guaranty where it indicts a man who is then a prisoner in a federal penitentiary in another state and, for six years thereafter, despite his repeated demands that it do so, takes no steps to bring him to trial:[6]

4. United States v. Ewell, 383 U.S. 116 (1966). *See also* Pollard v. United States, 352 U.S. 354 (1957) (dissenting opinion).

5. Klopfer v. North Carolina, 386 U.S. 213 (1967).

6. Smith v. Hooey, 393 U.S. 374 (1969).

This constitutional guarantee has universally been thought essential to protect at least three basic demands of criminal justice in the Anglo-American legal system: "[1] to prevent undue and oppressive incarceration prior to trial, [2] to minimize anxiety and concern accompanying public accusation and [3] to limit the possibilities that long delay will impair the ability of an accused to defend himself" . . . These demands are both aggravated and compounded in the case of an accused who is imprisoned by another jurisdiction . . .

. . . Texas concedes that if it [had made] an effort to secure a federal prisoner's appearance, he would, in fact, "be produced for trial in the state court" . . .

. . . Upon the petitioner's demand, Texas had a constitutional duty to make a diligent, good-faith effort to bring him before the [Texas] court for trial.

In a later similar case where the accused was indicted by the state in 1960 and finally was brought from federal prison in another state to stand trial and convicted in 1968, Douglas joined with the Court to hold that the state conviction must be reversed and all state proceedings on the same charge terminated, at least where there "is abundant evidence of actual prejudice to petitioner in the death of two potential witnesses, unavailability of another, and the loss of police records."[7]

7. Dickey v. Florida, 398 U.S. 30 (1970).

9 UNREASONABLE SEARCHES AND SEIZURES

The Fourth Amendment provides that, "The right of the people to be secure in their persons, houses, papers, and effects, against unreasonable searches and seizures, shall not be violated, and no Warrants shall issue, but upon probable cause, supported by Oath or affirmation, and particularly describing the place to be searched, and the persons or things to be seized."[1]

This provision governs both arrests and searches. Hence, when an officer seeks an arrest warrant from a magistrate he must make a showing of probable cause for arrest and describe the person to be arrested.[2] Douglas has voted with the Court to hold that a warrant is

1. Those who find this chapter hard going may take some comfort from the Court's statement in a recent decision under the Fourth Amendment: "Of course, it would be nonsense to pretend that our decision today reduces Fourth Amendment law to complete order and harmony." Coolidge v. New Hampshire, 403 U.S. 443 (1971).

2. In an opinion in which Douglas joined, the Court has said—though it did not hold—that, "A warrant of arrest can be based upon an indictment because the grand jury's determination that probable cause existed for the indictment also establishes that element for the purpose of issuing a warrant for the apprehension of the person so charged." Giordenello v. United States, 357 U.S. 480 (1958). *See also* McGrain v. Daugherty, 273 U.S. 135, 157 (1927). That procedure on indictments is now authorized by Rule 9 of the Federal Rules of Civil Procedure. *Cf.* Albrecht v. United States, 273 U.S. 1 (1927).

not properly issued on the sworn complaint of an officer that a named person "did receive, conceal, etc., narcotic drugs . . . with knowledge of unlawful importation." The purpose of the complaint is to enable the magistrate to judge whether probable cause for arrest exists. The magistrate "must judge for himself the persuasiveness of the facts relied on to show probable cause." But a complaint which "contains no affirmative allegation that the [officer] spoke with personal knowledge of the matters contained therein" and which "does not indicate any sources for the officer's belief," but merely asserts the officer's belief that a named person has committed a crime, gives the magistrate no basis for making a finding of probable cause.[3]

But a warrant is not always required before an arrest can be made. Douglas has joined in a decision of the Court which concludes that an officer may arrest without a warrant where a misdemeanor or a felony has been committed in his presence or where he has probable cause to believe—as distinguished from a good faith suspicion—that a felony has been committed or is about to be committed,[4] although he would limit the latter exception to cases where there is not time to obtain a warrant.[5] He has joined with the Court in cases holding that probable cause was not established[6] and has not always agreed with the Court when it was satisfied that probable cause had been established.[7]

One of the cases in which Douglas dissented from a finding of probable cause for arrest illustrates the difficulties of the problems in this area. The officers who had arrested defendant without a warrant on a narcotics charge had relied primarily on the statements of an informant, and they testified about the informants "previous reliability" but

3. Giordenello v. United States, note 2, *supra*. *See also* Whiteley v. Warden, 401 U.S. 560 (1971).

4. United States v. Di Re, 332 U.S. 581 (1948); Henry v. United States, 361 U.S. 98 (1959).

5. Jones v. United States, 362 U.S. 257 (1960) (dissenting in part); Wong Sun v. United States, 371 U.S. 497 (1963) (concurring opinion).

6. United States v. Di Re, note 4, *supra;* Henry v. United States, note 4, *supra;* Wong Sun v. United States, note 5, *supra* (concurring opinion); Beck v. Ohio, 379 U.S. 89 (1964); Recznik v. Lorain, 393 U.S. 166 (1968). *See also* Whiteley v. Warden, note 3, *supra.*

7. Draper v. United States, 358 U.S. 307 (1959) (dissenting opinion); Mc Cray v. Illinois, 386 U.S. 300 (1967) (dissenting opinion).

were not required to disclose the informant's name. Douglas did not consider it sufficient that the officers had testified in detail about what the informant had told them and why they considered him reliable:[8]

> Only through the informer's testimony can anyone other than the arresting officers determine "the persuasiveness of the facts relied on to show probable cause" . . . Without that disclosure neither we nor the lower courts can ever know whether there was "probable cause" for the arrest. Under the present decision we leave the Fourth Amendment exclusively in the custody of the police . . . Unless the identity of the informer is disclosed "the policeman himself conclusively determines the validity of his own arrest" . . .
>
> There is no way to determine the reliability of Old Reliable, the informer . . . Unless he is produced, the Fourth Amendment is entrusted to the tender mercies of the police . . . Except in rare and emergency cases, it requires magistrates to make the findings of "probable cause" [before issuing warrants]. We should be mindful of [the Fourth Amendment's] command that a judicial mind should be interposed between the police and the citizen.

Douglas has voted with the Court to hold that the officer arresting without a warrant must have probable cause to believe that the felony has been or is being committed *by the person arrested*—it is not enough that the warrantless officer smells opium fumes emanating from a hotel room and, without knowing who is in the room, knocks and is admitted and finds the defendant alone. "Thus the Government is obliged to justify the arrest by the search and at the same time to justify the search by the arrest. This will not do. An officer gaining access to private living quarters under color of his office and of the law which he personifies must then have some valid basis in law for the intrusion."[9]

For a search warrant to issue, the magistrate must again have some basis for finding probable cause that the search will produce relevant evidence, and the warrant must "particularly describe the place to be searched, and the . . . things to be seized."[10] Douglas has voted with the Court to hold insufficient an affidavit whose principal allegation was that a "confidential reliable informant" stated that the suspect was

8. Mc Cray v. Illinois, note 7, *supra* (dissenting opinion).
9. Johnson v. United States, 333 U.S. 10 (1948).
10. See text at note 1, *supra*.

violating the law,[11] or that asserted that affiants had "received reliable information from a credible person and do believe that . . . narcotics . . . are being kept" at described premises "for the purpose of sale and use contrary to . . . law."[12] And he has dissented when the Court was satisfied with affidavits stating that the affiant's belief of criminal conduct was based "upon observations made by me, and based upon information received from other Investigators,"[13] or that the affiant had been informed by an undisclosed informant, whose information on previous occasions had been reliable, and by "other sources of information" that the suspects were engaged in illicit heroin traffic and kept a supply of the drug in their apartment.[14]

Douglas also voted with the Court to hold that a search warrant authorizing the seizure of "books, records, pamphlets, cards, receipts, lists, memoranda, pictures, recordings and other written instruments concerning the Communist Party of Texas" did not satisfy the constitutional requirement that the warrant be one "particularly describing the . . . things to be seized."[15] He voted with the Court again to hold that a valid search warrant cannot be issued by a state attorney general who is in charge of the investigation of a murder and who later was the chief prosecutor at the trial,[16] and that a subpoena issued by the district attorney cannot serve the office of a warrant, which must be issued "by a neutral and detached magistrate instead of . . . the officer engaged in the often competitive enterprise of ferreting out crime."[17]

Here again, as in the case of arrest, a warrant is not always required for a search. While, with an exception to be noted later, a search may not be made merely because an officer has probable cause to believe that a crime has been or is being committed or that evidence of a crime

11. Spinelli v. United States, 393 U.S. 410 (1969).

12. Aguilar v. Texas, 378 U.S. 108 (1964).

13. United States v. Ventresca, 380 U.S. 102 (1965) (dissenting opinion).

14. Jones v. United States, note 5, *supra* (dissenting in part). *See also* United States v. Harris, 403 U.S. 573 (1971) (dissenting opinion).

15. Stanford v. Texas, 379 U.S. 476 (1965). *See also* Marcus v. Search Warrant, 367 U.S. 717 (1961) (concurring opinion).

16. Coolidge v. New Hampshire, 403 U.S. 443 (1971).

17. Mancusi v. De Forte, 392 U.S. 364 (1968).

will be produced,[18] some warrantless searching is allowed as an incident to a valid arrest whether the arrest is being made on warrant or on probable cause without a warrant.

Questions as to the validity of arrests and searches usually arise only where they produce some solid, incriminating evidence which defendant seeks to have excluded from his later trial because illegally obtained. Where they produce nothing, and the person searched is released, that is usually the end of the matter. Hence, in the cases which reach the courts, it frequently proves difficult to divorce the inquiry into the officer's probable cause for belief from the results of his arrest and search. Thus, in one case where an informer told officers that the defendant "was peddling narcotics to several addicts" and would arrive in the city by train at a designated time, the Court held that the officers, acting without a warrant, had probable cause to arrest defendant as he left the train and search him—a search which produced heroin and led to prosecution for illegally transporting it. Douglas said in dissent:[19]

> Decisions under the Fourth Amendment, taken in the long view, have not given the protection to the citizen which the letter and spirit of the Amendment would seem to require. One reason, I think, is that wherever a culprit is caught red-handed, as in leading Fourth Amendment cases, it is difficult to adopt and enforce a rule that would turn him loose. A rule protective of law-abiding citizens is not apt to flourish where its advocates are usually criminals. Yet the rule we fashion is for the innocent and guilty alike. If the word of the informer on which the present arrest was made is sufficient to make the arrest legal, his word would also protect the police who, acting on it, hauled the innocent citizen off to jail . . .

18. Weeks v. United States, 232 U.S. 383 (1914); Johnson v. United States, 333 U.S. 10 (1948); United States v. Jeffers, 342 U.S. 48 (1951); Jones v. United States, 357 U.S. 493 (1958).

19. Draper v. United States, 358 U.S. 307 (1959) (dissenting opinion). Douglas later voted with the Court to hold that illegally seized evidence is inadmissable in Court not only in criminal prosecutions but also in proceedings to forfeit property allegedly used in violation of law. One 1958 Plymouth Sedan v. Pennsylvania, 380 U.S. 693 (1965). *Cf.* United States v. United States Coin and Currency, note 55, p. 228, *infra*.

> . . . If an arrest is made without a warrant, the offense must be committed in the presence of the officer or the officer must have "reasonable grounds to believe that the person to be arrested has committed or is committing" a violation of the narcotics law. The arresting officers did not have a bit of evidence, known to them and as to which they could take an oath had they gone to a magistrate for a warrant, that petitioner had committed any crime. The arresting officers did not know the grounds on which the informer based his conclusion; nor did they seek to find out what they were. They acted solely on the informer's word. In my view that was not enough . . .
>
> . . . Evidence required to prove guilt is not necessary. But the attendant circumstances must be sufficient to give rise in the mind of the arresting officer at least to inferences of guilt . . . If he takes the law into his own hands and does not seek the protection of a warrant, he must act on some evidence known to him . . . This important requirement should be strictly enforced, lest the whole process of arrest revert . . . to whispered accusations by people.

The rule permitting search without a warrant where incidental to a valid arrest is justified "by the need to seize weapons and other things which might be used to assault an officer or effect an escape, as well as by the need to prevent the destruction of evidence of the crime—things which might easily happen where the weapon or evidence is on the accused's person or under his immediate control."[20] This rationale suggests more limits on the scope of the search than the Court has always imposed.

In 1947 Douglas voted with the Court in the *Harris* case to sustain a five-hour search of a suspect's four-room apartment incident to his valid arrest there, since the entire premises were "under his immediate control."[21] One year later he joined in a decision that, without overruling *Harris*, held that a seizure of evidence in plain view at the time of the suspect's valid arrest at his illegal still was improper where, unlike the situation in *Harris*, the officers had ample opportunity to obtain a search warrant.[22] But that decision was overruled two years later in a

20. Preston v. United States, 376 U.S. 364 (1964).

21. Harris v. United States, 331 U.S. 145 (1947).

22. Tropiano v. United States, 334 U.S. 699 (1948). *See also* Douglas' opinion for the Court in McDonald v. United States, 335 U.S. 451 (1948).

case in which Douglas did not participate.[23] As the Court has proceeded thereafter to test the validity of searches incident to valid arrest by the reasonableness of the scope of the search rather than by the practicability of obtaining a search warrant, he has voted with the Court to hold that an arrest of a suspect two blocks from his home,[24] in an automobile in front of his home,[25] or on the steps of his home[26] will not support a warrantless search of the house,[27] and that an arrest within the suspect's home will not support a warrantless searching of an entire three-bedroom house, including attic, garage, and workshop,[28] or of a sixteen-bedroom house of prostitution.[29] In 1967 he expressly repudiated the *Harris* decision,[30] and in 1971 he voted with a majority of the Court to repudiate it.[31]

The Court's decisions on search of automobiles have followed an even more torturous course than those dealing with the search of homes. They begin with the *Carroll* case, in the Prohibition era, upholding provisions of the National Prohibition Act authorizing seizure of autos carrying illegal liquor and the liquor, and arrest of the occupants, without a warrant. These provisions were held constitutional as applied to permit police to stop an automobile on the highway and search it for illegal liquor, not as an incident to a valid arrest, but where the officer has "reasonable or probable cause for believing that the automobile which he stops and seizes has contraband liquor therein which is being illegally transported." This distinction between a search of a building and a search of a movable vehicle was said to be justified by the fact that "the vehicle can be quickly moved out of the locality or jurisdic-

23. United States v. Rabinowitz, 339 U.S. 56 (1950).

24. James v. Louisiana, 382 U.S. 36 (1965).

25. Shipley v. California, 395 U.S. 818 (1969).

26. Vale v. Louisiana, 399 U.S. 30 (1970).

27. He also voted with the Court to invalidate a warrantless search of defendant's hotel room in California two days before his arrest in Nevada. Stoner v. California, 376 U.S. 483 (1964).

28. Chimel v. California, 395 U.S. 752 (1969). *See also* Kremen v. United States, 353 U.S. 346 (1957).

29. Von Cleef v. New Jersey, 395 U.S. 814 (1969).

30. Gilbert v. California, 388 U.S. 263 (1967) (concurring in part and dissenting in part).

31. Coolidge v. New Hampshire, 403 U.S. 443 (1971).

tion in which the warrant must be sought." Emphasis was also placed on the fact that Congress had provided that the illegal liquor should be destroyed and the automobile in which it was transported forfeited and sold so as to make the case similar to ancient common law practice, with which the framers of the Fourth Amendment must have been familiar, of seizing without warrant and forfeiting goods held in violation of the revenue laws. Here, unlike a case involving private books and papers, "the government is entitled to possession of the property." And where the search thus made without a warrant revealed the commission of a misdemeanor in the officer's presence, it apparently justified the following arrest of the auto's occupants without a warrant.[32]

Douglas later joined in a decision that refused to extend the doctrine of the *Carroll* case to permit the search of the occupant of a parked automobile, not incident to a valid arrest, by Office of Price Administration investigators looking for counterfeit gasoline rationing coupons. Assuming that the investigators had reasonable cause for searching the car under the *Carroll* doctrine, and even though counterfeit ration coupons, like illegal liquor, were contraband, the Court concluded that a right to make a warrantless search of the car did not confer a right to make a warrantless search of its occupants any more than a search warrant for a residence only would authorize a search of all persons found in it. But the opinion of the Court also raised substantial doubts as to whether a warrantless search of an auto on reasonable cause would be held "reasonable" under the Fourth Amendment unless expressly authorized by Congress, as it was in the *Carroll* case.[33] While Douglas

32. Carroll v. United States, 267 U.S. 132 (1925). *See also* Husty v. United States, 282 U.S. 694 (1931). *Cf.* Gambino v. United States, 275 U.S. 310 (1927). Scher v. United States, 305 U.S. 251 (1938), extended the doctrine of *Carroll* to permit the officer to pursue the automobile into the driver's own garage, holding that where a search just before the car entered the garage would have been legal, "passage of the car into the open garage closely followed by the observing officer" should not change matters.

33. United States v. Di Re, note 4, *supra. Cf.* Davis v. United States, 328 U.S. 582 (1946), where Douglas wrote for the Court to sustain a finding that an operator of a gasoline service station had voluntary surrendered unlawfully possessed ration coupons to inspectors for the Office of Price Administration who had first succeeded in making an illegal purchase of gasoline at his station without coupons. "The search was . . . where petitioner transacted his business. Moreover, the officers

also joined in a subsequent decision upholding a warrantless automobile search for illegally transported liquor where the facts were very similar to *Carroll* but the applicable federal statutes did not expressly authorize search without a warrant,[34] he wrote for the Court to invalidate a warrantless search of an auto, which produced stolen radios, where not incident to a valid arrest because the warrantless arrest which accompanied it was not justified by probable cause.[35]

He also voted with the Court in the *Preston* case to hold that a valid arrest of vagrancy suspects in a parked car will not support a search of the car in a garage to which it was towed after the suspects were booked and jailed, although the search produced loaded revolvers and evidence of conspiracy to rob a bank. "Once an accused is under arrest and in custody, then a search made at another place, without a warrant, is simply not incident to the arrest . . . At this point there was no danger that any of the men arrested could have used any weapons in the car or could have destroyed any evidence of a crime."[36]

But he dissented when the Court sustained the search of an auto, in a garage to which it had been towed a week after its occupants' arrest on a narcotics charge, because applicable law required the arresting officers to impound the car and hold it for forfeiture. Since the car was "validly held by officers," the Court thought the search reasonable. Douglas contended that the rule of *Preston* should be applied, since the police

---

demanded the coupons on the basis that they were the property of the Government . . . Where officers seek to inspect *public* documents at the place of business where they are required to be kept, permissible limits of persuasion are not so narrow as where *private* papers are sought. The demand is one of right. When the custodian is persuaded by argument that it is his duty to surrender them and he hands them over, duress and coercion will not be so readily implied as where private papers are involved." The surrender being voluntary, there was no "seizure" within the meaning of the Fourth Amendment.

34. Brinegar v. United States, 338 U.S. 160 (1949).

35. Henry v. United States, 361 U.S. 98 (1959). *See also* Rios v. United States, 364 U.S. 253 (1960), where he joined in an opinion indicating that the validity of a warrantless search of the taxicab in which the suspect was riding depended on probable cause for his warrantless arrest on a narcotics charge.

36. Preston v. United States, 376 U.S. 364 (1964). *Cf.* Dyke v. Taylor Implement Mfg. Co., 391 U.S. 216 (1968) (dissenting opinion).

there also held the car "validly," though they were under no obligation to hold it:[37]

There are those who do not like *Preston.* I think, however, it states a healthy rule, protecting the zone of privacy of the individual as prescribed by the Fourth Amendment. These days police often take possession of cars, towing them away when improperly parked. Those cars are "validly" held by the police. Yet if they can be searched without a warrant, the precincts of the individual are invaded and the barriers to privacy breached. Unless the search is incident to an arrest, I would insist that the police obtain a warrant to search a man's car just as they must do to search his home.

But Douglas voted with the Court in the *Chambers* case[38] sustaining the search of an auto where police, acting on reports describing the car and the dress of its occupants following a robbery, arrested the suspects in the car, drove the car to the police station, and then searched it. While the search was not incident to the arrest under the *Preston* rule, the decision in *Carroll*[39] was said to support the warrantless search because here the police had probable cause "to search the car for guns and stolen money," which they found. In *Preston*, it was now noted, the officers who arrested suspects for vagrancy had no cause to believe that evidence of crime was concealed in the auto. The Court also noted that, if a warrant were required, the car or its contents might be removed before a warrant could be obtained, so that it might be necessary to permit the police to immobilize the car until a warrant could be issued by a magistrate. And it could "see no difference between on the one hand seizing and holding a car before presenting the probable cause issue to a magistrate and on the other hand carrying out an immediate search without a warrant" subject to later review on the probable cause issue.

37. Cooper v. California, 386 U.S. 58 (1967) (dissenting opinion). But he concurred with the Court's decision that no search had occurred where, after a suspect's arrest on robbery charge, the police impounded his car as evidence, and after it was towed to the police station an officer, who was closing the windows in the car against rain, observed and took possession of the automobile registration card lying on the floor of the car. Harris v. United States, 390 U.S. 234 (1968) (concurring opinion).

38. Chambers v. Maroney, 399 U.S. 42 (1970).

39. Note 32, *supra.*

In the most recent case involving automobiles, Douglas voted with the Court to hold that a valid arrest of a murder suspect in his home three weeks after police began investigating him would not support the impounding of his auto parked in his driveway and the search of it two days later. But he also joined in a plurality opinion which would limit the "automobile exception" from search warrant requirements to cases where "it is not practicable to obtain a warrant."[40]

The suspect may, of course, consent to a search without a warrant, but that consent may not be given for him by hotel clerks or managers.[41] And, in a decision in which Douglas joined, the Court held that a consent to search given to an officer who claims to have a warrant, but who either has no warrant or has an invalid warrant, is not an effective consent but only an "acquiescence to a claim of lawful authority" which did not, in fact, exist.[42] Douglas wrote for the Court, however, to hold that a government contractor may waive his rights under both the Fourth and the Fifth Amendments by agreeing in his contract that his records shall be open at all times to government inspection.[43] And he voted with the Court to hold that there was no search, and hence no violation of the Fourth Amendment, where police interrogated a murder suspect's wife while he was in custody, and she voluntarily turned over his guns to them in "a spontaneous, good faith effort . . . to clear him of suspicion."[44]

The Court, in the *Miller* decision in which Douglas joined, has also held in the exercise of its supervisory powers over federal justice that, where an arrest and search would otherwise be lawful because the search was made by federal officers incident to an arrest on probable cause or pursuant to warrant, it becomes illegal where officers do not first identify themselves and state their purpose for demanding admis-

40. Coolidge v. New Hampshire, 403 U.S. 443 (1971).

41. United States v. Jeffers, 342 U.S. 48 (1951); Stoner v. California, 376 U.S. 483 (1964). *Cf.* Davis v. United States, 328 U.S. 582 (1946).

42. Bumper v. North Carolina, 391 U.S. 543 (1968).

43. Zap v. United States, 328 U.S. 624 (1946).

44. Coolidge v. New Hampshire, 403 U.S. 443 (1971). Douglas also concurred in a decision holding that, where defendant and a co-defendant both stored clothing in a duffel bag kept at the co-defendant's home, the latter as a joint user had authority to consent to a search of the bag. Frazier v. Cupp, 394 U.S. 731 (1969) (concurring in result).

sion, at least where there are no "exigent circumstances" arising out of peril to the officers or others or the possibility that the person to be arrested may flee or destroy evidence.[45]

But the Court later held that state officers did not violate the Fourth Amendment when, moving to arrest defendant on probable cause on a narcotics charge, they obtained a key from his apartment manager and entered his apartment surreptitiously. Assuming that the use of the manager's key was equivalent to a forcible entry, the Court concluded that the "no-knock" entry was reasonable because of "exigent circumstances." The danger that defendant would destroy narcotics in his possession, plus the fact that defendant had previously eluded the officers as they followed his car, which "was ground for the belief that he might well have been expecting the police," made a previous announcement of identity and purpose unnecessary. Douglas joined in a dissent which took the position that "the Fourth Amendment is violated by an unannounced police intrusion into a private home, with or without an arrest warrant, except (1) where the persons within already know of the officers' authority and purpose, or (2) where the officers are justified in the belief that persons within are in imminent peril of bodily harm, or (3) where those within, made aware of the presence of someone outside (because, for example, there has been a knock at the door), are then engaged in activity which justifies the officers in the belief that an escape or the destruction of evidence is being attempted":[46]

Any exception not requiring a showing of such awareness necessarily implies a rejection of the inviolable presumption of innocence. The excuse for failing to knock or announce the officer's mission where the occupants are oblivious to his presence can only be an almost automatic assumption that the suspect within will resist the officer's attempt to enter peacefully, or will frustrate the arrest by an attempt to escape, or will attempt to destroy whatever possibly incriminating evidence he may have. Such assumptions do obvious violence to the presumption of innocence. Indeed, the violence is compounded by another assumption,

45. Miller v. United States, 357 U.S. 301 (1958). *See also* Wong Sun v. United States, note 5, *supra* (concurring opinion).

46. Ker v. California, 374 U.S. 23 (1963) (dissenting opinion).

also necessarily involved, that a suspect to whom the officer first makes known his presence will further violate the law. It need hardly be said that not every suspect is in fact guilty of the offense of which he is suspected, and that not everyone who is in fact guilty will forcibly resist arrest or attempt to escape or destroy evidence . . .

. . . Practical hazards of law enforcement militate strongly against any relaxation of the requirement of awareness. First, cases of mistaken identity are surely not novel in the investigation of crime. The possibility is very real that the police may be misinformed as to the name or address of a suspect, or as to other material information. That possibility is itself a good reason for holding a tight rein against judicial approval of unannounced police entries into private homes. Innocent citizens should not suffer the shock, fright or embarrassment attendant upon an unannounced police intrusion. Second, the requirement of awareness also serves to minimize the hazards of the officers' dangerous calling. We expressly recognized in *Miller* v. *United States* . . . that the federal notice [requirement] "is also a safeguard for the police themselves who might be mistaken for prowlers and be shot down by a fearful householder."

The decision of the majority in this case doubtless facilitated the enactment by Congress in 1970 of a statute, applicable only in the District of Columbia, authorizing the issuance of arrest and search warrants which expressly permit forcible entry by officers without prior announcement of their identity.[47]

In 1921 the Court held that a search otherwise legal must be confined to the instrumentalities by which a crime is committed, such as burglar tools; the fruits of crime, such as stolen property; weapons by which an escape of a person arrested might be effected; and contraband—property the possession of which is a crime. But if the search went beyond that and produced "merely evidentiary materials" (in that case, documents taken from defendants's office), such materials could not be used against the defendant.[48] In 1967 the Court rejected that distinction in a case where the otherwise lawful search of the house of an armed robbery suspect had produced not only a shotgun and a pistol and

47. District of Col. Code §23-591.

48. Gouled v. United States, 255 U.S. 298 (1921). *See also* Harris v. United States, note 21, *supra.*

ammunition for both, but also items of clothing which were later admitted in evidence against him. "Privacy is disturbed no more," the Court said, "by a search directed to a purely evidentiary object than it is by a search directed to an instrumentality, fruit, or contraband. A magistrate can intervene in both situations, and the requirements of probable cause and specificity can be preserved intact." Douglas dissented:[49]

> [The Fourth Amendment] has been thought, until today, to have two faces of privacy:
>
> (1) One creates a zone of privacy that may not be invaded by the police through raids, by legislators through laws, or by magistrates through the issuance of warrants.
>
> (2) A second creates a zone of privacy that may be invaded either by the police in hot pursuit or by a search incident to arrest or by a warrant issued by a magistrate on a showing of probable cause . . .
>
> The right of privacy protected by the Fourth Amendment relates in part of course to the precincts of the home or the office. But it does not make them sanctuaries where the law can never reach . . . We have no such sanctuaries . . . A policeman in "hot pursuit" or an officer with a search warrant can enter any house, any room, any building, any office. The privacy of those *places* is of course protected against invasion except in limited situations. The full privacy protected by the Fourth Amendment is, however, reached when we come to books, pamphlets, papers, letters, documents, and other personal effects. Unless they are contraband or instruments of the crime, they may not be reached by any warrant . . . Any invasion whatsoever of those personal effects is "unreasonable" within the meaning of the Fourth Amendment . . .
>
> . . . The personal effects and possessions of the individual (all contraband and the like excepted) are sacrosanct from prying eyes, from the long arm of the law, from any rummaging by police. [The privacy protected by the Fourth Amendment] involves the choice of the individual to disclose or to reveal what he believes, what he thinks, what he possesses. The article may be a nondescript work of art, a manuscript of a book, a personal account book, a diary, invoices, personal clothing, jewelry or whatnot. Those who wrote the Bill of Rights believed that every individual needs both to communicate with others and to keep his affairs to himself. That dual aspect of privacy means that the individual should have the freedom to select for himself

49. Warden v. Hayden, 387 U.S. 294 (1967) (dissenting opinion).

the time and circumstances when he will share his secrets with others and to decide the extent of that sharing . . . The Framers . . . knew what police surveillance meant and how the practice of rummaging through one's personal effects could destroy freedom.

Where a search is illegal, both the evidence seized[50] and the "fruits of the poisonous tree"[51] —other evidence obtained as a consequence of the search—are inadmissible in evidence. Douglas concurred in a decision which held that statements made by defendant following an illegal arrest were included among the inadmissible "fruits."[52] He has disagreed with the Court's ruling that the exclusionary rule is available only to the persons whose rights are violated, so that evidence obtained by an illegal search of one defendant may be used against other defendants,[53] and has voted with the Court to hold that incriminating testimony given by the defendant about the search in an unsuccessful effort to exclude the evidence seized cannot be used against him, since that would force him "either to give up what he believed, with advice of counsel, to be a valid Fourth Amendment claim or, in legal effect, to waive his Fifth Amendment privilege against self-incrimination."[54] But he dissented when the Court held that illegally seized evidence could be admitted at the trial for the limited purpose of impeaching defendant's testimony.[55]

The practice of the police to "stop and frisk" suspects on the street has also presented Fourth Amendment problems for the Court. In one such case an officer, observing two men on a public street in the middle of the afternoon, noted that first one, then the other, would walk down the street a distance, look into the window of a particular store, and then return, and that they repeated this ritual five or six times apiece. Suspecting that they were "casing a stick-up" job, he stopped them, frisked them, and came up with two revolvers and some ammunition which were later used to convict them of carrying concealed weapons.

50. Weeks v. United States, note 18, *supra. See also* Fahy v. Connecticut, 375 U.S. 85 (1963).
51. Silverthorne Lumber Co., v. United States, 251 U.S. 385 (1920).
52. Wong Sun v. United States, note 5, *supra* (concurring opinion).
53. Alderman v. United States, 394 U.S. 165 (1969) (dissenting in part).
54. Simmons v. United States, 390 U.S. 377 (1968).
55. Walder v. United States, 347 U.S. 62 (1954).

The Court rejected arguments that the "stop and frisk" did not amount to an arrest and search, but it held that the "warrant clause" of the Fourth Amendment applied only "wherever practicable" and that, apart from that clause, the search and seizure here were "reasonable" within the meaning of that amendment. The governmental interest in effective crime prevention justified the officer's approaching the men, whose acts "warranted further investigation," even though there was no probable cause to make an arrest. And he was justified also in searching them for weapons which might be used against him while he was making a further investigation, since he had "reasonable grounds to believe" that they were "armed and dangerous." Ergo, the weapons were admissible in evidence. Douglas alone dissented:[56]

> The opinion of the Court disclaims the existence of "probable cause." If loitering were in issue and that was the offense charged, there would be "probable cause" shown. But the crime here is carrying concealed weapons; and there is no basis for concluding that the officer had "probable cause" for believing that that crime was being committed. Had a warrant been sought, a magistrate would, therefore, have been unauthorized to issue one, for he can act only if there is a showing of "probable cause." We hold today that the police have greater authority to make a "seizure" and conduct a "search" than a judge has to authorize such action. We have said precisely the opposite over and over again . . .
>
> There have been powerful hydraulic pressures throughout our history that bear heavily on the Court to water down constitutional guarantees and give the police the upper hand. That hydraulic pressure has probably never been greater than it is today.
>
> Yet if the individual is no longer to be sovereign, if the police can pick him up whenever they do not like the cut of his jib, if they can "seize" and "search" him in their discretion, we enter a new regime. The decision to make it should be made only after a full debate by the people of this country [and a constitutional amendment].

The Court in companion cases considered a state "stop and frisk" law authorizing an officer to act whenever he "reasonably suspects" that a person has committed, is committing, or is about to commit a felony. The state court had applied the law to allow the use, in a prosecution

56. Terry v. Ohio, 392 U.S. 1 (1968) (dissenting opinion).

for unlawful possession of heroin, of quantities of that drug found by an officer who stopped and frisked a man simply because he saw him talking to a number of known narcotics addicts over a period of eight hours. The Court invalidated this application of the law. Such observations were held not to supply a "reasonable inference" that the person observed was engaged in criminal traffic in narcotics nor the basis for "reasonable fear of life or limb on the part of the police officer." At the same time, however, the Court sustained a conviction under the law for possessing burglar tools with intent to commit a crime where an officer from his own apartment saw two men tiptoeing in the hallway of the building. They began running when he came through the door, he chased them down two flights, apprehended one, and took the tools from his pocket. This officer was held to be "reasonably suspicious" of the activities of the man he apprehended, and, once he had stopped him, the officer "reasonably suspected that he was in danger of life or limb, even though he held [the suspect] at gun point." Douglas concurred in both holdings, but thought as to the second that the officer had "probable cause" to believe that the suspect was on a burglary mission, so that the arrest was valid and the search was a lawful incident of the arrest.[57]

Douglas has also voted with the Court to hold that taking a person to police headquarters solely to take his fingerprints, during an "investigatory stage" wherein some twenty-four persons were rounded up and fingerprinted, was nonetheless an arrest under the Fourth Amendment which was invalid because of lack of probable cause or warrant, so that the fingerprints were not admissible in evidence.[58] He also wrote for the Court to hold that there was, in the circumstances of the case, no violation of the Fourth Amendment where a post office detained mailed packages for one day to enable police to make a sufficient investigation of the sender and the addressees to obtain probable cause for issuance of a search warrant—taking the occasion to reemphasize a much earlier decision that the postal authorities have no power to inspect first class mail without a warrant.[59]

57. Sibron v. New York, 392 U.S. 40 (1968) (concurring opinion).
58. Davis v. Mississippi, 394 U.S. 721 (1969).
59. United States v. Van Leeuwen, 397 U.S. 249 (1970).

When, in 1959, the Court held that a city could authorize its health inspectors to inspect private homes without warrants because "no evidence for criminal prosecution is sought to be seized," Douglas dissented on the ground that the invasion of privacy was as great, regardless of its purpose. "One invasion of privacy by an official of government can be as oppressive as another. Health inspectors are important. But they are hardly more important than the search for narcotic peddlers, rapists, kidnapers, murderers, and other criminal elements . . . Many today would think that the search for subversives was even more important than the search for unsanitary conditions. It would seem that the public interest in protecting privacy is equally as great in one case as in another."[60] He dissented again when an equally divided Court affirmed a state decision holding building inspectors free of the Fourth Amendment in their inspection of homes.[61] He also dissented when the Court permitted, in the trial of a Russian spy, the use of evidence obtained by a search of the suspect's hotel room incident to an "administrative arrest" made by the immigration service of the Justice Department on a warrant issued by the immigration service.[62] In cases decided in 1967 involving health inspection of a private home[63] and fire inspection of a commercial warehouse,[64] the Court adopted the dissenters' view: "It is surely anomalous to say that the individual and his private property are fully protected by the Fourth Amendment only when the individual is suspected of criminal behavior." Such routine administrative inspections of entire areas must be authorized by warrants issued on "probable cause" which, in this context, may be based on "appraisal of

60. Frank v. Maryland, 359 U.S. 360 (1959) (dissenting opinion).

61. Eaton v. Price, 364 U.S. 263 (1960) (dissenting opinion). *See also* Eaton v. Price, 360 U.S. 246 (1959).

62. Abel v. United States, 362 U.S 217 (1959) (dissenting opinion).

63. Camara v. Municipal Court, 387 U.S. 523 (1967).

64. See v. Seattle, 387 U.S. 541 (1967). Douglas wrote for the Court in Colonnade Catering Corp. v. United States, 397 U.S. 72 (1970), conceding that the rule of the *See* and *Camara* cases would not prevent Congress from authorizing administrative inspection without warrant of licensed liquor dealers suspected of trafficking in liquor on which no tax had been paid. But he concluded that where Congress had prescribed a criminal penalty for licensees who refused to permit the inspection, that was the sole sanction. Officials were not entitled to make a forcible entry, and where they did so, evidence which they seized could not be used in court.

conditions in the area as a whole, not on . . . conditions in each particular building."

But in 1971 the Court held that a state could deny welfare aid to a mother for her dependent child when the mother refused to permit a caseworker to visit her home without a warrant, even though she offered to supply all "reasonable and relevant information" elsewhere. The visit was not a "search" within the meaning of the Fourth Amendment, the Court said, even though the caseworker's purposes were "investigative" as well as "rehabilitative." The visit was "not forced or compelled," and when the welfare recipient refused to consent to it, there was no visit and the aid "merely ceased." Alternatively, if the visit was viewed as a search, it was a reasonable one within the meaning of the Fourth Amendment. "One who dispenses purely private charity naturally has an interest in and expects to know how his charitable funds are . . . put to work. The public, when it is the provider, rightly expects the same." And this proposed visit was no midnight raid. The recipient received written notice several days in advance. Douglas dissented:[65]

> We are living in a society where one of the most important forms of property is government largesse which some call the "new property." The payrolls of government are but one aspect of that "new property." Defense contracts, highway contracts, and the other multifarious forms of contracts are another part. So are subsidies to air, rail, and other carriers. So are disbursements for scientific research. So are TV and radio licenses to use the air space which of course is a part of the public domain. Our concern here is not with those subsidies but with grants that directly or indirectly implicate the *home life* of the recipient.
>
> In 1969 roughly 126 billion dollars were spent by the federal, state, and local governments on "social welfare." To farmers alone, whose numbers totalled 128,987, nearly four billion was paid, in part for not growing certain crops. Those payments were in some instances very large, a few running a million or more a year. But the majority were payments under $5,000 each.
>
> Yet almost every beneficiary whether rich or poor, rural or urban, has a "house"—one of the places protected by the Fourth Amendment . . . The question in this case is whether receipt of largesse from the

65. Wyman v. James, 400 U.S. 309 (1971) (dissenting opinion).

government makes the *home* of the beneficiary subject to access by an inspector of the agency of oversight, even though the beneficiary objects to the intrusion and even though the Fourth Amendment's procedure for access to one's *house* or *home* is not followed. The penalty here is not, of course, invasion of the privacy of Barbara James, only her loss of [government] largesse. That, however, is merely rephrasing the problem. Whatever the semantics, the central question is whether the government by force of its largesse has the power to "buy up" rights guaranteed by the Constitution . . .

If the welfare recipient was not Barbara James but a prominent, affluent cotton or wheat farmer receiving benefit payments for not growing crops, would not the approach be different? . . . But Constitutional rights—here the privacy of the home—are obviously not dependent on the poverty or the affluence of the beneficiary . . .

I would place the same restrictions on inspectors entering the *homes* of welfare beneficiaries as are on inspectors entering the *homes* of those on the payroll of the government, or the *homes* of those who contract with the government, or the *homes* of those who work for those having government contracts. The values of the home protected by the Fourth Amendment are not peculiar to capitalism as we have known it; they are equally relevant to the new form of socialism which we are entering. Moreover as the numbers of functionaries and inspectors multiply, the need for protection of the individual becomes indeed more essential if the values of a free society are to remain.

Closely akin to the search warrant is the administrative subpoena, issued by a department or agency investigating possible violations of a statute it is charged with administering, and enforcible, if it is resisted, by a court order. Douglas joined in a decision of the Court which treated such a subpoena as subject to the Fourth Amendment. Hence, when the agency sought a court order to compel compliance, the court could, if the party whose records are subpoened raised the points, inquire into whether the subpoena was sufficiently specific as to the evidence sought and as to whether there was "probable cause" for the inquiry, that is, whether the agency was authorized to make the investigation and whether the evidence sought was relevant to the investigation.[66]

66. Oklahoma Press Publishing Co. v. Walling, 327 U.S. 186 (1946). *See also* United States v. Morton Salt Co., 338 U.S. 632 (1950), a decision in which Douglas did not participate.

Long before Douglas came to the Court, it had held that no Fourth Amendment rights of a taxpayer were infringed when the Internal Revenue Service, investigating his tax liability, summoned his bank to produce *its* records pertaining to him.[67] In 1971 the Court applied the same rule to sustain an IRS summons to a taxpayer's former employer seeking the employer's records pertaining to the taxpayer. It held that the taxpayer had no standing to challenge the summons, even though a possible result of the investigation might be criminal prosecution, so long as no indictment was pending and the investigation was directed at least in part to tax liability and not "solely for criminal purposes." Douglas concurred, since the records sought were those of the employer rather than the taxpayer, but took the occasion to note his disagreement with the IRS position that, in its ensuing investigation, the taxpayer had no right to attend, to cross-examine other witnesses, and to offer rebutting evidence.[68]

As many of the decisions discussed above reveal, the Fourth Amendment is now applied to the states. That result came about by a two-step process. In 1949 in *Wolf v. Colorado*, the Court decided that the amendment's prohibition of unreasonable searches and seizures was implicit in "the concept of ordered liberty"[69] and therefore incorporated by the Fourteenth. But the exclusionary rule applied where federal authorities obtain evidence by illegal search, that it was to be excluded from evidence in any later trial,[70] was held not applicable to the states. They were left free to select "the means by which the right should be made effective," either by adopting their own exclusionary rules, by allowing the person whose rights were violated to recover damages from the police, or by disciplining the police. Hence, the Court affirmed a conviction in a state case in which illegally seized evidence had been used. Douglas dissented on the ground that this left the Fourth Amendment's application to the states with "no effective sanction."[71]

67. First National Bank of Mobile v. United States, 267 U.S. 576 (1925). *See also* Justice v. United States, 390 U.S. 199 (1968).

68. Donaldson v. United States, 400 U.S. 517 (1971) (concurring opinion). *See also* United States v. Minker, 350 U.S. 179 (1956) (concurring opinion).

69. See p. 177, *supra*.

70. Weeks v. United States, note 18, *supra*.

71. Wolf v. Colorado, 338 U.S. 25 (1949) (dissenting opinion).

For the next twelve years he persisted in that dissent as the Court refused to sanction injunctions against use of illegally obtained evidence by the states[72] or to upset convictions based on that use.[73] And he wrote for the Court to hold that, in the exercise of its supervisory authority over federal law enforcement, it would approve of an injunction against a federal agent testifying in a state prosecution on the basis of evidence illegally seized by that agent[74] and to interpret the Ku Klux Act of 1871[75] to provide a federal remedy in damages against state officers for the victim of an illegal arrest and search.[76] He also joined in decisions rejecting the notion that federal authorities could use in federal prosecutions evidence illegally seized by state officers and turned over to the federal officials "on a silver platter"—whether the federal officers had a hand in the search[77] or had nothing to do with it.[78]

Then in 1961, in a decision in which Douglas concurred,[79] the Court reconsidered its position, noted the "obvious futility of relegating the Fourth Amendment to the protection of other remedies," and concluded that the exclusionary rule was "an essential ingredient of . . . the Fourth Amendment," so that the states were constitutionally forbidden to use evidence obtained by illegal search.

Just as technological changes have raised problems about impartial grand juries and fair trials,[80] so they have raised problems under the Fourth Amendment. In *Olmstead v. United States*,[81] decided in 1928 over the dissents of Justices Holmes, Brandeis, Butler, and Stone, the Court held that government wiretapping did not violate the Fourth

72. Stefanelli v. Minard, 342 U.S. 117 (1951) (dissenting opinion).

73. Salsburg v. Maryland, 346 U.S. 545 (1954) (dissenting opinion); Irvine v. California, 347 U.S. 128 (1954) (dissenting opinion).

74. Rea v. United States, 350 U.S. 214 (1956). *See also* Wilson v. Schnettler, 365 U.S. 381 (1961) (dissenting opinion).

75. See p. 138, *supra*.

76. Monroe v. Pape, 365 U.S. 167 (1961).

77. Lustig v. United States, 338 U.S. 74 (1949) (concurring opinion). *See also* Byars v. United States, 273 U.S. 28 (1927).

78. Elkins v. United States, 364 U.S. 206 (1960); Rios v. United States, note 35, *supra*. *See also* Gambino v. United States, note 32, *supra*.

79. Mapp v. Ohio, 367 U.S. 643 (1961) (concurring opinion).

80. See pp. 168-170, *supra*.

81. 277 U.S. 438 (1928).

Amendment and that evidence so obtained could be used in a criminal trial. Thereafter, Congress enacted the Communications Act of 1934 containing a provision that "no person not being authorized by the sender shall intercept any communication and divulge or publish the . . . contents . . . of such intercepted communication to any person." [82] Before Douglas came to the Court, it had held that evidence obtained by a federal officer by tapping telephone wires was not admissible in a federal prosecution. "No person" was read to include federal agents, and to allow the federal agent to testify in court about the contents of the intercepted message would be to "divulge" those contents to "any person."[83] Douglas has since voted with the Court to hold that this provision is not confined to interstate communication, and that disclosure is not "authorized by the sender" when a co-defendant who has pleaded guilty to federal charges is willing to read the transcript of the federal government's tap of his telephone conversations with a defendant standing trial. Neither party to the conversation had authorized the interception, and the transcripts were revealed to the prosecutor prior to the co-defendant's "enforced agreement to publication."[84] He voted with the Court again to hold that the act forbade not only use in a federal prosecution of the contents of the intercepted message, but also the "fruit of the poisonous tree"—other evidence obtained as a consequence of the illegal tap.[85] And he also voted with the Court to hold that this sanction was not available to one not a party to the intercepted conversation—co-defendants who were not standing trial with defendant could testify after using the government's illegal taps of their conversations with each other to refresh their recollections.[86]

Thereafter, at a time when he was also dissenting from the Court's refusal to apply the exclusionary rule of the Fourth Amendment to the states so as to forbid their use of evidence obtained by unconstitutional searches, Douglas also dissented when the Court held in *Schwartz v. Texas* that the states might use evidence obtained by wiretaps illegal

82. 47 U.S.C. §605.
83. Nardone v. United States, 302 U.S. 379 (1937).
84. Weiss v. United States, 308 U.S. 321 (1939).
85. Nardone v. United States, 308 U.S. 338 (1939).
86. Goldstein v. United States, 316 U.S. 114 (1942).

under the Communications Act—basing his dissent on the ground that the wiretapping violated the Fourth Amendment.[87] He voted with the Court to hold that evidence obtained by state officers through illegal wiretaps without participation by federal officers could not be used in a federal prosecution,[88] and dissented in *Rathbun v. United States* [89] when the Court refused to apply the rule to the federal use of contents of a conversation with defendant overheard by a state officer on a telephone extension with the consent of the other party to the conversation. He rejected the Court's conclusion that such use of the extension phone was not an "interception" within the meaning of the Act and contended that it was illegal unless authorized by defendant.

In 1968 the Court overruled *Schwartz v. Texas* and narrowly confined *Rathbun v. United States*, to hold that the Communications Act forbids states to use evidence obtained by an illegal interception and to find one where the telephone company had, at the direction of local police, connected a telephone in a neighboring house to defendant's party line, from which vantage point the police listened to his telephone conversations.[90]

Meanwhile, more sophisticated methods of eavesdropping were being developed which were not covered by the Communications Act. Early in his service on the Court Douglas voted with a majority in *Goldman v. United States*[91] to hold, following the *Olmstead* decision,[92] that neither the Communications Act nor the Fourth Amendment was violated where the eavesdropping was done by means of a detectaphone applied, without "trespass," by federal agents in an adjoining office to the partition wall of defendant's office.

Ten years later he concluded that he had been wrong to concur in

87. Schwartz v. Texas, 344 U.S. 199 (1952) (dissenting opinion). *See also* Pugach v. Dollinger, 365 U.S. 458 (1961) (dissenting opinion).

88. Benanti v. United States, 355 U.S. 96 (1955). *Cf.* text at notes 77-78, *supra.*

89. 355 U.S. 107 (1957) (dissenting opinion).

90. Lee v. Florida, 392 U.S. 378 (1968). *See also* Douglas' dissent from the Court's refusal to review convictions based on conversations of defendants obtained when an informer placed telephone calls to defendants and then permitted government agents to listen to or record the conversations. Hudson v. United States, 402 U.S. 965 (1971).

91. 316 U.S. 129 (1942).

92. See text at note 81, *supra.*

that holding, however, and so announced in *On Lee v. United States*, where he dissented from a decision that there was no violation of the Fourth Amendment where the police sent into defendant's place of business an informer and erstwhile friend wired for sound:[93]

Since [the *Goldman* decision] various aspects of the problem have appeared again and again in the cases coming before us. I now more fully appreciate the vice of the practices spawned by *Olmstead* and *Goldman*. Reflecting on them has brought new insight to me. I now feel that I was wrong in the *Goldman* case. Mr. Justice Brandeis in his dissent in *Olmstead* espoused the cause of privacy—the right to be let alone. What he wrote is an historic statement of that point of view.

[Brandeis had said, in 1928, in part: "The progress of science in furnishing the Government with means of espionage is not likely to stop with wire-tapping. Ways may some day be developed by which the Government, without removing papers from secret drawers, can reproduce them in Court, and by which it will be enabled to expose to a jury the most intimate occurrences of the home. Advances in the psychic and related sciences may bring means of exploring unexpressed beliefs, thoughts and emotions . . . The makers of our Constitution . . . conferred, as against the Government, the right to be let alone—the most comprehensive of rights and the right most valued by civilized men. To protect that right, every unjustifiable intrusion by the Government upon the privacy of the individual, whatever the means employed, must be deemed a violation of the Fourth Amendment."]

. . . It is important to civil liberties that we pay more than lip service to the view [expressed by Justice Holmes in his dissent in *Olmstead*] that this manner of obtaining evidence against people is "dirty business."

Douglas continued to urge the overruling of *Olmstead* and *Goldman* as the Court found the Fourth Amendment violated by use of a "spike mike" inserted from a neighbor's adjoining row house through a crevice in the party wall, since this involved a "physical trespass," "an unauthorized physical penetration into the premises occupied by the petitioners,"[94] but no trespass and hence no violation where an Internal Revenue agent wired for sound gained admission to defendant's office by feigning willingness to accept a bribe.[95]

93. On Lee v. United States, 343 U.S. 747 (1952) (disserting opinion).
94. Silverman v. United States, 365 U.S. 505 (1961) (concurring opinion).
95. Lopez v. United States, 373 U.S. 427 (1963) (dissenting opinion).

Indeed, he has gone further with respect to the use of informers. The Court found no violation of the Fourth Amendment and affirmed a conviction in the *Hoffa* case, where an erstwhile friend of the defendant's repeated to the police conversations had with the defendant, whether or not the government had "placed" the friend in defendant's midst for that purpose, since the friend did not enter defendant's hotel room "by force or stealth." Douglas urged that the case should not be reviewed since the record was clear that the government had not "placed" the friend in defendant's councils—thus indicating that he regarded that factor as crucial.[96] At the same time he dissented from a holding in the *Lewis* case that the Fourth Amendment permitted a federal narcotics agent to testify to conversations with defendant after he gained entry to defendant's home by misrepresenting his identity and feigning willingness to buy narcotics.[97] He dissented also from a decision in the *Osborn* case permitting the use of a tape recording of conversations between Hoffa's lawyer and a police officer hired by the lawyer to assist in investigative work in a federal criminal trial, but who was at the same time working for the federal government on the case, and who, with the approval of the federal district court on the basis of a "detailed factual affidavit," was wired for sound in order to record conversations which were later used against the lawyer in a prosecution for attempted bribery of jurors.[98] In a single dissenting opinion he dealt with all three cases:

> We are rapidly entering the age of no privacy, where everyone is open to surveillance at all times; where there are no secrets from government. The aggressive breaches of privacy by the Government increase by geometric proportions. Wiretapping and "bugging" run rampant, without effective judicial or legislative control.
>
> Secret observation booths in government offices and closed television circuits in industry, extending even to rest rooms, are common. Offices, conference rooms, hotel rooms, and even bedrooms . . . are "bugged" for the convenience of government. Peepholes in men's rooms are there to catch homosexuals . . . Personality tests seek to ferret out a man's

96. Hoffa v. United States, 385 U.S. 293 (1966) (separate opinion).
97. Lewis v. United States, 385 U.S. 206 (1966) (dissenting opinion).
98. Osborn v. United States, 385 U.S. 323 (1966) (dissenting opinion).

innermost thoughts on family life, religion, racial attitudes, national origin, politics, atheism, ideology, sex and the like. Federal agents are often "wired" so that their conversations are either recorded on their persons . . . or transmitted to tape recorders some blocks away. The Food and Drug Administration recently put a spy in a church organization. Revenue agents have gone in the disguise of Coast Guard officers. They have broken and entered homes to obtain evidence.

Polygraph tests of government employees and of employees in industry are rampant. The dossiers on all citizens mount in number and increase in size. Now they are being put on computers so that by pressing one button all the miserable, the sick, the suspect, the unpopular, the off-beat people of the Nation can be instantly identified . . .

We have here in the District of Columbia squads of officers who work the men's rooms in public buildings trying to get homosexuals to solicit them . . . Undercover agents or "special employees" of narcotics divisions of city, state, and federal police actively solicit sales of narcotics . . . Police are instructed to pander to the weakensses and craven motives of friends and acquaintances of suspects, in order to induce them to inform . . . In many cases the crime had not yet been committed. The undercover agent may enter a suspect's home and make a search upon mere suspicion that a crime will be committed. He is indeed often the instigator of, and active participant in, the crime—an *agent provocateur*. Of course, when the solicitation by the concealed government agent goes so far as to amount to entrapment, the prosecution fails . . . But the "dirty business" does not begin or end with entrapment. Entrapment is merely a facet of a much broader problem. Together with illegal searches and seizures, coerced confessions, wiretapping, and bugging, it represents lawless invasion of privacy. It is indicative of a philosophy that the ends justify the means.

We are here concerned with the manner in which government agents enter private homes. In *Lewis* the undercover agent appeared as a prospective customer. Tomorrow he may be a policeman disguised as the grocery deliveryman or telephone repairman . . .

Entering another's home in disguise to obtain evidence is a "search" that should bring into play all the protective features of the Fourth Amendment. When the agent in *Lewis* had reason for believing that petitioner possessed narcotics, a search warrant should have been obtained . . .

The formula approved today by the Court in *Hoffa* . . . makes it possible for the Government to use willy-nilly, son against father, nephew against uncle, friend against friend to undermine the sanctity of the most private and confidential of all conversations. The Court takes the position that whether or not the Government "placed" Partin in Hoffa's counsels is immaterial . . . But very real differences underlie [that factor] . . . A person may take the risk that a friend will turn on him and report to the police. But that is far different from the Government's "planting" a friend in the person's entourage so that he can secure incriminating evidence . . . The Government has actively encouraged and participated in a breach of privacy by sending in an undercover agent . . . The Government unlawfully enters a man's home when its agent crawls through a window, breaks down a door, enters surreptitiously, or, as alleged here, gets in by trickery and fraud . . .

Once electronic surveillance . . . is added to the techniques of snooping which this sophisticated age has developed, we face the stark reality that the walls of privacy have broken down and all the tools of the police state are handed over to our bureaucracy on a constitutional platter. The Court pays lip service to this danger in *Osborn* . . . but goes on to approve what was done in that case for another reason. In *Osborn*, use of the electronic device was approved by . . . the District Court in advance of its use. But what the Court overlooks is that the Fourth Amendment does not authorize warrants to issue for *any* search even on a showing of probable cause . . .

It was . . . held in *Gouled* v. *United States*[99] . . . that a search warrant "may not be used as a means of gaining access to a man's house or office and papers solely for the purpose of making search to secure evidence to be used against him in a criminal or penal proceeding" but only to obtain contraband articles or the tools with which a crime had been committed . . .

I would adhere to *Gouled* and bar the use of all testimonial evidence obtained by wiretapping or by an electronic device.

In 1967 in the *Berger* case the Court invalidated a New York statute authorizing eavesdropping on a court order issued upon the oath or affirmation of a police officer, as used to authorize a "trepassory intrusion" consisting of the installing of recording devices in defendant's office. The statute was found to conflict with the Fourth Amendment in several particulars, some of which also characterize a new 1968 federal eavesdropping law:[100] (1) While it required the officer's statement to assert that "there is reasonable ground to believe

99. See text at note 48, *supra*.
100. 18 U.S.C. §2518.

that evidence of a crime may be thus obtained" and to "particularly describe the persons" whose conversations were to be overheard, it did not require particularity in the court order as to the specific crime involved, or the "place to be searched" or the "things [conversations] to be seized." (2) It authorized eavesdropping for a two-month period, renewable for additional two-month periods, during which "the conversations of any and all persons coming into the area covered by the device will be seized indiscriminately and without regard to their connection with the crime under investigation." (3) It did not provide for termination of the eavesdropping authority once the conversation sought was obtained. (4) It gave the suspect no notice, "as do conventional warrants," and did not "overcome this defect" by requiring a showing of "exigent circumstances." The Court also noted that the statute might be further defective in substituting "reasonable grounds" for "probable cause" and in failing to provide for a return on the warrant, "thereby leaving full discretion in the officer as to the use of seized conversations of innocent as well as guilty parties." Douglas concurred, "because at long last [the Court] overrules *sub silentio* *Olmstead* v. *United States* . . . and its offspring," but reiterated his objection to any use of electronic surveillance to obtain "mere evidence" as distinguished from contraband and instrumentalities of crime, which, as he had maintained in his recent dissent from the decision allowing searches for "mere evidence,"[101] "is a violation of the Fourth and Fifth Amendments, no matter with what nicety and precision a warrant may be drawn."[102]

Later in the same year, in the *Katz* case, the Court rejected its earlier notion that the Fourth Amendment was confined to a "trespass" or a "physical intrusion" of any given area—"the Fourth Amendment protects people, not places"—expressly overruled *Olmstead* and *Goldman*, and held illegal the interception of defendant's telephone conversations by means of an electronic device attached to the outside of a public telephone booth. The Court noted, however, that a judicial order "could constitutionally have authorized, with appropriate safeguards,

101. See text at note 49, *supra*.
102. Berger v. New York, 388 U.S. 41 (1967) (concurring opinion).

the very limited search and seizure that the Government asserts in fact took place." Justice White, in a concurring opinion, suggested that the decision did not mean that the Fourth Amendment required "the warrant procedure and the magistrate's judgment if the President of the United States or . . . the Attorney General has considered the requirements of national security and authorized electronic surveillance as reasonable." Douglas wrote a separate concurrence to reply to this suggestion:[103]

I feel compelled to reply to the separate concurring opinion of my Brother White, which I view as a wholly unwarranted green light for the Executive Branch to resort to electronic eavesdropping without a warrant in cases which the Executive Branch itself labels "national security" matters.

Neither the President nor the Attorney General is a magistrate. In matters where they believe national security may be involved they are not detached, disinterested, and neutral as a court or magistrate must be. Under the separation of powers created by the Constitution, the Executive Branch is not supposed to be neutral and disinterested. Rather it should vigorously investigate and prevent breaches of national security and prosecute those who violate the pertinent federal laws. The President and the Attorney General are properly interested parties, cast in the role of adversary, in national security cases. They may even be the intended victims of subversive action. Since spies and saboteurs are as entitled to the protection of the Fourth Amendment as suspected gamblers like petitioner, I cannot agree that where spies and saboteurs are involved adequate protection of Fourth Amendment rights is assured when the President and Attorney General assume both the position of adversary-and-prosecutor and disinterested, neutral magistrate.

There is, so far as I understand constitutional history, no distinction under the Fourth Amendment between types of crimes. Article III, § 3, gives "treason" a very narrow definition and puts restrictions on its proof. But the Fourth Amendment draws no lines between various substantive offenses . . .

I would respect the present lines of distinction and not improvise because a particular crime seems particularly heinous. When the Framers took that step, as they did with treason, the worst crime of all, they made their purpose manifest.

103. Katz v. United States, 389 U.S. 347 (1967) (concurring opinion).

In 1971 the Court refused to reverse a conviction based on conversations which defendant had with a police informer wired for sound. A majority agreed only that the *Katz* decision would not apply retroactively to invalidate police conduct which occurred before *Katz* was decided. But a plurality opinion of four justices took the position that *Katz* did not, in any event, require the overruling of *On Lee v. United States*, which had earlier sanctioned the use of an informer wired for sound.[104] *Katz* was limited, they said, to situations where the government intercepted conversations without the assistance of a party to the conversation,[105] and the Fourth Amendment was held not to protect the defendant's "expectations of privacy" in his conversations with the informer. Douglas, who had dissented from an earlier decision that *Katz* should not be given retroactive effect,[106] dissented again and addressed himself to the plurality opinion:[107]

Electronic surveillance is the greatest leveler of human privacy ever known. How most forms of it can be held "reasonable" within the meaning of the Fourth Amendment is a mystery . . . The concepts of privacy . . . enshrined in the Fourth Amendment vanish completely when we slavishly allow an all-powerful government, proclaiming law and order, efficiency, and other benign purposes, to penetrate all the walls and doors which men need to shield them from the pressures of a turbulent life around them and give them the health and strength to carry on.

That is why a "strict construction" of the Fourth Amendment is necessary if every man's liberty and privacy are to be constitutionally honored . . .

Today no one perhaps notices because only a small, obscure criminal is the victim. But every person is the victim, for the technology we exalt today is man's master . . .

Monitoring, if prevalent, certainly kills free discourse and spontaneous utterances. Free discourse—a First Amendment value—may be frivolous or serious, humble or defiant, reactionary or revolutionary, profane or in good taste; but it is not free if there is surveillance . . .

Now that the discredited [decision] in *On Lee* [is] resuscitated and revived, must everyone live in fear that every word he speaks may be

104. See text at note 93, *supra*.

105. *See also* Hudson v. United States, note 90, *supra*.

106. Desist v. United States, 394 U.S. 244 (1969) (dissenting opinion).

107. United States v. White, 401 U.S. 745 (1971) (dissenting opinion).

transmitted or recorded and later repeated to the entire world? I can imagine nothing that has a more chilling effect on people speaking their minds and expressing their views on important matters. The advocates of that regime should spend some time in totalitarian countries and learn firsthand the kind of a regime they are creating here.

In a series of cases which began reaching the Court in 1965, the solicitor general disclosed that FBI or other federal agents had engaged in illegal electronic interception. Douglas has joined with the Court in such cases to order a new trial where overheard conversations were between defendant and his lawyer,[108] and, where there was no intrusion into attorney-client discussions, to remand the case to the trial court for an evidentiary hearing on the question whether illegally obtained evidence had contributed to the conviction.[109] When the defendant in one case brought to the Court's attention the possibility of such illegal activity, and the solicitor general advised the Court that "the policy of the Department of Justice [is] to make disclosure to the courts if it finds (1) that a defendant was present or participated in a conversation overheard by unlawful electronic surveillance, and (2) that the government has thereby obtained any information which is arguably relevant to the litigation involved," Douglas joined with the Court in refusing to accept "the Department's *ex parte* determination" that nothing overheard was "arguably relevant" to the case, and in remanding to the trial court for hearing on the issue.[110] He voted with the Court again to reject the government's next argument, that the surveillance records should first be screened for "arguable relevance" by the trial judge and only those selected by him should be disclosed to defendant. The defendant was entitled to examine all records concerning him, including those containing "national security" information. And, since the Fourth Amendment protects "houses" as well as "effects," the defendant had standing to object to any evidence obtained by electronic surveillance of his own conversations or of those of third persons on his premises (Douglas would have extended the exclusion to

108. Black v. United States, 385 U.S. 26 (1966); O'Brien v. United States, 386 U.S. 345 (1967).

109. Hoffa v. United States, 387 U.S. 231 (1967); Roberts v. United States, 389 U.S. 18 (1967); Giordano v. United States, 394 U.S. 310 (1969).

110. Kolod v. United States, 390 U.S. 136 (1968).

all conversations of co-defendants and co-conspirators wherever overheard).[111]

Douglas dissented when the Court declined to review a case in which the trial court refused to exclude all evidence tainted by an "astounding record of lawless invasion" consisting of "bugging" defendant's office for over a year, his lawyer's office for almost six months, his secretary's office-apartment for eight months, forcible entry into the secretary's office by FBI agents who photographed files, and an illegal search of that office by Internal Revenue agents. In addition, both sets of agents kept the secretary's office under surveillance through a peephole in a door across the hall, and the Post Office Department kept a "mail cover" on defendant, recording the addressees and senders of all mail delivered to addresses believed connected with defendant.[112]

In the Court's most recent decision under the Fourth Amendment, Douglas voted with the majority to hold that the victim of a search and arrest by federal agents which violates the Fourth Amendment may maintain an action for damages in a federal court even though no federal statute authorizes such a remedy.[113] The Court rejected the government's argument that the only consequence of violation of the Fourth Amendment by federal agents should be to subject them to liability as measured by the applicable state law of trespass as between private citizens. The *Katz* case[114] was said to have "made it clear beyond peradventure that the Fourth Amendment is not tied to the niceties of local trespass laws." And one who alleges an unconstitutional search and seizure "states a cause of action under the Fourth Amendment."[115]

111. Alderman v. United States, note 53, *supra. See also* Cook v. United States, 401 U.S. 996 (1971), where Douglas dissented from the Court's refusal to review a case in which he was not satisfied with the government's denial that any electronic surveillance had occurred. *Cf.* Taglianetti v. United States, 394 U.S. 316 (1969), where he voted with the Court to hold that the trail judge could intervene to screen out those records of the conversations of others as to which defendant had no standing to object.

112. Balistrieri v. United States, 394 U.S. 985 (1969) (dissenting opinion).

113. The Ku Klux Act, under which Monroe v. Pape, note 76, *supra,* was decided applies only to persons acting under color of *state* law.

114. See text at note 103, *supra.*

115. Bivens v. Six Unknown Named Agents of Federal Bureau of Narcotics, 403 U.S. 388 (1971).

10 SELF–INCRIMINATION

The Fifth Amendment provides that no person "shall be compelled in any Criminal case to be a witness against himself." Long before Douglas came to the Court, it had been held that a witness who did not expressly invoke the privilege waived it,[1] and that the privilege was available in any federal proceeding, civil or ciminal, whenever "the answer might tend to subject to criminal responsibility him who gives it."[2] It had further been held that, where the Congress undertook to confer statutory immunity so as to make the privilege unavailable, the statute must confer immunity not only from use of the witness' testimony in a later criminal proceeding against him, but also from prosecution based on other evidence obtained by use of that testimony.[3] In other early cases the Court had also held that a federal immunity statute may,[4] but need not,[5] confer immunity from state prosecutions also, that (assuming a state immunity statute was subject to constitutional test under the Fourteenth Amendment) it need not confer immunity from federal prosecution,[6] and that a witness in a

1. Vajtauer v. Commissioner, 273 U.S. 103 (1927). *See also* United States v. Kordel, 377 U.S. 1 (1970).

2. McCarthy v. Arndstein, 266 U.S. 34 (1924).

3. Counselman v. Hitchcock, 142 U.S. 547 (1892).

4. Brown v. Walker, 161 U.S. 591 (1896).

5. Hale v. Henkel, 201 U.S. 43 (1906).

6. Jack v. Kansas, 199 U.S. 372 (1905).

federal proceeding could not base his claim of the privilege on fear of state prosecution.[7] But the privilege was held to be available in a proceeding to forfeit goods illegally imported without payment of customs duties.[8]

It had also been held that a corporate official had no privilege against disclosing corporate records, as distinguished from his private papers,[9] and that the privilege was not available to corporations.[10]

While early decisions had held that a bankrupt in his own bankruptcy proceeding who had not yet made "an actual admission of guilt or incriminating facts . . . is not deprived of the privilege of stopping short in his testimony wherever it may fairly tend to incriminate him,"[11] a different rule was applied to a defendant who took the stand in a criminal prosecution. He waived the privilege against self-incrimination as to all questions on cross-examination relevant to his testimony on direct examination,[12] although not as to "collateral crimes" unconnected with the charge.[13] While it was also held proper to instruct the jury, after a defendant in a criminal case had testified, to take into consideration his failure to deny or explain incriminating aspects of the prosecution's case,[14] a federal statute providing that the failure of a defendant in a criminal case to take the stand "shall not create any presumption against him"[15] was interpreted to mean that the prosecutor may not comment on the defendant's failure to testify.[16]

Douglas later voted with the Court to hold that the same statute entitles a nontestifying defendant to have the jury instructed, if he so requests, to give no weight to his failure to testify,[17] and wrote for the

7. United States v. Murdock, 284 U.S. 141 (1931).

8. Boyd v. United States, 116 U.S. 616 (1886).

9. Hale v. Henkel, note 5, *supra*.

10. Wilson v. United States, 221 U.S. 361 (1911); Essgee Co. v. United States, 262 U.S. 151 (1923). *See also* United States v. Kordel, note 1, *supra*.

11. McCarthy v. Arndstein, 262 U.S. 355 (1923); McCarthy v. Arndstein, note 2, *supra*.

12. Fitzpatrick v. United States, 178 U.S. 304 (1900); Raffel v. United States, 271 U.S. 494 (1926).

13. Boyd v. United States, 142 U.S. 450 (1892).

14. Caminetti v. United States, 242 U.S. 470 (1917).

15. Now 18 U.S.C. §3481.

16. Wilson v. United States, 149 U.S. 60 (1895).

17. Bruno v. United States, 308 U.S. 287 (1939).

Court to hold that where a testifying defendant claimed the privilege and the court sustained his claim it was improper for the prosecutor to comment upon his invocation of the privilege.[18] But he joined dissenters when the Court held, at a time when the Fifth Amendment privilege was not held applicable to the states, that the federal government could prosecute a defendant on the basis of testimony he was compelled to give in a state proceeding so long as federal officials were not a party to the compulsion, contending that the Fifth Amendment forbade the federal government to use compelled incriminating testimony no matter what government supplied the compulsion.[19]

Douglas voted with the Court to hold that an officer of an unincorporated labor union had no privilege with respect to union records and that the privilege was not available to the union.[20] He voted with a unanimous Court to hold, however, that a union official can invoke the privilege when asked of his knowledge of the whereabouts of union records, though he had no privilege as to the records themselves.[21] And, as previously noted, he wrote for the Court to hold that an individual contracting with the government may waive his rights under both the Fourth and Fifth Amendments by agreeing in his contract that his records shall be open at all times to government inspection.[22] But he dissented when the Court interpreted a federal immunity statute to confer immunity on a witness who testified before a grand jury without invoking his privilege against self-incrimination or in any way indicating that his testimony was being given in return for the statutory immunity.[23] Thereafter, however, he voted with the Court to hold that a witness who first claimed the privilege, answered some questions, and later answered further questions after specifically disclaiming immunity

18. Johnson v. United States, 318 U.S. 189 (1943). Douglas later dissented when the Court held that no reversible error was committed when a federal prosecutor called two co-defendants on a gambling charge who had pleaded guilty and, knowing that they would invoke the privilege, asked them questions about their relationships with the defendant. Namet v. United States, 373 U.S. 179 (1963) (dissenting opinion). Compare text at notes 6-7, p. 280, *infra*.

19. Feldman v. United States, 322 U.S. 487 (1944) (dissenting opinion).

20. United States v. White, 322 U.S. 694 (1944).

21. Curcio v. United States, 354 U.S. 118 (1957).

22. Zap v. United States, note 43, p. 193, *supra*.

23. United States v. Monia, 317 U.S. 424 (1943) (dissenting opinion).

as to them, was entitled to immunity from prosecution for matters covered by the answers as to which the privilege was asserted.[24]

He also joined in decisions of the Court holding that witnesses before a federal grand jury could decline to answer questions concerning their connections with the Communist Party of Colorado, since the answers "would have furnished a link in the chain of evidence needed in a prosecution of petitioner for violation of (or conspiracy to violate) the Smith Act."[25] But he joined in dissent from a decision that another witness before the same grand jury who testified in September 1948 that she had been treasurer of the Communist party of Denver until January 1948, and in that capacity had possession of the membership lists and dues records of the organization but testified that she had since turned them over to another, had gone so far in her testimony that she had waived her privilege and could not invoke it when asked to name the person to whom she had delivered the records. The dissenters thought this ruling left witnesses in a dilemma:[26] "On the one hand, they risk imprisonment for contempt by asserting the privilege prematurely; on the other, they might lose the privilege if they answer a single question. The Court's view makes the protection depend on timing so refined that lawyers, let alone laymen, will have difficulty in knowing when to claim it."

As previously noted, Douglas later voted with the Court to hold that witnesses summoned before the House Un-American Activities Committee could invoke the privilege when questioned about alleged membership in the Communist party,[27] or about membership in organizations cited by the Committee as "Communist fronts," or about associations with persons suspected of having Communist affiliations.[28]

Douglas joined the dissenters again when the Court held that the defendant in a denaturalization proceeding who takes the stand and testifies in his own behalf is to be treated like a defendant in a criminal case, rather than like a bankrupt summoned to testify in his own

24. Smith v. United States, 337 U.S. 137 (1949).

25. Blau v. United States, 340 U.S. 159 (1950); Blau v. United States, 340 U.S. 332 (1951).

26. Rogers v. United States, 340 U.S. 367 (1951) (dissenting opinion).

27. Quinn v. United States, note 124, p. 81, *supra*.

28. Emspak v. United States, note 124, p. 81, *supra*.

bankruptcy proceedings,[29] and cannot on cross-examination invoke the privilege as to any matters relevant to his direct examination. Again the dissenters thought the decision placed the witness in a dilemma:[30]

> The rule of waiver now applied in criminal cases, although long accepted, is itself debatable and should not be carried over to any new area absent the most compelling justification. By likening the position of a defendant who voluntarily takes the stand in a civil case to that of an accused testifying on his own behalf in a criminal prosecution the majority unfortunately fails to give due consideration to material differences between the two situations. For example failure of a criminal defendant to take the stand may not be made the subject of adverse comment by prosecutor or judge, nor may it lawfully support an inference of guilt. *Wilson* v. *United States* . . . [31] On the other hand the failure of a party in a civil action to testify may be freely commented on by his adversary and the trier of fact may draw such inferences from the abstention as he sees fit on the issues in the case . . . Thus to apply the criminal rule of waiver to a civil proceeding may place a defendant in a substantial dilemma. If he testifies voluntarily he can be compelled to give incriminating evidence against himself; but, unlike a defendant in a criminal case, if he remains off the stand his silence can be used against him.

Douglas joined in dissent again when the Court, at a time when the Fifth Amendment's privilege was not held applicable to the states, affirmed an earlier holding[32] that no federal constitutional provision was violated where a state compelled a witness to testify by granting immunity from state but not federal prosecution. The dissenters urged a reconsideration of the earlier decision[33] that testimony compelled by state authorities could be used in a federal prosecution, so that a person could not be "whipsawed into incriminating himself under both state and federal law even though there is a privilege against self-incrimination in the Constitution of each."[34]

29. See text at note 11, *supra.*
30. Brown v. United States, 356 U.S. 148 (1958) (dissenting opinion).
31. Note 16, *supra.*
32. See text at note 6, *supra.*
33. Feldman v. United States, note 19, *supra.*
34. Knapp v. Schweitzer, 357 U.S. 371 (1958) (dissenting opinion). *See also* Mills v. Louisiana, 360 U.S. 230 (1959) (dissenting opinion).

Douglas thereafter voted with the Court when it avoided reconsideration of an earlier decision that the federal privilege does not extend to testimony which may incriminate under state law[35] by construing a federal immunity statute to confer immunity from both state and federal prosecution and by reaffirming another early decision[36] that Congress had power to grant such immunity.[37]

Earlier, he had dissented when the Court held sufficient to eliminate the Fifth Amendment privilege of a grand jury witness, questioned about his and others' membership in the Communist party, the federal Immunity Act of 1954, which confers immunity from state or federal prosecution. He urged that the decision in *Boyd v. United States*, [38] holding the privilege available in a proceeding to forfeit goods illegally imported without payment of custom duties, should be read to entitle the witness to invoke the privilege despite the Immunity Act or, alternatively, that the decision in *Brown v. Walker*,[39] first finding a similar immunity law sufficient to eliminate the privilege, should be overruled:[40]

There are numerous disabilities created by federal law that attach to a person who is a Communist. These disabilities include ineligibility for employment in the Federal Government and in defense facilities, disqualification for a passport, the risk of internment, the risk of loss of employment as a longshoreman—to mention only a few. These disabilities imposed by federal law are forfeitures . . .

The forfeiture of property on compelled testimony [as in the *Boyd* case] is no more abhorrent than the forfeiture of rights of citizenship. Any forfeiture of rights as a result of compelled testimony is at war with the Fifth Amendment.

The Court apparently distinguishes the *Boyd* case on the ground that the forfeiture of property was a penalty affixed to a criminal act. The loss of a job and the ineligibility for a passport are also penalties affixed to a criminal act. For the case of *Dennis* v. *United States* . . . [41] makes

35. United States v. Murdock, note 7, *supra.*

36. Brown v. Walker, note 4, *supra.*

37. Reina v. United States, 364 U.S. 507 (1960). *See also* Adams v. Maryland, 347 U.S. 179 (1954).

38. Note 8, *supra.*

39. Note 4, *supra.*

40. Ullman v. United States, 350 U.S. 422 (1956) (dissenting opinion).

41. Note 83, p. 68, *supra.*

plain that membership in the Communist Party is a crucial link of evidence for conviction under the Smith Act . . . When a man loses a job because he is a Communist, there is as much a penalty suffered as when an importer loses property because he is a tax evader . . . And the Constitution places the property rights involved in the *Boyd* case no higher than the rights of citizenship involved here. . .

Second, as to *Brown* v. *Walker*. The difficulty I have with that decision and with the majority of the Court in the present case is that they add an important qualification to the Fifth Amendment . . . Wisely or not, the Fifth Amendment protects against the compulsory self-accusation of crime without exception or qualification. In *Counselman* v. *Hitchcock*[42] . . . Mr. Justice Blatchford said, "The privilege is limited to criminal matters, but it is as broad as the mischief against which it seeks to guard."

The "mischief" to be prevented falls under at least three heads.

(1) One "mischief" is not only the risk of conviction but the risk of prosecution . . . [The Immunity Act] protects the accused only on account of the "transaction, matter, or thing" concerning which he is compelled to testify . . . The forced disclosure may open up vast new vistas for the prosecutor with leads to numerous accusations not within the purview of the question and answer. What related offenses may be disclosed by leads furnished by the confession? How remote need the offense be before the immunity ceases to protect it? How much litigation will it take to determine it? . . .

The Court leaves all those uncertainties to another day, saying that the immunity granted by Congress will extend to its constitutional limits and that those constitutional limits will be determined case by case in future litigation. That means that no one knows what the limits are . . .

The concession of the Court underlines my point. It shows that the privilege of silence is exchanged for a partial, undefined, vague immunity. It means that Congress has granted far less than it has taken away.[43]

42. Note 3, *supra*.

43. Douglas later dissented when, after the Fifth Amendment had been held applicable to the states, the Court declined to review a New York prosecution which he thought conferred only a "use" immunity and not the full "transactional" immunity required by the Fifth Amendment. Under grant of immunity the defendant had admitted before a grand jury that he had assaulted another with tire irons. A police officer then testified before the grand jury that he had arrested the defendant and taken the tire irons from him and that defendant tried to bribe him to "get rid of" the tire irons. Defendant was then indicted for and convicted of

(2) The guarantee against self-incrimination . . . is not only a protection against conviction and prosecution but a safeguard of conscience and human dignity and freedom of expression as well. My view is that the Framers put it beyond the powr of Congress to *compel* anyone to confess his crimes. The evil to be guarded against was partly self-accusation under legal compulsion. But that was only a part of the evil . . . The Framers . . . created the federally protected right of silence and decreed that the law could not be used to pry open one's lips and make him a witness against himself.

A long history and a deep sentiment lay behind this decision . . .

The Court, by forgetting that history, robs the Fifth Amendment of one of the great purposes it was designed to serve . . . The Fifth Amendment protects the conscience and the dignity of the individual, as well as his safety and security, against the compulsion of government.

(3) This right of silence . . . serves another high purpose. Mr. Justice Field, one of the four dissenters in *Brown* v. *Walker*, stated that it is the aim of the Fifth Amendment to protect the accused from compulsory testimony "which would expose him to infamy and disgrace" as well as that which might lead to a criminal conviction . . .

There is great infamy involved in the present case, apart from the loss of rights of citizenship under federal law which I have already mentioned. The disclosure that a person is a Communist practically excommunicates him from society. School boards will not hire him . . . A lawyer risks exclusion from the bar . . . a doctor, the revocation of his license to practice . . . If an actor, he is on a blacklist . . . And he will be able to find no employment in our society except at the lowest level, if at all . . .

It is no answer to say that a witness who exercises his Fifth Amendment right of silence . . . may bring himself into disrepute. If so, that is the price he pays for exercising the right of silence granted by the Fifth Amendment. The critical point is that the Constitution places the right of silence *beyond the reach of government* . . . When public opinion casts a person into outer darkness, as happens today when a person is exposed as a Communist, the government brings infamy on the head of the witness when it compels disclosure. That is precisely what the Fifth Amendment prohibits.

---

attempted bribery, the New York Court of Appeals ruling that the immunity statute did not prevent the prosecution because defendant gave no testimony as to the bribery attempt. Piccirillo v. New York, 400 U.S. 548 (1971) (dissenting opinion).

Consistently with these views, Douglas joined with the Court in the *Slochower* case to hold that a city may not discharge a college professor solely because he invokes his federal privilege against self-incrimination when questioned about past Communist party membership by the Senate Internal Security Subcommittee. To infer guilt from invocation of a privilege available to the innocent as well as the guilty is to violate due process.[44] And he dissented where the Court held that the state could, without denial of due process, dismiss a subway conductor who, when questioned by state authorities about Communist party membership, invoked the Fifth Amendment privilege at a time when it was not held applicable to the states. The Court found that no inference of guilt had been drawn from the erroneous claim of the privilege, but that a justifiable inference of "unreliability" had been based on the conductor's "lack of frankness." Douglas contended that the action violated the Fifth Amendment, which he considered applicable to the states.[45] He dissented again when the Court found no denial of due process where a state discharged a social worker because he refused, on First and Fifth Amendment grounds, to answer questions about his political affiliations when summoned by the House Committee on Un-American Activities. The Court found the case different from *Slochower* because the state had ordered the employee in advance to answer the Committee's questions and had "not predicated discharge on any 'built-in' inference of guilt . . . but solely on employee insubordination for failure to give information which . . . the state has a legitimate interest in securing." The dissenters saw no difference between this case and *Slochower*, since the employee's "insubordination" consisted exclusively of his refusal to answer the Committee's questions

44. Slochower v. Board of Education, 350 U.S. 551 (1956) (concurring opinion). *See also* his votes with the Court to hold that due process is denied where a state refuses to admit an applicant to practice law because of irrational inferences of lack of "moral character" drawn from the applicant's good faith belief that the First Amendment allowed him to refuse to answer the examining committee's questions about political associations and beliefs, Konigsberg v. State Bar, note 107, p. 76, *supra*, or because of such inferences drawn from the fact of Communist party membership fifteen years earlier. Schware v. Board of Bar Examiners, note 107, p. 76, *supra*.

45. Lerner v. Casey, 357 U.S. 468 (1958) (dissenting opinion).

and a ground for refusal was the privilege against self-incrimination: [46] "The Federal Constitution told [the employee] he could, without penalty, refuse to incriminate himself before any arm of the Federal Government; California, however, has deprived him of his job solely because he exercised this federal constitutional privilege . . . I would hold that no state can put any kind of penalty on any person for claiming a privilege authorized by the Federal Constitution."

Douglas joined the dissenters once more when, in *Cohen v. Hurley*, [47] the Court held a state could disbar a lawyer who, in a state inquiry into "ambulance chasing," invoked his state constitutional privilege against self-incrimination. Again the Court was satisfied that the state had not drawn any irrational inference of guilt which would violate the due process clause—the state had found the lawyer's refusal to answer "contrary to the standards of candor and frankness that are required and expected of a lawyer to the court." Douglas contended that the Fifth Amendment's privilege should be held applicable to the states and that, in any event, the Court disposed of the case "on a ground that, from the standpoint of the legal profession, is the most far-reaching possible—that lawyers have fewer constitutional rights than others." "If the legal profession can, with the aid of those members of the profession who have become judges, exclude any member it wishes even though such exclusion could not be accomplished within the limits of the same kind of due process that is accorded to other people, how is any lawyer going to be able to take a position or defend a cause that is likely to incur the displeasure of the judges or whatever group of his fellow lawyers happens to have authority over him? The answer is that

46. Nelson v. Los Angeles County, 362 U.S. 1 (1960) (dissenting opinions). *See also* Beilan v. Board of Education, note 101, p. 73, *supra* (dissenting opinion). Douglas dissented also when the Court later held that states could deny a license to practice law to applicants who "obstructed" investigation into their moral character by refusing to answer questions about their political beliefs and associations. The Court was satisfied that no impermissible inferences had been drawn from the applicant's refusal to provide "unprivileged answers to questions" which were relevant to their qualifications and not protected by the First Amendment. The dissenters contended that the action violated the First Amendment, Konigsberg v. State Bar, note 107, p. 76, *supra* (dissenting opinion); *In re* Anastaplo, note 107, p. 76, *supra* (dissenting opinion).

47. 366 U.S. 117 (1961) (dissenting opinion).

in many cases he is not going to be able to take such a position or to defend such a cause and the public will be deprived of just those legal services that, in the past, have given lawyers their most bona fide claim to greatness."

Douglas dissented again from the treatment given to an alien, who, in deportation proceedings, invoked the Fifth Amendment's privilege when asked if he was a member of the Communist party. The Immigration Act authorizes the immigration service to suspend deportation of an alien who is eligible for admission to the United States and "who has proved good moral character." But that act also provides that members of the Communist party are not eligible for admission. The service declined to suspend deportation on the grounds that the alien had failed to prove good moral character and had not shown that he was not a member of the Communist party. The Court affirmed that action on the sole ground that the alien had not met his burden of proving that he was not a member of the Communist party. Douglas thought that, in the complete absence of any evidence that the alien was a Communist party member, he had no burden of proof to meet:[48]

> Today we allow invocation of the Fifth Amendment to serve, in effect though not in terms, as proof that an alien lacks the "good moral character" which he must have . . . to become eligible for [suspension of deportation].
>
> The statute says nothing about the need of an alien to prove he never was a Communist. If the question of Communist Party membership had never been asked and petitioner had never invoked the Fifth Amendment, can it be that he would still be ineligible for suspension? It is for me unthinkable. Presumption of innocence is too deeply ingrained in our system for me to believe that an alien would have the burden of establishing a negative.

In 1965 Douglas voted with a unanimous Court[49] to hold unconstitutional under the Fifth Amendment those provisions of the Internal Security Act of 1950 which required, once the Subversive Activities Control Board had labeled the Communist party of the United States a "Communist action group," that the group should file a registration

48. Kimm v. Rosenberg, 363 U.S. 405 (1960) (dissenting opinions).
49. Albertson v. Subversive Activities Control Board, 382 U.S. 70 (1965).

statement, including a list of its members, and that, if the group did not do so, the obligation to register should fall upon each member.[50] The party, though labeled by the board, had not registered. The board had found certain persons to be members and ordered them to register for the party. The risks of incrimination which this order placed on them were, to the Court, "obvious." The registration would require them to admit Communist party membership and the admission could be used against them under, "to mention only two federal criminal statutes," the Smith Act or another provision of the Internal Security Act making it a crime to conspire "to perform any act which would substantially contribute to the establishment within the United States of a totalitarian dictatorship." And an immunity provision in the act was not broad enough to eliminate the privilege. Since it only forbade admission of the registration statement in evidence and did not forbid its use as an investigatory lead, it was insufficient under standards established in 1892.[51]

Douglas had long taken the view that other federal statutes were subject to the same constitutional infirmity. He had voted with the Court to establish the "required records" doctrine in a case holding that, where Congress in the World War II Emergency Price Control Act required sellers to maintain sales records "of the same kind customarily kept" in order that "there may be suitable information of transactions which are the appropriate subjects of governmental regulation and the enforcement of restrictions validly established," such records were not "exclusively private" but had "public aspects" and, like the records of corporations, were not protected by the Fifth Amendment.[52] But he took a different view of a provision in the federal revenue act which imposed an excise tax on persons engaged in the business of accepting wagers, required such persons to register annually with the Collector of Internal Revenue, disclosing name and residence, each place of business where wagers were accepted, and the names and addresses of employees, and required that registrants post "conspicuously" in their principal place of business the revenue stamps which denoted payment

50. See p. 76, *supra*.
51. Counselman v. Hitchcock, note 3, *supra*.
52. Shapiro v. United States, 335 U.S. 1 (1948).

of the tax. When in 1953 the Court affirmed the conviction of a Pennsylvanian who had failed to register or pay the tax (gambling being a state crime in Pennsylvania), it held that the registration provisions did not violate the Fifth Amendment because defendant was "not compelled to confess to acts already committed, he is merely informed by the statute that in order to engage in the business of wagering in the future he must fulfill certain conditions." Douglas joined in a brief dissent contending that the federal act "creates a squeezing device contrived to put a man in federal prison if he refuses to confess himself into a state prison as a violator of state gambling laws," and that such use of federal compulsion should be held to violate the Fifth Amendment.[53]

He continued to urge that view as the Court upheld the same act, as applied to one doing business in the District of Columbia, where another federal statute makes wagering a crime.[54] Finally, in 1968, the Court overruled its prior decisions and adopted the dissenting view[55] — when a defendant prosecuted for failure to register and pay the tax properly asserts the Fifth Amendment's privilege against self-incrimination that provides "a complete defense to his prosecution" because the information required to be disclosed would expose him to both federal and state prosecutions. The additional fact that the federal act required registrants to preserve daily records indicating the gross amount of their wagers did not bring the case within the "official records" doctrine,[56] because this was not a requirement that the registrant keep records "of the same kind as he has customarily kept" and there were no "public aspects" to the information required to be kept, which related not to

53. United States v. Kahriger, 345 U.S. 22 (1953) (dissenting opinions). *See also* Irvine v. California, 347 U.S. 128 (1954) (dissenting opinion), where the Court sustained the use of federal tax stamps to obtain a conviction under state anti-gambling laws.

54. Lewis v. United States, 348 U.S. 419 (1955) (dissenting opinions).

55. Marchetti v. United States, 390 U.S. 39 (1968). *See also* Grosso v. United States, 390 U.S. 62 (1968). *Cf.* United States v. Knox, 396 U.S. 77 (1969) (dissenting opinion). Douglas voted with the Court to hold that the claim of privilege also bars an action to forfeit property used in unregistered gambling activities. United States v. United States Coin and Currency, 401 U.S. 715 (1971). *Cf.* One 1958 Plymouth Sedan v. Pennsylvania, note 19, p. 187, *supra*.

56. See text at note 52, *supra*.

"an essentially noncriminal and regulatory area of inquiry" but to a "selective group inherently suspect of criminal activities," as was true of the registration requirements of the Internal Security Act.[57]

Thereafter, Douglas voted with the Court to invalidate on similar grounds the registration provisions of the National Firearms Act[58] and of the federal Marijuana Tax Act.[59] He wrote for the Court, however, to sustain an amended Firearms Act which imposed registration requirements only on the sellers of firearms, forbade persons with prior criminal records to buy firearms, required sellers to obtain from buyers their photographs and fingerprints and a certificate from police officials that the firearm was intended for lawful use, and provided that the information so obtained could not be used, directly or indirectly, in any criminal proceeding for prior or concurrent offenses. To the argument that the immunity conferred did not extend to future crimes, he replied that the privilege against self-incrimination does not supply "insulation for a career of crime about to be launched."[60]

But when the Court upheld a California "hit and run" statute requiring an automobile driver involved in an accident to stop and give his name and address (there are similar statutes in all of the states), he dissented. Reversing the state Supreme Court, which had held that the Fifth Amendment forbade the use of the information required to be disclosed, the Court concluded that this statute, unlike those previously invalidated, was not aimed at persons "inherently suspect of criminal activities" but was, like the reporting requirements of the federal income tax law, "directed at the public at large." Douglas joined in a dissenting opinion which did not so view it:[61]

These suggestions ignore the fact that *this particular respondent* would have run a serious risk of self-incrimination by complying with the disclosure statute. Furthermore, it is hardly accurate to suggest that the activity of driving an automobile in California is not "an area per-

57. See text at notes 50-51, *supra*.

58. Haynes v. United States, 390 U.S. 85 (1968).

59. Leary v. United States, 395 U.S. 6 (1969); United States v. Covington, 395 U.S. 57 (1969).

60. United States v. Freed, 401 U.S. 601 (1971).

61. California v. Byers, 402 U.S. 424 (1971) (dissenting opinion).

meated with criminal statutes" . . . And it is unhelpful to say the statute is not aimed at an "inherently suspect" group because it applies to "all persons who drive automobiles in California" . . . The compelled disclosure is required of all persons who drive automobiles in California *who are involved in accidents causing property damage.* If this group is not "suspect" of illegal activities, it is difficult to find such a group . ,.

I can only assume that the unarticulated premise of the decision is that there is so much crime abroad in this country at present that Bill of Rights' safeguards against arbitrary government must not be completely enforced. I can agree that there is too much crime in the land for us to treat criminals with favor. But I can never agree that we should depart in the slightest way from the Bill of Rights' guarantees that give this country its high place among the free nations of the world. If we affirmed the State Supreme Court, California could still require persons involved in accidents to stop and give their names and addresses. The state would only be denied the power to violate the Fifth Amendment by using the fruits of such compelled testimony against them in criminal proceedings. Instead of criticizing the Supreme Court of California for its rigid protections of individual liberty, I would without more ado affirm its judgment.

As earlier noted, when the Court in 1947 reaffirmed its 1908 decision that the Fourteenth Amendment did not make the Fifth's guarantee against self-incrimination applicable to the states, Douglas joined in a dissent which urged both that the Fourteenth Amendment should be read to incorporate all of the Bill of Rights and that, on any process of "selective incorporation," the privilege against self-incrimination should be made applicable.[62] He continued to urge the privilege's incorporation as the Court held that the forcible use of a stomach pump to recover morphine capsules swallowed by a suspect violated the due process clause of the Fourteenth Amendment and rendered the capsules inadmissible in evidence because it did not "respect certain decencies of civilized conduct" and "shocks the conscience" of the Court,[63] but that the results of a blood test administered to an unconscious drunken driving suspect were constitutionally admissible.[64] He again urged that the privilege should apply to the states when the Court held that a state

62. See pp. 177-178, *supra.*
63. Rochin v. California, 342 U.S. 165 (1952) (concurring opinion).
64. Breithaupt v. Abram, 352 U.S. 432 (1957) (dissenting opinions).

may compel a policeman to waive his rights under an immunity statute by threatening to discharge him and then, after his resignation, hold him in criminal contempt when he fails to answer incriminating questions.[65] He urged the same view in dissent when the Court declined to review a conviction in a state proceeding where the court had instructed the jury that it might take into consideration the defendant's failure to take the witness stand.[66] He dissented again when the Court upheld the contempt conviction of one under state indictment who refused to answer questions of a United States Senate Committee, but did not base his refusal to answer on the Fifth Amendment because a claim of the privilege before the Congressional Committee could have been used against him in his later state trial.[67]

Once more, his views ultimately prevailed. In 1964 the Court held the Fifth Amendment's privilege sufficiently "fundamental" to be applied to the states "according to the same standards that protect . . . against federal encroachment"—including the rule excluding the use of evidence illegally obtained and overruled prior decisions to the contrary.[68] Douglas concurred, but expressed his preference for general rather than selective incorporation of the Bill of Rights into the due process clause of the Fourteenth Amendment.[69]

At the same time Douglas voted with the Court to overrule more prior decisions[70] and to hold that, where either state or federal governments compel testimony by granting immunity, the immunity will protect from prosecution by either—the immediate consequence of the decision being that a witness in a state proceeding who persisted in his refusal to answer questions after grant of immunity because of fear of federal prosecution might be punished by the state for contempt.[71]

Thereafter, Douglas wrote for the Court to hold that the Fifth

65. Regan v. New York, 349 U.S. 58 (1955) (dissenting opinion).

66. Scott v. California, 364 U.S. 471 (1960) (dissenting opinion).

67. Hutcheson v. United States, 369 U.S. 599 (1962) (dissenting opinion). *See also* Cohen v. Hurley, note 47, *supra* (dissenting opinion).

68. Twining v. New Jersey, note 94, p. 176, *supra;* Adamson v. California, note 97, p. 177, *supra.*

69. Malloy v. Hogan, 378 U.S. 1 (1964) (concurring opinion).

70. United States v. Murdock, note 7, *supra;* Feldman v. United States, note 19, *supra.*

71. Murphy v. Waterfront Commission, 378 U.S. 52 (1964).

Amendment forbade a state court to instruct a jury to consider, or the prosecutor to comment on, a defendant's failure to testify in a criminal case. Although the long-standing federal rule to the same effect was embodied in a statute,[72] the requirements of the Fifth Amendment were said to be identical.[73] He wrote for the Court also to overrule *Cohen v. Hurley*[74] and to hold that a lawyer could not be disbarred for invoking his privilege against self-incrimination,[75] and again to hold that policemen who refrained from asserting their privilege because of a state statute providing for the discharge of those who invoked it could not be convicted on the basis of their testimony because it was coerced—the state could not put them to "a choice between the rock and the whirlpool," between loss of employment and forfeiture of constitutional rights.[76]

In other cases Douglas has voted with the Court to hold that a state may not discharge a policeman for his refusal to sign a general waiver of immunity before being called before a grand jury, although, if the policeman had been granted immunity and "had refused to answer questions specifically, directly, and narrowly relating to the performance of his official duties . . . the privilege against self-incrimination would not have been a bar to his dismissal,"[77] and that the same rule applies to sanitation workers.[78]

When, however, the Court held that application of the privilege against self-incrimination to the states did not preclude them from using the results of blood tests taken over the objection of a suspect drunken driver because the privilege extends only to compelled "communications" or "testimony," including documents, but not to "real or

72. See text at notes 15-16, *supra.*

73. Griffin v. California, 380 U.S. 609 (1965). *See also* Chapman v. California, 386 U.S. 18 (1967); Anderson v. Nelson, 390 U.S. 523 (1968).

74. Note 47, *supra.*

75. Spevack v. Klein, 385 U.S. 511 (1967).

76. Garrity v. New Jersey, 385 U.S. 493 (1967). Douglas also wrote for the Court in Stevens v. Marks, 383 U.S. 234 (1966), where, without deciding whether a policeman's waiver of immunity on threat of loss of his job was valid, it was held that he had effectively withdrawn the waiver.

77. Gardner v. Broderick, 392 U.S. 273 (1968).

78. Uniformed Sanitation Men Association, Inc. v. Commissioner, 392 U.S. 280 (1968).

physical evidence," Douglas joined in a dissent which rejected the distinction between "communicative" or "testimonial" evidence and "physical" evidence and contended also that this "forcible blood-letting" violated due process and the right of privacy which in *Griswold v. Connecticut*[79] was held "to be within the penumbra" of several of the specific guarantees of the Bill of Rights.[80] Douglas has continued to dissent as the Court has applied its "testimonial compulsion" test to conclude that the Fifth Amendment does not apply to defendant's handwriting samples[81] and to police lineups.[82]

Douglas dissented also from a decision that a state does not violate the Fifth Amendment when it requires a defendant, in advance of trial, to give the prosecutor notice if he intends to assert an alibi defense and to furnish the prosecutor with the details of his alibi and the names of witnesses he intends to use in support of the defense.[83] He dissented again when the Court held that a closely held family corporation had no standing to challenge a state statute terminating all contracts of the corporation with the state and disqualifying the corporation for five years thereafter from contracting with the state whenever a corporate officer invokes the privilege against self-incrimination before a grand jury, where the statute had been invoked against it because its president had invoked the privilege. Douglas thought that the corporation had standing to seek relief for damage to shareholders resulting from damage to the corporation, and that the damage here was illegally inflicted:[84]

> A corporation, to be sure, is not a beneficiary of the Self-Incrimination Clause, in the sense that it may invoke it . . . Yet placing this family corporation on the blacklist . . . is one way of reaching the economic

79. Note 177, p. 100, *supra.*

80. Schmerber v. California, 384 U.S. 757 (1966) (dissenting opinions).

81. Gilbert v. California, 388 U.S. 263 (1967) (concurring in part and dissenting in part).

82. Gilbert v. California, note 81, *supra;* United States v. Wade, 388 U.S. 218 (1967) (concurring in part and dissenting in part).

83. Williams v. Florida, 399 U.S. 78 (1970) (concurring in part and dissenting in part).

84. George Campbell Painting Corp. v. Reid, 392 U.S. 286 (1968) (dissenting opinion).

interest of the recalcitrant president. If, as I felt in *Spevack* v. *Klein*, . . .[85] placing the penalty of disbarment on a lawyer for invoking the Self-Incrimination Clause is unconstitutional, so is placing a monetary penalty on a businessman for doing the same. Reducing the value of appellant corporation by putting it on the State's blacklist is a penalty which every stockholder suffers. If New York provided that where a businessman invokes the Self-Incrimination Clause . . . he shall forfeit, say, $10,000, the law would plainly be unconstitutional as exacting a penalty for asserting a constitutional privilege . . . Yet penalizing this man's family corporation for his assertion of immunity has precisely that effect.[86]

85. Note 75, *supra.*

86. The development of additional rules governing police interrogations, to implement both the Fifth Amendment's privilege against self-incrimination and the Sixth Amendment's guaranty of a right to counsel, are discussed in Chapter 11.

11 COUNSEL

The Sixth Amendment provides that, "In all criminal prosecutions, the accused shall enjoy the right . . . to have the Assistance of Counsel for his defense."

Shortly before Douglas came to the Court, it read this requirement to mean that, in a federal prosecution for passing counterfeit bills, the government must provide counsel at its expense for an indigent defendant who did not knowingly and intelligently waive his right to counsel.[1] Thereafter, in cases involving federal prosecutions, Douglas voted with the Court to hold that the defendant in a bank robbery case was entitled to the appointment of counsel before entering his plea to the charge,[2] that a defendant who had retained his own lawyer was deprived of his Sixth Amendment rights when the trial court appointed that lawyer also to represent a co-defendant with conflicting interests,[3] and dissented from a decision that the defendant in a prosecution for using the mails to defraud had knowingly and intelligently waived his

1. Johnson v. Zerbst, 304 U.S. 458 (1939). Since 1964 indigent defendants in federal criminal cases, "charged with a felony or a misdemeanor not petty," also have a statutory right to have counsel appointed under the Criminal Justice Act (18 U.S.C. §3006A). *See* Wood v. United States, 389 U.S. 20 (1967).

2. Walker v. Johnston, 312 U.S. 275 (1941). *See also* Von Moltke v. Gillies, 332, U.S. 708 (1948); United States v. Morgan, 346 U.S. 502 (1954).

3. Glasser v. United States, 315 U.S. 60 (1942).

right to the assistance of counsel and his right to jury trial. Douglas did not believe, in view of the complications of the mail fraud law, that a man without legal advice was competent to choose between trial by judge and trial by jury.[4]

In 1932, in the famed *Scottsboro* case,[5] the Court held that young, illiterate defendants prosecuted by the state in a capital case and unable to employ counsel were denied due process of law where the state failed to provide counsel for them in time to prepare their defense. When ten years later, in *Betts v. Brady*, the Court refused to extend this ruling to the case of a farm hand of little education convicted by the state of robbery and sentenced to eight years—holding that the Sixth Amendment right to counsel was not so "fundamental" as to be incorporated by the Fourteenth and that there was no denial of due process because the procedure was not offensive to "common and fundamental ideas of fairness and right"—Douglas joined in a dissent which said in part:[6]

> I believe that the Fourteenth Amendment made the Sixth applicable to the states . . .
>
> A practice cannot be reconciled with "common and fundamental ideas of fairness and right" which subjects innocent men to increased dangers of conviction merely because of their poverty. Whether a man is innocent cannot be determined from a trial in which, as here, denial of counsel has made it impossible to conclude, with any satisfactory degree of certainty, that the defendant's case was adequately presented. No one questions that due process requires a hearing before conviction and sentence for the serious crime of robbery. As the Supreme Court of Wisconsin said, in 1859, " . . . would it not be a little like mockery to secure to a pauper these solemn constitutional guarantees for a fair and full trial of the matter with which he was charged, and yet to say to him when on trial, that he must employ his own counsel, who could alone render these guarantees of any real permanent value to him . . . ? Why this great solicitude to secure him a fair trial if he cannot have the benefit of counsel?"

4. Adams v. McCann, 317 U.S. 269 (1942) (dissenting opinion).
5. Powell v. Alabama, 287 U.S. 45 (1932).
6. Betts v. Brady, 316 U.S. 455 (1942) (dissenting opinion).

Thereafter, in a long series of cases, the Court evolved a test for state prosecutions which it once stated as follows:[7]

When a crime subject to capital punishment is not involved, each case depends on its own facts . . . Where the gravity of the crime and other factors—such as the age and education of the defendant, the conduct of the court or the prosecuting officials, and the complicated nature of the offense charged and the possible defenses thereto—render criminal proceedings without counsel so apt to result in injustice as to be fundamentally unfair . . . the accused must have legal assistance . . . whether he pleads guilty or elects to stand trial, whether he requests counsel or not. Only a waiver of counsel, understandingly made, justifies trial without counsel.

When, in the application of that test, the Court concluded that counsel was required, Douglas voted with the Court.[8] He also voted with the Court to hold that a state denies due process when it requires a defendant in a burglary case to plead to the charge without giving him an opportunity to consult with counsel retained by him,[9] when it requires a defendant to go to trial on habitual criminal charges without giving him an opportunity to retain a lawyer,[10] or when it does not appoint counsel in a capital case until after indictment when, by state law, any challenge to the grand jury on the ground of systematic exclusion of blacks therefrom must be made before indictment.[11] And he wrote for the Court to hold that in a capital case where, by state law, the arraignment is a "critical stage in a criminal proceeding"—because pleas in abatement and challenges to the grand jury must be

7. Uveges v. Pennsylvania, 335 U.S. 437 (1948).

8. *Ex parte* Hawk, 321 U.S. 114 (1944); Williams v. Kaiser, 323 U.S. 471 (1945); Tomkins v. Missouri, 323 U.S. 485 (1945); Rice v. Olson, 324 U.S. 786 (1945); De Meerleer v. Michigan, 329 U.S. 663 (1947); Townsend v. Burke, 334 U.S. 736 (1948); Wade v. Mayo, 334 U.S. 672 (1948); Uveges v. Pennsylvania, note 7, supra; Gibbs v. Burke, 337 U.S. 773 (1949) (concurring opinion); Moore v. Michigan, 355 U.S. 155 (1957); Cash v. Culver, 358 U.S. 633 (1959); McNeal v. Culver, 365 U.S. 109 (1961) (concurring opinion); Chewning v. Cunningham, 368 U.S. 443 (1962); Carnley v. Cochran, 369 U.S. 506 (1962) (concurring opinion).

9. House v. Mayo, 324 U.S. 42 (1945).

10. Chandler v. Fretag, 348 U.S. 3 (1954).

11. Reece v. Georgia, 350 U.S. 85 (1955). *See also* Douglas' dissent in Michel v. Louisiana, 350 U.S. 91 (1955).

made at that time and a defense of insanity can be pleaded thereafter only in the unreviewable discretion of the trial judge—counsel must be provided at arraignment.[12]

But where the Court's case-by-case analysis led it to conclude that no counsel was required in a particular case, Douglas dissented and urged that *Betts v. Brady* be overruled.[13] And he dissented also when the Court found that the defendant in a capital case had knowingly and intelligently waived his right to counsel.[14]

In 1963, in *Gideon v. Wainwright*,[15] a decision in which all of the justices concurred, *Betts v. Brady* was overruled and the Sixth Amendment right to counsel in criminal cases was made applicable to the states.[16]

Since that time Douglas has voted with the Court to hold that where by state law a defendant enters his plea to the charge at a "preliminary hearing" in advance of arraignment, that hearing is a "critical stage in a criminal proceeding" at which he must have counsel.[17] For some time, however, Douglas had been suggesting that, at least where confessions of a defendant were used at his trial, counsel should be required at an even earlier time. In 1958, in *Crooker v. California*, when the Court

12. Hamilton v. Alabama, 368 U.S. 52 (1961).

13. Foster v. Illinois, 332 U.S. 134 (1947) (dissenting opinion); Bute v. Illinois, 333 U.S. 640 (1948) (dissenting opinion); Gryger v. Burke, 334 U.S. 728 (1948) (dissenting opinion). *See also* Gibbs v. Burke, note 8, *supra* (concurring opinion); McNeal v. Culver, note 8, *supra* (concurring opinion); Carnley v. Cochran, note 8, *supra* (concurring opinion).

14. Carter v. Illinois, 329 U.S. 173 (1946) (dissenting opinion).

15. 372 U.S. 335 (1963).

16. It cannot be said with assurance that the Sixth Amendment right to counsel extends to *all* criminal cases. As indicated at pages 21-22, *supra*, and pages 252-253, *infra*, the Court over Douglas' dissent has held that the Sixth Amendment right to jury trial does not extend to "petty offenses," the draftsmen of the Criminal Justice Act (note 1, *supra*) have hazarded that the right to counsel does not extend to "petty" misdemeanors, and the Court recently promulgated, over the dissents of Justices Black and Douglas, Rules of Procedure for The Trial of Minor Offenses before United States Magistrates which make no provision for assignment of counsel or for jury trial in minor offenses which are "petty." 400 U.S. 1031 (1971). As indicated on p. 21, *supra*, a federal statute provides that any federal misdemeanor for which the penalty does not exceed six months imprisonment or a $500 fine is a "petty offense."

17. White v. Maryland, 373 U.S. 59 (1963). *Cf.* text at notes 11 and 12, *supra*, and Coleman v. Alabama, 399 U.S. 1 (1970) (concurring opinion).

found no violation of the due process clause where the state arrested defendant and denied his request for an opportunity to call a lawyer until some five or six hours of interrogation had produced the confession used at his trial, Douglas dissented, protesting that "what takes place in the secret confines of the police station may be more critical than what takes place at the trial," and urging that "the accused who wants counsel should have one at any time after the moment of arrest."[18] When in a later case the Court found that a confession obtained after an indicted defendant had surrendered himself to the police was involuntary and reversed the conviction for that reason, Douglas suggested that, since defendant's request to consult with his counsel had been denied during interrogation, there was "an even more important ground for decision":[19]

We do not have here mere suspects who are being secretly interrogated by the police as in *Crooker* v. *California* . . . This is a case of an accused, who is scheduled to be tried by a judge and jury, being tried in a preliminary way by the police. This is a kangaroo court procedure whereby the police produce the vital evidence in the form of a confession which is useful or necessary to obtain a conviction. They in effect deny him effective representation by counsel. This seems to me to be a flagrant violation of the principle announced in *Powell* v. *Alabama* . . .[20] that the right of counsel extends to the preparation for trial, as well as to the trial itself. As Professor Chafee once said, "A person accused of crime needs a lawyer right after his arrest probably more than at any other time" . . . When he is deprived of that right after indictment and before trial, he may indeed be denied effective representation by counsel at the only stage when legal aid and advice would help him.

As indicated earlier, Douglas had previously argued that confessions obtained while the accused was being held without the arraignment required by state law should be held inadmissible.[21] In 1961 he combined his arguments: "I would hold that any confession obtained

18. Crooker v. California, 357 U.S. 433 (1958) (dissenting opinion). *See also* Ashdown v. Utah, 357 U.S. 426 (1958) (dissenting opinion); Cicenia v. Lagay, 357 U.S. 504 (1958) (dissenting opinion).

19. Spano v. New York, 360 U.S. 315 (1959) (concurring opinion).

20. Note 5, *supra*.

21. Page 167, *supra*.

by the police while the defendant is under detention is inadmissible, unless there is prompt arraignment and unless the accused is informed of his right to silence and accorded an opportunity to consult counsel."[22]

The Court accepted a part of these views in 1964 when it held inadmissible in a federal prosecution conversation overheard by a narcotics agent while defendant, who had been arrested, arraigned, indicted, and released on bail, was sitting in the car of an erstwhile friend which the narcotics agent had wired for sound. Defendant was denied the "basic protections" of the right to counsel, the Court said, "when there was used against him at his trial evidence of his own incriminating words, which federal agents had deliberately elicited from him after he had been indicted and in the absence of his counsel."[23]

More of Douglas' views were adopted in the same year when the Court held inadmissible in a state trial incriminating statements elicited from defendant at the police station, after his arrest but before indictment and after the denial of his request to see his attorney. "Where, as here, the investigation is no longer a general inquiry into an unsolved crime but has begun to focus on a particular suspect, the suspect has been taken into police custody, the police carry out a process of interrogation that lends itself to eliciting incriminating statements, the suspect has requested and been denied an opportunity to consult with his lawyer, and the police have not effectively warned him of his absolute constitutional right to remain silent, the accused has been denied 'the Assistance of Counsel' in violation of the Sixth Amendment." To the state's argument that the decision would mean that "the number of confessions obtained by the police will diminish significantly, because most confessions are obtained during the period between arrest and indictment," the Court replied that that fact merely points up the "critical nature" of that period and that, "If the exercise of constitutional rights will thwart the effectiveness of a system of law enforcement, then there is something very wrong with that system." [24]

Finally, in 1966, the Court adopted Douglas' views on the right to

22. Reck v. Pate, note 42, p. 161, *supra* (concurring opinion). *See also* Culombe v. Connecticut, 367 U.S. 568 (1961) (concurring opinion).

23. Massiah v. United States, 377 U.S. 201 (1964).

24. Escobedo v. Illinois, 378 U.S. 478 (1964). *Cf.* Frazier v. Cupp, 394 U.S. 731 (1969).

counsel entirely in the *Miranda* case,[25] which, in order to implement both the right to counsel and the privilege against self-incrimination, laid down the rules for police officers, state and federal, where statements stemming from custodial interrogation are used in evidence. "Unless other fully effective means are devised to inform accused persons of their right of silence and to assure a continuous opportunity to exercise it," law enforcement officers must observe the following rules "after a person has been taken into custody or otherwise deprived of his freedom in any significant way": (1) "At the outset, if a person in custody is to be subjected to interrogation, he must be informed in clear and unequivocal terms that he has the right to remain silent." (2) "The warning of the right to remain silent must be accompanied by the explanation that anything said can and will be used against the individual in court." (3) "An individual held for interrogation must [also] be clearly informed that he has the right to consult with a lawyer and to have the lawyer with him during interrogation" and "that if he is indigent a lawyer will be appointed to represent him." (4) "If the individual indicates in any manner, at any time prior to or during questioning, that he wishes to remain silent, the interrogation must cease." (5) "If the individual states that he wants an attorney, the interrogation must cease until an attorney is present." (6) While the accused may waive his Fifth Amendment right to remain silent and his Sixth Amendment right to counsel, if the interrogation goes on "without the presence of an attorney and a statement is taken, a heavy burden rests on the government to demonstrate that the defendant knowingly and intelligently waived" those rights.

In cases decided since *Miranda*, Douglas, while disagreeing with the Court's conclusion that placing the defendant in a police lineup does not violate the Fifth Amendment because not involving "testimonial compulsion,"[26] has agreed with the Court that conducting the lineup without notice to and in the absence of his counsel violates the Sixth Amendment. The consequence was, the Court held, that eyewitnesses to the crime charged who identify defendant on the basis of both that observation and such a later police lineup should not be allowed to

25. Miranda v. Arizona, 384 U.S. 436 (1966).

26. See text at note 82, p. 233, *supra*.

identify him in court unless the government establishes "by clear and convincing evidence that the in-court identifications were based upon observations of the suspect other than the lineup identification." And witnesses who did not witness the crime charged, but who identified defendant at such a lineup as one who had committed other crimes should not be allowed to identify him in court. This was necessary, the Court thought, to protect the accused from "instances of suggestive procedures" such as the use of lineups where "all in the lineup but the suspect were known to the identifying witness," or "other participants in a lineup were grossly dissimilar in appearance to the suspect," or where "only the suspect was required to wear distinctive clothing which the culprit allegedly wore."[27]

Douglas also agreed with the Court's suggestion in those cases that the same rule would apply where the suspect alone is presented to witnesses for identification. And he would have applied the rule retroactively, where the Court declined to do so. Hence he dissented when the Court affirmed the conviction in a murder case, in which the victim's wife was also injured, where the defendant was brought to her hospital room and, as he stood handcuffed to a police officer and the only black person in the room, she identified him as the culprit, and both she and several police officers testified at the trial to her previous identification.[28] In another case where an equally divided Court affirmed a conviction based on a rape victim's station-house identification of defendant, Douglas dissented on due process grounds because he thought the police had "maximized the suggestion that petitioner committed the crime."[29] He has also joined with the Court in recognizing that the use of photographs of the suspect and others to enable witnesses to identify the culprit is subject to the same abuses as the police lineup and may be "so impermissibly suggestive as to give rise to a very substantial likelihood of irreparable misidentification," although he agreed that in the particular case no such abuse had been shown.[30]

27. United States v. Wade, note 82, p. 233, *supra* (concurring in part and dissenting in part); Gilbert v. California, note 81, p. 233, *supra* (concurring in part and dissenting in part); Coleman v. Alabama, note 17, *supra* (concurring opinion).
28. Stovall v. Denno, 388 U.S. 293 (1967) (dissenting opinion).
29. Biggers v. Tennessee, 390 U.S. 404 (1968) (dissenting opinion).
30. Simmons v. United States, 390 U.S. 377 (1968).

In later cases Douglas has voted with the Court to hold that a convicted defendant is entitled to counsel when his probation is revoked and sentence imposed,[31] that the *Miranda* rules apply where a suspect is questioned by the police in his own bedroom, since the police admitted that he was "under arrest" and not free to leave,[32] and that they apply also when a defendant serving a term in a state prison is interrogated there by federal Internal Revenue agents and his incriminatory statements are later used in a federal tax fraud prosecution.[33]

But when the Court held in 1971 that statements taken from a defendant in violation of the *Miranda* rules, and hence inadmissible as part of the prosecution's case, could nonetheless be used by the prosecutor on cross-examination of the defendant to impeach his testimony by asking him if he had not earlier made statements to the police which were inconsistent with that testimony,[34] Douglas joined the dissenters. To the Court's assertion that "The shield provided by *Miranda* cannot be perverted into a license to use perjury by way of defense, free from the risk of confrontation with prior inconsistent utterances," they replied:[35]

> [The privilege against self-incrimination] is fulfilled only when an accused is guaranteed the right "to remain silent unless he chooses to speak in the *unfettered* exercise of his own will . . . " The choice of whether to testify in one's own defense must therefor be "unfettered," since that choice is an exercise of the constitutional privilege. *Griffin* v. *California* . . .[36] held that comment by the prosecution upon the accused's failure to take the stand or a court instruction that such silence is evidence of guilt is impermissible because it "fetters" that choice—" [i]t cuts down on the privilege by making its assertion costly" . . . For precisely the same reason the constitutional guarantee forbids the prosecution from using a tainted statement to impeach the accused who takes the stand. The prosecution's use of the tainted statement "cuts down on the privilege by making its assertion costly" . . . Thus the accused is denied an "unfettered" choice when the

31. Mempa v. Rhay, 389 U.S. 128 (1967).
32. Orozco v. Texas, 394 U.S. 324 (1957).
33. Mathis v. United States, 391 U.S. 1 (1968).
34. *Cf.* Walder v. United States, note 55, p. 197, *supra.*
35. Harris v. New York, 401 U.S. 222 (1971) (dissenting opinion).
36. Note 73, p. 232, *supra.*

decision whether to take the stand is burdened by the risk that an illegally obtained prior statement may be introduced to impeach his direct testimony denying complicity in the crime charged against him . . .

The objective of deterring improper police conduct is only part of the larger objective of safeguarding the integrity of our adversary sustem. The "essential mainstay" of that system . . . is the privilege against self-incrimination . . . [As was said in *Miranda*], "the constitutional foundation underlying the privilege is the respect a government . . . must accord to the dignity and integrity of its citizens" . . . These values are plainly jeopardized if an exception against admission of tainted statements is made for those used for impeachment purposes. Moreover, it is monstrous that courts should aid or abet the law-breaking officer. It is abiding truth that "[n]othing can destroy a government more quickly than its failure to observe its own laws, or worse, its disregard of the charter of its own existence" . . . Thus even to the extent that *Miranda* was aimed at deterring police practices in disregard of the Constitution . . . today's holding will seriously undermine the achievement of that objective. The Court today tells the police that they may freely interrogate an accused incommunicado and without counsel and know that although any statement they obtain in violation of *Miranda* cannot be used on the state's direct case, it may be introduced if the defendant has the temerity to testify in his own defense. This goes far toward undoing much of the progress made in conforming police methods to the Constitution.

In one remaining area Douglas' views on the right to counsel remain minority views. Prior to the application of the Sixth Amendment to the states, he joined in a dissent which maintained that persons were illegally incarcerated by the state where, following a fire on their business premises, the fire marshal conducted a hearing to investigate its causes, they were subpoenaed to testify in a nonpublic hearing, they declined to do so unless their counsel could be present and were committed to jail by the marshal until they were ready to testify. The dissenters maintained that the commitment violated due process not only because it occurred in a secret proceeding but also since, the fire marshal having the "ordinary duties of policemen" with respect to arson and similar crimes, the witnesses were entitled to have counsel present when interrogated by him.[37] Again at a time before the Sixth

37. *In re* Groban, 352 U.S. 330 (1957) (dissenting opinion).

Amendment was applied to the states, he joined in a dissent on the same grounds from a holding that a state judge investigating alleged "ambulance chasing" could, consistent with due process, sentence licensed private detectives to jail for criminal contempt when they refused to answer questions because he would not permit their counsel to be present.[38]

38. Anonymous v. Baker, 360 U.S. 287 (1959) (dissenting opinion).

12 JURY TRIAL

The original Constitution provides, in Article III dealing with the federal judiciary, that, "The Trial of all Crimes . . . shall be by Jury."[1] The Sixth Amendment adds, "In all criminal prosecutions, the accused shall enjoy the right to . . . trial, by an impartial jury."

The application of the Sixth Amendment's jury trial guaranty to criminal contempt proceedings,[2] the application of the equal protection clauses's prohibition against systematic exclusion of qualified groups from jury panels,[3] and the application of the due process clause's protection against the prejudicing of the jury by adverse publicity[4] have been previously considered.

In one early case the Court read both the Article III and the Sixth Amendment guarantees of jury trial as incorporating common law principles under which certain "petty offenses" were not entitled to a jury trial. But it held that a charge that union members had conspired to prevent nonunion members from working, and to boycott those who employed them, was not such a petty offense. Hence a conviction on that charge in a District of Columbia police court without a jury, and a sentence to pay a fine of $25 or to serve thirty days in jail, were

1. U.S. Const., Art. III, §2, Cl. 3.
2. See pp. 21-22, *supra.*
3. See pp. 125-126, 139-140, *supra.*
4. See pp. 168-170, *supra.*

unconstitutional, even though the defendants could appeal to a higher court and there have a jury trial.[5] In another case these guarantees were held applicable to other federal territories and construed to require a jury "as it was at common law, of twelve persons." Hence it was held that when Utah became a state and applied its constitutional provisions for a jury of eight to try a defendant for a crime committed there while Utah was a territory, the application violated a prohibition in the federal Constitution against ex post facto laws.[6] (As noted earlier, however, the Court soon thereafter decided that the Fourteenth Amendment did not incorporate the Sixth Amendment right to jury trial, so that Utah could use its eight-man jury to try defendants for offenses committed there after Utah became a state.[7])

Other early cases held that Congress could not authorize the Territory of Alaska to convict a defendant by a jury of six of the offense of keeping a disreputable house,[8] and that the Sixth Amendment was not violated by a federal statute giving the defendant ten peremptory challenges to jurors but providing that where there was more than one defendant they should together have only ten such challenges.[9]

In a 1930 decision,[10] where a defendant in a federal prosecution for bribery of a prohibition agent agreed during a trial in which one juror became ill that the trial should proceed with eleven jurors, the Court assumed that Article III and the Sixth Amendment also incorporate the common law requirement of a unanimous verdict[11] and hence treated the case as no different than one where defendant had waived his right to jury entirely, but held that the right could be waived by a knowing and intelligent defendant, with the consent of the government. And in 1937 the Court held that a prosecution for selling second-hand goods without a license, an offense for which the penalty was a fine of not

5. Callan v. Wilson, 127 U.S. 540 (1888).

6. Thompson v. Utah, 170 U.S. 343 (1898). *Ex post facto* laws are considered in more detail in Chapter 19.

7. Maxwell v. Dow, note 92, p. 176, *supra.*

8. Rassmussen v. United States, 197 U.S. 516 (1905).

9. Stilson v. United States, 250 U.S. 583 (1919).

10. Patton v. United States, 281 U.S. 276 (1930).

11. See also Andres v. United States, 333 U.S. 740 (1948). *Cf.* Parker v. Gladden, 385 U.S. 363 (1966).

more than $300 or ninety days imprisonment and for which the defendant had been sentenced to pay $300 or serve sixty days, was, in view of the limited punishment authorized, a prosecution for a "petty offense" for which no jury trial was required.[12]

As previously indicated, Douglas dissented when the Court found a knowing and intelligent waiver of jury trial by a defendant who had also waived his right to counsel, contending that defendant in a complicated mail fraud case needed legal advice before he could make an intelligent choice between trial by jury and trial by judge.[13] He dissented again when the Court rejected an argument that a defendant in a federal narcotics prosecution in the District of Columbia had been denied the "impartial jury" required by the Sixth Amendment when he was tried by a jury made up of twelve employees of the federal government. Because defendant had not shown systematic exclusion of private employees from the panel from which the jury was drawn, had used nine of his ten peremptory challenges to remove private employees from the jury, and had an unlimited number of challenges whenever he could persuade the trial court that a juror was subject to actual bias, the Court was not persuaded that defendant was deprived of an impartial jury. The Court also took note of the difficulties of obtaining juries in the District of Columbia prior to 1935 when the common law disqualification of government employees to serve on juries was removed by statute. Douglas joined in a dissenting opinion which said in part:[14]

> On one proposition I should expect trial lawyers to be nearly unanimous: that a jury, every member of which is in the hire of one of the litigants, lacks something of being an impartial jury . . .
>
> . . . This criminal trial was an adversary proceeding, with the Government both an actual and nominal litigant. It was the patron and benefactor of the whole jury, plus one juror's wife for good measure. At the same time that it made its plea to them to convict, it had the upper hand of every one of them in matters such as pay and promotion. Of late years, the Government is using its power as never before to pry into their lives and thoughts upon the slightest suspicion of less than

12. District of Columbia v. Clawans, 300 U.S. 167 (1937).
13. Adams v. McCann, note 4, p. 236, *supra*.
14. Frazier v. United States, 335 U.S. 497 (1948) (dissenting).

complete trustworthiness. It demands not only probity but unquestioning ideological loyalty . . . Even if we have no reason to believe that an acquitting juror would be subjected to embarrassments or reprisals, we cannot expect every clerk and messenger in the great bureaucracy to feel so secure as to put his dependence on the Government wholly out of mind . . . [E]ven if this suspicion can be dismissed by the Court as a mere phantasy, it cannot deny that such a jury has a one-sided outlook on problems before it and an appearance of government leverage which is itself a blemish on the name of justice in the District of Columbia . . .

The cause of overloading this jury with persons beholden to the Government is no mystery and no accident. It is due to a defect in a system which will continue to operate in the same direction so long as the same practice is followed . . . [W]hen the panel of jurors was drawn, the Court appears to have asked all those who did not wish to serve to step aside, and they were excused from serving.

This amiable concession in some jurisdictions might produce no distortion of the composition of the panel; but it is certain to do just that in the District of Columbia because of the dual standard and dubious method of jury compensation. The nongovernment juror receives $4 per day, which under present conditions is inadequate to be compensatory to nearly every gainfully employed juror. But the government employee is not paid specially; instead, he is given leave from his government work with full pay while serving on the jury . . .

The Government was confronted by no occasion to use any of its [ten] peremptory challenges to get rid of its adversary's employees. The defendant was. But if the defendant should try to use his challenges to excuse employees of the Government, he would dismiss one only to incur a probability of getting another. If he exhausted his challenges in this effort, it would still be futile, for no one claims he had enough to displace them all. It might not be wise tactics to show suspicion or disapproval of a class some of whom will have to sit anyway. Moreover, if he used his challenges as far as they would go to dislodge government servants, it would leave him helpless to challenge any of the non-government jurors, for which challenge he might have good reason.

Douglas did not participate in a later decision which affirmed a trial court ruling that, in a criminal prosecution of the General Secretary of the Communist party of the United States for contempt of the House Un-American Activities Committee, defendant had not shown actual bias, so as to be entitled to challenge jurors for cause, merely by showing that the jurors were federal employees, at least where the jurors had denied on *voir dire* examination that they would be intimidated by the federal loyalty program.[15] But in a later case involving another prosecution for contempt of the same committee, a conviction was reversed because the trial court did not permit defendant's counsel to interrogate prospective jurors about the possible influence of the loyalty program on them. Douglas concurred on the ground that all government employees should have been excluded from the jury without necessity for showing actual bias.[16]

Douglas voted with the Court in a later case to hold, in the exercise of its supervisory powers over federal justice, that a conviction under the Food, Drug and Cosmetic Act for dispensing toxic drugs without a doctor's prescription must be reversed because several jurors had read in newspapers during the trial that defendant had previously been convicted of forgery and had admitted before a state legislative committee that he had practiced medicine without a license and had written prescriptions for drugs—matters on which the trial judge had refused to allow the government to introduce evidence.[17]

He voted with the Court also to hold that a federal conviction must be reversed because an FBI agent during the trial interviewed a juror about a suggestion made by a private party to the juror, and reported by the juror to the judge, that the juror should solicit a bribe from the defendant. The combination of private, and official intrusions on the juror had subjected him "to extraneous influences to which no juror should be subjected."[18] And he voted with the Court to apply the same rule to a union officer convicted of filing a false non-Communist affidavit with the government, where an FBI agent, investigating another similar case, mistakenly called three of the jurors or their families to inquire whether they had received any "propaganda." This "official intrusion" on the jurors was no less prejudicial because unintentional.[19]

15. Dennis v. United States, 339 U.S. 162 (1950).
16. Morford v. United States, 339 U.S. 258 (1950) (concurring opinion).
17. Marshall v. United States, 360 U.S. 310 (1959).
18. Remmer v. United States, 350 U.S. 377 (1956).
19. Gold v. United States, 352 U.S. 985 (1957).

Before the Sixth Amendment's guaranty of jury trial was held applicable to the states, Douglas also voted with the Court to hold that it was a denial of due process for the state during trial to put the jury in the custody of two deputy sheriffs who were also two principal witnesses for the prosecution, even though there was no showing that the deputies had discussed the case with the jurors.[20] After the Sixth Amendment guaranty was held applicable to the states, he voted with the Court again to hold that defendant was denied an impartial jury where the bailiff in charge of the jurors had said to at least one regular juror or an alternate that defendant was a "wicked fellow" who "is guilty" and that if there was anything wrong in finding him guilty "the Supreme Court will correct it."[21]

Douglas also joined with a unanimous Court to uphold a Federal Rule of Criminal Procedure which conditions a defendant's right to waive jury trial on "approval of the court and the consent of the government," as applied in a case where the court approved the waiver but the government would not consent. Finding that the common law did not recognize a *right* to waive jury trial and that the "ability to waive a constitutional right does not ordinarily carry with it the right to insist upon the opposite," the Court pointed out that if either the court or the government refused to consent to the waiver "the result is simply that the defendant is subject to an impartial trial by jury—the very thing that the Constitution guarantees him."[22]

Douglas also voted with the Court to invalidate a provision in the federal Kidnaping Act providing for the death penalty if a kidnap victim is not liberated unharmed "and if the verdict of the jury shall so recommend." Since a defendant could put himself in jeopardy of the death penalty only by asserting his right to jury trial, the statute "needlessly penalizes the assertion of a constitutional right." Its purpose, to mitigate the severity of capital punishment, could be achieved without such penalizing by letting the jury decide on the penalty in every case, regardless of whether judge or jury had determined the issue

20. Turner v. Louisiana, 379 U.S. 466 (1968).
21. Parker v. Gladden, note 11, *supra*.
22. Singer v. United States, 380 U.S. 24 (1965).

of guilt.[23] The similar death penalty provision of the federal Bank Robbery Act was later invalidated for the same reason.[24] But in a decision in which Douglas joined, the Court rejected the contention of one convicted under the Kidnaping Act and sentenced to thirty years that his guilty plea had been coerced by the invalid provision as to the death penalty, concluding that he had changed his plea from not guilty to guilty because his co-defendant pleaded guilty and became available to testify against him.[25]

In 1968, in a case involving a defendant convicted in a state court of simple battery, for which the maximum punishment was two years imprisonment and a $300 fine and for which he received sixty days and a $150 fine, the Court held that "the Fourteenth Amendment guarantees a right of jury trial in all criminal cases which—were they to be tried in a Federal court—would come within the Sixth Amendment's guarantee." While the Court had "no constitutional doubts about the practices, common in both federal and state courts, of accepting waivers of jury trial and prosecuting petty crimes without extending a right to jury trial," it held that the offense here involved was not, in view of the maximum punishment authorized, a "petty offense." Douglas joined in a concurring opinion which reiterated his view that the Fourteenth Amendment generally incorporated all of the guarantees of the Bill of Rights, but noted that at least the "selective incorporation process has the virtue of having already worked to make most of the Bill of Rights protections applicable to the states."[26] And, as previously indicated,[27] he has consistently dissented when, in applying the Sixth Amendment to criminal contempt proceedings, the Court has taken six months as the maximum penalty that can be imposed without a jury trial. As he once expressed his views on this issue:[28]

I cannot say what is and what is not a "petty crime." I certainly believe, however, that where punishment of as much as six months *can*

23. United States v. Jackson, note 33, p. 159, *supra.*
24. Pope v. United States, note 33, p. 159, *supra.*
25. Brady v. United States, note 34, p. 159, *supra.*
26. Duncan v. Louisiana, 391 U.S. 145 (1968) (concurring opinion).
27. See pp. 21-22, *supra. See also* note 16, p. 238, *supra.*
28. Frank v. United States, note 50, p. 22, *supra* (dissenting opinion).

be imposed, I would not classify the offense as "petty" if that means that people tried for it are to be tried as if we had no Bill of Rights . . . I do not deny that there might possibly be some offenses charged for which the punishment is so minuscule that it might be thought of as petty. But to my way of thinking, when a man is charged by a governmental unit with conduct for which the Government can impose a penalty of imprisonment for any amount of time, I doubt if I could ever hold it petty.

In 1970 Douglas concurred in a decision invalidating the New York practice of trying without a jury those accused of misdemeanors punishable by a maximum of one year's imprisonment. But, while the plurality opinion again suggested that the most relevant criterion "reflecting the seriousness with which society regards the offense" was the "maximum authorized penalty," Douglas joined in a concurring opinion which now rejected the notion that an exception for "petty offenses" could be read into the federal constitutional guarantees of jury trial.[29]

Shortly after holding the Sixth Amendment's jury trial requirements applicable to the states, the Court considered one state's practice of allowing the prosecutor to exclude from the jury in a capital case all prospective jurors who expressed qualms about the death penalty, regardless of the potential juror's view as to whether his reservations about that penalty would prevent him from voting to impose it or from rendering an impartial verdict as to defendant's guilt. That state also submitted to the jury in capital cases both the responsibility of determining guilt or innocence and the responsibility of determing whether the death penalty should be imposed. The Court held that a jury so selected could be allowed to determine the guilt issue, but could not, consistently with due process, be allowed to impose the death penalty. As to guilt, defendant had failed to prove "that jurors not opposed to the death penalty tend to favor the prosecution in the determination of guilt." But "a jury that must choose between life imprisonment and capital punishment can do little more—and must do nothing less—than express the conscience of the community . . . Yet, in a nation less than

29. Baldwin v. New York, 399 U.S. 66 (1970).

half of whose people believe in the death penalty, a jury composed exclusively of such people cannot speak for the community . . . Such a jury can speak only for a distinct and dwindling minority. If the State had excluded only those prospective jurors who stated in advance of trial that they would not even consider returning a verdict of death, it could argue that the resulting jury was simply 'neutral' with respect to the penalty. But when it swept from the jury all who expressed conscientious or religious scruples against capital punishment and all who opposed it in principle, the State crossed the line of neutrality. In its quest for a jury capable of imposing the death penalty, the State produced a jury uncommonly willing to condemn a man to die." Douglas did not agree with this disposition of the issue:[30]

The Court permits a State to eliminate from juries some of those who have conscientious scruples against the death penalty; but it allows those to serve who have no scruples against it as well as those who, having such scruples, nevertheless are deemed able to determine after a finding of guilt whether the death penalty or a lesser penalty should be imposed. I fail to see or understand the constitutional dimensions of those distinctions.

The constitutional question is whether the jury must be "impartially drawn from a cross-section of the community" or whether it can be drawn with systematic and intentional exclusion of some qualified groups, to use Mr. Justice Murphy's words in his dissent in *Fay* v. *New York* . . .[31]

A fair cross-section of the community may produce a jury almost certain to impose the death penalty if guilt were found; or it may produce a jury almost certain not to impose it . . . If a particular community were overwhelmingly opposed to capital punishment, it would not be able to exercise a discretion to impose or not impose the death sentence. A jury representing the conscience of that community would . . . avoid the death penalty by recommending mercy or it would avoid it by finding guilt of a lesser offense.

In such instance, why should not an accused have the benefit of that controlling principle of mercy in the community? Why should his fate be entrusted exclusively to a jury that was either enthusiastic about

30. Witherspoon v. Illinois, 391 U.S. 510 (1968) (separate opinion).
31. Note 11, p. 126, *supra*.

capital punishment or so undecided that it could exercise a discretion to impose it or not, depending on how it felt about the particular case?

I see no constitutional basis for excluding those who are so opposed to capital punishment that they would never inflict it on a defendant. Exclusion of them means the selection of jurors who are either protagonists of the death penalty or are neutral concerning it. That results in a systematic exclusion of qualified groups, and the deprivation of the accused of a cross-section of the community for decision on both his guilt and his punishment.

Although the Court reverses as to penalty, it declines to reverse the verdict of guilt rendered by the same jury. It does so on the ground that petitioner has not demonstrated . . . that the jury which convicted him was "less than neutral with respect to guilt" . . . because of the exclusion of all those opposed in some degree to capital punishment . . . But we do not require a showing of specific prejudice when a defendant has been deprived of his right to a jury representing a cross-section of the community . . . We can as easily assume that the absence of those opposed to capital punishment would rob the jury of certain peculiar qualities of human nature as would the exclusion of women from juries. *Ballard* v. *United States.*[32]

In a companion case involving similar procedures, the Court found no constitutional objection where the jury that convicted defendant of rape recommended a life sentence rather than the death penalty. Douglas disagreed because a jury from which those with scruples against capital punishment had not been excluded might have, and under the applicable state law could have, found defendant guilty of the lesser offense of assault with intent to commit rape.[33]

Only a few states which submit issues of punishment as well as of guilt to the jury provide for separate proceedings before the jury on the two issues. Douglas has twice dissented when the Court held that such separate proceedings were not constitutionally required. One case involved a state's habitual criminal statute which, as applied to defendant in a murder case, allowed the jury in a single proceeding to hear the evidence on that charge and to hear evidence of a prior murder

32. Note 9, p. 125, *supra*.
33. Bumper v. North Carolina, 391 U.S. 543 (1968) (concurring in part and dissenting in part).

conviction. The jury was instructed that it was not to consider the prior conviction as any evidence of guilt on the current charge, that if it found defendant guilty of the current charge and that he had been previously convicted it should sentence him to death or life imprisonment, but that if it found that he was guilty on the current charge but that he had not been previously convicted it should sentence him to death or for a prison term of not less than two years. The jury found him guilty and sentenced him to death. The Court held that this procedure did not violate due process, pointing out that while evidence of prior crimes was generally excluded because of its prejudicial effect, there were widely recognized exceptions which permitted introduction of evidence of prior crimes where relevent to the issue of intent with respect to the crime charged, or to rebut the evidence of character witnesses called by the defendant, or to impeach defendant's credibility when he takes the stand. Douglas joined in a dissent which pointed out that all of the exceptions to which the Court referred were instances in which the prior convictions had some probative value on the issue of current guilt, whereas the general exclusion of evidence of prior crimes was a recognition of the danger that, despite cautionary instructions, the jury "might punish an accused for being guilty of a previous offense, or feel the incarceration is justified because the accused is a 'bad man,' without regard to his guilt of the crime currently charged." Hence, the dissenters would have read the due process clause to require that the jury reach its conclusion on the issue of guilt before hearing evidence of prior crimes.[34]

The second case, decided in 1971, involved a murder conviction in Ohio of a defendant who pleaded not guilty and not guilty by reason in insanity, but who was found guilty and sentenced to death by the jury in a single proceeding in which he did not take the stand. When the Court held that this procedure did not violate the privilege against self-incrimination or otherwise deny due process by requiring defendant to waive the privilege on the issue of guilt or remain silent on the issue of punishment, Douglas again dissented:[35]

34. Spencer v. Texas, 385 U.S. 554 (1967) (dissenting opinion).
35. McGautha v. California, 402 U.S. 183 (1971) (dissenting opinion).

On the issue of guilt the state was required to produce evidence to establish it. On the issue of insanity the burden was on the petitioner to prove it . . . On the issue of mercy, *viz.* life imprisonment rather than death, petitioner . . . was banned from offering any specific evidence directed only toward a claim of mercy.

If a defendant wishes to testify in support of the defense of insanity or in mitigation of what he is charged with doing, he can do so only if he surrenders his right to be free from self-incrimination. Once he takes the stand he can be cross-examined not only as respects the crime charged but also on other misdeeds. In Ohio impeachment covers a wide range of subjects: prior convictions for felonies and statutory misdemeanors, prior convictions in military service and dishonorable discharges. Once he testifies he can be recalled for cross-examination in the State's case in rebuttal.

On the question of insanity and punishment the accused should be under no restraints when it comes to putting before the court and jury all the relevant facts. Yet he cannot have that freedom where these issues are tied to the question of guilt. For on that issue he often dare not speak lest he in substance be tried not for this particular offense but for all the sins he ever committed.

The unitary trial . . . has a constitutional infirmity because it is not neutral on the awesome issue of capital punishment. The rules are stacked in favor of death. It is one thing if the legislature decides that the death penalty attaches to defined crimes. It is quite another to leave the judge or jury the discretion to sentence an accused to death or to show mercy under procedures that make the trial death oriented. Then the law becomes a mere pretense, lacking the procedural integrity that would likely result in a fair resolution of the issues.

In the same case the Court held that defendants were not denied due process of law by the states of California and Ohio where the question whether they should live or die was left to the absolute discretion of the jury without any governing standards. "In the light of history, experience, and the present limitations of human knowledge," the Court did not believe any such standards could be devised. Douglas joined in a dissent on this point also:

The question . . . is whether the rule of law, basic to our society and binding upon the States by virtue of the Due Process Clause of the Fourteenth Amendment, is fundamentally inconsistent with capital sentencing procedures that are purposely constructed to allow the maximum possible variation from one case to the next, and provide no mechanism to prevent that consciously maximized variation from reflecting merely random or arbitrary choice. The Court does not, however, come to grips with that fundamental question. Instead, the Court misapprehends petitioners' argument and deals with the cases as if petitioners contend that due process requires capital sentencing to be carried out under predetermined standards so precise as to be capable of purely mechanical application . . . This misapprehended question is then treated in the context of the Court's assumption that the legislatures in Ohio and California are incompetent to express with clarity the bases upon which they have determined that some persons guilty of some crimes should be killed, while others should live—an assumption that, significantly, finds no support in the arguments made by those States in these cases. With the issue so polarized, the Court is led to conclude that the rule of law and the power of the States to kill are in irreconcilable conflict. This conflict the Court resolves in favor of the State's power to kill.

In my view the Court errs on all points from its premises to its conclusions. Unlike the Court, I do not believe that the legislatures of the 50 states are so devoid of wisdom and the power of rational thought that they are unable to face the problem of capital punishment directly, and to determine for themselves the criteria under which convicted capital felons should be chosen to live or die. We are thus not, in my view, faced by the dilemma perceived by the Court, for cases in this Court have for almost a century and a half approved a multiplicity of imaginative procedures designed by the state and federal legislatures to assure evenhanded treatment and ultimate legislative control regarding matters which the legislatures have deemed either too complex or otherwise inapposite for regulation under predetermined rules capable of automatic application. Finally, even if I shared the Court's view that the rule of law and the power of the States to kill are in irreconcilable conflict, I would have no hesitation in concluding that the rule of law must prevail.

Except where it incorporates specific substantive constitutional guarantees against state infringement, the Due Process Clause of the Fourteenth Amendment does not limit the power of the States to choose among competing social and economic theories in the ordering of life within their respective jurisdictions. But it does require that, if state power is to be exerted, these choices must be made by a responsible organ of state government. For if they are not, the very best that may be hoped for is that state power will be exercised not upon the basis of any social choice made by the people of the State, but instead merely on the basis of social choices made at the whim of the particular state official wielding the power . . . Government by whim is the very antithesis of due process . . .

It is of critical importance . . . to emphasize that we are not called upon to determine the adequacy or inadequacy of any particular legislative procedure designed to give rationality to the capital sentencing process. For the plain fact is that the legislatures of California and Ohio . . . have sought no solution at all. We are not presented with a State's attempt to provide standards, attacked as impermissible or inadequate. We are not presented with a legislative attempt to draw wisdom from experience through a process looking towards growth in understanding through the accumulation of a variety of experiences. We are not presented with the slightest attempt to bring the power of reason to bear on the considerations relevant to capital sentencing. We are faced with nothing more than stark legislative abdication. Not once in the history of this Court, until today, have we sustained against a due process challenge such an unguided, unbridled, unreviewable exercise of power. Almost a century ago, we found an almost identical California procedure constitutionally inadequate to license a laundry[36] . . . Today we hold it adequate to license a life. I would reverse the petitioners' sentences of death.

In 1970 the Court reconsidered prior readings of the federal guaranty of jury trial to require a common law jury of twelve[37] and, in a decision which Douglas joined on this issue, rejected them. Finding the history of both Article III and the Sixth Amendment inconclusive on this point, the Court turned to the function which the jury performed—"the interposition between the accused and his accuser of the commonsense judgment of a group of laymen, and . . . the community participation and shared responsibility that results from that group's determination of guilt or innocence"—and concluded that that function could be as well performed by a state's jury of six as by a jury of twelve.[38]

The Seventh Amendment adds another guaranty of jury trial in many

36. Yick Wo v. Hopkins, 118 U.S. 356 (1886).

37. Thompson v. Utah, note 6, *supra;* Rassmussen v. United States, note 8, *supra;* Patton v. United States, note 10, *supra.*

38. Williams v. Florida, 399 U.S. 78 (1970) (concurring in part and dissenting in part).

civil cases: "In suits at common law, where the value in controversy shall exceed twenty dollars, the right of jury trial shall be preserved."

The 1875 decision that this guaranty is not made applicable to the states by the Fourteenth Amendment[39] remains unchallenged. When the Supreme Court held that the Sixth Amendment guaranty of jury trial in criminal case was applicable to the states, it noted that most of the debate about the merits of the jury as a fact-finding device "has centered on the jury in civil cases."[40]

In civil cases tried in the federal courts, Douglas has consistently voted against use of the devices of directed verdicts and judgments notwithstanding the verdict where he thought they infringed on the jury trial guaranteed by the Seventh Amendment.[41] And he voted with the Court when it reaffirmed earlier decisions that the Seventh Amendment guaranty is not applicable to suits at equity, rather than at common law, in the federal courts.[42] But he also voted with the Court to hold that, where an established motion picture exhibitor was charged by a newcomer with violation of the antitrust laws, it could not, in anticipation of a damage action by the newcomer in which a jury trial would be available, defeat the right to jury trial by getting first to the federal courthouse with a suit in equity to enjoin the bringing of the damage action.[43]

39. Walker v. Sauvinet, note 89, p. 176, *supra.*

40. Duncan v. Louisiana, note 26, *supra.*

41. Berry v. United States, 312 U.S. 450 (1941); Conway v. O'Brien, 312 U.S. 492 (1941); Halliday v. United States, 315 U.S. 94 (1942); Galloway v. United States, 319 U.S. 372 (1943) (dissenting opinion); Bailey v. Central Vermont Railway, Inc. 319 U.S. 350 (1943); Brady v. Southern Ry. Co., 320 U.S. 476 (1943) (dissenting opinion); Blair v. Baltimore & Ohio R.R., 323 U.S. 600 (1945); Wilkerson v. McCarthy, 336 U.S. 53 (1949) (concurring opinion); Dice v. Akron, C. & Y. R.R., 342 U.S. 359 (1952); Schulz v. Pennsylvania R.R., 350 U.S. 523 (1956); Harris v. Pennsylvania R.R., 361 U.S. 15 (1959) (concurring opinion); Inman v. Baltimore & Ohio R.R. 361 U.S. 138 (1959) (dissenting opinion); A. & G. Stevedores, Inc. v. Ellerman Lines, Ltd., 369 U.S. 355 (1962); International Terminal Operating Co. v. N.V. Nederl. Amerik Stoomv. Maats; 393 U.S. 74 (1968). *See also* cases cited in note 4, p. 321, *infra.*

42. Yakus v. United States, 321 U.S. 414 (1944).

43. Beacon Theatres v. Westover, 359 U.S. 500 (1959). *See also* Katchen v. Landy, 382 U.S. 323 (1966) (dissenting opinion).

13 DOUBLE JEOPARDY

The Fifth Amendment provides that no person shall "be subject for the same offense to be twice put in jeopardy of life or limb."

In 1904, construing a federal statute for the government of the Philippine Islands which contained a Bill of Rights including a provision that "no person shall be twice put in jeopardy of punishment," the Court concluded that this provision forbade an appeal by the government where defendant had been acquitted by a court sitting without a jury. In the course of its opinion the Court stated that where a jury is used, "no legal jeopardy can attach until a jury has been called and charged with the deliverance of the accused."[1] That notion, that jeopardy does not attach until the jury is impanelled and sworn, was later employed to sustain the constitutionality under the Fifth Amendment of statutes allowing the United States to appeal where the trial court dismisses an indictment before the jury is called—"before the moment of jeopardy is reached."[2]

Despite the notion that jeopardy attaches when the jury is sworn, this guaranty has long been construed not to forbid a second trial where the jury at the first trial is unable to reach a verdict and is discharged.[3]

1. Kepner v. United States, 195 U.S. 100 (1904).

2. Taylor v. United States, 207 U.S. 120 (1907); United States v. Bitty, 208 U.S. 393 (1908).

3. United States v. Perez, 9 Wheat. 579 (1824); Logan v. United States, 144 U.S. 263 (1892).

Early cases also held that reprosecution was not barred where the trial judge properly declared a mistrial because a letter published in a newspaper and read by several jurors raised doubts as to the impartiality of one juror,[4] or because the judge discovered that one juror had served on the grand jury which had indicted the defendant.[5]

As indicated earlier, Douglas dissented when the Court later held that a defendant was not placed twice in jeopardy when, after a court martial began taking evidence against him, it was dissolved for "tactical reasons" and he was later tried again.[6] He later wrote for the Court to hold that where the jury, after being sworn, was discharged because two of the prosecution's key witnesses were not present for trial, defendant could not be retried.[7] But he dissented again in *Gori* v. *United States* when the Court permitted a second prosecution of a defendant after the judge at the first trial had declared a mistrial, apparently because he thought the prosecutor guilty of a prejudicial line of questioning on the direct examination of a government witness. The record in the case was too skimpy to permit the Court to rule on the propriety of the trial judge's action, but it was satisfied that, even though he acted out of "overeager solicitude," he acted "in the sole interest of the defendant" and concluded that a second trial was not barred. Douglas was not persuaded.[8]

Today the Court phrases the problem in terms of whether a mistrial has been granted "to help the prosecution" on the one hand or "in the sole interest of the defendant" on the other. The former is plainly in violation of [the double jeopardy clause] . . . But not until today, I believe, have we ever intimated that a mistrial ordered "in the sole interest of the defendant" was no bar to a second trial where the mistrial was not ordered at the request of the defendant or with his consent.

There are occasions where a second trial may be had, although the jury which was impanelled for the first trial was discharged without reaching a verdict and without the defendant's consent. Mistrial because

4. Simmons v. United States, 142 U.S. 148 (1891).
5. Thompson v. United States, 155 U.S. 271 (1894).
6. Wade v. Hunter, note 33, p. 117, *supra* (dissenting opinion).
7. Downum v. United States, 372 U.S. 734 (1963).
8. Gori v. United States, 367 U.S. 364 (1961) (dissenting opinion).

the jury was unable to agree is a classic example . . . Discovery by the judge during the trial that "one or more members of a jury might be biased against the Government or the defendant" has been held to warrant discharge of the jury and direction of a new trial . . . That is to say, "a defendant's valued right to have his trial completed by a particular tribunal must in some instances be subordinated to the public's interest in fair trials designed to end in just judgments" . . .

To date these exceptions have been narrowly confined. Once a jury has been impanelled and sworn, jeopardy attaches and a subsequent prosecution is barred, if a mistrial is ordered—absent a showing of imperious necessity . . .

. . . I read the Double Jeopardy Clause as applying a strict standard. "The prohibition is not against being twice punished; but against being twice put in jeopardy" . . . It is designed to help equalize the position of government and the individual, to discourage abusive use of the awesome power of society. Once a trial starts jeopardy attaches. The prosecution must stand or fall on its performance at the trial. I do not see how a mistrial directed because the prosecutor has no witnesses is different from a mistrial directed because the prosecutor has abused his office and is guilty of misconduct. In neither is there a breakdown in judicial machinery such as happens when the judge is stricken, or a juror has been discovered to be disqualified to sit . . . The policy of the Bill of Rights is to make rare indeed the occasions when the citizen can for the same offense be required to run the gantlet twice.

Thereafter Douglas voted with the Court to hold that a defendant could not be retried after the trial judge interrupted the prosecution's presentation of evidence to direct a verdict of acquittal, either because he thought the prosecutor guilty of misconduct or because he thought the government's witnesses lacked credibility. This case was said to be different from *Gori*, where the first trial terminated "prior to entry of judgment" because here it "terminated with the entry of a final judgment of acquittal."[9]

In 1971, in a decision in which Douglas joined, the Court rejected the suggestion in *Gori* that vulnerability to reprosecution should depend on an appellate court's assessment of "the motivation underlying the trial judge's action in declaring a mistrial." Rather, the test was said to be whether the mistrial was properly ordered because "there is a manifest

9. Fong Foo v. United States, 369 U.S. 141 (1962).

necessity for the act, or the ends of public justice would otherwise be defeated." Hence, where the trial judge concluded, after inadequate inquiry, that prosecuting witnesses had not been adequately warned by the government of the privilege against self-incrimination and their right to counsel, and then proceeded, without giving defendant a chance to object, to direct a mistrial where a continuance would in any event have been more appropriate, reprosecution was held barred.[10]

It was long ago held that where one defendant was acquitted by the jury and two others convicted, and those convicted appealed and got their convictions reversed because of defects in the indictment on which all three were tried, the one acquitted could not be tried on a new indictment for the same offense, but those who appealed and obtained reversals of their convictions could be. The Fifth Amendment's prohibition was "not against being twice punished, but against being twice put in jeopardy; and the accused, whether convicted or acquitted, is equally put in jeopardy at the first trial." But that reading of the guaranty did not help the other two—they could not plead former conviction because they had obtained a reversal of their convictions on appeal, and "it is quite clear that a defendant who procures a judgment against him upon an indictment to be set aside, may be tried anew upon the same indictment, or upon another indictment, for the same offense of which he had been convicted."[11]

Douglas has since voted with the Court to hold that when a case is submitted to the jury on instructions that it could find defendant guilty of either first or second degree murder, the jury convicts him of second degree murder, and that conviction is reversed on his appeal for insufficient evidence, he can again be tried for murder in the second degree but not in the first. The purpose of the double jeopardy guaranty was to make sure that the government "should not be allowed to make repeated attempts to convict an individual for an alleged offense, thereby subjecting him to embarrassment, expense and ordeal and compelling him to live in a continuing state of anxiety and insecurity, as well as enhancing the possibility that even though innocent he may

10. United States v. Jorn, 400 U.S. 470 (1971).
11. United States v. Ball, 163 U.S. 662 (1896).

be found guilty." And the defendant here was placed in jeopardy on the first degree charge "once he [was] put to trial before a jury" and the jury did not convict him of that charge, although the procedure did not require that it formally acquit him either. "He was forced to run the gantlet once on that charge," and that was all the double jeopardy clause permits.[12]

When in a later case the government had dismissed an indictment at the close of its case but thereafter tried the defendant again for the same offense and obtained a conviction, and the Supreme Court ordered the second proceeding dismissed on motion of the solicitor general as contrary to Justice Department policy, Douglas joined in a concurring opinion which would have put the decision not on the basis of departmental policy but on the ground that the defendant had been placed twice in jeopardy.[13] And he joined in a dissent when the Court allowed retrial on the same charge where defendant's first conviction had been vacated, on his motion and after he had served seven years in prison, because his guilty plea, entered during trial, was coerced by the trial judge. The dissenters could see no significant difference between one deprived of his right to have his trial completed after the jury was sworn because of the failure of the prosecution to have its witnesses present[14] and one who was so deprived by a trial judge's threats.[15]

Douglas has voted with the Court also to hold that defendant may be retried where on his appeal his earlier conviction is reversed because of erroneous instructions to the jury.[16] But he joined in dissent when, after defendants' motions to vacate a conviction for selling narcotics without an order from one authorized to buy such drugs had been granted because of a defective indictment, the Court permitted a reindictment in three counts for selling narcotics without a proper order, for sales of narcotics not bearing tax stamps, and for sale of illegally imported narcotics, all based on the same sale charged in the

12. Green v. United States, 355 U.S. 184 (1957).

13. Petite v. United States, note 34, p. 19, *supra* (concurring opinion).

14. See text at note 7, *supra.*

15. United States v. Tateo, 377 U.S. 463 (1964) (dissenting opinion).

16. Forman v. United States, 361 U.S. 416 (1960). *See also* Bryan v. United States, 338 U.S. 552 (1950).

original indictment. The dissenters thought this procedure constituted a denial of due process:[17]

Under the original one-count indictments . . . Dennis faced a sentence of from five to 20 years; Ewell, a second offender, 10 to 40 years. Under the new three-count indictment, the District Court may cumulate the sentences on the three counts and impose terms of from 12 to 50 years upon Dennis and from 25 to 100 years upon Ewell . . . In my opinion, however, the Government may not, following vacation of a conviction, reindict a defendant for additional offenses arising out of the same transaction but not charged in the original indictment.

In a different setting this Court has vividly criticized the Government's attempt to penalize a successful appellant by retrying him on an aggravated basis. *Green* v. *United States* . . . [18] Although the decision in *Green* was premised upon the Double Jeopardy Clause, its teaching . . . also demonstrates this Court's concern to protect the right of appeal in criminal cases. It teaches that the Government, in its role as prosecutor, may not attach to the exercise of the right to appeal the penalty that if the appellant succeeds, he may be retried on another and more serious charge . . .

In the present case it appears that the purpose as well as the effect of the Government's action was to discourage the exercise of the right . . . to seek review of criminal convictions. According to the District Court, the only reason advanced by the Government for the multiplication of charges against appellees was that the prosecutor wanted to discourage others from attacking their convictions . . . The prosecutor's concern is understandable, but the right to . . . review is granted by law. The prosecutor may not consistently with the Due Process clause boobytrap this right, either to punish or to frighten.

As previously indicated, the Court in 1937 held the double jeopardy clause inapplicable to the states.[19] In 1947 the Court found it unnecessary to reconsider that ruling because it held that the guaranty would not in any event be violated by a state's second attempt to electrocute a convicted murderer after the first attempt had failed. Douglas dissented, but on the ground that the second attempt would constitute the

17. United States v. Ewell, 383 U.S. 116 (1966) (dissenting opinion).
18. Note 12, *supra.*
19. Palko v. Connecticut, note 96, p. 177, *supra.*

infliction of cruel and unusual punishment in violation of the Eighth Amendment.[20]

In another case in which the defendant in a state proceeding did not invoke the Fifth Amendment's double jeopardy clause, the Court held that there was no denial of due process where the state tried defendant again after the trial court had in a first prosecution declared a mistrial because co-defendants, who had been already convicted but who planned appeals, had invoked their state privilege against self-incrimination when called to testify for the state. Douglas dissented on the ground that due process should not permit "the prosecution to have a jury discharged so that it could obtain better evidence against the accused."[21] Thereafter he continued to dissent as due process was held to permit the state, after defendant was acquitted of charges of robbing three persons, to try him for robbery of a fourth person in the same transaction;[22] or, after defendant was convicted in two successive trials of murder of his wife and one child, but received only sentences of terms of years, to try him a third time (and finally to get a death sentence) for murder of a second child in the same occurrence;[23] or, after defendant was convicted of murder and sentenced to life imprisonment, to try him again for kidnaping the murder victim, for which he was sentenced to death;[24] or, after defendant was tried for manslaughter and the lesser offense of reckless homicide, convicted of the lesser offense, but had the conviction reversed on appeal, to try him again on both charges, resulting in a second conviction on the lesser offense.[25] He also dissented from decisions holding that after state conviction the federal government could prosecute defendant for a federal crime based on the same act,[26] and that after federal acquittal the state could convict of a crime based on the same act.[27]

20. Francis v. Resweber, 329 U.S. 459 (1947) (dissenting opinion). The prohibition against cruel and unusual punishment is considered in Chapter 18.

21. Brock v. North Carolina, 344 U.S. 424 (1953) (dissenting opinion).

22. Hoag v. New Jersey, 356 U.S. 464 (1958) (dissenting opinion).

23. Ciucci v. Illinois, 356 U.S. 571 (1958) (dissenting opinion).

24. Williams v. Oklahoma, 358 U.S. 576 (1959) (dissenting opinion).

25. Cichos v. Indiana, 385 U.S. 76 (1966) (dissenting opinion). *See also* Brantley v. Georgia, note 96, p. 177, *supra.*

26. Abbate v. United States, 359 U.S. 187 (1959) (dissenting opinion).

27. Bartkus v. Illinois, 359 U.S. 121 (1959) (dissenting opinion).

Finally, in 1969, in a decision in which Douglas joined, the Court held the double jeopardy clause of the Fifth Amendment applicable to the states under the Fourteenth Amendment and reversed the larceny conviction of a defendant who was first convicted of burglary but acquitted of larceny, had his burglary conviction reversed on appeal because of an invalid indictment, and was then reindicted for and convicted of both burglary and larceny.[28] In a companion case the Court also held that the double jeopardy guaranty "protects against multiple punishments for the same offense," so that a defendant who gets his first conviction set aside and is retried and convicted again must be given credit on his second sentence for time served on the first. But it also held that the double jeopardy clause did not forbid a more excessive penalty on the second conviction, although it would be a denial of due process if the penalty was increased *because* defendant had succeeded in having the first conviction reversed or set aside. Douglas would have gone further and read the double jeopardy guaranty to forbid any increase in penalty on the second conviction:[29]

The theory of double jeopardy is that a person need run the gantlet only once. The gantlet is the risk of the range of punishment which the State or Federal Government imposes for that particular conduct . . . He risks the maximum permissible punishment when first tried. That risk having been faced once need not be faced again . . .

The Fourteenth Amendment would now prohibit [a state], after trial, from retrying . . . these defendants in the bald hope of securing a more favorable verdict . . . But here, because these defendants were successful in appealing their convictions, the Court allows . . . just that. It is said that events subsequent to the first trial may justify a new and greater sentence. Of course that is true. But it is true, too, in *every* criminal case. Does that mean that the State should be allowed to reopen every verdict and readjust every sentence by coming forward with new evidence concerning guilt and punishment? If not, then why should it be allowed to do so merely because the defendant has taken the initiative in seeking an error-free trial? It is doubtless true that the State has an interest in adjusting sentences upward when it discovers new evidence warranting that result. But the individual has an interest in remaining free of double punishment. And in weighing those inter-

28. Benton v. Maryland, 395 U.S. 784 (1969).
29. North Carolina v. Pearce, 395 U.S. 711 (1969) (concurring opinion).

ests against one another, the Constitution has decided the matter in favor of the individual.

In two later cases, Douglas voted with the Court to hold that what due process formerly permitted, the double jeopardy clause now forbids. Where a defendant is acquitted of robbing one victim he may not thereafter be convicted of robbing another victim in the same episode.[30] And where a defendant is tried for murder and the lesser offense of manslaughter, convicted of manslaughter, but has his conviction reversed on appeal, he may not again be tried for murder.[31]

Whether the application of the double jeopardy clause to both state and federal governments will prevent successive prosecutions by each for the same acts,[32] remains to be determined. The Court did not reach that question in unanimously concluding that that clause forbids such successive prosecutions by city and state, since "both are arms of the same sovereign."[33]

Closely related to the policy of the double jeopardy guaranty is another series of cases which thus far have been disposed of not on constitutional grounds but on the interpretation of federal criminal statutes. Prosecutors are not infrequently prone to an ingenious reading of those statutes so as to divide one crime into many for the purpose of increasing the penalty or of multiplying the number of convictions defendant will have to attack on appeal.[34]

Douglas has voted with the Court to hold that a single agreement contemplating the possible commission of seven substantive crimes will not support a conviction of seven conspiracies,[35] although, to the extent that substantive crimes are also committed pursuant to the conspiracy, the defendant may be convicted of conspiracy and of substantive offenses;[36] that an employer who fails to make a withhold-

30. Ashe v. Swenson, 397 U.S. 436 (1970). *Cf.* Hoag v. New Jersey, note 22, *supra.*

31. Price v. Georgia, 398 U.S. 323 (1970). *Cf.* Brantley v. Georgia, note 96, p. 177, *supra;* Cichos v. Indiana, note 25, *supra.*

32. See text at notes 26 and 27, *supra.*

33. Waller v. Florida, 397 U.S. 387 (1970).

34. See United States v. Ewell, note 17, *supra.*

35. Braverman v. United States, 317 U.S. 49 (1942).

36. Pinkerton v. United States, 328 U.S. 640 (1946). *See also* Pereira v. United States, 347 U.S. 1 (1954) (concurring in part and dissenting in part).

ing tax return covering 101 employees can be convicted of only one crime;[37] that a defendant who transports two women in interstate commerce on a single automobile trip for purposes of prostitution commits only one violation of the Mann Act;[38] that a defendant whose single shotgun blast hits two federal officers is guilty of a single assault;[39] and that one who on one occasion enters and robs a federally insured bank cannot be convicted both of robbery and of entering the bank with intent to rob,[40] or both of taking money and of receiving stolen money.[41] But he dissented when the Court held that an employer who violated the minimum wage, overtime, and record-keeping requirements of the Fair Labor Standards Act over a period of time could be charged with only one crime for each of the three types of violation, since each involved a "single course of conduct" regardless of the number of employees affected:[42]

I think the question whether an employer has violated the criminal provisions of the Act is determined by reference to what he has done to a particular employee. The Act does not speak of "course of conduct" . . . [It] requires the employer to pay "each of his employees" not less than 75 cents an hour, prohibits him from employing "any of his employees" for more than 40 hours a week unless overtime is paid, and requires him to keep records of "the persons employed by him" and the wages, hours, etc. . . . And the Act makes it unlawful for an employer to violate "any of the provisions" of those sections . . .

It therefore seems clear to me that if an employer pays one employee less than 75 cents an hour *or* fails to pay overtime to one employee *or* fails to keep the required records for one employee, a crime has been established if *scienter* is shown. And it seems equally clear to me that if an employer wilfully fails to pay one employee the minimum wage, *and* wilfully fails to pay him the required overtime, *and* wilfully fails to keep the required records for him, three crimes have been committed. The crime is defined with reference to the individual employee. The

37. United States v. Carroll, 345 U.S. 457 (1953). *See also* Yates v. United States, 355 U.S. 66 (1957) (dissenting opinion).

38. Bell v. United States, 349 U.S. 81 (1955).

39. Ladner v. United States, 358 U.S. 169 (1958).

40. Prince v. United States, 352 U.S. 322 (1957).

41. Heflin v. United States, 358 U.S. 415 (1959).

42. United States v. Universal CIT Credit Corp., 344 U.S. 218 (1952) (dissenting opinion).

crime may be a single, isolated act. It may or may not be recurring or continuous. The violation may affect one employee one week or one month, and another employee another week or another month; and it may affect one employee in one way, another employee in a different way. The violations may be continuous, and follow a set pattern; or they may be sporadic and erratic. The Act does not differentiate between them . . . Perhaps a committee of Congress would be receptive to the suggestion now made. But it should be received there, not here . . . [U]ntil this case no court, so far as I can learn, has ever had the inventive genius to suggest that "course of conduct" rather than the "employee" is the unit of the crime.

Douglas dissented also when the Court, following a 1932 decision, held that a single sale of narcotics would support three convictions—one for sale without a written order from one authorized to buy such drugs, one for sale of drugs not bearing tax stamps, and one for sale of drugs unlawfully imported—and that no double jeopardy was involved:[43]

Plainly, Congress defined three distinct crimes, giving the prosecutor on these facts a choice. But I do not think the courts were warranted in punishing petitioner three times for the same transaction. I realize that *Blockburger* v. *United States* . . . holds to the contrary. But I would overrule that case.

I find that course necessary because of my views on double jeopardy, recently expressed in *Hoag* v. *New Jersey* . . .[44] Once a crucial issue is litigated in a criminal case that issue may not be the basis of another prosecution. Here the same sale is made to do service for three prosecutions.

He dissented again when the Court in another case held that one found in possession of heroin could be convicted both of purchasing heroin not bearing tax stamps and of receiving heroin knowing it to have been unlawfully imported, and that proof of possession of the unstamped heroin alone, aided by a statutory presumption of purchase from the absence of tax stamps and a statutory presumption of receipt from the possession, was sufficient to sustain both convictions.[45]

43. Gore v. United States, 357 U.S. 386 (1955) (dissenting opinion). *Cf.* United States v. Ewell, note 17, *supra.*

44. Note 22, *supra.*

45. Harris v. United States, 359 U.S. 19 (1959) (dissenting opinion).

14 GRAND JURY INDICTMENT

The Fifth Amendment provides that, "No person shall be held to answer for a capital or otherwise infamous crime, unless on a presentment or indictment of a Grand Jury, except in cases arising in the land and naval forces."[1]

In a series of early cases the Court concluded that an "infamous crime" within the meaning of this guaranty is one for which the authorized punishment includes imprisonment at hard labor or in a penitentiary—regardless of the punishment actually imposed in the particular case.[2] Under current federal law this embraces all crimes for which a term of more than one year is authorized, since anyone sentenced to more than a year may be required to serve his term in a penitentiary.[3] Crimes neither capital nor infamous may be prosecuted on an information filed by a prosecuting attorney.[4]

1. The "presentment" referred to in the Fifth Amendment was formerly used when the grand jury filed a charge on its own initiative rather than acting on a bill of indictment brought before it by the prosecuting attorney. Under current federal practice all criminal charges by a grand jury are by indictment. Rule 7, Federal Rules of Criminal Procedure.

2. *Ex parte* Wilson, 114 U.S. 417 (1885); Mackin v. United States, 117 U.S. 348 (1886); Wong Wing v. United States, 163 U.S. 228 (1896); United States v. Moreland, 258 U.S. 433 (1922); Brede v. Powers, 263 U.S. 4 (1923).

3. 18 U.S.C. §4083.

4. Duke v. United States, 301 U.S. 492 (1937).

The question of the application of this guaranty to the states has not been raised since it was last rejected in 1928.[5] But, as previously indicated, though the states are not required to use grand juries and may prosecute on the charge of a prosecuting official, where they do employ a grand jury they are forbidden by the equal protection clause systematically to exclude persons from the grand jury on the basis of race.[6]

The Court has said that "the most valuable function of the grand jury [is] not only to examine into the commission of crimes, but to stand between the prosecutor and the accused, and to determine whether the charge was founded upon credible testimony or was dictated by malice or personal ill will."[7] But in a 1956 decision in which Douglas joined, it held that an indictment is valid although the grand jury heard only hearsay testimony which would not be admissible at trial:[8]

> Our constitutional grand jury was intended to operate substantially like its English progenitor. The basic purpose of the English grand jury was to provide a fair method for instituting criminal proceedings against persons believed to have committed crimes. Grand jurors were selected from the body of the people and their work was not hampered by rigid procedural or evidential rules. In fact, grand jurors could act on their own knowledge and were free to make their presentments or indictments on such information as they deemed satisfactory. Despite its broad power to institute criminal proceedings the grand jury grew in popular favor with the years. It acquired an independence in England free from control by the Crown or judges. Its adoption in our constitution as the sole method for preferring charges in serious criminal cases shows the high place it held as an instrument of justice. And in this country as in England of old the grand jury has convened as a body of laymen, free from technical rules, acting in secret, pledged to indict no one because of prejudice and to free no one because of special favor . . .
>
> . . . If indictments were held open to challenge on the ground that there was inadequate or incompetent evidence before the grand jury, the resulting delay would be great indeed. The result of such a rule

5. Gaines v. Washington, note 90, p. 176, *supra*.
6. See pp. 139-140, *supra*.
7. Hale v. Henkel, 201 U.S. 43, 59 (1906).
8. Costello v. United States, 350 U.S. 359 (1956). *See also* Holt v. United States, 218 U.S. 245 (1910).

would be that before trial on the merits a defendant could always insist on a kind of preliminary trial to determine the competency and adequacy of evidence before the grand jury. This is not required by the Fifth Amendment. An indictment returned by a legally constituted and unbiased grand jury, like an information drawn by the prosecutor, if valid on its face, is enough to call for a trial on the merits . . .

. . . In a trial on the merits, defendants are entitled to a strict observance of all the rules designed to bring about a fair verdict. Defendants are not entitled, however, to a rule which would result in interminable delay but adding nothing to the assurance of a fair trial.

In a number of other cases, as previously indicated, Douglas has been willing to give less latitude to other investigating agencies. The Court has held that persons subpoenaed by a fire marshal, investigating a fire on their business premises, to testify in a non-public hearing are not entitled to counsel. In reaching this conclusion it endorsed lower court decisions holding that one called before a grand jury has no right to counsel and concluded that the same rule should apply to the fire marshal's investigation. Douglas joined in a dissent which did not challenge the assumption as to grand juries, but said in part:[9]

I believe that it violates the protections guaranteed every person by the Due Process Clause . . . for a state to compel a person to appear alone before any law enforcement officer and give testimony in secret against his will . . .

Any surface support the grand jury practice may lend disappears upon analysis of that institution. The traditional English and American grand jury is composed of 12 to 23 members selected from the general citizenry of the locality where the alleged crime was committed. They bring into the grand jury room the experience, knowledge and viewpoint of all sections of the community. They have no axes to grind and are not charged personally with the administration of the law. No one of them is a prosecuting attorney or law-enforcement officer ferreting out crime. It would be very difficult for officers of the state seriously to abuse or deceive a witness in the presence of a grand jury. Similarly the presence of the jurors offers a substantial safeguard against the officers' misrepresentations, unintentional or otherwise, of the witness' statement and conduct before the grand jury. The witness

9. *In re* Groban, note 37, p. 244, *supra* (dissenting opinion).

can call on the grand jurors if need be for their normally unbiased testimony as to what occurred before them.

When the Court later applied the same rule to an investigation of "ambulance chasing" by a state judge, he again dissented.[10]

Again, when the Court in *Hannah v. Larche* held that state voting registrars suspected of violating federal voting rights laws were not entitled to confront and cross-examine witnesses against them when summoned before the federal Civil Rights Commission, he dissented:[11]

The Civil Rights Commission . . . is an arm of the Executive. There is, in my view, only one way the Chief Executive may move against a person accused of crime and deny him the right of confrontation and cross-examination and that is by grand jury.

. . . The Grand jury brings suspects before neighbors, not strangers . . . "The very purpose of the requirement that a man be indicted by grand jury is to limit his jeopardy to offenses charged by a group of his fellow citizens acting independently of either prosecuting attorney or judge."

This Commission has no such guarantee of fairness. Its members are not drawn from the neighborhood. The members cannot be as independent as grand juries because they meet not for one occasion only; they do a continuing job for the executive and, if history is a guide tend to acquire a vested interest in that role.

Grand juries have their defects. They do not always return a true bill, for while the prejudices of the community may radiate through them, they also have the saving quality of being familiar with the people involved. They are the only accusatory body in the Federal Government that is recognized by the Constitution. I would allow no other engine of government, either executive or legislative, to take their place—at least when the right of confrontation and cross examination are denied the accused as is done in these cases.

When the Court later held in *Jenkins v. McKeithen* that persons summoned before a state commission investigating violations of criminal laws in the labor-management relations field were entitled to confront and cross-examine witnesses against them, Douglas concurred. He did not base his concurrence on the conclusion that, since the state

10. Anonymous v. Baker, note 38, p. 245, *supra* (dissenting opinion).
11. Hannah v. Larche, note 12, p. 147, *supra* (dissenting opinion).

commission's function was confined solely to criminal law violations, it, unlike the Civil Rights Commission, "exercises a function very much akin to making an official adjudication of criminal culpability." He concurred for the reasons stated in his dissent in *Hannah v. Larche.*[12]

Douglas concurred again when the Court held that a taxpayer had no standing to challenge summonses of a special agent of the Internal Revenue Service to a former employer to produce records pertaining to the taxpayer. But he wrote a separate opinion to challenge the assumption of the IRS that the taxpayer would have no right to confront, cross-examine, and rebut evidence taken against him in its investigation:[13]

The Internal Revenue Service is clearly conducting a criminal investigation of the petitioner. That is the function of special agents. The purpose of the summonses is to gather evidence for a criminal prosecution. At such "investigations" the summoned party may or may not be put under oath, at the discretion of the agent. He does have the right to be accompanied by counsel or an accountant. But the Internal Revenue Service has taken the position that the taxpayer who is being investigated is not entitled to be present at such "ex parte investigations." Moreover, he normally is not given notice of the issuance of the summons to the third party. Our decisions, however, make clear that the taxpayer has the right to be present at the hearing and to confront and cross-examine witnesses and inspect evidence against him . . .

. . . The Court held [in *Jenkins v. McKeithan*] that the [state] commission exercised an accusatory function and was empowered to brand people as criminals . . . Therefore, due process required the commission to afford a person being investigated the right to confront and cross-examine the witnesses against him.

Given the identity of purpose of the investigations in *Jenkins* and in this case, the rule of *Jenkins* clearly applies . . .

. . . The special agent will perform the function traditionally reserved to the grand jury in our Federal Government. The teaching of the *Jenkins* case is that such a proceeding may not be held without affording the taxpayer an opportunity to attend, to cross-examine, and to rebut.

12. Jenkins v. McKeithen, 395 U.S. 411 (1969) (concurring opinion).
13. Donaldson v. United States, note 68, p. 203, *supra* (concurring opinion).

In an early case the Court held that, where the Fifth Amendment requires an indictment and one is returned by the grand jury, it may not be amended by the court or the prosecutor in any respect without resubmission to the grand jury, even where the amendment merely removes language which is surplusage in that it does not state an essential element of the crime.[14] In 1960 Douglas voted with the Court to hold that where the indictment charges interference by extortion with the shipment of sand into a state, but the proof also shows such interference with the shipment of steel out of the same state, it is reversible error for the trial court to tell the jury that it can base a conviction on the latter shipments. "After an indictment has been returned its charges may not be broadened through amendment except by the grand jury itself . . . The very purpose of the requirement that a man be indicted by grand jury is to limit his jeopardy to offenses charged by a group of his fellow citizens acting independently of either prosecuting attorney or judge."[15]

A Federal Rule of Criminal Procedure provides that capital offenses shall be prosecuted by indictment, but that the defendant may waive his right to grand jury indictment in any noncapital case.[16] Douglas also voted with the Court to hold, assuming that the Fifth Amendment guaranty could be knowingly and intelligently waived, that the federal rule forbade its waiver in a capital case, and that a prosecutor's charge by information under the Federal Kidnaping Act was invalid when it did not allege that the victim was released unharmed, since proof of harm to the victim (which did not in fact emerge in the particular case) would have supported a death sentence.[17]

As previously noted, however, Douglas has dissented from the Court's refusal to hold that defendants in a federal criminal contempt proceeding based on conduct which occurs outside the courtroom are not entitled to all the procedural safeguards required by the Constitution for criminal prosecutions, including indictment by a grand jury.[18]

14. *Ex parte* Bain, 121 U.S. 1 (1887).
15. Stirone v. United States, 361 U.S. 212 (1960).
16. Rule 7, Federal Rules of Criminal Procedure.
17. Smith v. United States, 360 U.S. 1 (1959).
18. Green v. United States, note 48, p. 21, *supra* (dissenting opinion).

15 COMPULSORY PROCESS

The Sixth Amendment provides that, "In all criminal prosecutions, the accused shall enjoy the right . . . to have compulsory process for obtaining witnesses in his favor."

Douglas voted with the Court in 1967, in its only significant consideration of this guaranty, to hold it applicable to the states and to construe it to guarantee the "right to offer the testimony of witnesses, and to compel their attendance, if necessary, . . . the right to present the defendant's version of the facts as well as the prosecution's." Hence, a state was held to have violated the Constitution, not by refusing to subpoena a defense witness, but by applying a state rule that co-participants in the same crime could not testify for one another, though they could testify for the prosecution.[1]

1. Washington v. Texas, 388 U.S. 14 (1967). *Cf.* Blackmer v. United States, 284 U.S. 421 (1932).

16 CONFRONTATION AND CROSS–EXAMINATION

The Sixth Amendment also provides that, "In all criminal prosecutions the accused shall enjoy the right . . . to be confronted with the witnesses against him."

This provision is construed not to forbid the admission into evidence in a second prosecution of the testimony at the first trial of a witness now deceased or a witness unavailable because of defendant's wrongful procurement where the witness had testified and the defendant had an opportunity to cross-examine at the former trial.[1] But it does not permit such use of former testimony where the witness is now unavailable due to the negligence of the government.[2] As the Court once said, the purpose of this guaranty is "to secure the accused in the right to be tried, so far as facts provable by witnesses are concerned, by only such witnesses as meet him face to face at the trial, who give their testimony

1. Reynolds v. United States, 98 U.S. 145 (1878); Mattox v. United States, 156 U.S. 237 (1895).

2. Motes v. United States, 178 U.S. 458 (1900). *See also* Kirby v. United States, 174 U.S. 47 (1899), holding that in a prosecution for receiving stolen property the government cannot introduce the record of the conviction of another person for theft to prove that the property was stolen.

in his presence, and give to the accused an opportunity of cross-examination."[3]

In 1959, the Court considered a case involving the Defense Department's security clearance program for the employees of private manufacturers who produce goods for the armed services. In a decision in which Douglas joined, it noted that the department's clearance boards relied on the statements of informants who did not appear for cross-examination in the hearings before the boards and noted also that due process had frequently been held to require in civil cases whenever "government action seriously injures an individual" what the Sixth Amendment requires in criminal cases. Finding that the boards' procedures "raised serious constitutional problems," the Court concluded that Congress and the president had not intended to authorize it.[4]

On the Court's next consideration of the confrontation guaranty, Douglas joined in a decision that it was applicable to the states and was violated by the use at trial of testimony given at a preliminary hearing by a witness who had since left the state, where defendant was present at the hearing but had no counsel to assist in cross-examining the witness.[5] Douglas also joined in the decision in a companion case holding the guaranty violated where, after a co-defendant who had been convicted and had an appeal pending invoked his privilege against self-incrimination when called by the state, his confession implicating defendant was read to the jury at defendant's trial.[6] But he later concurred in a decision holding that defendant's right of confrontation was not violated where the prosecutor in his opening statement to the jury gave "an objective summary of evidence" which he expected to produce, including the expected testimony of a co-defendant who had pleaded guilty and whom the prosecutor expected would testify, where the co-defendant when called invoked his privilege against self-incrimination, and where the jury was instructed that statements made by

3. Dowdell v. United States, 221 U.S. 325 (1911).

4. Greene v. McElroy, note 98, p. 73, *supra.* For Douglas' views where the president had authorized such procedures, see Bailey v. Richardson, note 8, p. 145, *supra.*

5. Pointer v. Texas, 380 U.S. 400 (1965).

6. Douglas v. Alabama, 380 U. S. 415 (1965).

counsel concerning the facts in the case should not be regarded as evidence.[7]

Douglas voted with the Court to hold that a defendant had not made a knowing and intelligent waiver of his right to confrontation where he stated in open court that, although he would put in no evidence, he did not plead guilty to the charge, and his appointed counsel thereafter agreed that he would not cross-examine the state's witnesses.[8] He also joined in a decision that the guaranty was violated when, after an informant testifying for the prosecution admitted on cross-examination that the name he had given on direct examination was not his real name, counsel for defendant was not allowed to ask him his correct name and address.[9] And he agreed that there had been another violation when the state was allowed to use at trial the testimony given by a witness at a preliminary hearing where defendant's counsel was present but did not cross examine and where the state made no good faith effort to obtain the witness from federal prison in another state and present him at the trial. The exception permitting use of the prior testimony of an unavailable witness where defendant had a prior opportunity to cross-examine was limited to cases of necessity. The right to cross-examine was said to be "basically a trial right" that gives the jury an opportunity to "weigh the demeanor of the witness," and a preliminary hearing, which is conducted only to determine whether there is probable cause to hold the accused for trial, "is ordinarily a much less searching exploration into the merits of a case than a trial."[10] Douglas later voted with the Court to hold that this ruling would not apply to bar the use of testimony given by a witness at the preliminary hearing where the witness was subjected to extensive cross-examination by defendant's counsel, or where he took the stand and was available for cross-examination at the trial.[11]

7. Frazier v. Cupp, 394 U.S. 731 (1969). *Cf.* Namet v. United States, note 18, p. 218, *supra.*

8. Brookhart v. Janis, 384 U.S. 1 (1966).

9. Smith v. Illinois, 390 U.S. 129 (1968).

10. Barber v. Page, 390 U.S. 719 (1968). *See also,* Berger v. California, 393 U.S. 314 (1969). *Cf.* the similar rule applied to defendants under the "speedy trial" guaranty, discussed at pp. 181-182, *supra.*

11. California v. Green, 399 U.S. 149 (1970).

Douglas joined in dissent when, in 1957, the Court held that it was not reversible error in a federal prosecution to admit in evidence the confession of a co-defendant who did not take the stand where the confession implicated the defendant, but where the trial court instructed the jury that it was not to be considered as evidence against defendant and where "the other evidence against [defendant] was sufficient to sustain his conviction." The dissenters did not believe that defendant's fate should be left to "the psychological feat" which this practice demanded of the jury. Nor did they believe that an appellate court could know how the jury's mind would have operated on the other evidence against defendant "if powerfully improper evidence had not in effect been put in the scale against" him.[12]

Twelve years later the Court overruled that decision in the *Bruton* case,[13] where the co-defendant who did not take the stand but whose confession was admitted under cautioning instructions that it was not to be used against defendant had obtained a reversal of his conviction because the confession was obtained without observing the *Miranda* requirements.[14] The Court now concluded that, "because of the substantial risk that the jury, despite instructions to the contrary, looked to the incriminating extrajudicial statements in determining petitioner's guilt, admission of [the] confession in this joint trial violated petitioner's right of cross-examination secured by the Confrontation Clause of the Sixth Amendment."

In 1971, the Court limited the *Bruton* ruling to a case where the co-defendant did not take the stand. Where he did take the stand and repudiate his confession, the confession could be admitted in evidence, with a cautionary instruction that it was not to be considered against the defendant, since defendant had an opportunity to cross-examine his co-defendant at the trial. Douglas joined in a dissent which said in part:[15]

12. Delli Paoli v. United States, 352 U.S. 232 (1957).

13. Bruton v. United States, 391 U.S. 123 (1968). *See also*, Roberts v. Russell, 392 U.S. 293 (1968).

14. See p. 241, *supra*.

15. Nelson v. O'Neil, 402 U.S. 622 (1971) (dissenting opinion).

With all deference, I think the Court asks and answers the wrong question in this case. Under the law of California . . . admissions to a police officer by a criminal defendant after his arrest could not be used as substantive evidence against other defendants, whether or not the declarant testified at trial [and the California trial court so instructed the jury in this case] . . .

Bruton and *Roberts*[16] . . . compel the conclusion that the Federal Constitution forbids the states from assuming that juries can follow instructions which tell them to wipe their minds of highly damaging, incriminating admissions of one defendant which simultaneously incriminate another defendant whose guilt or innocence the jury is told to decide . . . Under *Bruton* and *Roberts*, California having made the determination that [the confession] could not be considered as evidence against [the defendant] may not subvert its own judgment in some but not all cases by presenting the inadmissible evidence to the jury and telling the jury to disregard it. For the inevitable result of this procedure is that, in fact, different rules of evidence will be applied to different defendants depending solely upon the fortuity of whether they are jointly or separately tried.

Douglas wrote for the Court to hold that a denial of confrontation was harmless error, not requiring reversal of the conviction, where the confessions of three co-defendants were admitted with limiting instructions under very special circumstances. One of these co-defendants testified that defendant had participated in an attempted robbery and resulting murder and was cross-examined by defendant's counsel. Defendant admitted that he was present at the scene of the crimes and fled with the other three but denied that he was a participant. The confessions of the others were not as damaging as that of the co-defendant who testified.[17]

As previously indicated, Douglas protested that the record was inadequate to decide the issue when the Court concluded that a defendant who so disrupts the trial as to prevent its continuance forfeits his right of confrontation and can be removed from the courtroom and tried *in absentia* until he is willing to conduct himself properly.[18]

16. Note 13, *supra*.
17. Harrington v. California, 395 U.S. 250 (1969).
18. Illinois v. Allen, note 51, p. 22, *supra*.

Quite apart from the confrontation clause of the Constitution, federal and state rules of evidence include a hearsay rule which, like the confrontation clause, is designed to preserve for parties in civil and criminal litigation the opportunity to cross-examine those whose testimony is used against them. But, to date, there are many more recognized exceptions to the hearsay rule than to the confrontation guaranty, and they vary from jurisdiction to jurisdiction. When one of those exceptions is invoked against the defendant in a criminal case, it is subject to constitutional challenge under the confrontation clause. Indeed, many of the cases previously considered in this chapter doubtless involved rulings by at least the trial judge that the statements in question were admissible under exceptions both to the hearsay rule and to the confrontation clause.

One exception to the hearsay rule, developed in federal cases where no constitutional challenge was made, is for the testimony of co-conspirator. His out-of-court statements, whether or not he is charged as a defendant or present for cross-examination at trial, are admissible if made in furtherance of the conspiracy on the theory that he is acting as an agent for the other conspirators so that his statements may be treated as admissions by them.[19] But the Court has held that statements of conspirators made after the conspiracy has terminated are not admissible in federal courts since not made in furtherance of the conspiracy.[20] And Douglas wrote for the Court to hold that this limitation precluded admission against others of an incriminating statement made by one co-conspirator after he had been apprehended by the FBI, since such a statement "is not in any sense a furtherance of the criminal enterprise. It is rather a frustration of it." Even if it be assumed that the conspirators were engaged in a second conspiracy to conceal the first, "the admissions made to the officers ended it. So far as each conspirator who confessed was concerned, the plot was then terminated."[21]

19. Clune v. United States, 159 U.S. 590 (1895).

20. Brown v. United States, 150 U.S. 93 (1893); Krulewitch v. United States, 336 U.S. 400 (1949); Lutwak v. United States, 344 U.S. 604 (1953).

21. Fiswick v. United States, 329 U.S. 211, 217 (1946).

Some states follow a different rule and permit the introduction of such statements on the theory that they are made as part of a conspiracy to conceal the crime charged. In 1970 the Court held that the confrontation clause did not forbid a state to apply this rule in a prosecution not for conspiracy but for murder, to allow a witness to testify in defendant's trial to an incriminating statement made by a co-defendant (who was separately tried and previously convicted) after he had been apprehended by the police. In the plurality opinion the federal rule was said to be a product not of the confrontation clause, but of the Court's disfavor of "attempts to broaden the already pervasive and wide-sweeping nets of conspiracy prosecutions." And there was no violation of the confrontation clause here because the co-defendants statement, "If it hadn't been for [defendant], we wouldn't be in this now," was of only "peripheral significance"; he clearly spoke from personal knowledge as evidenced by the testimony of a second co-defendant and by his own prior conviction, and the statement was not an attempt to exculpate himself. With such "indicia of reliability" the statement could be used without cross-examination since the possibility that cross-examination could have shown it unreliable "was wholly unreal." Douglas joined in a dissent which said in part.[22]

[The plurality opinion] characterizes as "wholly unreal" the possibility that cross-examination of [the co-defendant] himself would change the picture presented by [the witness' account of what the co-defendant had said]. A trial lawyer might well doubt, as an article of the skeptical faith of that profession, such a categorical prophecy about the likely results of careful cross-examination . . . The plurality concedes that the remark is ambiguous . . . At his trial [defendant] himself gave unsworn testimony to the effect that the murder prosecution might have arisen from enmities which [defendant's] own law enforcement activities had stirred up in the locality. Did [the co-defendant's] accusation relate to [defendant] as a man with powerful and unscrupulous enemies, or [defendant] as a murderer? The plurality opts for the latter interpretation for it concludes that [the co-defendant's] remark was "against his own penal interest" and hence to be believed. But at this great distance from events, no one can be certain. The point is that absent cross-ex-

22. Dutton v. Evans, 400 U.S. 74 (1970) (dissenting opinion).

amination of [the co-defendant] himself, the jury was left with only the unelucidated, apparently damning, and patently damaging accusation as told by the witness.

...The state was able to use [the witness] to present the damaging evidence and thus to avoid confronting [defendant] with the person who allegedly gave witness against him. I had thought that this was precisely what the Confrontation Clause . . . prevented.

While the Sixth Amendment's confrontation guaranty applies only in "all criminal prosecutions," Douglas dissented, as previously indicated, when the Court in *Hannah v. Larche*[23] found no denial of due process where the federal Civil Rights Commission, investigating state voting registrars suspected of violating federal law, summoned the registrars to testify without disclosing the identity of their accusers or allowing them to confront and cross-examine others who had testified. When the Court later distinguished *Hannah v. Larche* and found a denial of due process where a state commission followed similar procedures, because the commission's function was limited entirely to investigating criminal law violations, Douglas concurred for the reasons stated in his dissenting opinion in *Hannah v. Larche.*[24]

Judicial rules of evidence, including the hearsay rule, are not applied by administrative agencies and departments. In 1971 the Court sustained the action of the Secretary of Health, Education and Welfare in denying a disability claim under the Social Security Act after an administrative hearing. At the hearing four doctors, who had examined the claimant at the request of the government and who submitted reports adverse to his claim, did not testify, but their reports were admitted in evidence. A fifth doctor, retained as a "medical adviser" to HEW for the case, who had not examined the claimant, testified and summarized the contents of the adverse reports. All other testimony, including that of two doctors, was supplied by the claimant and supported his claim of back injury. Douglas dissented from the approval of the secretary's action:[25]

23. Note 12, p. 147, *supra.*

24. Jenkins v. McKeithen, note 12, p. 276, *supra* (concurring opinion). *See also* Donaldson v. United States, note 13, p. 276, *supra* (concurring opinion).

25. Richardson v. Perales, 402 U.S. 389 (1971) (dissenting opinion).

[The reports of the four doctors] may be received as the Administrative Procedure Act . . . provides that "any oral or documentary evidence may be received." But this hearsay evidence cannot by itself be the basis for an adverse ruling. The same section of the Act states that "a party is entitled . . . to conduct such cross-examination as may be required for a full and true disclosure of the facts" . . .

Cross-examination of doctors in these physical injury cases is, I think, essential to a full and fair disclosure of the facts.

. . . Although Congress provided in the Social Security Act that "[e]vidence may be received at any hearing before the Secretary even though inadmissible under rules of evidence applicable to court procedure" . . . Congress also provided that findings of the Secretary were to be conclusive only *"if supported by substantial evidence"* . . . Uncorroborated hearsay untested by cross-examination does not by itself constitute "substantial evidence" . . . Particularly where, as in this case, a disability claimant appears and testifies as to the nature and extent of his injury and his family doctor testifies in his behalf supporting the fact of his disability, the Secretary should not be able to support an adverse determination on the basis of medical reports from doctors who did not testify or the testimony of an HEW employee who never even examined the claimant as a patient.

This case is minuscule in relation to the staggering problems of the Nation. But when a grave injustice is wreaked on an individual by the presently powerful federal bureaucracy, it is a matter of concern to everyone, for these days the average man can say "There but for the grace of God go I."

One doctor whose word cast this claimant into the limbo never saw him, never examined him, never took his vital statistics nor saw him try to walk or bend or lift weights.

He was a "medical advisor" to HEW. The use of circuit-riding doctors who never see or examine claimants to defeat their claims should be beneath the dignity of a great nation. Three other doctors who were not subject to cross-examination were experts retained and paid by the Government. Some, we are told, who were subject to no cross-examination were employed by the workmen's compensation insurance company to defeat respondent's claim . . .

Review of the evidence is of no value to us. The vice is in the procedure which allows it without testing it by cross-examination. Those defending a claim look to defense-minded experts for their salvation. Those who press for recognition of a claim look to other experts. The problem of the law is to give advantage to neither, but to let trial by ordeal of cross-examination distill the truth.

17 BAIL

The Eighth Amendment provides that "Excessive bail shall not be required."

From the first Judiciary Act of 1789 to the Bail Reform Act of 1966 and the present Federal Rules of Criminal Procedure, legislation has provided for bail for persons arrested for federal prosecution. The Bail Reform Act provides that a person arrested for a noncapital offense *shall* be released pending trial on his own recognizance or on bail, unless it is determined that "such a release will not reasonably assure the appearance of the person as required," and that a person arrested on a capital offense and a person convicted of an offense but unsentenced or with an appeal pending *may* be released pursuant to the same standards.[1] The federal rules provide also that the amount of bail shall be such as "will insure the presence of the defendant" at trial, "having regard to . . . the policy against unnecessary detention of defendants pending trial."[2]

In 1951, in a decision in which Douglas joined, the Court held that the fixing of bail at $50,000 for each of four defendants indicted in

1. 18 U.S.C. §§3146, 3148.

2. Rule 46, Federal Rules of Criminal Procedure. The Congress in 1970 enacted a different policy for cases in the District of Columbia—one of preventive detention to hold in custody prior to trial those considered likely to commit other offenses. District of Col. Code §23-1321 to § 23-1331.

California for violation of the Smith Act was not sustained by proof that four others previously convicted of violation of the Smith Act in New York had forfeited bail and failed to report for imprisonment, or "by assuming, without the introduction of evidence, that each petitioner is a pawn in a conspiracy and will, in obedience to a superior, flee the jurisdiction. To infer from the fact of indictment alone a need for bail in an unusually high amount is an arbitrary act." "The right to release before trial" was said to be "conditioned on the accused's giving adequate assurance that he will stand trial and submit to sentence if found guilty . . . Bail set at a figure higher than an amount reasonably calculated to fulfill this purpose is 'excessive' under the Eighth Amendment."[3]

In 1967, in a decision which did not involve interpretation of the Eighth Amendment, the Court unanimously held that the fact that a defendant in a mail fraud prosecution was thirty-seven minutes late in appearing at one session of his trial did not justify the trial court in ordering him into custody without bail for the balance of his trial:[4] "A trial judge indisputably has broad powers to ensure the orderly and expeditious progress of a trial. For this purpose, he has the power to revoke bail and to remit the defendant to custody. But this power must be exercised with circumspection. It may be invoked only when and to the extent justified by danger which the defendant's conduct presents or by danger of significant interference with the progress or order of the trial." Since the defendant's commitment was found to have placed a burden on him and his counsel in the conduct of the case, his conviction was reversed.

In 1952 the Court held that the Eighth Amendment did not require bail for aliens held in custody pending deportation proceedings, because deportation "is not a criminal proceeding," because even in criminal proceedings that amendment does not "accord a right to bail in all cases, but merely [provides] that bail shall not be excessive in those cases where it is proper to grant bail," and because the aliens, who were alleged to be deportable as past or present members of the Communist

3. Stack v. Boyle. 342 U.S. 1 (1951).

4. Bitter v. United States, 389 U.S. 15 (1967). For other remedies available to a trial judge confronted with actual disobedience, see p. 22, *supra*.

party, were shown to be "active in Communist work" and hence might be detained "as a menace to the security of the United States." Douglas dissented[5] for reasons that "strike deeper than the bail provisions of the Eighth Amendment." He thought the statute under which the aliens were alleged to be deportable was unconstitutional, so that the aliens were "illegally detained and should be set free, making the issue of bail meaningless."[6]

5. Carlson v. Landon, 342 U.S. 524 (1952) (dissenting opinion).
6. See text at note 4, p. 143, *infra.*

18 CRUEL AND UNUSUAL PUNISHMENT; EXCESSIVE FINES

The Eighth Amendment also provides that "excessive fines" shall not be imposed, "nor cruel and unusual punishments inflicted."

Early decisions held only that this guaranty was not made applicable to the states by the Fourteenth Amendment, and that it was not a denial of due process of law for the state to substitute electrocution for hanging as a means of executing the death penalty for murder,[1] or to impose a sentence of ten years for conspiracy to defraud involving the sale of "a pretended gold brick."[2] Where the Eighth Amendment did apply, it was held not to be violated by the Territory of Utah when it ordered execution for murder by firing squad.[3] But a provision in the Philippine bill of rights forbidding cruel and unusual punishments, which was said to be "taken from the Constitution of the United States" and therefore to have "the same meaning," was held violated when a coast guard disbursing officer was convicted of making two false entries in his cash book indicating payments of 208 and 408 pesos, without regard to whether he intended or committed any fraud, and sentenced to fifteen years imprisonment at hard labor with his wrists

1. *In re* Kemmler, note 91, p. 176, *supra*.
2. Howard v. Fleming, 191 U.S. 126 (1903).
3. Wilkerson v. Utah, 99 U.S. 139 (1878).

chained to his ankles, deprived of his civil rights, perpetually disfranchised and disqualified for public office, subjected to official surveillance for life, and fined four thousand pesetas.[4]

In 1947 the Court considered the punishment inflicted in a contempt proceeding where a labor union had violated a federal injunction against a strike in a coal mines operated by the United States. The trial court had found both the union and its president guilty of civil and criminal contempt and fined the president $10,000 and the union $3,500,000. Without express reference to the Eighth Amendment the Court held that the fine against the president was warranted but that an unconditional fine of $3,500,000 against the union was "excessive as punishment for the criminal contempt" and that $2,800,000 of it should be converted to a civil sanction, payable only if the union did not cease the strike within a reasonable time. Douglas dissented on the issue, contending that the $10,000 fine on the president and the remaining unconditional fine of $700,000 against the union were excessive under the Eighth Amendment, since they believed in good faith, though erroneously, that the injunction was illegal and since the War Labor Disputes Act under which the mines were seized prescribed a maximum punishment of one year and $5,000 for interference with properties taken over by the United States. He believed that only conditional civil fines should have been imposed.[5]

In the same year, assuming without deciding that the Eighth Amendment's prohibition against cruel and unusual punishment applied to the states, the Court held it would not be violated by a state's second attempt to electrocute one convicted of murder where the first attempt had failed. Douglas joined in a dissent which said in part:[6]

The contrast is that between instantaneous death and death by installments—caused by electric shocks administered after one or more intervening periods of complete consciousness of the victim. Electrocution, when instantaneous, *can* be inflicted by a state in conformity with due process of law . . .

4. Weems v. United States, 217 U.S. 349 (1910).

5. United States v. United Mine Workers, note 52, p. 23, *supra* (concurring in part and dissenting in part).

6. Francis v. Resweber, note 20, p. 267, *supra*.

The all-important consideration is that the execution shall be so instantaneous and substantially painless that the punishment shall be reduced, as nearly as possible, to no more than that of death itself. Electrocution has been approved only in a form that eliminates suffering . . .

If the state officials deliberately and intentionally had placed the [defendant] in the electric chair five times and, each time, had applied electric current to his body in a manner not sufficient, until the final time, to kill him, such a form of torture would rival that of burning at the stake. Although the failure of the first attempt, in the present case, was unintended, the reapplication of the electric current will be intentional. How many deliberate and intentional reapplications of the electric current does it take to produce a cruel, unusual and unconstitutional punishment? While five applications would be more cruel and unusual than one, the uniqueness of the present case demonstrates that, today, two separated applications are sufficiently "cruel and unusual" to be prohibited. If five attempts would be "cruel and unusual," it would be difficult to draw the line between two, three, four and five. It is not difficult, however, as we here contend, to draw the line between the one continuous application . . . and any other application of the current.

A later case was disposed of on procedural grounds. A man convicted of burglary in Alabama and sentenced to the state penitentiary escaped after serving six years. He was later apprehended in Ohio and held for extradition back to Alabama. While so held, he filed a petition for habeas corpus in federal court, alleging that he had been brutally mistreated in the Alabama prison and would be subjected to the same treatment if returned there. The Court held that before he could seek federal relief he must first exhaust his state remedies by returning to the custody of Alabama prison authorities and presenting his claims to the Alabama courts. Douglas dissented from the denial of a hearing in federal court:[7]

The petition presents facts which, if true, make this a shocking case in the annals of our jurisprudence.

[Petitioner] offered to prove that the Alabama jailers have a nine-pound strap with five metal prongs that they use to beat prisoners, that they used this strap against him, that the beatings frequently caused

7. Sweeney v. Woodall, 344 U.S. 86 (1952) (dissenting opinion).

him to lose consciousness and resulted in deep wounds and permanent scars.

He offered to prove that he was stripped to his waist and forced to work in the broiling sun all day long without a rest period.

He offered to prove that on entrance to the prison he was forced to serve as a "gal-boy" or female for homosexuals among the prisoners.

Lurid details are offered in support of these main charges. If any of them is true, [petitioner] has been subjected to cruel and unusual punishment in the past and can be expected upon his return to have the same awful treatment visited upon him.

. . . If the allegations of the petition are true, this [petitioner] must suffer torture and mutilation or risk of death itself to get relief in Alabama.

. . . I rebel at the thought that any human being . . . should be forced to run a gamut of blood and terror . . . to get his constitutional rights. That is too great a price to pay for the legal principle that before a state prisoner can get federal relief he must exhaust his state remedies.

. . . The infliction of "cruel and unusual punishments" against the command of the Eighth Amendment is a violation of the Due Process Clause of the Fourteenth Amendment, whether that clause be construed as incorporating the entire Bill of Rights or only some of its guaranties . . . Even under the latter and more restricted view, the punishments inflicted here are so shocking as to violate the standards of decency implicit in our system of jurisprudence.

Five years later Douglas wrote for the Court to invalidate, as a denial of due process, the conviction of one who had previously been convicted of forgery because she had failed to comply with a city ordinance requiring all convicted felons to register with the police. The defendant had resided in the city for years and did not know of the ordinance until she was arrested by the police on suspicion of another offense and charged with failure to register:[8]

We do not go with Blackstone in saying that "a vicious will" is necessary to constitute a crime . . . for conduct alone without regard to the intent of the doer is often sufficient. There is a wide latitude in the lawmakers to declare an offense and to exclude elements of knowledge and diligence from its definition . . . But we deal here with conduct that is wholly passive—mere failure to register. It is unlike the commission of

8. Lambert v. California, 355 U.S. 225 (1957).

acts, or the failure to act under circumstances that should alert the doer to the consequences of his deed . . . The rule that "ignorance of the law will not excuse" . . . is deep in our law, as is the principle that of all the powers of local government, the police power is "one of the least limitable" . . . On the other hand, due process places some limits on its exercise. Engrained in our concept of due process is the requirement of notice . . . Notice is required in a myriad of situations where a penalty or forfeiture might be suffered for mere failure to act . . . [Prior] cases involved only property interests in civil litigation. But the principle is equally appropriate where a person, wholly passive and unaware of any wrongdoing, is brought to the bar of justice for condemnation in a criminal case.

. . . This appellant on first becoming aware of her duty to register was given no opportunity to comply with the law and avoid its penalty, even though her default was entirely innocent . . . We believe that actual knowledge of the duty to register or proof of the probability of such knowledge and subsequent failure to comply are necessary before a conviction under the ordinance can stand. As Holmes wrote in *The Common Law*, "A law which punished conduct which would not be blameworthy in the average member of the community would be too severe for that community to bear."

As previously indicated, Douglas in 1958 joined in a plurality opinion which concluded that a federal statute forfeiting the citizenship of a serviceman convicted of desertion by court martial imposed an additional, and a cruel and unusual, punishment.[9]

In 1962, in *Robinson v. California*, the Court held the prohibition against cruel and unusual punishment applicable to the states and violated when the state convicted defendant of the crime of being "addicted to the use of narcotics." The state might impose criminal sanctions against unauthorized manufacture, prescription, sale, purchase, possession, or use, or against disorderly or antisocial behavior resulting from use, of narcotics. And it might establish a program of compulsory treatment for addicts involving involuntary confinement. But it could not make the mere status of being an addict a criminal offense, any more than it could make it a crime to be mentally ill, or a leper, or afflicted with a venereal disease. Narcotic addiction is also an

9. Trop v. Dulles, note 16, p. 39, *supra*.

illness. Even though defendant had been sentenced to only ninety days, so that "in the abstract," the punishment was not cruel and unusual, "even one day in prison would be a cruel and unusual punishment for the 'crime' of having a common cold." Douglas concurred in that decision:[10]

> In Sixteenth Century England one prescription for insanity was to beat the subject "until he had regained his reason" . . . In America "the violently insane went to the whipping post and into prison dungeons or, as sometimes happened, were burned at the stake or hanged;" and "the pauper insane often roamed the countryside as wild men and from time to time were pilloried, whipped and jailed" . . .
>
> Today we have our differences over the legal definition of insanity. But however insanity is defined, it is in end effect treated as a disease. While afflicted people may be confined either for treatment or for the protection of society, they are not branded as criminals.
>
> Yet terror and punishment linger on as means of dealing with some diseases . . . That approach continues as respects drug addicts . . .
>
> The impact that an addict has on a community causes alarm and often leads to punitive measures. Those measures are justified where they relate to acts of transgression. But I do not see how under our system *being an addict* can be punished as a crime. If addicts can be punished for their addiction, then the insane can be punished for their insanity. Each has a disease and each must be treated as a sick person . . .
>
> The question presented in the earlier cases concerned the degree of severity with which a particular offense was punished or the element of cruelty present. A punishment out of all proportion to the offense may bring it within the ban against "cruel and unusual punishments" . . . So may the cruelty of the method of punishment, as, for example, disemboweling a person alive . . . But the principle that would deny power to exact capital punishment for a petty crime would also deny power to punish a person by fine or imprisonment for being sick . . .
>
> By the [early Seventeenth Century] enlightenment was coming as respects the insane . . . We should show the same discernment respecting drug addiction.

Thereafter, the Court refused to hold similarly unconstitutional the Texas conviction of a defendant for being "found in a state of intoxica-

10. Robinson v. California, 370 U.S. 660 (1962) (concurring opinion).

tion in a public place." Although defendant had suffered approximately one hundred convictions for the same offense in the past seventeen years, and there was psychiatric testimony that he was a "chronic alcoholic," the state court had ruled that chronic alcoholism was not a defense. There were differences from the case of the drug addict. The record showed "little about the circumstances surrounding the drinking bout which resulted in this conviction, or about [defendant's] drinking problem, or indeed about alcoholism itself." On "the comparatively primitive state of our knowledge on the subject," it could not be said that imprisonment "as a means of dealing with the public aspects of problem drinking can never be defended as rational." And defendant was convicted, "not for being a chronic alcoholic, but for being in public while drunk on a particular occasion." The Court should not so read the Eighth Amendment as to formulate a test of legal responsibility for one's acts in constitutional terms. Douglas joined in a dissent:[11]

The issue posed in this case is a narrow one. There is no challenge here to the validity of public intoxication statutes in general or to the Texas public intoxication statute in particular. This case does not concern the infliction of punishment upon the "social" drinker—or upon anyone other than a "chronic alcoholic" who, as the [trial judge] here found, cannot "resist the constant, excessive consumption of alcohol" . . .

. . . It is true, of course, that there is a great deal that remains to be discovered about chronic alcoholism . . . We are similarly woefully deficient in our medical, diagnostic, and therapeutic knowledge of mental disease and the problem of insanity; but few would urge that, because of this, we should totally reject the legal significance of what we do know about these phenomena . . .

It is entirely clear that the jailing of chronic alcoholics is punishment. It is not defended as therapeutic, nor is there any basis for claiming that it is therapeutic (or indeed a deterrent). The alcoholic offender is caught in a "revolving door"—leading from arrest on the street through a brief, unprofitable sojourn in jail, back to the street, and eventually another arrest. The jails, overcrowded and put to a use for which they are not suitable, have a destructive effect upon alcoholic inmates.

11. Powell v. Texas, 392 U.S. 514 (1968) (dissenting opinion).

. . . Most commentators, as well as experienced judges, are in agreement that "there is probably no drearier example of the futility of using penal sanctions to solve a psychiatric problem than the enforcement of the laws against drunkenness" . . .

Robinson stands upon a principle which, despite its subtlety, must be simply stated and respectfully applied because it is the foundation of individual liberty and the cornerstone of the relations between a civilized state and its citizens: Criminal penalties may not be inflicted upon a person for being in a condition he is powerless to change. In all probability, Robinson at some time before his conviction elected to take narcotics. But the crime as defined did not punish this conduct. The statute imposed a penalty for the offense of "addiction"—a condition which Robinson could not control. Once Robinson had become an addict, he was utterly powerless to avoid criminal guilt. He was powerless to choose not to violate the law.

In the present case, appellant is charged with a crime composed of two elements—being intoxicated and being found in a public place while in that condition. The crime, so defined, differs from that in *Robinson.* The statute covers more than a mere status. But the essential constitutional defect here is the same as in *Robinson* . . . I read [the trial court's] findings to mean that appellant was powerless to avoid drinking; that having taken his first drink, he had "an uncontrollable compulsion to drink" to the point of intoxication; and that, once intoxicated, he could not prevent himself from appearing in public places . . .

The findings in this case, read against the background of the medical and sociological data to which I have referred, compel the conclusion that the infliction upon appellant of a criminal penalty for being intoxicated in a public place would be "cruel and inhuman punishment" within the prohibition of the Eighth Amendment.

Douglas dissented, too, from the Court's refusal to review a District of Columbia vagrancy conviction:[12]

Our vagrancy laws stem from a series of [English] Statutes of Labourers . . . first passed in 1349 and amended and modified from time to time over the next 200 years . . . They "confined the labouring population to stated places of abode, and required them to work at specified rates of wages. Wandering or vagrancy thus became a crime." History

12. Hicks v. District of Columbia, 383 U.S. 252 (1966) (dissenting opinion). *See also* Edelman v. California, 344 U.S. 357 (1953) (dissenting opinion).

tells the story from the point of view of the Establishment: that wandering bands of people, who had left their masters, committed all sorts of crimes and hence must be punished for wandering. That philosophy obtains in this country . . .

The wanderer, the pauper, the unemployed—all were deemed to be potential criminals. As stated by the Court of Appeals for the District of Columbia . . . "A vagrant is a probable criminal; and the purpose of the statute is to prevent crimes which may likely flow from his mode of life." The vagrant, therefore, is not necessarily one who has committed any crime but one who reflects "a present condition or status" . . . That condition is not a failure to make a productive contribution to society, for the idle rich are not reached. The idle pauper is the target. Insofar as that status reflects pauperism it suggests the need for welfare; and insofar as it reflects idleness it suggests the need for the intervention of employment agencies. I do not see how under our system either of those elements can be made a crime. To do so serves the cause either of arrests and convictions on suspicion or of arrests and convictions of unpopular minorities—procedures very convenient to the police but foreign to our system.

I do not see how economic or social status can be made a crime any more than being a drug addict can be.

Douglas also joined in a dissent when the Court declined to review a case in which a convicted rapist had been sentenced to death. The dissenters thought that the case presented at least three questions:[13]

(1) In light of the trend both in this country and throughout the world against punishing rape by death, does the imposition of the death penalty by those States which retain it for rape violate "evolving standards of decency that mark the progress of [our] maturing society," or "standards of decency more or less universally accepted"?

(2) Is the taking of human life to protect a value other than human life consistent with the constitutional proscription against "punishments which by their excessive . . . severity are greatly disproportioned to the offenses charged"?

(3) Can the permissible aims of punishment (*e.g.*, deterrence, isolation, rehabilitation) be achieved as effectively by punishing rape less severely than by death (*e.g.*, by life imprisonment); if so, does the imposition of the death penalty for rape constitute "unnecessary cruelty"?

13. Rudolph v. Alabama, 375 U.S. 889 (1963) (dissenting opinion).

19 EX POST FACTO LAWS

Not all limitations on arbitrary governmental action are contained in the Bill of Rights. Article I of the original Constitution forbids both the federal government and the states to pass any "ex post facto Law."[1] In a very early decision the Supreme Court held that this prohibition applied only to criminal laws. Justice Chase, in a frequently quoted passage, defined an ex post facto law as one "that makes an action done before the passing of the law, and which was *innocent* when done, criminal," or which "*aggravates* a crime, or makes it *greater* than it was, when committed," or which "inflicts a *greater punishment*, than the law annexed to the crime, when committed," or which "alters the *legal* rules of *evidence*, and receives less, or different, testimony, than the law required at the time of the commission of the offence."[2]

Since 1920 the Immigration Law has forbidden the entry into this country of aliens who advocate or teach, or are members of or affiliated with any organization that advocates or teaches, forcible overthrow of the government. In 1939, in a decision in which Douglas joined, the Court held that this prohibition did not authorize the deportation of an alien who entered the United States in 1912, joined the Communist

1. U.S. Const. Art. I, §9, Cl. 3; Art. I, §10, Cl. 1.

2. Calder v. Bull, 3 Dall. 386 (1798). *See also* Thompson v. Utah, note 6, p. 247, *supra*.

party in 1932, and left the party in 1933.[3] Thereafter, the Communist party dropped all aliens from formal membership. In 1940, Congress amended the law to exclude any alien who "was at the time of entering the United States, or has been at any time thereafter, a member of" a proscribed organization. In 1952 the Court upheld that amendment as applied to aliens who entered in 1920 and belonged to the Communist party from 1923 to 1929, as well as to one who entered in 1916, joined the party in 1925, and was dropped from the party's membership roles in 1939 along with all other aliens. The amendment was held not to be an ex post facto law because not penal legislation nor a law which imposed "really criminal penalties for which civil form was a disguise." Douglas dissented:[4]

There are two possible bases for sustaining this Act:

(1) A person who was once a Communist is tainted for all time and forever dangerous to our society; or

(2) Punishment through banishment from the country may be placed upon an alien not for what he did, but for what his political views once were.

Each of these is foreign to our philosophy. We repudiate our tradition of tolerance and our articles of faith based upon the Bill of Rights when we bow to them by sustaining an Act of Congress which has them as a foundation.

... We have long held that a resident alien is a "person" within the meaning of the Fifth and the Fourteenth Amendments. He therefore may not be deprived either by the National Government or by any state of life, liberty, or property without due process of law. Nor may he be denied the equal protection of the laws ...

The right to be immune from arbitrary decrees of banishment certainly may be more important to "liberty" than the civil rights which all aliens enjoy when they reside here. Unless they are free from arbitrary banishment, the "liberty" they enjoy while they live here is indeed illusory. Banishment is punishment in the practical sense. It may deprive a man and his family of all that makes life worth while. Those who have their roots here have an important stake in this country. Their plans for themselves and their hopes for their children all depend

3. Kessler v. Strecker, 307 U.S. 22 (1939).

4. Harisiades v. Shaughnessy, 342 U.S. 580 (1952) (dissenting opinion). *See also* Carlson v. Landon, note 5, p. 290, *supra* (dissenting opinion).

on their right to stay. If they are uprooted and sent to lands no longer known to them, no longer hospitable, they become displaced, homeless people condemned to bitterness and despair.

This drastic step may at times be necessary in order to protect the national interest. There may be occasions where the continued presence of an alien, no matter how long he may have been here, would be hostile to the safety or welfare of the Nation due to the nature of his conduct. But unless such condition is shown, I would stay the hand of the Government and let those to whom we have extended our hospitality and who have become members of our communities remain here and enjoy the life and liberty which the Constitution guarantees.

Congress has not proceeded by that standard. It has ordered these aliens deported not for what they are but for what they once were. Perhaps a hearing [on that issue] would show that they continue to be people dangerous and hostile to us. But the principle of forgiveness and the doctrine of redemption are too deep in our philosophy to admit that there is no return for those who have once erred.

When a 1952 retroactive amendment was employed to deport an alien because he had been convicted of a marihuana offense in 1928, Douglas again dissented, protesting that, "In the absence of a rational connection between the imposition of the penalty of deportation and the *present* desirability of the alien as a resident in this country, the conclusion is inescapable that the [amendment] merely adds a new punishment for a past offense. That is the very injustice that the *Ex Post Facto* Clause was designed to prevent."[5] He dissented also in *Galvan v. Press*[6] when an alien who entered in 1918 and belonged to the Communist party from 1944 to 1946 was deported under another amendment, added by the Internal Security Act of 1950, authorizing deportation of aliens who at the time of entry or at any time thereafter were members of the Communist party.

But a later amendment provided that the proscribed membership must be "voluntary" and not include membership which was solely

5. Marcello v. Bonds, 349 U.S. 302 (1955) (dissenting opinion). Douglas has continued to dissent from retroactive applications of the 1952 amendment. Lehmann v. Carson, 353 U.S. 685 (1957) (dissenting opinion); Mulcahey v. Catalanotte, 353 U.S. 692 (1957) (dissenting opinion).

6. 347 U.S. 522 (1954) (dissenting opinion).

"when under sixteen years of age, by operation of law, or for purposes of obtaining employment, food rations, or other essentials of living, and were necessary for such purposes." The Court read this provision as "illustrative of the spirit in which the rigorous provisions regarding deportability . . . are to be construed," so that there must be "a substantial basis for finding that an alien committed himself to the Communist party in consciousness that" he was "joining an organization." This was not shown, the Court concluded, with respect to an alien who entered the country in 1914, joined the party briefly in 1935, not for the purpose "of overthrowing anything" but because there were "no jobs at that time" and because "it seemed to me that it came hand in hand—the Communist Party and the fight for bread." This evidence was insufficient to show that his brief membership had any "political" implications.[7] Douglas joined in that interpretation of the statute and dissented in a later case[8] when the Court held that it would not save an alien who entered in 1908, belonged to the party from 1937 to 1939, and, according to two ex Communists who testified against him, discussed only problems such as "labor conditions and the like" and did not advocate forcible overthrow of the government.[9]

7. Rowoldt v. Perfetto, 355 U.S. 115 (1957).

8. Niukkanen v. McAlexander, 362 U.S. 390 (1960) (dissenting opinion).

9. Cases finding legislation to violate both the prohibition against ex post facto laws and the prohibition against bills of attainder are discussed in the next chapter.

20 BILLS OF ATTAINDER

Article I of the Constitution also forbids the federal government and the states to pass any "Bill of Attainder."[1]

The Court in the *Cummings* case held this prohibition violated when, after the Civil War, a state amended its constitution to forbid, among others, a Catholic priest to practice his profession without first taking an oath that he had not supported the Confederate cause.[2] At the same time, in the *Garland* case, it held the prohibition violated also when the federal government, by both a federal statute and a rule adopted by the Supreme Court, excluded attorneys from practice in federal courts until they took a similar oath.[3] A bill of attainder was defined as "a legislative act which inflicts punishment without judicial trial." Deprivation of "political or civil rights" was held to constitute punishment. While the English bills of attainder which inspired their prohibition here were usually directed at named individuals, no difference was seen in provisions which "presume the guilt" of priests and lawyers and "adjudge the deprivation of their right" to preach or practice "unless the presumption be first removed by their expurgatory oath." "As the

1. U.S. Const., Art. I, §9, Cl. 3; Art. I, §10, Cl. 1.
2. Cummings v. Missouri, 4 Wall. 277 (1866).
3. *Ex parte* Garland, 4 Wall. 333 (1866). A state statute conditioning a defendant's right to defend a civil suit in the state courts on the taking of a similar oath met the same fate in Pierce v. Corskadon, 16 Wall, 234 (1872).

oath prescribed cannot be taken by those parties, the act, as against them, operates as a legislative decree of perpetual exclusion. And exclusion from the professions or any of the ordinary avocations of life for past conduct can be regarded in no other light than as punishment." The net result was that "the legislative body, in addition to its legitimate functions, exercises the powers and office of judge . . . it pronounces upon the guilt of the party, without any of the forms or safeguards of trial; it determines the sufficiency of the proofs produced, whether conformable to the rules of evidence or otherwise; and it fixes the degree of punishment in accordance with its own notions of the enormity of the offence." That was a "legislative enactment creating the deprivation without any of the ordinary forms and guards provided for the security of the citizen in the administration of justice by the established tribunals." Since the effect of the oaths was also to impose punishment for some acts which were not offenses when committed and to add new punishment for other acts which were offenses when committed, they were also invalid as ex post facto laws. Finally, the Supreme Court rule incorporating the statutory oath for lawyers, "having been unadvisedly adopted," was rescinded.

In 1946, in *United States v. Lovett*,[4] Douglas joined with the Court to hold the prohibition against bills of attainder violated by a rider to a Congressional Appropriation Act which forbade the payment of the salaries of named federal employees who had incurred the displeasure of Chairman Dies of the House Committee on Un-American Activities. Although a subcommittee of the Appropriations Committee had held hearings on Dies' charges in secret executive session in which the accused employees were permitted to testify but from which their lawyers were excluded, and had concluded that the employees were guilty of "subversive activity" as the Appropriations Committee had defined that term for the purposes of the hearing, this did not cure the attainder. The principle of the cases involving the post–Civil War oaths was said to be "that legislative acts, no matter what their form, that apply either to named individuals or to easily ascertainable members of a group in such a way as to inflict punishment on them without a

4. 328 U.S. 303 (1946).

judicial trial are bills of attainder prohibited by the Constitution." And the "permanent proscription from any opportunity to serve the Government is punishment," just as was the permanent exclusion from private vocations in the earlier cases. "The effect was to inflict punishment without the safeguards of a judicial trial and 'determined by no previous law or fixed rule.' " "An accused in court must be tried by an impartial jury, has a right to be represented by counsel, he must be clearly informed of the charge against him, the law which he is charged with violating must have been passed before he committed the act charged, he must be confronted by the witnesses against him, he must not be compelled to incriminate himself, he cannot twice be put in joepardy for the same offense, and even after conviction no cruel and unusual punishment can be inflicted upon him."

A later decision in the first *Douds* case[5] upheld a federal statute, since repealed, which forbade unions access to the facilities of the National Labor Relations Board until their officers had filed an oath disclaiming membership in the Communist party or belief in, or membership in or support of an organization that believed in, or taught, overthrow of the government of the United States by force or by any illegal or unconstitutional methods. A majority held that the First Amendment was not violated because the purpose of Congress was not to interfere with speech, but to protect interstate commerce against political strikes. The public interest in avoiding such strikes was said to be "substantial," and therefore to outweigh the "relatively small" impact of the oath requirement on First Amendment rights. And the oath requirement was said not to constitute a bill of attainder because it, unlike the previous legislative acts invalidated as attainders, did not punish for "*past* actions," but made union officers subject to possible loss of position "only because there is substantial ground for the congressional judgment that their beliefs and loyalties will be transformed into *future* conduct. Of course, the history of the past conduct is the foundation for the judgment as to what the future conduct is likely to be; but that does not alter the conclusion that [the statute] is intended to prevent future action rather than to punish past action."

5. American Communication Association v. Douds, 339 U.S. 382 (1950).

Here, "there is no one who may not, by a voluntary alteration of the loyalties which impel him to action, become eligible to sign" the oath. Douglas did not participate in that decision, but in the second *Douds* case indicated his view that so much of the oath as inquired into personal beliefs did violate the First Amendment and that this was enough to invalidate the entire oath requirement.[6]

Shortly thereafter, however, he dissented when the Court sustained a city ordinance requiring municipal employees to take an oath that they did not, and for the past five years had not, advocated overthrow of the government by force or other unlawful means and were not, and during the past five years had not been, members of organizations so advocating. The majority held that the oath did not violate the First Amendment, was not a bill of attainder because it did not inflict punishment but merely prescribed "qualifications for office," and was not an ex post facto law even if viewed as imposing punishment because a state statute had forbidden the employment of persons with the same proscribed beliefs and affiliations for seven years before the oath requirement was imposed. Douglas urged that the oath was a bill of attainder, just as were the post–Civil War oaths:[7]

> There are, of course, differences between the present case and the *Cummings* and *Garland* cases. Those condemned by the Los Angeles ordinance are municipal employees; those condemned in the others were professional people. Here the past conduct for which punishment is exacted is single—advocacy within the past five years of the overthrow of the Government by force and violence. In the other cases the acts for which Cummings and Garland stood condemned covered a wider range and involved some conduct which might be vague and uncertain. But those differences . . . are wholly irrelevant. Deprivation of a man's means of livelihood by reason of past conduct, not subject to this penalty when committed, is punishment whether he is a professional man, a day laborer who works for private industry, or a government employee. The deprivation is nonetheless unconstitutional whether it be for one single past act or a series of past acts. The degree of particularity with which the past act is defined is not the criterion.

6. Osman v. Douds, note 81, p. 67, *supra* (dissenting opinion).

7. Garner v. Los Angeles Board of Public Works, 341 U.S. 716 (1951) (dissenting opinion).

> We are not dealing here with the problem of vagueness in criminal statutes. No amount of certainty would have cured the laws in the *Cummings* and *Garland* cases. They were stricken down because of the mode in which punishment was inflicted.
>
> Petitioners were disqualified from office not for what they are today, not because of any program they currently espouse . . . not because of standards related to fitness for the office . . . but for what they once advocated. They are deprived of their livelihood by legislative act, not by judicial processes. We put the case in the aspect most invidious to petitioners [who had refused to take the oath and were, therefore, discharged]. Whether they actually advocated the violent overthrow of Government does not appear. But here, as in the *Cummings* case, the vice is in the presumption of guilt which can only be removed by the expurgatory oath. That punishment, albeit conditional, violates here as it did in the *Cummings* case the constitutional prohibition against bills of attainder. Whether the ordinance also amounts to an *ex post facto* law is a question we do not reach.

A few years later the Court had the attainder question in a different context. The Social Security Act of 1935 imposed a payroll tax on employees and their employers and provided for retirement benefits for the employees. An alien who entered this country in 1913 was employed so as to be covered by the act from 1936 to 1955, after which he became eligible for retirement and was awarded $55.60 per month. But he had also been a member of the Communist party from 1933 to 1939. In 1950 the Immigration Law was amended to make party membership a specific ground for deportation and the alien was deported in 1956. Because a 1954 amendment to the Social Security Act also provided for termination of benefits for one deported on that ground, his retirement benefits were also terminated. There was no similar provision for termination of the benefits of an alien who left the country voluntarily nor for all aliens who were deported. In a case involving only the validity of the termination of benefits and not of the deportation,[8] the Court held the 1954 amendment to the Social Security Act not invalid as a bill of attainder. The Court was not satisfied

8. For the validity of the deportation, see text at note 6, p. 290, *supra*.

there was "unmistakable evidence of punitive intent" as there was in the *Cummings*, *Garland* and *Lovett* cases. Douglas dissented:[9]

> Punishment in the sense of a bill of attainder includes [as was said in *Cummings*] the "deprivation or suspension of political or civil rights" . . . In that case it was barring a priest from practicing his profession. In *Ex parte Garland* . . . it was excluding a man from practicing law in the federal courts. In *United States* v. *Lovett* . . . it was cutting off employee's compensation and barring them permanently from government service. Cutting off a person's livelihood by denying him accrued social benefits—part of his property interests—is no less a punishment. Here, as in the other cases cited, the penalty exacted has one of the classic purposes of punishment—"to reprimand the wrongdoer, to deter others" . . .
>
> Social Security payments are not gratuities. They are products of a contributory system, the funds being raised by payment from employees and employers alike . . .
>
> Social Security benefits have rightly come to be regarded as basic financial protection against the hazards of old age and disability . . .
>
> Congress could provide that only people resident here could get Social Security benefits. Yet both the House and the Senate rejected any residence requirements . . . Congress concededly might amend the program to meet new conditions. But may it take away Social Security benefits from one person or from a group of persons for vindictive reasons? Could Congress on deporting an alien for having been a Communist confiscate his home, appropriate his savings accounts, and thus send him out of the country penniless? I think not. Any such Act would be a bill of attainder. The difference, as I see it, between that case and this is one merely of degree. Social Security benefits, made up in part of this alien's own earnings, are taken from him because he once was a Communist . . .
>
> . . . The aim and purpose are clear—to take away from a person by legislative *fiat* property which he has accumulated because he has acted in a certain way or embraced a certain ideology. That is a modern version of the bill of attainder . . .

The Court thereafter held that provisions of the Internal Security Act of 1950, requiring the Communist party to register with the Subversive

9. Flemming v. Nestor, 363 U.S. 603 (1960) (dissenting opinion).

Activities Control Board as a "Communist action" group, did not constitute a bill of attainder because the act did not designate specific persons or groups to which it applied, but prescribed a general standard to be applied after full administrative hearings subject to judicial review. Douglas dissented, but on the ground—later adopted by the Court—that the registration provisions violated the Fifth Amendment privilege against self-incrimination.[10]

A few years later, Douglas voted with the Court, in *United States v. Brown* to strike down as a bill of attainder a 1959 federal statute which replaced the non-Communist oath for union officers with a provision making it a crime for a member of the Communist party to serve as a union official.[11] This statute had been used to convict a union official who had been "an open and avowed Communist, for more than a quarter of a century." Under the *Cummings*, *Garland*, and *Lovett* cases, the statute was said "plainly" to constitute a bill of attainder, since it did "not set forth a generally applicable rule decreeing that any person who commits certain acts or possesses certain characteristics (acts and characteristics which, in Congress' view, make them likely to initiate political strikes) shall not hold union office, and leave to courts and juries the job of deciding what persons have committed the specified acts or possess the specified characteristics." "The moment [the statute] was enacted, respondent was given the choice of declining a leadership position in his union or incurring criminal liability." "In a number of decisions, this Court has pointed out the fallacy of the suggestion that membership in the Communist party, or any other political organization, can be regarded as an alternative, but equivalent, expression for a list of undesirable characteristics." This decision was "not necessarily controlled by" the first *Douds* decision,[12] which held that the purpose of the former non-Communist oath requirement was not punishment, but the prevention of political strikes, but "the Court

10. See Communist Party v. Subversive Activities Control Board, note 111, p. 77, *supra;* Albertson v. Subversive Activities Control Board, note 49, p. 226, *supra.*

11. United States v. Brown, 381 U.S. 437 (1965).

12. Note 5, *supra.*

in *Douds* misread *United States v. Lovett*" as limiting "punishment" to "retribution." "We do not hold today that Congress cannot weed dangerous persons out of the labor movement, any more than the Court held in *Lovett* that subversives must be permitted to hold sensitive government positions. Rather, we make again the point made in *Lovett:* that Congress must accomplish such results by rules of general applicability. It cannot specify the people upon whom the sanction it prescribes is to be levied. Under our Constitution, Congress possesses full legislative authority, but the task of adjudication must be left to other tribunals."

The Court later held, in a prosecution of union leaders for conspiracy to defraud the government by filing false non-Communist oaths under the now-repealed oath requirement, that the constitutionality of the oath could not be litigated in that prosecution because its validity could have been challenged by other means than "an alleged conspiracy, cynical and fraudulent, to circumvent the statute." Douglas joined in an opinion which maintained that the defendants could not have conspired to interfere with "lawful" and "proper" functions of government, as the indictment alleged, if the oath requirement was unconstitutional, and which contended also that it was unconstitutional as a bill of attainder. The dissenters could see no distinction between the statute which put union officers to a choice between giving up their offices and committing a crime, which the Court had held to be a bill of attainder in the *Brown* case, and one which gave them a choice between giving up their offices or filing a false affidavit, which was also a crime. "The heart of the holding in *Brown* was that Communists had been . . . attainted through legislative findings rather than a due process judicial trial. [The now repealed oath requirement] amounts to exactly the same sort of attainder by legislative fiat . . . I must say with considerable regret that future historians reporting this case may justifiably draw an inference that it is the petitioners, whatever may be their offense, and not the Government, who have been defrauded. For petitioners, if convicted and sentenced . . . unlike the Government, actually will have been deprived of something—their freedom. They will be in jail, having been denied by their Government the right to challenge the constitutionality of [the oath requirement] which, when it is challenged, must in my judgment be held to be the constitutionally doubly prohibited freedom-destroying, legislative bill of attainder."[13]

13. Dennis v. United States, 384 U.S. 855 (1966) (concurring in part and dissenting in part).

PART III THE ECONOMY

In Douglas' time on the Court there has been a major shift in the bulk of the Court's work. The problems dealt with in Parts I and II—problems of the structure of government and the power of government to restrict individual freedom—formed a small part of the Court's caseload prior to 1939. Until that time the Court had been primarily concerned with disputes between individuals and with the power of government to control the ownership and use of property.

These economic problems have not disappeared from the Court's docket and continue to constitute an important part if it. But with the shift in constitutional interpretation which has permitted a greater scope for governmental regulation of the economy, the Court has been less concerned with the power to regulate and more involved in implementing that regulation.

21 GOVERNMENTAL POWER TO REGULATE

The notion that the due process clauses of the Fifth and Fourteenth Amendments impose not only requirements of procedural fairness but also substantive limitations that empower the courts to test statutes regulating economic activity for their reasonabless had begun to crumble two years before Douglas joined the Court. In 1937 the Court sustained a state minimum wage law for women[1] that was indistinguishable from one invalidated a year earlier.[2]

Douglas has made his contribution to the demise of substantive due process. Writing for a unanimous Court in 1941 to uphold a state law regulating the fees of private employment agencies and overruling an earlier case in which Holmes and Brandeis had dissented, Douglas declared that the Court was not concerned "with the wisdom, need, or appropriateness of the legislation." Those questions were, under our constitutional system, committed to the legislators. The "only constitutional prohibitions or restraints which [the employment agencies] have suggested for the invalidation of this legislation are those notions of public policy embedded in earlier decisions of this Court but which, as

1. West Coast Hotel Co. v. Parrish, 300 U.S. 379 (1937).
2. Morehead v. New York *ex rel.* Tipaldo, 298 U.S. 587 (1936).

Mr. Justice Holmes long admonished, should not be read into the Constitution."[3]

In 1937 also the Court had concluded that the power of Congress to "regulate Commerce ... among the several states"[4] would reach to what previously had been viewed as a "purely local activity" beyond federal regulation—production. The National Labor Relations Act was upheld in its application to a major steel producer's plant in Pennsylvania[5] and to the operations of a trailer manufacturer in Detroit[6] and a maker of men's suits in Richmond, Virginia.[7]

Early in his tenure Douglas joined with a unanimous Court to confirm the congressional power to regulate manufacturing which had been approved only by 5 to 4 votes in 1937.[8] And in 1940 he wrote for the Court to uphold federal power to fix the prices for bituminous coal sold in interstate commerce:[9]

There are limits on the powers of the states to act as respects these interstate industries ... If the industry acting on its own had endeavored to stabilize the markets through price-fixing agreements it would have run afoul of the Sherman [Anti-Trust] Act ... But that does not mean that there is a no man's land between the state and federal domains ... Congress under the commerce clause is not impotent to deal with what it may consider to be dire consequences of laissez-faire

3. Olsen v. Nebraska, 313 U.S. 236 (1941). *See also* his opinions in Queenside Hills Realty Co. v. Saxl, 328 U.S. 80 (1946); California Auto Assn. v. Maloney, 341 U.S. 105 (1951); Day-Brite Lighting, Inc. v. Missouri, 342 U.S. 421 (1952); Williamson v. Lee Optical Co., 348 U.S. 483 (1955), and his votes where others wrote for the Court in Daniel v. Family Security Insurance Co., 336 U.S. 220 (1949), and Cities Service Gas Co. v. Peerless Oil & Gas Co., 340 U.S. 179 (1950).

4. U.S. Const., Art. I, §8, Cl. 3.

5. National Labor Relations Board v. Jones & Laughlin Steel Corp., 301 U.S. 1 (1937).

6. National Labor Relations Board v. Fruehauf Trailer Co., 301 U.S. 49 (1937).

7. National Labor Relations Board v. Friedman-Harry Marks Clothing Co., 301 U.S. 58 (1937). The metamorphosis of the Constitution, at a time when President Franklin D. Roosevelt was pressing his abortive "Court-packing" plan, is treated in more detail in V. Countryman, *Douglas of the Supreme Court* (New York: Doubleday, 1959), ch. 1.

8. United States v. Darby, 312 U.S. 100 (1941); Opp Cotton Mills, Inc. v. Administrator, 312 U.S. 126 (1941).

9. Sunshine Coal Co. v. Adkins, 310 U.S. 381 (1940).

. . . The commerce clause empowers it to undertake stabilization of an interstate industry . . . by . . . price control.

Perhaps the most important of the commerce clause cases was *Wickard v. Filburn*,[10] where a unanimous Court in 1942 upheld federal regulation of wheat production which reached to the fixing of quotas on wheat produced for the farmers' own consumption. One of the primary purposes of the regulation was to increase the price for wheat in the interstate market, and the amount raised for home consumption would obviously compete with wheat on the market and might thus frustrate the proper congressional objective. "Once an economic measure of the reach of the power granted to Congress in the Commerce Clause is accepted, questions of federal power cannot be decided simply by finding the activity in question" to be "of local character."

Other vestiges of the restrictive view of the commerce clause were also disposed of. In 1944 a majority including Douglas voted to reject an earlier notion that the insurance business, even when transacted across state lines, was not subject to the commerce clause because "contracts of insurance are not commerce at all."[11] And in 1971 Douglas wrote for the Court to sustain a federal statute aimed at "loan sharking" which Congress had found to be in large part under the control of organized crime. The statute made it a federal crime to use extortionate means to collect or attempt to collect any extension of credit. There was no question that the defendant was a "loan shark" who had loaned money at usurious rates to a New York butcher and then threatened the borrower and his family with physical injury in an effort to collect. But the defendant contended that his conduct was too local for federal regulation:[12]

The Commerce Clause reaches in the main three categories of problems. First, the use of channels of . . . commerce which Congress deems are being misused, as for example, the shipment of stolen goods . . . or of persons who have been kidnapped . . . Second, protection of the instrumentalities of . . . commerce, as for example, the destruction of

10. 317 U.S. 111 (1942).
11. United States v. South-Eastern Underwriters Ass'n., 322 U.S. 533 (1944).
12. Perez v. United States, 402 U.S. 146 (1971).

an aircraft, or persons or things in commerce, as for example, thefts from interstate shipments . . . Third, those activities affecting commerce. It is with this last category that we are here concerned . . .

[In *Wickard v. Filburn*[13] the Court said] "even if appellee's activity be local and though it may not be regarded as commerce, it may still, whatever its nature, be reached by Congress if it exerts a substantial economic effect on interstate commerce . . . "

As pointed out in *United States v. Darby*[14] . . . the decision sustaining an Act of Congress which prohibited the employment of workers in the production of goods "for interstate commerce" at other than prescribed wages and hours—*a class of activities*—was held properly regulated by Congress without proof that the particular intrastate activity . . . had an effect on commerce . . .

Where the *class of activities* is regulated and that *class* is within the reach of federal power, the courts have no power "to excise, as trivial, individual instances" of the class . . .

Extortionate credit transactions, though purely intrastate, may in the judgment of Congress affect interstate commerce .,. In the setting of the present case there is a tie-in between loan sharks and interstate crime.

The findings by Congress are quite adequate on that ground . . .

. . . It appears . . . that loan sharking in its national setting is one way organized interstate crime holds its guns to the heads of the poor and the rich alike and syphons funds from numerous localities to finance its national operations.

Early in his tenure on the Court, Douglas expressed doubts "concerning the propriety of the judiciary acting to nullify state legislation on the ground that it burdens interstate commerce."[15] Later cases providing examples of obvious burdens, due to the possibilities of conflicting state regulation, or multiple taxation, or the assertion by a state of power to halt interstate operations through licensing regulations, led him to resolve the doubts in favor of the judicial power and to favor its exercise in many cases where the Court did not.[16] But he has also

13. Note 10, *supra.*
14. Note 8, *supra.*
15. Nippert v. City of Richmond, 327 U.S. 416 (1946) (dissenting opinion).
16. The cases are too numerous for comprehensive citation. Illustrative are: Panhandle Eastern Pipeline Co. v. Michigan Public Service Commission, 341 U.S. 329 (1951) (dissenting opinion); Breard v. Alexandria, 341 U.S. 622 (1951) (dissenting opinion); Buck v. California, 343 U.S. 99 (1952) (dissenting opinion);

found an absence of invalidating burdens, again in many cases disagreeing with the Court.[17] And when Congress exercised its newly recognized power to deal with insurance under the commerce clause, by enacting a statute providing that the states should remain free to regulate and tax that business in areas not covered by federal law, Douglas voted to give generous rein to such state regulation and taxation.[18]

Lloyd A. Fry Roofing Co. v. Wood, 344 U.S. 157 (1952) (dissenting opinion); Public Service Commission v. Wycoff Co., 344 U.S. 237 (1952) (dissenting opinion); Chicago v. Willett, 344 U.S. 574 (1953) (dissenting opinion); Bibb v. Navajo Freight Lines, 359 U.S. 520 (1959). *See also* Huron Portland Cement Co. v. City of Detroit, 362 U.S. 440 (1960) (dissent).

17. Southern Pacific Co., v. Arizona, 325 U.S. 761 (1945) (dissenting opinion); Joseph v. Carter & Weekes Stevedoring Co., 330 U.S. 422 (1947) (dissenting opinion); Central Greyhound Lines v. Mealey, 334 U.S. 653 (1948) (dissenting opinion); Ott v. Mississippi Valley Barge Line Co., 336 U.S. 169 (1949); Dean Milk Co. v. City of Madison, 340 U.S. 349 (1951) (dissenting opinion); Spector Motor Service, Inc., v. O'Connor, 340 U.S. 602 (1951) (dissenting opinion); Bode v. Barrett, 344 U.S. 583 (1953); Colorado Anti-Discrimination Commission v. Continental Air Lines, 372 U.S. 714 (1963).

18. Prudential Insurance Co. v. Benjamin, 328 U.S. 408 (1946); Robertson v. California, 328 U.S. 440 (1946) (dissenting in part); Travelers Health Association v. Virginia, 339 U.S. 643 (1950) (concurring opinion). Further on Douglas' views on the power of government to regulate the economy, see H. Linde, "Justice Douglas on Freedom in the Welfare State," 39 *Wash. L. Rev.* 4 (1964); *40 Wash. L. Rev.* 10 (1965).

22 LABOR

One of the most pervasive uses made by the Congress of its power to regulate interstate commerce is in the field of labor-management relations. It has enacted a body of legislation dealing with the compensation of injured employees, the collective bargaining process, and the internal operations of labor unions. Just as Douglas has been liberal in his interpretation of the constitutional power to enact such legislation, he has been hospitable in his interpretation of the congressional policy embodied in that legislation.

Thus, he has consistently voted with those favoring a broad coverage,[1] and a broad standard of liability[2] under federal statutes providing for the compensation of injured railway employees, seamen, longshoremen and federal employees, and for a similar breadth in the scope of remedies for injured employees created by the courts under the ad-

1. *See, e.g.*, O'Donnell v. Great Lakes Dredge & Dock Co., 318 U.S. 36 (1943); Desper v. Starved Rock Ferry Co., 342 U.S. 187 (1952) (dissent); Johanson v. United States, 343 U.S. 427 (1952) (dissenting opinion); Ward v. Atlantic Coast Line R. Co., 362 U.S. 396 (1960); Roper v. United States, 368 U.S. 20 (1961) (dissenting opinion); Hellenic Lines. Ltd. v. Rhoditis, 398 U.S. 306 (1970); Moragne v. States Marine Lines, 398 U.S. 375 (1970).

2. *See, e.g.*, South Chicago Coal & Dock Co. v. Bassett, 309 U.S. 251 (1940); Farrell v. United States, 336 U.S. 511 (1949) (dissenting opinion); Palermo v. Luckenbach SS. Co., 355 U.S. 20 (1957); Kernan v. American Dredging Co., 355 U.S. 426 (1958); Morales v. City of Galveston, 370 U.S. 165 (1962) (dissenting opinion); Grunenthal v. Long Island R. Co., 393 U.S. 156 (1968); Usner v. Luckenbach Overseas Corp., 400 U.S. 494 (1971) (dissenting opinion).

miralty jurisdiction—although he has drawn the line where he detects the limits of policy or power.[3] Similarly, he has persisted, over the substantial opposition of some members of the Court, in preserving the jury trial provided for by some of these remedies from encroachment through the judge-created devices of directed verdicts and judgments notwithstanding the verdict.[4] And he has been vigilant to protect employees from inadvertent or confused loss of their rights to compensation through the execution of releases.[5]

Douglas voted to sustain the constitutionality of the Fair Labor Standards Act, forbidding the employment of child labor and prescribing maximum hours and minimum wages for employees "engaged in [interstate] commerce or in the production of goods for" such commerce.[6] Here again, in the enforcement of this act, he has favored a generous interpretation of its coverage[7] and of the remedies it provides

3. Swanson v. Marra Bros., 328 U.S. 1 (1946); Lauritzen v. Larsen, 345 U.S. 571 (1953); Herdman v. Pennsylvania R. Co., 352 U.S. 518 (1957); Dennis v. Denver & Rio Grande W. R. Co., 375 U.S. 208 (1963) (dissenting opinion); Edwards v. Pacific Fruit Express Co., 390 U.S. 538 (1968). *See also* O'Keeffe v. Smith Associates, 380 U.S. 359 (1965) (separate opinion).

4. *See, e.g.*, Jenkins v. Kurn, 313 U.S. 256 (1941); Stewart v. Southern Ry. Co., 315 U.S. 283 (1942) (dissenting opinion); Tiller v. Atlantic Coast Line R. Co., 318 U.S. 54 (1943); De Zon v. American President Lines Ltd., 318 U.S. 660 (1943) (dissenting opinion); Brady v. Southern Ry. Co., 320 U.S. 476 (1943) (dissenting opinion) Lavender v. Kurn, 327 U.S. 645 (1946); Eckenrode v. Pennsylvania R. Co., 335 U.S. 329 (1948) (dissent); Wilkerson v. McCarthy, 336 U.S. 53 (1949) (concurring opinion); Moore v. Chesapeake & Ohio Ry., 340 U.S. 573 (1951) (dissenting opinion); Senko v. La Crosse Dredging Corp., 352 U.S. 370 (1957); Gibson v. Thompson, 355 U.S. 18 (1957); Stevenson v. Atlantic Coast Line R. Co., 355 U.S. 62 (1957); Grimes v. Raymond Concrete Pile Co., 356 U.S. 252 (1958); Butler v. Whiteman, 356 U.S. 271 (1958); Harris v. Pennsylvania R. R., 361 U.S. 15 (1959) (concurring opinion); Inman v. Baltimore & O. R. Co., 361 U.S. 138 (1959) (dissenting opinion); New York, N.H. & H. R. Co. v. Henagan, 364 U.S. 441 (1960) (dissenting opinion); Davis v. Baltimore & O. R. Co., 379 U.S. 671 (1965); Rodicker v. Illinois Central R. Co., 400 U.S. 1012 (1971) (dissenting opinion).

5. Duncan v. Thompson, 315 U.S. 1 (1942); Garrett v. Moore-McCormack Co. Inc., 317 U.S. 239 (1942); Callen v. Pennsylvania R. Co., 332 U.S. 625 (1948) (dissenting opinion); Dice v. Akron, C. & Y. R. R., 342 U.S. 359 (1952); Maynard v. Durham & S. Ry. Co., 365 U.S. 160 (1961); Hogue v. Southern Ry. Co., 390 U.S. 516 (1968).

6. United States v. Darby, note 8, p. 316, *supra;* Opp Cotton Mills v. Administrator, note 8, p. 316, *supra;* Overnight Motor Co. v. Missel, 316 U.S. 572 (1942).

7. *See, e.g.*, A. B. Kirschbaum Co. v. Walling, 316 U.S. 517 (1942); Overnight Motor Co. v. Missel, note 6, *supra;* McLeod v. Threlkeld, 319 U.S. 491 (1943) (dissenting opinion); Western Union Telegraph Co., v. Lenroot, 323 U.S. 490

for workers employed in violation of its provisions.[8] Thus, he voted with the Court to construe the act to cover portal-to-portal time in the coal and iron mines and in a pottery factory,[9] and the on-call time of company firemen outside of regular hours.[10] Congress responded to these decisions with an amendment excluding from coverage traveling time and activities preliminary or postliminary to the "principal activities" of the employees. Thereafter Douglas voted with a unanimous Court to hold the time spent by employees of a battery manufacturer using showers and clothes-changing facilities required by state law in order to minimize the risk of lead poisoning was "an integral and indispensable part of [their] principal activities" and hence within the coverage of the act.[11]

Here again, however, he has found limitations in coverage under an act which does not by its terms invoke the full range of the federal commerce power[12] and which also contains several exceptions from its application.[13] And when Congress again amended the act to extend its coverage to state hospitals and schools, he contended in dissent that the

---

(1945) (dissenting opinion); Morris v. Mc Comb, 332 U.S. 422 (1947) (dissenting opinion); Farmers Reservoir & Irr. Co. v. McComb, 337 U.S. 755 (1949); Mitchell v. Kentucky Finance Co., 359 U.S. 290 (1959); Mitchell v. H. B. Zachry Co., 362 U.S. 310 (1960) (dissenting opinion); Idaho Sheet Metal Works, Inc. v. Wirtz, 383 U.S. 190 (1966).

8. Overnight Motor Co. v. Missel, note 6, *supra;* Walling v. Belo Corp., 316 U.S. 625 (1942) (dissenting opinion); Walling v. Helmerich & Payne, Inc., 323 U.S. 37 (1944); Gemsco, Inc. v. Walling, 324 U.S. 244 (1945); Brooklyn Savings Bank v. O'Neil, 324 U.S. 697 (1945); Walling v. Harnischfeger Corp., 325 U.S. 427 (1945); D. A. Schulte, Inc. v. Gangi, 328 U.S. 108 (1946); Mitchell v. Robert De Mario Jewelry, Inc., 361 U.S. 288 (1960) (concurring opinion).

9. Tennessee Coal, Iron & R. Co. v. Muscoda Local, 321 U.S. 590 (1944); Jewell Ridge Coal Corp. v. Local No. 6167, U.M.W., 325 U.S. 161 (1945); Anderson v. Mt. Clemens Pottery Co., 328 U.S. 680 (1941).

10. Skidmore v. Swift & Co., 323 U.S. 134 (1944).

11. Steiner v. Mitchell, 350 U.S. 247 (1956). *See also* Mitchell v. King Packing Co., 350 U.S. 260 (1955).

12. 10 East 40th Building, Inc. v. Callus, 325 U.S. 578 (1945); Alstate Construction Co. v. Durken, 345 U.S. 13 (1953) (dissenting opinion); Thomas v. Hempt Bros., 345 U.S. 19 (1953) (dissenting opinion).

13. Boutell v. Walling, 327 U.S. 463 (1946) (dissenting opinion); Walling v. General Industries Co., 330 U.S. 545 (1947); Levinson v. Spector Motor Service, 330 U.S. 649 (1947); Pyramid Motor Freight Corp. v. Ispass, 330 U.S. 695 (1947).

extension invalidly impinged upon rights reserved to the states under the Tenth Amendment.[14]

Most pervasive of the federal laws relating to labor is the National Labor Relations Act of 1935, guaranteeing to employees the right to organize in labor unions and engage in collective bargaining, proscribing a number of employer anti-union "unfair labor practices" and creating a National Labor Relations Board to administer its provisions. In this area Douglas has frequently been willing to allow the board more leeway than would a majority of the Court, in interpreting and applying substantive provisions of the act[15] as well as in fashioning remedies to protect employees' rights.[16] But he dissented from the approval of a back pay formula devised by the board which would give an unlawfully discharged employee more than he had lost in wages.[17] And he wrote for the Court to sustain a board finding that a large international union had been unlawfully assisted by an employer[18] and voted with it to hold that employers were entitled to lock out their employees in some circumstances.[19] He also voted with the Court to hold that a finding

14. Maryland v. Wirtz, 392 U.S. 183 (1968) (dissenting opinion).

15. NLRB v. American National Insurance Co., 343 U.S. 395 (1952) (dissenting opinion); NLRB v. Rockaway News Supply Co., Inc., 345 U.S. 71 (1953) (dissenting opinion); NLRB v. Local Union No. 1229, 346 U.S. 464 (1953) (dissenting opinion); NLRB v. United Steelworkers of America, 357 U.S. 357 (1958) (dissenting opinion).

16. National Licorice Co. v. NLRB, 309 U.S. 350 (1940) (dissenting opinion); Republic Steel Corp. v. NLRB, 311 U.S. 7 (1940) (dissenting opinion); NLRB v. Express Publishing Co., 312 U.S. 426 (1941) (dissenting opinion); Phelps Dodge Corp. v. NLRB, 313 U.S. 177 (1941) (dissenting opinion); Continental Oil Co. v. NLRB, 313 U.S. 212 (1941) (dissenting opinion); Southern Steamship Co. v. NLRB, 316 U.S. 31 (1942) (dissenting opinion); NLRB v. Indiana & Michigan Electric Co., 318 U.S. 9 (1943) (dissenting opinion); NLRB v. Crompton-Highland Mills, Inc., 337 U.S. 217 (1949) (dissenting in part); H. K. Porter Co., Inc. v. NLRB, 397 U.S. 99 (1970) (dissenting opinion).

17. NLRB v. Seven-Up Bottling Co., 344 U.S. 344 (1953) (dissenting opinion).

18. International Association of Machinists v. NLRB, 311 U.S. 72 (1940).

19. NLRB v. Truck Drivers Local, 353 U.S. 87 (1957). Douglas also voted with the Court to hold that while an employer may liquidate his entire business even for anti-union purposes, he may not liquidate a part of it if his purpose is to discourage the employees in his remaining operations from exercising their rights to organize and bargain collectively. Textile Workers Union v. Darlington Manufacturing Co., 380 U.S. 263 (1965).

that an employer had dominated a union could not be based upon the employer's exercise of rights of free speech guaranteed by the First Amendment,[20] and dissented from a decision that foremen were employees within the coverage of the act[21] —a position later substantially adopted by Congress.[22] And he concurred with the Court's reading of the amendments effected by the Labor Management Relations Act of 1947 to mean that henceforth the United States courts of appeal were to have a greater role, and the Supreme Court a lesser one, in reviewing board action, and were to impose a more severe standard of proof on board findings.[23]

The 1947 act also defined a new set of proscribed unfair labor practices which might be committed by unions, but preserved the guarantees of employees' rights to organize and bargain collectively. Douglas has on occasion protested that a majority of the Court has so interpreted the proscriptions as to impair the guarantees.[24] But he dissented from a holding that the typographers union had not "exacted" money for "services not performed" where it insisted on setting "bogus" type, which was not used, whenever a newspaper publisher used mats to reproduce advertising.[25] And he voted with the

20. NLRB v. Virginia Electric & Power Co., 314 U.S. 469 (1941). *See also* Virginia Electric & Power Co. v. NLRB, 319 U.S. 533 (1943); NLRB v. United Steelworkers of America, 357 U.S. 357 (1958) (dissenting opinion); NLRB v. Gissel Packing Co., 395 U.S. 575 (1969).

21. Packard Motor Car Co. v. NLRB, 330 U.S. 485 (1947) (dissenting opinion).

22. 29 U.S.C. §§152(3), 164(a). *See also* Marine Engineers Beneficial Association v. Interlake Steamship Co., 370 U.S. 173 (1962) (dissenting opinion). Douglas also voted with the Court to uphold the board in its determination that plant guards were employees who could be organized into separate bargaining units. NLRB v. E.C. Atkins & Co., 331 U.S. 398 (1947); NLRB v. Jones & Laughlin Steel Corp., 331 U.S. 416 (1947). That interpretation was later expressly approved by Congress. 29 U.S.C. §159(b).

23. Universal Camera Corp. v. NLRB, 340 U.S. 474 (1951) (concurring opinion); NLRB v. Pittsburgh Steamship Co., 340 U.S. 498 (1951). *See also* NLRB v. J.H. Rutter-Rex Manufacturing Co., 396 U.S. 258 (1969) (dissenting opinion).

24. *See, e.g.*, NLRB v. Denver Building & Construction Trades Council, 341 U.S. 675 (1951) (dissenting opinion); International Brotherhood of Electrical Workers v. NLRB, 341 U.S. 694 (1951) (dissenting opinion); Local 74 v. NLRB, 341 U.S. 707 (1951) (dissenting opinion); Local 1976 v. NLRB, 357 U.S. 93 (1958) (dissenting opinion). *See also* NLRB v. Local 825, 400 U.S. 297 (1971) (dissenting opinion).

25. American Newspaper Publishers Ass'n. v. NLRB, 345 U.S. 100 (1953) (dissenting opinion). At the same time he voted with the Court to hold that the

Court to require the board to process an unfair labor practice charge filed against a union, as employer, by its employees.[26]

Other provisions of the 1947 act authorized suits in the federal district courts for violation of collective bargaining contracts between employers and unions and for damages caused by the unfair labor practices of unions. Douglas wrote for the Court to sustain a damage award obtained by an employer against a union for unfair labor practices.[27] He wrote for the Court again to hold that a union could maintain an action for specific performance to compel an employer to comply with a provision in a collective bargaining contract for compulsory arbitration of grievances.[28] But when the converse situation was presented and an employer sued a union for specific performance of a collective bargaining contract containing a no-strike clause and an arbitration clause, a majority concluded that the new statute did not override a provision of the Norris–La Guardia Act of 1932 forbidding injunctions against strikes in labor disputes. Although Douglas had previously given generous adherence to the policy of the Norris–La Guardia Act,[29] he joined in a dissent in that case urging that the two statutes be reconciled to permit injunctions against strikes over grievances the parties had agreed to arbitrate, since "the availability of the injunctive remedy in this setting is far more necessary to the accom-

musicians' union did not violate the same provision by insisting on the hiring of a "stand-by" local band whenever a theater employed a traveling band, since the stand-by musicians' services were actually used by the theaters. NLRB v. Gamble Enterprises, 345 U.S. 117 (1953).

26. Office Employees International Union v. NLRB, 353 U.S. 313 (1957).

27. International Longshoremen's Union v. Juneau Spruce Corp., 342 U.S. 237 (1952).

28. Textile Workers Union v. Lincoln Mills, 353 U.S. 448 (1957). *See also* General Electric Co. v. Local 205, 353 U.S. 547 (1957); Goodall-Sanford, Inc. v. United Textile Workers, 353 U.S. 550 (1957); United Steelworkers of America v. Warrior & Gulf Navigation Co., 363 U.S. 574 (1960); United Steelworkers of America v. American Mfg. Co., 363 U.S. 564 (1960); United Steelworkers of America v. Enterprise Wheel & Car Corp., 363 U.S. 593 (1960). *Cf.* U.S. Bulk Carriers, Inc. v. Arguelles, 400 U.S. 351 (1971).

29. Milk Wagon Drivers Union v. Lake Valley Farm Products, Inc., 311 U.S. 91 (1940); Brotherhood of Railroad Trainmen v. Toledo, P. & W. R. Co., 321 U.S. 50 (1944); Order of Railroad Telegraphers v. Chicago & North Western Ry. Co., 362 U.S. 330 (1960); Marine Cooks & Stewards v. Panama Steamship Co., Ltd., 362 U.S. 365 (1960). *See also* Chicago & North Western Ry. Co. v. United Transportation Union, 402 U.S. 570 (1971) (dissenting opinion).

plishment of the purposes of [the Labor Management Relations Act] than it would be detrimental to those of Norris–La Guardia."[30] Eight years later, when the question was again presented, the Court reversed itself and adopted the dissenters' view.[31]

In another context the Labor Management Relations Act specifically amended the Norris–La Guardia Act: federal injunctions are authorized for strikes that "will imperil" the "national health or safety." When the Court interpreted this provision to sustain an injunction against an industrywide steelworkers' strike, Douglas dissented, contending that the court issuing the injunction had found no more than that the strike would impair "the economic well-being or general welfare of the country," whereas "Congress, when it used the words 'national health,' was safeguarding the heating of homes, the delivery of milk, the protection of hospitals, and the like."[32]

Douglas has voted with the majority to hold that nothing in the Constitution forbids the states to enact open-shop laws.[33] He has also written for the Court to hold that Congress may override such laws and permit union-shop agreements in areas subject to the commerce power,[34] but has insisted that funds collected by the union from a member under a union-shop arrangement may not be used, consistently with the First Amendment, to further political causes which the member opposes.[35] Similarly, he has consistently voted with the Court to

30. Sinclair Refining Co. v. Atkinson, 370 U.S. 195 (1962) (dissenting opinion). *See also* International Longshoremen's Ass'n. v. Philadelphia Marine Trade Ass'n., 389 U.S. 64 (1967) (dissenting opinion). Douglas had previously voted with the Court for a similar accommodation between the Norris–La Guardia Act and the Railway Labor Act. Brotherhood of Railroad Trainmen v. Chicago River & I. Railroad Co., 353 U.S. 30 (1957). And when the president, acting pursuant to statute during a time of declared war, seized the coal mines during a labor dispute, he agreed that the United States was not subject to the Norris–La Guardia Act. United States v. United Mine Workers, note 52, p. 23, *supra*.

31. The Boys Markets, Inc. v. Retail Clerk's Union, 398 U.S. 235 (1970).

32. United Steelworkers of America v. United States, 361 U.S. 39 (1959) (dissenting opinion).

33. Lincoln Federal Labor Union v. Northwestern Iron & Metal Co., 335 U.S. 525 (1949); American Federation of Labor v. American Sash & Door Co., 335 U.S. 538 (1949).

34. Railway Employees' Department v. Hanson, 351 U.S. 225 (1956).

35. International Association of Machinists v. Street, 367 U.S. 740 (1961) (concurring opinion). *See also* Lathrop v. Donohue, 367 U.S. 820 (1961) (dissenting

hold that unions which, by enrolling a majority of the employees in a bargaining unit have qualified as the exclusive bargaining representative for all employees in the unit under federal legislation, must represent all employees fairly and may not discriminate against some on racial[36] or other[37] grounds. He has also voted to uphold state legislation forbidding unions to engage in racial discrimination.[38]

Labor legislation apart, Douglas early voted with a majority to hold that peaceful picketing was protected from injunction by the First Amendment,[39] and, while recognizing that the protection does not extend to violent conduct[40] or to picketing designed solely to force an employer to engage in illegal conduct,[41] he has frequently dissented where he viewed the majority as erroneously permitting restraint of the use of nonviolent picketing as a means of publicizing the union's position in a labor dispute.[42]

---

opinion), where he took the same position with respect to a state requirement that all lawyers join an "integrated" state bar association.

36. Steele v. Louisville & Nashville Railroad Co., 323 U.S. 192 (1944); Brotherhood of Railway Trainmen v. Howarn, 343 U.S. 768 (1952); Conley v. Gibson, 355 U.S. 41 (1957).

37. Czosek v. O'Mara, 397 U.S. 25 (1970). *See also* his vote with the Court in Wirtz v. Hotel, Motel & Club Employees, 391 U.S. 492 (1968), to invalidate a union bylaw limiting eligibility for elective office in the union to those who had previously held such office.

38. Railway Mail Association v. Corsi, note 55, p. 131, *supra*.

39. Thornhill v. Alabama, 310 U.S. 88 (1940); Carlson v. California, 310 U.S. 106 (1940); American Federation of Labor v. Swing, 312 U.S. 321 (1941) (concurring opinion); Bakery & Pastry Drivers & Helpers Local v. Wohl, 315 U.S. 769 (1942) (concurring opinion); Cafeteria Employees Union v. Angelos, 320 U.S. 293 (1943); Amalgamated Food Employees Union v. Logan Valley Plaza, 391 U.S. 308 (1968). *See also* Thomas v. Collins, 323 U.S. 516 (1945) (concurring opinion), invalidating a state licensing requirement as applied to union organizers.

40. Hotel & Restaurant Employees Local v. Board, 315 U.S. 437 (1942).

41. Giboney v. Empire Storage Co., 336 U.S. 490 (1949); Journeymen Plumbers Local Union v. Graham Bros., 345 U.S. 192 (1952) (dissenting opinion).

42. Milk Wagon Drivers Union v. Meadowmoor Dairies, 312 U.S. 287 (1941) (dissenting opinion); Carpenters and Joiners Union v. Ritters Cafe, 315 U.S. 722 (1942) (dissenting opinion); Journeymen Plumbers Local Union v. Graham Bros. note 41, *supra* (dissenting opinion); International Brotherhood of Teamsters v. Vogt, 354 U.S. 284 (1957) (dissenting opinion).

23 THE ANTITRUST LAWS

In 1890 Congress enacted the Sherman Act, making illegal "every . . . combination in restraint of trade" in interstate or foreign commerce. Long before Douglas came to the Court that body had interpreted the act only to forbid "unreasonable" restraints.[1]

Early in his tenure Douglas wrote for the Court to establish a large exception to the earlier decision and to lay the foundation for the development of a body of effective antitrust laws during the last three decades. A combination to fix prices was held to be illegal per se, without necessity for further inquiry into reasonableness:[2]

The reasonableness of prices has no constancy due to the dynamic quality of business facts underlying price structures. Those who fixed reasonable prices today will perpetuate unreasonable prices tomorrow, since those prices would not be subject to continuous administrative supervision and readjustment in light of changed conditions. Those who controlled the prices would control or effectively dominate the market. And those who were in that strategic position would have it in their power to destroy or drastically impair the competitive system. But the thrust of the rule is deeper and reaches more than monopoly power. Any combination which tampers with price structures is engaged in an unalwful activity. Even though the members of the price-fixing group

1. Standard Oil Co. v. United States, 221 U.S. 1 (1911).
2. United States v. Socony-Vacuum Oil Co., 310 U.S. 150 (1940).

were in no position to control the market, to the extent that they raised, lowered or stabilized prices they would be directly interfering with the free play of market forces. The Act places all such schemes beyond the pale and protects that vital part of our economy against any degree of interference. Congress has not left with us the determination of whether or not particular price-fixing schemes are wise or unwise, healthy or destructive.

In a later case he wrote for the Court again to sustain the power of a lower court, on finding an illegal monopoly and a use of monopoly power in illegal restraint of trade in the exhibition of motion pictures, to order the defendant to divest itself of theaters unlawfully acquired or used.[3]

In this type of case we start from the premise that an injunction against future violations is not adequate to protect the public interest. If all that was done was to forbid a repetition of the illegal conduct, those who had unlawfully built their empires could preserve them intact. They could retain the full dividends of their monopolistic practices and profit from the unlawful restraints of trade which they had inflicted on competitors. Such a course would make enforcement of the Act a futile thing unless perchance the United States moved at the incipient stages of the unlawful project . . .

To require diversiture of theatres unlawfully acquired is not to add to the penalties that Congress has provided in the anti-trust laws. [Divestiture] merely deprives a defendant of the gains from his wrongful conduct. It is an equitable remedy designed in the public interest to undo what could have been prevented had the defendants not out-distanced the government in their unlawful project.

In a long list of other cases, in many of which he wrote for the Court, Douglas has voted for a rigorous application of the Sherman Act and a variety of other federal laws forbidding mergers, price discrimination, tie-in sales, and other practices harmful to free competition.[4] And he

3. Schine Theaters v. United States, 334 U.S. 110 (1948). *See also* his opinion for the Court in United States v. Crescent Amusement Co., 323 U.S. 173 (1944), his dissent in Timkin Roller Bearing Co. v. United States, 341 U.S. 593 (1951), and his vote with the Court in United States v. E. I. Du Pont De Nemours & Co., 366 U.S. 316 (1961).

4. *See, e.g.*, United States v. Bausch & Lomb Optical Co., 321 U.S. 707 (1944); Georgia v. Pennsylvania Railroad Co., 324 U.S. 439 (1945); Associated Press v.

has frequently protested that a majority was not rigorous enough in its application of those laws.[5] One such protest came when the Court adhered to previous decisions that size alone, accomplished without resort to illegal predatory practices, was not a violation of the Sherman Act. It therefore concluded that no violation of that act was to be found when United States Steel Corporation, the country's largest producer of unfinished rolled steel, which also produced fabricated steel products, purchased the properties of Consolidated Steel Corporation, the largest independent steel fabricator on the West Coast. Douglas dissented:[6]

We have here the problem of bigness. Its lesson should by now have been burned into our memory by Brandeis. [His book] *The Curse of Bigness* shows how size can become a menace—both industrial and social. It can be an industrial menace because it creates gross inequali-

United States, 326 U.S. 1 (1945) (concurring opinion); Federal Trade Commission v. Morton Salt Co., 334 U.S. 37 (1948); United States v. National Association of Real Estate Boards, 339 U.S. 485 (1950); Standard Oil Co. v. Federal Trade Commission, 340 U.S. 231 (1951); Lorain Journal Co. v. United States, 342 U.S. 143 (1951); United States v. Shubert, 348 U.S. 222 (1955); Radovich v. National Football League, 352 U.S. 445 (1957); Federal Maritime Board v. Isbrandtsen Co., 356 U.S. 481 (1958); International Boxing Club v. United States, 358 U.S. 242 (1959); Poller v. Columbia Broadcasting System, 368 U.S. 464 (1962); Silver v. New York Stock Exchange, 373 U.S. 341 (1963); United States v. Philadelphia National Bank, 374 U.S. 321 (1963); United States v. Aluminum Company of America, 377 U.S. 271 (1964); United States v. General Motors Corp., 384 U.S. 127 (1966); Federal Trade Commission v. Texaco Co., 393 U.S. 223 (1968); Fortner Enterprises, Inc. v. United States Steel Corp., 394 U.S. 495 (1969); Perkins v. Standard Oil Co., 395 U.S. 642 (1969); United States v. Greater Buffalo Press, Inc., 402 U.S. 549 (1971).

5. FTC v. Bunte Bros., 312 U.S. 349 (1941) (dissenting opinion); Mc Lean Trucking Co. v. United States, 321 U.S. 67 (1944) (dissenting opinion); Bruce's Juices v. American Can Co., 330 U.S. 743 (1947) (dissenting opinion); Federal Trade Commission v. Ruberoid Co., 343 U.S. 470 (1952) (dissenting opinion); Times-Picayuine Publishing Co. v. United States, 345 U.S. 594 (1953) (dissenting opinion); Automatic Canteen Co. v. Federal Trade Commission, 346 U.S. 61 (1953) (dissenting opinion); United States v. E. I. Du Pont De Nemours & Co., 351 U.S. 377 (1956) (dissenting opinion); Nashville Milk Co. v. Carnation Co., 355 U.S. 373 (1958) (dissenting opinion); Federal Trade Commission v. Standard Oil Co., 355 U.S. 396 (1957) (dissenting opinion); United States v. Armour & Co., 402 U.S. 673 (1971) (dissenting opinion).

6. United States v. Columbia Steel Co., 334 U.S. 498 (1948) (dissenting opinion).

ties against existing or punative competitors. It can be a social menace—because of its control of prices. Control of prices in the steel industry is powerful leverage on our economy. For the price of steel determines the price of hundreds of other articles. Our price level determines in large measure whether we have prosperity or depression—an economy of abundance or scarcity . . . In final analysis, size in steel is the measure of the power of a handful of men over our economy. That power can be utilized with lightning speed. It can be benign or it can be dangerous. The philosophy of the Sherman Act is that it should not exist. For all power tends to develop into a government in itself. Power that controls the economy should be in the hands of elected representatives of the people, not in the hands of an industrial oligarchy. Industrial power should be decentralized. It should be scattered into many hands so that the fortunes of the people will not be dependent on the whim or caprice, the political prejudices, the emotional stability of a few self-appointed men. The fact that they are not vicious men but respectable and social-minded is irrelevant. That is the philosophy and the command of the Sherman Act. It is founded on a theory of hostility to the concentration in private hands of power so great that only a government of the people should have it.

Douglas has agreed with the majority in finding no violation, though, where the government prosecutes in reliance on illegal acts which it has failed to prove;[7] where Congress has enacted exemptions for certain kinds of resale price maintenance laws,[8] for industry practices subject to other regulation,[9] and for certain agricultural groups;[10] or where the antitrust laws are invoked against conduct not fairly covered by them, such as a combination of railroads to lobby for exemption from the

7. United States v. Oregon State Medical Society, 343 U.S. 326 (1952). *See also* White Motor Co. v. United States, 372 U.S. 253 (1963).

8. *See* Schwegmann Bros. v. Calvert Distillers Corp., 341 U.S. 384 (1951); United States v. Mc Kesson & Robbins, Inc., 351 U.S. 305 (1956); Hudson Distributors, Inc. v. Eli Lilly Co., 377 U.S. 386 (1964).

9. Pan American World Airways v. United States, 371 U.S. 296 (1963). *Cf.* McLean Trucking Co. v. United States, note 5, *supra* (dissenting opinion); Pennsylvania Water Power Co. v. Federal Power Commission, 343 U.S. 414 (1952) (dissenting opinion); Carnation Co. v. Pacific Westbound Conference, 383 U.S. 213, 932 (1966).

10. Sunkist Growers, Inc. v. Winckler & Smith Citrus Products Co., 370 U.S. 19 (1962).

antitrust laws[11] or certain labor union practices[12] not undertaken in combination with nonlabor groups.[13]

He has on occasion also thought that the majority went too far in interpreting the antitrust laws to cover situations not within his reading. Thus, in *Standard Oil Company v. United States*, the Court held that the largest seller of gasoline on the West coast, which distributed some of its products through its own service stations and some through independent stations, violated the Clayton Act by requiring the independent stations handling its gasoline to buy from it all of their requirements of petroleum products. Although all of the defendant's major competitors employed similar exclusive dealing arrangements, and defendant's comparative competitive position had not improved as a consequence of its resort to the practice, the Court said the effect of such arrangements "may be to substantially lessen competition," since the effect was to foreclose competition for defendant's share of the market. The Court also suggested that the defendant could as effectively protect its competitive position by hiring the independent operators as its agents or by buying them up and thus adding to its owned outlets. Douglas dissented:[14]

It is plain that a filling station owner who is tied to an oil company for his supply of products [by an exclusive dealing contract] is not an available customer for the products of other suppliers. The same is true of a filling station owner who purchases his inventory a year in advance. His demand is withdrawn from the market for the duration of the contract in one case and for a year in the other. The result in each case is to lessen competition if the standard is day-to-day purchases.

11. Eastern Railroad Presidents Conference v. Noerr Motor Freight, Inc., 365 U.S. 127 (1961).

12. Apex Hosiery Co. v. Leader, 310 U.S. 469 (1940); United States v. Hutcheson, 312 U.S. 219 (1941); Hunt v. Crumboch, 325 U.S. 821 (1945); United Mine Workers v. Pennington, 381 U.S. 657 (1965) (concurring opinion); American Federation of Musicians v. Carroll, 391 U.S. 99 (1968). *See also* Los Angeles Meat & Provision Drivers Union v. United States, 371 U.S. 94 (1962) (dissenting opinion).

13. Allen Bradley Co. v. Electrical Workers Local, 325 U.S. 797 (1945); United Brotherhood of Carpenters v. United States, 330 U.S. 395 (1947). *See also* Meat Cutters Local v. Jewel Tea Co., 381 U.S. 676 (1965) (dissenting opinion).

14. Standard Oil Co. v. United States, 337 U.S. 293 (1949) (dissenting opinion).

Whether it is a substantial lessening of competition within the meaning of the anti-trust laws is a question of degree and may vary from industry to industry.

The Court answers the question for the oil industry by a formula which . . . promises to wipe out large segments of independent filling station operators. The method of doing business under requirements contracts at least keeps the independents alive. They survive as small business units. The situation is not ideal from either their point of view or that of the nation. But the alternative which the Court offers is far worse from the point of view of both.

The elimination of these requirements contracts sets the stage for Standard and the other oil companies to build service station empires of their own. The opinion of the Court does more than set the stage for that development. It is an advisory opinion as well, stating to the oil companies how they can with impunity build their empires. The formula suggested by the Court is either the use of the "agency" device, which in practical effect means control of filling stations by the oil companies . . . or the outright acquisition of them by subsidiary corporations or otherwise . . . Under the approved judicial doctrine either of those devices means increasing the monopoly of the oil companies over the retail field.

When the choice is thus given, I dissent from the outlawry of the requirements contract on the present facts. The effect which it had on competition in this field is minor as compared to the damage which will flow from the judicially approved formula for the growth of bigness tendered by the Court as an alternative. Our choice must be made on the basis not of abstractions but of the realities of modern industrial life.

Today there is vigorous competition between the oil companies for the market. That competition has left some room for the survival of the independents. But when this inducement for their survival is taken away, we can expect that the oil companies will move in to supplant them with their own stations. There will still be competition between the oil companies. But there will be a tragic loss to the nation. The small, independent businessman will be supplanted by clerks.

24 THE PATENT AND COPYRIGHT SYSTEMS

The Constitution empowers Congress to "promote the Progress of Science and useful Arts, by securing for limited Times to Authors and Inventors the exclusive Right to their respective Writings and Discoveries."[1] Congress has exercised this power by providing that an inventor may receive a patent giving him the exclusive right for seventeen years to use, make, and sell the patented invention and that an author may receive a copyright for twenty-eight years, renewable for another twenty-eight, which will give him the right to prevent the copying of his work. Both systems contemplate that one way in which the inventor or author may realize upon his monopoly is by licensing others to use it.

PATENTS

Douglas has long insisted that the patent grant must be confined to its constitutional purpose, the promotion of "the progress of science and useful arts," and has complained that the Patent Office has been too lax in its standards of what rises to the level of patentable invention. Thus he once provided a partial list of "incredible patents which the Paten Office has spawned"—including such gadgets as a rubber cap eraser fo

1. U.S. Const., Art. I, §8, Cl. 8.

pencils, a revolving cue rack, rubber hand grips for bicycle handlebars, and a metal washer on a wire staple.[2]

In 1941 he wrote for the Court to announce that "if an improvement is to obtain the privileged position of a patent more ingenuity must be involved than the work of a mechanic skilled in the art . . . The new device, however useful it may be, must reveal the flash of creative genius, not merely the skill of the calling."[3] The cordless cigarette lighter for automobiles involved in that case did not survive the test, where the only improvement over prior cordless lighters was to install a thermostatic control which would disconnect the lighter from the circuit when it was sufficiently hot for use, and where thermostatic controls for heating units had long been employed in a variety of electrical designs.

A number of other patents, including some of Marconi's on the telegraph,[4] succumbed to the rigors of that test in cases during the succeeding nine years in which Douglas voted with and frequently wrote for the Court,[5] and in several cases he dissented when he thought the Court too easily satisfied.[6] Thereafter the Court left the question of patent validity to the lower federal courts for fifteen years. When it considered the question again in 1966 it did so under a 1952 revision of the Patent Act. The new law added to previous requirements that a patentable invention be "new and useful" the further provision that it

2. Great At. & Pac. Tea Co. v. Supermarket Equipment Corporation, 340 U.S. 147 (1950) (concurring opinion).

3. Cuno Engineering Corp. v. Automatic Devices Corp., 314 U.S. 84 (1941).

4. Marconi Wireless Telegraph Co. v. United States, 320 U.S. 1 (1943).

5. Muncie Gear Works, Inc. v. Outboard, Marine & Mfg. Co., 315 U.S. 759 (1942); Universal Oil Products Co. v. Globe Oil & Refining Co., 322 U.S. 471 (1944); Dow Chemical Co. v. Haliburton Oil Well Cementing Co., 324 U.S. 320 (1945); General Electric Co. v. Jewel Incandescent Lamp Co., 326 U.S. 242 (1945); Funk Bros. Seed Co. v. Kalo Inoculant Co., 333 U.S. 127 (1948); Mandel Bros. v. Wallace, 335 U.S. 291 (1948) (concurring opinion); Jungersen v. Ostby & Barton Co., 335 U.S. 560 (1949). *See also* Halliburton Oil Well Cementing Co. v. Walker, 329 U.S. 1 (1946); Graver Tank & Mfg. Co. v. Linde Air Products Co., 336 U.S. 271 (1949) (concurring opinion).

6. Exhibit Supply Co. v. Ace Patents Corp., 315 U.S. 126 (1942) (dissenting opinion); Williams Manufacturing Co., v. United Shoe Mach. Corp., 316 U.S. 364 (1942) (dissenting opinion); Goodyear Tire & Rubber Co. v. Ray-o-vac Co., 321 U.S. 275 (1944) (dissenting opinion). *See also* Graver Tank & Mfg. Co. v. Linde Air Products Co., 339 U.S. 605 (1950) (dissenting opinions).

not have been "obvious at the time the invention was made to a person having ordinary skill in the art." It also added that, "Patentability shall not be negatived by the manner in which the invention was made." While conceding that the new language was aimed at the "flash of creative genius" test which Douglas had formulated, a majority with whom he joined concluded that, construed in the light of the constitutional purpose, the amendment made no change in "the general level of patentable invention" or in "the general strictness with which the overall test is to be applied."[7] Since that decision, Douglas has dissented from a holding that a chemical process was not "useful" within the meaning of the statute because no present use for its product could be identified, contending that the majority overlooked the possibility that it might contribute to research which would produce useful products.[8] He has also written for a unanimous Court to invalidate a combination patent on an improved paving machine, where all that was involved was the assembly on one chasis of four devices known in the prior art.[9]

The patent, where valid, authorizes the patentee to make, use, and sell his invention. But the patent laws do not expressly require him to do any of these things, and the Supreme Court long ago held that his suppression of the patent did not affect its validity.[10] When the Court reaffirmed that ruling in 1945, Douglas dissented, contending that it was inconsistent with the constitutional purpose of the patent grant:[11]

> Of the various enumerated powers [the power to grant patents] is the only one which states the purpose of the authority granted Congress. "The Congress is given no general power to issue letters patent or to reward inventors as it will. An experience with grants of monopoly in England was fresh in the minds of the Fathers; the lesson had been underlined in recent differences with the Crown." Hamilton, *Patents and Free Enterprise* (1941), p. 152 . . .

7. Graham v. John Deere Co., 383 U.S. 1 (1966). *See also* United States v. Adams, 383 U.S. 39 (1966).
8. Brenner v. Manson, 383 U.S. 519 (1966) (dissenting opinion).
9. Anderson's Black Rock, Inc. v. Pavement Salvage Co., 396 U.S. 57 (1969).
10. Continental Paper Bag Co. v. Eastern Paper Bag Co., 210 U.S. 405 (1908).
11. Special Equipment Co. v. Coe, 324 U.S. 370 (1945) (dissenting opinion).

It is a mistake therefore to conceive of a patent as another form of private property. The patent is a privilege "conditioned by a public purpose" . . . The public purpose is "to promote the progress of science and useful arts." The exclusive right of the inventor is but the means to that end. But the [original decision allowing patent suppression] marked a radical departure from that theory. It treated the "exclusive" right of the inventor as something akin to an "absolute" right. It subordinated the public purpose of the grant to the self-interest of the patentee.

The result is that suppression of patents has become commonplace. Patents are multiplied to protect an economic barony or empire, not to put new discoveries to use for the common good. "It is common practice to make an invention and to secure a patent to block off a competitor's progress. By studying his ware and developing an improvement upon it, a concern may 'fence in' its rival; by a series of such moves, it may pin the trade enemy within a technology which rapidly becomes obsolete. As often as not such maneuvers retard, rather than promote, the progress of the useful arts. Invariably their effect is to enlarge and to prolong personal privilege within the public domain." Hamilton, p. 161. One patent is used merely to protect another. The use of a new patent is suppressed so as to preclude experimentation which might result in further invention by competitors. A whole technology is blocked off. The result is a clog to our economic machine and a barrier to an economy of abundance.

Where the patent is used, Douglas has been vigilant to detect uses which would extend the legitimate monopoly to nonpatentable items, either by collecting royalties on the manufacture, sale, or use of such items, or by basing infringement suits on their manufacture, sale, or use.[12] Such practices violate the policy of the antitrust laws, just as the

12. Ethyl Gasoline Corp. v. United States, 309 U.S. 436 (1940); Morton Salt Co. v. G. S. Suppiger Co., 314 U.S. 488. (1942); B. B. Chemical Co. v. Ellis, 314 U.S. 495 (1942); United States v. Univis Lens Co., 316 U.S. 241 (1942); United States v. Masonite Corp., 316 U.S. 265 (1942); Mercoid Corp. v. Mid-Continent Investment Co., 320 U.S. 661 (1944); Transparent-Wrap Machine Corp. v. Stokes & Smith Co., 329 U.S. 637 (1947); International Salt Co. v. United States, 332 U.S. 392 (1947); Automatic Radio Mfg. Co. v. Hazeltine Research, Inc., 339 U.S. 827 (1950) (dissenting opinion); Aro Mfg. Co. v. Convertible Top Replacement Co., 365 U.S. 336 (1961); Aro Mfg. Co. v. Convertible Top Replacement Co., 377 U.S. 476 (1964) (dissenting opinion).

application of state law for the protection of unpatented "trade secrets" may violate the antitrust laws.[13]

Douglas has also voted with the Court to hold that when the patentee has misused his patents in violation of the antitrust laws an appropriate sanction may be to require him to license his competitors to use them.[14] But he has dissented from the Court's refusal to order the compulsory licensing on a royalty-free basis, contending that to allow the patentees to exact royalties was to allow them to "reap dividends from their unlawful activities."[15]

Before Douglas reached the Court, it was held in the *General Electric* case that one of the perquisites of the patentee, when licensing others to make and sell the patented article, is to fix the price at which his licensees can sell the finished product.[16] Douglas has joined in later decisions holding that there is nonetheless a violation of the antitrust laws when patentees combine to exercise this price-fixing power.[17] But he has also insisted that the earlier decision was wrong—that the provision in the patent laws giving the patentee the "exclusive right to make, use, and vend" his invention should not be construed to legitimatize a price-fixing agreement between the patentee and his licensees which would otherwise violate the antitrust laws:[18]

> [The *General Electric* case] saddled the economy with a vicious monopoly. In the first place, this form of price-fixing underwrites the high-cost producer. By protecting him against competition from low-cost producers, it strengthens and enlarges his monopoly. It is said in

13. Fashion Originators' Guild v. Federal Trade Commission, 312 U.S. 457 (1941); Millinery Creator's Guild v. Federal Trade Commission, 312 U.S. 469 (1941); Compco Corp. v. Day-Brite Lighting, Inc., 376 U.S. 234 (1964); Sears, Roebuck & Co. v. Stiffel Co., 376 U.S. 225 (1964). *See also* United States v. Sealy, Inc., 388 U.S. 350 (1967), where Douglas voted with the Court to find a violation of the antitrust laws through the licensing of the use of trademarks, which are not expressly authorized by the Constitution but are provided for by federal statute.

14. International Salt Co. v. United States, 332 U.S. 392 (1947); Besser Mfg. Co. v. United States, 343 U.S. 444 (1952).

15. United States v. National Lead Co., 332 U.S. 319 (1947) (dissenting opinion).

16. United States v. General Electric Co., 272 U.S. 476 (1926).

17. United States v. United States Gypsum Co., 333 U.S. 364 (1948); United States v. New Wrinkle, Inc., 342 U.S. 321 (1952).

18. United States v. Line Material Co., 333 U.S. 287 (1948) (concurring opinion).

reply that he, the patentee, has that monopoly anyway—that his exclusive right to make, use and vend would give him the right to exclude others and manufacture the invention and market it at any price he chose. That is true. But what he gets by the price-fixing agreement with his competitors is much more than that. He then gets not a benefit inherent in the right of exclusion but a benefit which flows from suppression of competition by combination with his competitors. Then he gets the benefit of the production and marketing facilities of competitors without the risks of price competition . . . In short, he and his associates get the benefits of a conspiracy or combination in restraint of competition. That is more than an "exclusive right" to an invention; it is an "exclusive right" to form a combination with competitors to fix the prices of the products of invention. The patentee creates by that method a powerful inducement for the abandonment of competition, for the cessation of litigation concerning the validity of patents, for the acceptance of patents no matter how dubious, for the abandonment of research in the development of competing patents. Those who can get stabilized markets, assured margins, and freedom from price cutting will find a price-fixing license an attractive alternative to the more arduous methods of maintaining their competitive positions. Competition tends to become impaired not by reason of the public's preference for the patented article but because of the preference of competitors for the price-fixing and for the increased profits which that method of doing business promises.

Another great advantage of the licensing system to the patentee was the Court-created doctrine that a licensee was estopped from challenging the validity of the patent.[19] Douglas concurred in decisions limiting the estoppel doctrine so as not to prevent a challenge to validity where the patentee's conduct would violate the antitrust laws if the patent was invalid,[20] or where a licensee sued for infringement was able to show that the alleged infringing device consisted solely of an invention covered by an expired patent.[21] But he has also objected to any application of the doctrine of license estoppel:[22]

19. United States v. Harvey Steel Co., 196 U.S. 310 (1905).

20. Sola Electric Co. v. Jefferson Electric Co., 317 U.S. 173 (1942); Edward Katzinger Co. v. Chicago Metallic Mfg. Co. 329 U.S. 394 (1947); MacGregor v. Westinghouse Electric Mfg. Co., 329 U.S. 402 (1947).

21. Scott Paper Co. v. Marcalus Mfg. Co., 326 U.S. 249 (1945).

22. Automatic Radio Mfg. Co. v. Hazeltine Research, Inc., 339 U.S. 827 (1950) (dissenting opinion).

> It is only right and just that the licensee be allowed to challenge the validity of the patents. A great pooling of patents is made; and whole industries are knit together in the fashion of the unholy alliances revealed in [prior Supreme Court cases finding an illegal combination of patents to fix prices]. One who wants the use of one patent may have to take hundreds. The whole package may contain many patents that have been foisted on the public. No other person than the licensee will be interested enough to challenge them. He alone will be apt to see and understand the basis of their illegality.
>
> The licensee protects the public interest in exposing invalid or expired patents and freeing the public of their toll. He should be allowed that privilege. He would be allowed it were the public interest considered the dominant one. Ridding the public of stale or specious patents is one way of serving the end of the progress of science.

In 1969 the Court adopted that view and rejected the doctrine of patent license estoppel.[23]

When a patentee sues for alleged infringement of his patent, the defendant in the infringement action typically has two possible defenses: (1) he is not infringing, and (2) the patent is invalid. Either defense, if established, is enough to defeat the suit. The first defense, obviously, would relate to the nature of the device, design, or process being used by the particular defendant. The second would relate to the novelty and usefulness of the patent on which the suit was based. In 1936 the Court held that a patentee who had lost one infringement suit on the ground that his patent was invalid could thereafter sue a second alleged infringer and relitigate the validity issue. In 1971 Douglas voted with a unanimous Court to overrule that decision and to hold that the patentee's second suit would be barred by the prior decision that his patent was invalid unless he could show that, for some reason, he did not have "a full and fair chance to litigate the validity of his patent" in the first suit.[24]

COPYRIGHT

The Court has had fewer occasions to consider problems of copyright, which the Constitution authorizes Congress to grant to "authors" for

23. Lear, Inc. v. Adkins, 395 U.S. 653 (1969). *See also* Standard Industries, Inc. v. Tigrett Industries, Inc., 397 U.S. 586 (1970) (dissenting opinion).

24. Blonder-Tongue Laboratories, Inc. v. University of Illinois Foundation, 402 U.S. 313 (1971).

their "writings." But two early decisions sustained action of the Copyright Office in granting copyrights to photographs[25] and to chromolithographs used as circus posters.[26] Congress has also included in the copyright laws musical and dramatic compositions, motion pictures, and "works of art." In the only case involving the issue since he came to the Court—an action for infringement of a copyright on lamp bases in the form of statuettes of male and female dancing figures—Douglas dissented from the refusal of the Court to order argument on the question whether the statuettes were eligible for copyright:[27]

> Is a sculptor an "author" and is his statue a "writing" within the meaning of the Constitution?
>
> The interests involved in the category of "works of art," as used in the copyright law, are considerable. The Copyright Office has supplied us with a long list of such articles which have been copyrighted—statuettes, book ends, clocks, lamps, door knockers, candlesticks, inkstands, chandeliers, piggy banks, sundials, salt and pepper shakers, fish bowls, casseroles, and ash trays. Perhaps these are all "writings" in the constitutional sense. But to me, at least, they are not obviously so.

In other cases Douglas voted with the Court to hold that the copyright grant does not immunize authors and composers who combine to fix license fees from the application of state antitrust laws,[28] and he wrote for the Court to hold that copyrights of motion pictures do not exempt from the Sherman Act combinations among motion picture producers to fix the admission prices charged by exhibitors of their copyrighted films.[29]

25. Burrow-Giles Lithographic Co. v. Sarony, 111 U.S. 53 (1884).

26. Bleistein v. Donaldson Lithographing Co., 188 U.S. 239 (1903).

27. Mazer v. Stein, 347 U.S. 201 (1954).

28. Watson v. Buck, 313 U.S. 387 (1941); Marsh v. Buck, 313 U.S. 406 (1941). *See also* Compco Corp. v. Day-Brite Lighting, Inc., note 13, *supra*, and Sears Roebuck & Co. v. Stiffel Co., note 13, *supra*, where Douglas voted with the Court to hold that state laws against unfair competition may not be applied to prevent copying of uncopyrighted pole lamps and designs for a reflector for fluorescent lighting fixtures.

29. United States v. Paramount Pictures, 334 U.S. 131 (1948).

25 UTILITY RATES

At the turn of the century, in *Smyth v. Ames*,[1] the Court launched a series of decisions reading the doctrine of substantive due process to mean that if a governmental rate-fixing authority fixed a public utility's rates so low as not to permit a "fair return" on the "fair value" of its property, there was an unconstitutional "confiscation" of that property.

For purposes of that doctrine the determination of the "fair value" of the property required a consideration of a variety of factors, including original cost, the cost of permanent improvements, reproduction cost less depreciation, and probable earning capacity. The "fair return" on that base was to be measured by the return customarily paid on investments of a similar nature. Justices Brandeis and Holmes protested this doctrine. They pointed out that the various measures of value which were to be considered were frequently contradictory, and that one of them—earning capacity—led to no result at all since earnings would be determined by the rate fixed. They pointed out also that customary rates of return had little or nothing to do with the total needs of any particular utility. In their view, "The thing devoted by the investor to the public use is not specific property" but the capital "prudently invested" in the enterprise, and on this investment the

1. 169 U.S. 466 (1898).

utility was entitled to a return adequate to pay its costs, including interest on its debt, and dividends on its shares which would reflect returns on similar stock investments.[2]

When, in 1942, a majority of the Court concluded that the provision in the Natural Gas Act authorizing the Federal Power Commission to fix "just and reasonable rates" imposed a test which "coincides with the Constitution" and held that test satisfied by a rate which would return 6 1/2 percent on a reproduction cost base, Douglas joined in a separate concurrence contending: (1) that the Constitution did not authorize the Court to review the reasonableness of rates, (2) while the statute did authorize such review, the Court should "lay the ghost of *Smyth* v. *Ames*" and adopt the views of Brandeis and Holmes.[3]

Two years later Douglas wrote the majority opinion in the *Hope Natural Gas* case that embodied these views:[4]

Rate-making is indeed but one species of price-fixing . . . The fixing of prices, like other applications of the police power, may reduce the value of the property which is being regulated. But the fact that the value is reduced does not mean that the regulation is invalid . . . It does, however, indicate that "fair value" is the end product of the process of rate-making not the starting point . . . The heart of the matter is that rates cannot be made to depend upon "fair value" when the value of the going enterprise depends on earnings under whatever rates may be anticipated . . .

The rate-making process under the Act, i.e., the fixing of "just and reasonable" rates, involves a balancing of the investor and the consumer interests . . . The investor interest has a legitimate concern with the financial integrity of the company whose rates are being regulated. From the investor or company point of view it is important that there be enough revenue not only for operating expenses but also for the capital costs of the business. These include service on the debt and dividends on the stock . . . By that standard the return to the equity owner should be commensurate with returns on investments in other enterprises having corresponding risks. That return, moreover, should

2. Southwestern Bell Telephone Co. v. Public Service Commission, 262 U.S. 276 (1923) (dissenting opinion).

3. Federal Power Commission v. National Gas Pipeline Co., 315 U.S. 575 (1942) (concurring opinion).

4. Federal Power Commission v. Hope Natural Gas Co., 320 U.S. 591 (1946).

be sufficient to assure confidence in the financial integrity of the enterprise, so as to maintain its credit and to attract capital.

That remains the standard for rate-making under the Natural Gas Act,[5] although Douglas has been more insistent than some other members of the Court that the rate-making authority provide an adequate record by which its action can be tested under that standard.[6] He has also expressed the view in dissent that the ICC does not fix a "reasonable" rate under its statutory authority when it fixes a commodity rate for railroads that does not cover the cost of carrying the commodity, even though the complaining railroad does not show a loss on its entire operations.[7]

Congress may, of course, impose additional standards, and has frequently required that the rates be nondiscriminatory. Where such a requirement is imposed, Douglas has been alert to detect rates which discriminate among consumers or against regions and competing forms of service.[8] And he has dissented from approval of a rate order that, in his view, perpetuated a relationship between the utility and a customer which violated the antitrust laws.[9]

He dissented again when a majority construed a section of the Shipping Act requiring Federal Maritime Commission approval of maritime agreements "fixing or regulating transportation rates or fares"

5. Panhandle Eastern Pipe Line Co. v. Federal Power Commission, 324 U.S. 635 (1945); Colorado Interstate Gas Co. v. Federal Power Commission, 324 U.S. 581 (1945); Colorado-Wyoming Gas Co. v. Federal Power Commission, 324 U.S. 626 (1945).

6. Permian Basin Area Rate Cases, 390 U.S. 747 (1968) (dissenting opinion).

7. Baltimore & Ohio Railroad Co. v. United States, 345 U.S. 146 (1953) (dissenting opinion).

8. L. T. Barringer & Co. v. United States, 319 U.S. 1 (1943) (dissenting opinion); ICC v. Inland Waterways Corp., 319 U.S. 671 (1943) (dissenting opinion); United States v. Wabash R.R., 321 U.S. 403 (1944); El Dorado Oil Works v. United States, 328 U.S. 12 (1946) (dissenting opinion); ICC v. Mechling, 330 U.S. 567 (1947); New York v. United States, 331 U.S. 284 (1947); Ayrshire Collieries Corp. v. United States, 335 U.S. 573 (1949); Swift & Co. v. United States, 343 U.S. 373 (1952) (dissenting opinion); Dixie Carriers v. United States, 351 U.S. 56 (1956); Chicago & Eastern Illinois R.R. v. United States, 375 U.S. 150 (1963) (dissenting opinion).

9. Pennsylvania Water & Power Co. v. Federal Power Commission, 343 U.S. 414 (1952) (dissenting opinion).

to apply to a collective bargaining agreement. Under the agreement a longshoremen's union permitted the introduction of labor-saving devices in return for the agreement of an employers organization to create a Mechanization Fund to mitigate the impact upon employees of technological unemployment. The employers determined to raise the fund by assessing shippers a fixed amount per revenue ton:[10]

If the tariff exacted from [shippers] is discriminatory or unreasonable [other sections of the Act] provide a remedy. If it violates the antitrust laws, there is also a remedy . . . But to require the funding part of maritime collective bargaining agreements to receive prior approval from the Maritime Commission is to use a sledge hammer to fix a watch. I cannot . . . attribute to Congress such a heavy-handed management of sensitive labor problems . . .

. . . A collective bargaining agreement is the product of negotiations. How can negotiators sitting at a table arrive at an agreement if they know that a major part of it depends on the approval of the . . . Commission? How many months—or years—will it take to get approval? What will happen meanwhile? Will not the imposition of that kind of administrative supervision bring an end to, or at least partially paralyze, collective bargaining? . . .

. . . To meet the costs increased by any collective bargaining agreement, a company might have to raise its prices and pass at least part of the added cost on to the consumer. But this happens all the time in the maritime industry, as well as in other industries, and does not constitute rate fixing of the type at which the Shipping Act is aimed. There is nothing in the legislative history of the Shipping Act which suggests that [it] gives the FMC the power or license to oversee labor negotiations.

10. Volkswagenwer Aktiengesellschaft v. Federal Maritime Commission, 390 U.S. 261 (1968) (dissenting opinion).

26 BUSINESS ORGANIZATIONS

The structure of business organizations and the powers, rights, and responsibilities of their officers and constituents are for the most part left to state law in our system. Federal law touches these matters only peripherally. But on a few occasions Justice Douglas has had an opportunity to draw upon his academic and SEC experience in this area.[1]

The administration of the federal Bankruptcy Act has provided some opportunities. Prior to the mid-thirties, the reorganization of financially distressed corporations had been undertaken in a loose receivership practice under which the courts had little opportunity to rule on either the feasibility of the reorganization plan or its fairness to public investors and with most aspects of the reorganization being left in the hands of management, its investment bankers, and larger creditors. Douglas had supervised a monumental study of these practices for the SEC[2] and in the 1930's Congress added new provisions to the Bankruptcy Act to remedy old abuses. In a series of opinions written for the Court, he later interpreted those provisions to deal with those abuses. The matter is complicated, but two aspects are of primary importance.

1. For a more detailed account, see R. Jennings, "Mr. Justice Douglas: His Influence on Corporate and Securities Regulation," 73 *Yale L. J.* 920 (1964).

2. SEC, Report on the Study and Investigation of the Work, Activities, Personnel and Functions of Protective and Reorganization Committees, vols. 1-8 (1937-40).

The new laws required the reorganization plan to be feasible. This meant, Douglas said, that the new capital structure of the reorganized company—its stock and its debt—must be based on a valuation of the enterprise. But here, unlike the rule then applicable to rate making, the valuation was to be made by "a capitalization of prospective earnings . . . Findings as to the earning capacity of an enterprise are essential to a determination of . . . feasibility . . . Whether or not the earnings may reasonably be expected to meet the interest and dividend requirements of the new securities is a *sine qua non* to a determination of the integrity and practicability of the new capital structure."[3] "Mr. Justice Brandeis once stated that 'value is a word of many meanings' . . . It gathers its meaning in a particular situation from the purpose for which a valuation is being made. Thus the question in a valuation for rate making is how much a utility will be allowed to earn. The basic question in a valuation for reorganization purposes is how much the enterprise in all probability can earn . . . A basic requirement of any reorganization is the determination of a capitalization which makes it possible . . . to give the new company a reasonable prospect for survival . . . Only 'meticulous regard for earning capacity' . . . can give the new company some safeguards against the scourge of overcapitalization."[4]

The new laws also required the reorganization plan to be "fair and equitable." This term, Douglas wrote, meant that the plan must observe a rule of "absolute priority" in the distribution of the new securities of the organized company. Under this rule there could be no distribution to unsecured creditors until secured creditors were fully compensated in new securities, and no distribution to stockholders until unsecured creditors were fully compensated. This meant, if the corporation was insolvent, that there could be no distribution to its stockholders save and to the extent that they made a new contribution "in money or in money's worth."[5]

Another case arising under the liquidation provisions of the Bankruptcy Act provided an occasion for considering the responsibilities of

3. Consolidated Rock Products Co. v. Du Bois, 312 U.S. 510 (1941).

4. Group of Institutional Investors v. Chicago, Milwaukee, St. Paul & Pacific Railroad Co., 318 U.S. 523 (1943).

5. Case v. Los Angeles Lumber Products Co., 308 U.S. 106 (1939).

corporate management to creditors. The case involved the competing claims of a contract creditor of the bankrupt corporation and of its president, who was also a director and its controlling shareholder, for back salary. Prior to the bankruptcy, the president had used his control of the company to cause it to confess judgment on his claim, thereby enabling him to levy on and sell most of its assets before the other creditor could reach them. Douglas wrote for a unanimous court that this abuse of the president's power would justify disallowance of his claim in the bankruptcy proceeding:[6]

> A director is a fiduciary . . . So is a dominant or controlling stockholder . . . Their powers are powers in trust . . . Their dealings with the corporation are subjected to rigorous scrutiny and where any of their contracts or engagements with the corporation is challenged the burden is on the director or stockholder not only to prove the good faith of the transaction but also to show its inherent fairness from the viewpoint of the corporation and those interested therein . . . That standard of fiduciary obligation is designed for the protection of the entire community of interests in the corporation—creditors as well as stockholders.[7]

Another case, arising under a now-repealed statute imposing on stockholders in national banks a "double liability" (that is, a second assessment of the par value of their stock) where necessary to pay creditors' claims, provided the occasion for Douglas to write for the Court in prescribing a rule of stockholder liability to the creditors of undercapitalized corporations which is of general applicability. The case involved the failure in 1931 of a national bank, all of whose stock was held by the Banco Kentucky Company, which also held the stock of several other banks. The double liability obviously fell on Banco, but it had

6. Pepper v. Litton, 308 U.S. 295 (1939). *See also* his opinion for the Court in Woods v. City Bank, 312 U.S. 263 (1941), denying compensation in a corporate reorganization case to an indenture trustee, a bondholders' committee, and the committee's counsel because of their representation of conflicting interests.

7. For a more detailed examination of Douglas' extensive contribution to the administration of the Bankruptcy Act, see V. Countryman, "Justice Douglas: Expositor of the Bankruptcy Law," 16 *UCLA L. Rev.* 773 (1969); J. Hopkirk, "William O Douglas—His Work in Policing Bankruptcy Proceedings," 18 *Vand. L. Rev.* 663 (1965).

also failed and Douglas found that, in view of its potential liability on the bank stock, liability should be imposed on the stockholders of Banco—both those who had originally held stock of the national bank but had exchanged it for stock in Banco and those who had purchased stock in Banco or who had acquired Banco stock in exchange for stock in other banks:[8]

> It is clear by reason of [an earlier decision] that if a stockholder of the Bank had transferred his shares to his minor children, he would not have been relieved from liability for this assessment . . . One who is legally irresponsible cannot be allowed to serve as an insulator from liability, whether that was the purpose or merely the effect of the arrangement . . . The same result will at times obtain where the transferee is financially irresponsible. This does not mean that every stockholder of a national bank who sells his shares remains liable because his transferee turns out to be irresponsible or impecunious. It is clear that he does not . . . But where after the sale he retains through his transferee an investment position in the bank, including control, he cannot escape the statutory liability if his transferee does not have resources commensurate with the risks of these holdings. In such a case he remains liable as a "stockholder" . . . within the meaning of [the double liability statute] . . . For he retains control and the other benefits of ownership without substituting in his stead anyone who is responsible for the risks of the banking business . . .
>
> . . . By that test it is clear to us that the old stockholders of the Bank are liable. For they retained through Banco their former investment positions in the Bank, including control, and did not constitute Banco as an adequate financial substitute in their stead . . . [Banco's] main assets were stocks in banks, stocks which carried double liability . . . Such an arrangement, if successful, would allow stockholders of banks to retain all of the benefits of ownership without the double liability which Congress had prescribed. The only substitute which depositors of one bank would have for that double liability would be the stock in another bank carrying a like liability. The sensitiveness of one bank in the group to the disaster of another would likely mean that at the only time when double liability was needed the financial responsibility of the holding company as stockholder would be lacking . . .
>
> That is a basis of liability sufficiently broad to include also the stockholders of Banco who had not been stockholders of the Bank . . .

8. Anderson v. Abbott, 321 U.S. 349 (1944).

It seems clear that Banco's stockholders are bound by the decisions of the directors which determined . . . the kind and quality of the corporate undertaking . . . The legality of the investments of Banco's funds . . . falls indeed into the category of acts of directors which normally cannot be challenged by stockholders. These principles, basic in general corporation law, are relevant here as indicating that the stockholders of Banco cannot escape responsibility for the inadequacy of Banco's resources merely because the choice of its investments was made by the officers and directors . . . The fact that they may have claims against an officer or director for mismanagement does not relieve them from liability to the depositors of the subsidiary banks.

Normally the corporation is an insulator from liability on claims of creditors . . . But there are occasions when the limited liability sought to be obtained through the corporation will be qualified or denied. The cases of fraud make up part of that exception. But they do not exhaust it. An obvious inadequacy of capital, measured by the nature and magnitude of the corporate undertaking, has frequently been an important factor in cases denying stockholders their defense of limited liability.

The legislation which Congress has enacted to regulate the issuance of and trading in corporate securities bears on many problems of business structure and responsibility. In many of the cases which have reached the Supreme Court under these laws, Justice Douglas has been disqualified because of his prior involvement in the matter while with the SEC. That was not true in a 1962 case which involved a provision of the Securities Exchange Act designed to deal with the problem of "insider trading"—the corporate officer who takes advantage of knowledge which he has acquired about the company's affairs by speculating in the company's securities on "short swing" transactions. To obviate the difficult problem of proving that such inside knowledge was employed, the Securities Exchange Act provides that where any officer or director purchases and sells, or sells and purchases, shares in his corporation within any period of less than six months, any profit realized shall be recoverable by the corporation.

The case before the Court arose out of the practice of investment banking firms of installing one of their partners on the board of directors of corporations whose securities issues they handle. It involved a firm with partners installed as directors on the boards of one hundred companies. The firm, not the partner-director, had engaged in short swing transactions in stock of one company and had realized profits of nearly $100,000. The Court held that the partner-director was liable for his proportionate share of his firm's profit—about $4,000—but that neither he nor his firm was liable for the balance. Douglas dissented, contending that the firm itself, rather than its partner, should be treated as the "director" on whom the statute imposed liability:[9]

> We forget much history when we give [the statute] a strict and narrow construction. Brandeis in [his book] *Other People's Money* spoke of the office of "director" as "a happy hunting ground" for investment bankers. He said that, "The goose that lays golden eggs has been considered a most valuable possession. But even more profitable is the privilege of taking the golden eggs laid by somebody else's goose. The investment bankers and their associates now enjoy that privilege" . . .
>
> What we do today allows all but one partner to share in the feast which the one places on the partnership table. They in turn can offer feasts to him in the 99 other companies of which they are directors . . . This result is a dilution of the fiduciary principle that Congress wrote into . . . the Act.

Half a century ago in *Eisner v. Macomber*,[10] the Court decided over four dissents, including those of Holmes and Brandeis, that common stock dividends on common stock were not taxable to the stockholder because not "income" to him within the meaning of the Sixteenth Amendment.[11] This decision took the majority into an analysis of

9. Blau v. Lehman, 368 U.S. 403 (1962) (dissenting opinion).

10. 252 U.S. 189 (1920).

11. The original Constitution required that "direct taxes" levied by Congress be apportioned among the states according to population (U.S. Const., Art. I, §2, Cl. 3; Art. I, §9, Cl. 4), and that duties, imports, and excises ("indirect taxes") be uniform throughout the United States (*Id.*, Art. I, §8, Cl. 1). In 1895 the Court held that a federal income tax, as applied to rents from real property and interest from bonds, was a direct tax on the real and personal property and void because not apportioned among the states according to population. Pollock v. Farmers' Loan & Trust Co., 157 U.S. 429 (1895), 158 U.S. 601 (1895). The Sixteenth Amendment, adopted in 1913, provides that Congress may tax "incomes, from whatever source derived," without apportionment among the states according to population.

corporate ownership. Stock dividends, it reasoned, are issued against accumulated corporate profits which, while held by the corporation, represent merely an increase in the value of each stockholder's proportionate interest in the corporation. While this was an "increase in capital," it was not "income" to the stockholder until "severed from the capital." And it was not "severed" by the issuance of stock dividends, since that did not change the stockholder's proportionate interest. He derived no taxable income until he sold the stock he had received as a dividend. A later decision in *Koshland v. Helvering* [12] limited that holding to a case where the stock dividend was on stock of the same kind—a common stock dividend on preferred changed the stockholder's proportionate interest and that was enough to make the dividend taxable income. Thereafter, Congress amended the Internal Revenue Code to define taxable income to include "dividends" but added that a stock dividend should not be so treated "to the extent that it does not constitute income to the shareholder within the meaning of the sixteenth amendment."

In a case arising after this statutory amendment, involving a dividend of common on common, the Court read the statute as accepting, rather than challenging, the *Macomber* decision's interpretation of the Sixteenth Amendment, and held, without reconsidering the constitutional question, that the statute did not make the dividend taxable. Douglas dissented from this reading of the statute to say that stock dividends were taxable only when they "constitute income to the shareholder within the meaning of the Sixteenth Amendment as construed by *Eisner* v. *Macomber*." He thought that the purpose of the statutory formulation was to challenge that decision, and he thought the decision was wrong: [13]

As Mr. Justice Brandeis stated in his dissent in *Eisner* v. *Macomber*, [the Sixteenth Amendment] was designed to include "everything which by reasonable understanding can fairly be regarded as income." Stock dividends representing profits certainly are income in the popular sense. "From a practical commonsense point of view there is something

12. 298 U.S. 441 (1936).
13. Helvering v. Griffiths, 318 U.S. 371 (1943) (dissenting opinion).

strange in the idea that a man may indefinitely grow richer without ever being subject to an income tax." Powell, Income from Corporate Dividends, 35 Harv. L. Rev. 363, 376. The wealth of stockholders normally increases as a result of the earnings of the corporation in which they hold shares. I see no reason why Congress could not treat that increase in wealth as "income" to them . . . The notion that there can be no "income" to the shareholders in such a case within the meaning of the Sixteenth Amendment unless the gain is "severed from" capital and made available to the recipient for his "separate use, benefit and disposal" . . . will not stand analysis. In cases like *Koshland* v. *Helvering* . . . where stock dividends were held to be taxable as income, both the original investment and the accumulations were retained by the company. Yet those cases hold that the stockholders may receive "income" from the operations of their corporation though the corporation makes no distribution of assets to them. Other cases make plain that there may be "income" though neither money nor property has been received by the taxpayer. Benefits accruing as the result of the discharge of the taxpayer's indebtedness or obligations constitute familiar examples. And increases in the value of property as a result of improvements made by the lessee are taxable income to the lessor even though the taxpayer could not "sever the improvement begetting the gain from his original capital" . . . The declaration of a stock dividend normally will not increase the wealth of the stockholders. Its accrual will usually antedate that event. For it is the accumulation of corporate earnings over a period of time which marks any real accrual of wealth to the stockholders. The narrow question here is whether Congress has the power to make the receipt of a stock dividend based on earnings an occasion for recognizing that accrual of wealth for income tax purposes. Congress has done so through the formula of computing the "income" to the stockholders at the "fair market value" of the stock dividends received. Whether that is the most appropriate procedure which could be selected for the purpose may be arguable. But I can see no constitutional reason for saying that Congress cannot make that choice if it so desires.[14]

14. For detailed reviews of Douglas' votes in federal tax cases, see B. Wolfman, J. Silver and M. Silver, "The Behavior of Justice Douglas in Federal Tax Cases," 122 *U. Pa. L. Rev.* 235 (1973); H. Cohn, "Mr. Justice Douglas and Federal Taxation," 45 *Conn. B. J.* 218 (1971).

27 CONSUMERS

The Court has not had many occasions to deal with the problems of consumer protection. The Constitution does not speak directly to that matter, and, until recently, neither Congress nor most state legislatures have been extensively concerned with the consumer. Two federal statutes have provided some cases for the Court in this area, however.[1]

One is the Federal Trade Commission Act, which authorizes the commission to act against "unfair and deceptive acts or practices" in interstate commerce. Under that act, Douglas has voted with the Court to sustain commission action against misleading advertising in the sale of an anti-obesity remedy,[2] against advertising offering one "free" can of paint with every can purchased where the price for one can was the price of two,[3] and against a television commercial for shaving cream which so softened sandpaper that it could instantly be shaved clean—where the "sandpaper" used in the advertisement was made of plexiglass, to which sand had been applied.[4] He also wrote for the Court in a

1. See also Douglas' opinion for the Court upholding provisions in the federal Consumer Credit Protection Act outlawing loan sharking as a valid exercise of the commerce power in Perez v. United States, note 12, p. 317, *supra.* Consumers are also the chief beneficiaries of his opinion for the Court in Sniadach v. Family Finance Corp., note 80, p. 174, *supra,* invalidating under the due process clause a state law allowing a suing creditor to attach the debtor's wages prior to judgment.

2. FTC v. Raladam Co., 316 U.S. 149 (1942).

3. FTC v. Mary Carter Paint Co., 382 U.S. 46 (1965).

4. FTC v. Colgate-Palmolive Co., 380 U.S. 374 (1965).

case sustaining the Commission's finding that the sale under the trade name "Alpacuna" of coats containing alpaca but no vicuna was deceptive. But it was held also that the commission could not prohibit all further use of that name without first considering whether use of it in conjunction with qualifying language would eliminate the deception. Trade names are "valuable business assets" which should not be destroyed "if less drastic means will accomplish the same result."[5]

The other statute is the Food, Drug, and Cosmetic Act, which forbids the shipment or receipt in interstate commerce of adulterated or misbranded food, drugs, cosmetics, or devices. Administration of the act is vested in part in the Food and Drug Administration, forfeiture of offending articles is authorized,[6] and criminal penalties are also prescribed for violators.[7] Douglas has voted with the Court to hold that the shipment of a machine branded "Sinuothermic" is a shipment of a misbranded machine where there was also shipped to the recipient separately a leaflet which made false claims about the machine's curative and therapeutic powers,[8] and to sustain an FDA order forbidding the use of coal-tar coloring on oranges where the coloring had poisonous properties, even though there was no finding that the amount used on the oranges rendered them poisonous.[9] But he dissented when the Court held that a disc used by physicians to test patients' sensitivity to antibiotic drugs was a "drug" subject to governmental testing before marketing rather than a "device" subject to the sanctions against misbranding and adulteration but not to pretesting.[10]

5. Siegel Co. v. FTC, 327 U.S. 608 (1946). Douglas also wrote for the Court to sustain, with some modification, an FTC cease-and-desist order against false labeling under the Fur Products Labeling Act. FTC v. Mandel Bros., Inc., 359 U.S. 385 (1959).

6. Douglas wrote for the Court to hold that multiple forfeitures of offending articles are not unconstitutional. Ewing v. Mytinger & Casselberry, 339 U.S. 594 (1950).

7. Douglas voted with the Court to hold that the criminal penalties are applicable to the officers of corporate offenders as well as to the corporations. United States v. Dotterweich, 320 U.S. 277 (1943). *See also* United States v. Walsh, 331 U.S. 432 (1947); United States v. Sullivan, 332 U.S. 689 (1948).

8. United States v. Urbuteit, 335 U.S. 355 (1948), 336 U.S. 804 (1949). *See also* Kordel v. United States, 335 U.S. 345 (1948).

9. Flemming v. Florida Citrus Exchange, 358 U.S. 153 (1958).

10. United States v. Bacto-Unidisk, 394 U.S. 784 (1969) (dissenting opinion). *Cf.* 62 Cases of Jam v. United States, 340 U.S. 593 (1951) (dissenting opinion).

28 THE POOR

As with consumers, the Constitution does not speak directly to the problems of the poor. But in 1941, when the Court held that one state's efforts to close its borders to the indigent imposed an unconstitutional burden on interstate commerce, Douglas concurred on the different ground that the state's action violated the freedom to travel from state to state, which he viewed as an incident of national citizenship conferred by the Fourteenth Amendment that occupies an even "more protected position in our constitutional system than does the movement of cattle, fruit, steel and coal across state lines."[1] He later voted with the Court to hold that state statutes making it a crime to take pay in advance for work which the taker intends not to perform, and making the failure to perform the work presumptive evidence of the proscribed intent, violate the Thirteenth Amendment's prohibition of involuntary servitude and the federal Anti-Peonage Act.[2] And, as previously indicated, he has dissented from the Court's refusal to review a case involving the constitutionality of a conviction for "vagrancy," since "I do not see how economic or social status can be made a crime."[3]

1. Edwards v. California, 314 U.S. 160 (1941) (concurring opinion).

2. Taylor v. Georgia, 315 U.S. 25 (1942); Pollock v. Williams, 322 U.S. 4 (1944). *See also* Bailey v. Alabama, 219 U.S. 219 (1911).

3. Hicks v. District of Columbia, note 12, p. 298, *supra. See also* Edelman v. California, 344 U.S. 357 (1953) (dissenting opinion).

As previous discussion has indicated, Douglas preceded the Court in concluding that the right to counsel in criminal prosecutions is so vital that, for defendants who cannot afford to retain an attorney, the government is required to provide one.[4] In addition, in a series of decisions in which Douglas joined, the equal protection clause has been construed to mean that where the state provides for those who can afford it certain remedies and procedures in criminal cases which may not be constitutionally required, it must make it possible for the indigent to invoke the same remedies and procedures. These cases originated in 1956 in a decision holding that, where the state provides an appeal from criminal convictions and where a stenographic transcript of the trial is essential to adequate and effective review, the state must provide such a transcript without cost for indigent defendants. "Destitute defendants must be afforded as adequate appellate review as defendants who have money enough to buy transcripts."[5] Subsequent cases have applied this doctrine to a filing fee required for an appeal,[6] to counsel on appeal,[7] to transcripts for appeal from trial court actions denying writs of habeas corpus which challenge the original conviction,[8] to fees for the filing of applications for such writs,[9] and to transcripts of preliminary hearings for use on trial.[10]

Early in 1971, in *Boddie v. Connecticut*, the Court concluded that in at least one sort of civil action the Constitution required free access to

4. See pp. 235-238, *supra*.

5. Griffin v. Illinois, 351 U.S. 12 (1956). *See also* Eskridge v. Washington, 357 U.S. 214 (1958); Williams v. Oklahoma City, 395 U.S. 458 (1969). Douglas also joined with the Court in finding a denial of equal protection where a state provides a transcript for appeal but requires incarcerated prisoners whose appeals are unsuccessful to reimburse it for the cost out of institutional wages, since no similar requirement was imposed on those who received suspended sentences or were placed on probation. Rinaldi v. Yeager, 384 U.S. 305 (1966).

6. Burns v. Ohio, 360 U.S. 252 (1959); Douglas v. Green, 363 U.S. 192 (1960); Draper v. Washington, 372 U.S. 487 (1963). *See also* Coppedge v. United States, 369 U.S. 438 (1962), and Hardy v. United States, 375 U.S. 277 (1964), enforcing an indigent's statutory rights to appeal *in forma pauperis* and to receive a free transcript on appeal in federal criminal prosecutions.

7. Douglas v. California, 372 U.S. 353 (1963).

8. Lane v. Brown, 372 U.S. 477 (1963); Long v. District Court, 385 U.S. 192 (1966). *See also* Gardner v. California, 393 U.S. 367 (1969).

9. Smith v. Bennett, 365 U.S. 708 (1961).

10. Roberts v. LaVallee, 389 U.S. 40 (1967).

the courts for plaintiffs. Indigent welfare mothers must be allowed to bring divorce actions without the payment of filing fees and costs for service of process on their spouses. Since the state had "monopolized" the procedure for "the adjustment of a fundamental human relationship" (unlike other contracts which the parties could voluntarily rescind without resort to the courts), the state denied the women due process of law by "denying them an opportunity to be heard upon their claimed right to a dissolution of their marriages." Douglas concurred, but he would have based the decision on the equal protection clause:[11]

Whatever residual element of substantive law the Due Process Clause may still have . . . it essentially regulates procedure. The Court today puts "flesh" upon the Due Process Clause by concluding that marriage and its dissolution are so important that an unhappy couple who are indigent should have access to the divorce courts free of charge. Fishing may be equally important to some communities. May an indigent be excused if he does not obtain a license which requires payment of money that he does not have? How about a requirement of an onerous bond to prevent summary eviction from rented property? . . . Is housing less important to the mucilege holding society together than marriage? . . . I do not see the length of the road we must follow if we accept [the Court's] invitation. The question historically has been whether the right claimed is "of the very essence of a scheme of ordered liberty." *Palko* v. *Connecticut* . . .[12]

An invidious discrimination based on poverty is adequate for this case. While Connecticut has provided a procedure for severing the bonds of marriage, a person can meet every requirement save court fees or the cost of service of process and be denied a divorce . . .

Thus under Connecticut law divorces may be denied or granted solely on the basis of wealth. Just as denying further judicial review in *Burns*[13] and *Smith*,[14] appellate counsel in *Douglas*,[15] and a transcript in *Griffin*[16] created an invidious distinction based on wealth, so too,

11. Boddie v. Connecticut, 401 U.S. 371 (1971).
12. Note 96, p. 177, *supra.*
13. Note 6, *supra.*
14. Note 9, *supra.*
15. Note 7, *supra.*
16. Note 5, *supra.*

does making the grant or denial of a divorce to turn on the wealth of the parties. Affluence does not pass muster under the Equal Protection Clause for determining who must remain married and who shall be allowed to separate.

Later in the year, the Court agreed to review a case involving an indigent who could not post the bond required to appeal an adverse judgment in a housing eviction case[17] and declined to review another similar case,[18] as well as the cases of indigents who could not pay the filing fee to initiate a bankruptcy proceeding in federal court[19] or the fee to appeal denial of a child guardianship claim,[20] the case of an indigent mother denied court-appointed counsel to contest a state determination that she should be deprived of custody of her children,[21] and a case involving a procedure whereby a tenant defending an eviction action was subjected to penalty of double the rent due if he lost.[22] It also remanded to state courts for reconsideration in the light of its decision in *Boddie* judgments against indigents sustaining a requirement of a fee to file a divorce action but with provision for extensions of time to pay the fee,[23] and a requirement of a fee to appeal denial of a welfare claim.[24] Douglas thought the Court should have taken all of the cases for review.[25]

All [of these cases] except *Kaufman v. Carter*[26] involve people who are denied access to the judicial process solely because of their indigency. *Kaufman* presents a distinctly different problem. There the state commenced a civil suit in 1963, declared petitioner an unfit mother and took five of her seven children away from her. The status of the children is reviewed annually as required by state law. She did not initially seek counsel; but in the 1968 review proceedings, she did.

17. Lindsey v. Normet, 402 U.S. 941 (1971).
18. Beverly v. Scotland Urban Enterprises, Inc., 402 U.S. 936 (1971).
19. *In re* Garland, 402 U.S. 966 (1971).
20. Bourbeau v. Lancaster, 402 U.S. 964 (1971).
21. Kaufman v. Carter, 402 U.S. 964 (1971).
22. Meltzer v. LeCraw, 402 U.S. 954 (1971).
23. Sloatman v. Gibbons, 402 U.S. 939 (1971).
24. Frederich v. Schwartz, 402 U.S. 937 (1971).
25. Meltzer v. LeCraw, note 22, *supra.*
26. Note 21, *supra.*

The State is enforcing its view of proper public policy. That procedure has consequences for the citizen so great that it is hardly an extension to say the rationale of *Douglas* v. *California*[27] . . . demands that she be provided counsel. I would grant centiorari and reverse in this case.

I believe a proper application of the Equal Protection Clause also requires that the access cases be reversed . . . All of these cases contain an invidious discrimination based on poverty . . .

Today's decisions underscore the difficulties with the *Boddie* approach. In *Boddie* the majority found marriage and its dissolution to be so fundamental as to require allowing indigents access to divorce courts without costs. When indigency is involved I do not think there is a hierarchy of interests. Marriage and its dissolution are of course fundamental. But the parent-child relationship is also of sufficient importance to require appointment of counsel when the state initiates and maintains proceedings to destroy it. Similarly obtaining a fresh start in life through bankruptcy proceedings or securing adequate housing[28] and the other procedures in these cases seemingly come within the Equal Protection clause.

Douglas voted with the Court in 1970 when it found a denial of equal protection where an indigent, who received the maximum penalty for his crime of petty theft of one year in jail and a $500 fine, was continued in custody after having served the year because of his inability to pay the fine.[29] But he made clear that he would reach the same conclusion with respect to jailing indigents for their inability to pay fines whether or not the fine is accompanied by a jail term and whether or not the total period of incarceration exceeds the maximum period of imprisonment fixed for the crime.[30] In the following year he

27. Note 7, *supra*.

28. Douglas did not participate in the decision in James v. Valtierra, 402 U.S. 137 (1971), holding that a state does not deny equal protection by subjecting all low-rent housing projects to approval of a majority of the voters. *Cf.* Hunter v. Erickson, note 74, p. 136, *supra*. And he previously dissented from refusals to review cases involving indigents subjected to a requirement of posting bond to appeal from a housing eviction, Simmons v. West Haven Housing Authority, 399 U.S. 510 (1970) (dissenting opinion), or confronted with a procedure whereby they could be summarily evicted without trial unless they posted bond. Williams v. Shaffer, 385 U.S. 1037 (1967) (dissenting opinion).

29. Williams v. Illinois, 399 U.S. 235 (1970).

30. Morris v. Schoonfield, 399 U.S. 508 (1970) (concurring opinion).

voted with the Court to find a denial of equal protection where an indigent with a total of $425 in fines for nine traffic offenses was jailed for 85 days to work them off at $5 per day.[31]

In the same year he dissented from the Court's refusal to review a state decision holding that where the court had appointed a psychiatrist to conduct an examination into defendant's competency to stand trial, the privilege which the state usually extended to a patient to bar a psychiatrist's testimony as to other matters was not available to the defendant because the psychiatrist was a "witness for the court" and no relationship of psychiatrist and patient existed:[32]

> If every court-appointed psychiatrist is only an agent of the state, not a confidant and adviser of the accused, then the potential of using him to deprive the accused of his constitutional rights is great, as evident from *Leyra* v. *Denno*[33] ... In that case a state psychiatrist did what police could not do—"an already physically and emotionally exhausted suspect's ability to resist interrogation was broken to almost trance-like submission by use of the arts of a highly skilled psychiatrist" ...
>
> Would not abolishing the attorney-client privilege for indigents who had court-appointed counsel violate both the Sixth and Fourteenth Amendments? ... If so, why is the psychiatrist-patient privilege different? Can the psychiatrist-patient privilege be constitutionally limited to those with a money relationship? Does "the kind of a trial a man gets depend on the amount of money he has?"

In recent years cases involving the rights of beneficiaries of welfare legislation have also begun to reach the Court, most of them arising under state-administered programs to which the federal government contributes funds so long as the state programs meet federal standards. In these cases Douglas has voted with the Court to hold that a tenant in a federally assisted municipal housing project could not be evicted without the notice and hearing provided by a Department of Housing and Urban Development regulation.[34] He voted with the Court also to

31. Tate v. Short, 401 U.S. 395 (1971).
32. Massey v. Georgia, 401 U.S. 964 (1971) (dissenting opinion).
33. Note 43, p. 162, *supra*.
34. Thorpe v. Housing Authority, 393 U.S. 268 (1969).

hold that, in the absence of proof of actual contribution by a non-adoptive stepfather or a man with whom the mother is living, a state which treated the income of such person as a "resource" of the child in computing the amount of aid to dependent children violated federal regulations issued under the Social Security Act and therefore forfeited its right to federal contributions to its program.[35] And he joined the Court again in holding that a state which disregarded some items of need in computing the amount of such aid similarly violated the act.[36] But he dissented when the Court held that a state which properly considered all items of need could then impose a flat maximum on the total grant to any one family. Since the effect of this practice was to reduce the amount of aid per child in large families and thus to provide an incentive to "farm out" some children with other relatives in order to escape the limitation, he argued that the practice violated the policy of the federal act to keep the children with their mother in their own home.[37]

Douglas voted with the Court to hold that a state denies equal protection of the law by conditioning eligibility for welfare payments on one year's residence.[38] Although the residence requirement might serve to discourage the influx of indigents or of recipients from other states seeking larger benefits, such a basis for classification was held impermissible as an infringement of the constitutional right of citizens to travel from state to state—a right which the Court found to be an established constitutional right, although it did not determine whether it was inherent in national citizenship, as Douglas had earlier contended, or was based on some other constitutional provision. Douglas agreed with the Court also that state welfare programs which exclude aliens entirely, or which exclude aliens who cannot meet a durational

35. Lewis v. Martin, 397 U.S. 552 (1970). The Court had earlier held that a less sophisticated "substitute father" rule, which simply denied aid to dependent children whose mothers had extramarital relations, volated the Social Security Act. Douglas concurred on the ground that the state had denied equal protection, since "the immorality of the mother has no rational connection with the need of her children." King v. Smith, 392 U.S. 309 (1968).

36. Rosado v. Wyman, 397 U.S. 397 (1970) (concurring opinion).

37. Dandridge v. Williams, 397 U.S. 471 (1970) (dissenting opinion).

38. Shapiro v. Thompson, 394 U.S. 618 (1969).

residence requirement, are also invalid, both under the equal protection clause and because of conflict with federal statutes which provide for deportation of aliens who become public charges only if they do so for causes existing at the time they entered the country.[39] He voted with the Court again to hold that a state violates the due process clause of the Fourteenth Amendment when it terminates welfare payments without notice and hearing.[40] The Court later held that a state's practice of suspending unemployment compensation benefits for which an applicant had been found eligible while the former employer appeals an eligibility finding violated a provision of the Social Security Act stating that the benefits must be paid "when due." Douglas concurred, pointing out that the employer's "experience rating," which determines the amount of his contribution to the unemployment fund, was not finally affected until the decision on appeal, so that he had no conceivable due process objection.[41]

39. Graham v. Richardson, 403 U.S. 365 (1971).

40. Goldberg v. Kelly, 397 U.S. 254 (1970); Wheeler v. Montgomery, 397 U.S. 280 (1970). *Cf.* Sniadach v. Family Finance Corp., note 80, p. 174, *supra.*

41. California Dept. of Human Resources Development v. Java, 402 U.S. 121 (1971) (concurring opinion). *Cf.* Sherbert v. Verner, note 21, p. 47, *supra,* where a state's administration of the unemployment compensation program was held to violate the First Amendment's guaranty of religious freedom, and Wyman v. James, note 65, p. 201, *supra,* where Douglas dissented from a holding that a state could deny welfare aid to a recipient who refused to permit a caseworker to visit her home.

29 THE PUBLIC DOMAIN

The federal government owns almost one fifth of the total land area of 1,900 million acres in the continental United States. Part of those federal holdings were ceded to the Union by the states. The balance of the federal lands were acquired by purchase from the states, by purchase or conquest from foreign nations, or by condemnation. As new states were formed from federal territory and admitted to the Union, Congress has traditionally reserved federal ownership of a part of the lands within their boundaries. As a consequence, the United States now owns land in every state. The states have also withheld some lands from private ownership and have reacquired some by purchase or condemnation.

The Constitution, written at a time when public land ownership was already divided between the nation and the states, does not undertake to define their respective boundaries. Those definitions are to be found in state acts of cession, in treaties, in federal acts admitting new states, and in the records of condemnation proceedings.

But these sources are silent as to the ownership of the great areas covered by the coastal seas and the inland waterways. In 1845 the Court decided that, as between the nations and the states, ownership and power to dispose of coastal tidelands between high- and low-water marks belonged to the states as a necessary part of their power to govern local affairs.[1]

1. Pollard's Lessee v. Hagan, 3 How. 212 (1845).

In a series of cases beginning a century later, the Court decided remaining questions involving the power to dispose of submerged coastal lands below the low-water mark. These questions were precipitated by the discovery of oil in some of these lands and the consequent assertion by the coastal states of jurisdiction over the ocean beds for various distances seaward for the purpose of selling drilling rights to private operators. In the first of these cases, California asserted the power to dispose of oil rights three geographical miles seaward from the low-water mark, the three-mile marginal belt being an area generally recognized in international law as a zone over which a nation can exercise broad dominion. Douglas voted with the Court to reject the California claim, finding that the same reasoning which gave the states control over and disposition rights in submerged lands above the low-water mark required that the federal government have similar control over and disposition rights in lands beyond that mark in order to protect itself from external dangers, to conduct its relations with other nations, and to foster and protect foreign commerce.[2] He wrote for the Court to dispose, on similar grounds, of a claim of Lousiana extending into the Gulf of Mexico twenty-seven marine miles beyond the low-water mark,[3] and he wrote for the Court again to reject a Texas claim which reached seaward to the continental shelf. Texas based its claim largely on the fact that it had existed for nine years as an independent republic before admission to the Union. But Douglas pointed out that the federal statute which admitted Texas to the Union, like those admitting California and Louisana, provided for admission "on an equal footing with the original states" and concluded that this "prevents extension of the sovereignty of a State into a domain of political and sovereign power of the United States from which the other States have been excluded just as it prevents a contraction of sovereignty which would produce inequality among the States."[4]

Congress reacted to these decisions with the Submerged Lands Act of 1953, which relinquished to the coastal states all interest in the submerged lands seaward to the states' boundaries as they existed at the

2. United States v. California, 332 U.S. 19 (1947).
3. United States v. Louisiana, 339 U.S. 699 (1950).
4. United States v. Texas, 339 U.S. 707 (1950).

time of admission to the Union, but not to exceed three geographical miles into the ocean or three marine leagues (nine nautical miles) into the Gulf of Mexico—subject to federal regulation for purposes of "commerce, navigation, national defense and international affairs."

When the Court upheld this act as a valid exercise of the power of Congress under the Constitution to "dispose of . . . the Territory or other Property belonging to the United States,"[5] Douglas dissented:[6]

The entire point of the earlier litigation . . . was that more than property rights was involved. As we said in *United States* v. *Texas*[7] . . . "once low-water mark is passed the international domain is reached. Property rights must then be so subordinated to political rights as in substance to coalesce and unite in the national sovereign." Any "property interests" which the states may *earlier* have held in the bed of the marginal sea were "so subordinated to the right of sovereignty as to follow sovereignty" . . .

It is said, however, that the interests in the marginal sea may be chopped up, the State being granted the economic ones and the Federal Government keeping the political ones. We rejected, however, that precise claim in the earlier cases. We said, for example, that the "equal footing" clause in the Joint Resolution admitting Texas to the Union precluded the argument that Texas surrendered only political rights over the marginal sea and retained all property rights.

If it were necessary for Texas to surrender all her property and political rights in the marginal sea in order to enter the Union on an "equal footing" with the other states, pray how can she get back some of those rights and still remain on an "equal footing" with the other States? . . . The "equal footing" clause, in other words, prevents one State from laying claim to a part of the national domain from which the other States are excluded.

In later decisions interpreting the Submerged Lands Act, Douglas has voted with the Court to hold that the claims of Alabama, Louisiana, and Mississippi extend three geographical miles into the Gulf of Mexico and the claims of Florida extend three marine leagues into the Gulf. But he has dissented from the further holding that the claims of Texas likewise extend three marine leagues into the Gulf, contending that

5. U.S. Const., Art. 4, §3, Cl. 2.
6. Alabama v. Texas, 347 U.S. 272 (1954) (dissenting opinion).
7. Note 4, *supra*.

Texas had not established that her boundaries had ever extended so far.[8] He dissented also from a decision defining California's claim below the low-water mark because he thought the Court had not given California an adequate opportunity to establish its historic boundaries.[9]

Another area of the public domain with which the Court has been much concerned consists of the great navigable rivers of the country. Here it has long been recognized that ownership of the river beds, like ownership of submerged coastal lands above low-water mark and, since 1953, for some distance below that mark, was vested in the states.[10] But it has also been recognized that this ownership is subject to federal regulation in the exercise of the commerce power.[11]

Prior to 1940 the Court had not recognized that the commerce power could be exercised in this connection for any purpose other than the promotion of navigation.[12] But in that year, in a decision in which Douglas joined,[13] the Court sustained provisions in the Federal Power Act which required private concerns who wished to construct power plants on navigable streams to obtain licenses from the Federal Power Commission. In so doing, it approved of a congressional definition of "navigable waters" as those which either were or by reasonable improvements could be made navigable. It also approved of statutory conditions on the license which were not related to navigation and rejected the notion that the commerce power was "limited to control for navigation."[14] That power might also be used, the Court said, for

8. United States v. Louisiana, 363 U.S. 1 (1960) (dissenting in part); United States v. Florida, 363 U.S. 121 (1960). *See also* United States v. Louisiana, 394 U.S. 1, 11 (1969).

9. United States v. California, 381 U.S. 139 (1965) (dissenting opinion). In other cases of congressional dispositions not raising constitutional issues, Douglas twice voted with and once wrote for the Court to hold that federal grants of rights of way to railroads did not include mineral rights. Great Northern Ry. Co. v. United States, 315 U.S. 262 (1942); United States v. Union Pacific R.R. Co., 353 U.S. 112 (1957).

10. Barney v. Keokuk, 94 U.S. 324 (1877).

11. Gibson v. United States, 166 U.S. 269 (1897).

12. The Court adhered to that concept but invoked the war power also (future production of munitions) to uphold the creation of the Tennessee Valley Authority. Ashwander v. TVA, 297 U.S. 288 (1936).

13. United States v. Appalachian Electric Power Co., 311 U.S. 377 (1940).

14. Instances of control for navigation still arise. *See* Douglas' opinion for the Court in United States v. Republic Steel Corp., 362 U.S. 482 (1960), construing a

flood protection and watershed development. And the water power which was developed as an inevitable incident of any of these uses was likewise subject to federal control. Thereafter, Douglas wrote for the Court to uphold the power of the United States to construct a multiple-purpose flood control, navigation, and power project on the non-navigable tributary of a navigable river.[15]

But he dissented when a majority held that Congress had not withdrawn the Roanoke Rapids power site from the authority of the FPC to license it to private concerns by authorizing its development by the federal government. While recognizing that "Congress in the Federal Power Act left part of the public domain to be exploited by private interests, if the Federal Power Commission so orders," he thought it perfectly clear that Congress meant to withdraw the Roanoke site for federal development "when conditions warranted . . . and budgetary requirements permitted":[16]

The true character of this raid on the *public domain* is seen when Roanoke Rapids is viewed in relation to the other projects in the comprehensive plan [approved by Congress]. Roanoke Rapids is the farthest downstream of the eleven units in the plan. Upstream from Roanoke Rapids is Buggs Island (now under construction with federal funds) with an ultimate installed capacity of 204,000 kw. and a controlled reservoir capacity of over 2,500,000 acre-feet. Roanoke Rapids is indeed the powerhouse of the Buggs Island Reservoir. That reservoir increases the dependable capacity of Roanoke Rapids from 4 hours during the peak month of December to 288 hours in the same peak month. Buggs Island contributes 70,000,000 kw.-hr. to the Roanoke Rapids project. There is evidence that this energy will have a value in excess of $700,000 a year.

That $700,000 of value is created by the taxpayers of this country. Though it derives from the investment of federal funds, it will now be appropriated by private power groups for their own benefits. The master plan now becomes clear: the Federal Government will put up

federal statute controlling the creation of any "obstruction" in navigable rivers to apply to the discharge into such rivers of industrial solids which reduce the depth of the channel.

15. Oklahoma v. Atkinson Co., 313 U.S. 508 (1941). *See also* his opinion for the Court in United States v. Grand River Dam Authority, 363 U.S. 229 (1960).

16. United States v. Chapman, 348 U.S. 153 (1953) (dissenting opinion).

the auxiliary units—the unprofitable ones; and the private power interests will take the plums—the choice ones.

One recent case in this area has involved the possible application of the National Environmental Policy Act of January 1970. That act requires that every federal agency shall include in every recommendation for "major federal actions significantly affecting the quality of the human environment" a detailed study of, among other things, any adverse environmental effects, possible alternatives to the proposed action, and "any irreversible and irretrievable commitment of resources which would be involved in the proposed action." The case arose out of efforts of citizens of San Antonio, unsuccessful in lower federal courts, to enjoin federal funding of the construction of a state highway through a public park in that city. At the time of suit, the secretary of transportation had only approved, and proposed to begin funding construction on, two segments of the highway entering the park from the north and south. He had not yet approved a connecting middle section. But he contended that his approval of these two segments had occurred in 1969 so that compliance with the 1970 act was not required. When the Court declined to review the case, Douglas dissented.[17]

The Solicitor General contends that the two end segments were approved in 1969. But the facts are that while Secretary Volpe gave preliminary approval of these segments [in December 1969], he withheld authorization of federal funds pending an agreement by the state to study further the middle segment . . . Texas agreed to the end segments [in August 1970] and the Secretary gave his "unqualified approval" and authorization of them [in August 1970], long after the new Act became effective . . .

The legal questions posed by [the act] include at least the following:

Should any piece of the park be destroyed to accommodate a freeway?

How can end segments of a highway aimed at the heart of a park he approved without appraising the dangers of drawing a dotted line between the two segments?

17. Named Individual Members of San Antonio Conservation Society v. Texas Highway Department, 400 U.S. 968 (1971).

How important is the park to the people of San Antonio? How many use it? For what purposes? What wildlife does it embrace? To what extent will a massive eight and six-lane highway decrease the value of the park as a place of solitude or recreation?

What are the alternatives that would save the park completely? Could a passage by way of tunnels be devised? Could the freeway be relocated so as to avoid the parkland completely and leave it as a sanctuary?

Is not the ruination of a sanctuary created for urban people an "irreversible and irretrievable loss" within the meaning of [the act]?

I do not think we will have a more important case this Term. Congress has been moving with alarm against the perils to the environment. One need not be an expert to realize how awful the consequences are when urban sanctuaries are filled with structures, paved with concrete or asphalt, and coverted into thoroughfares of highspeed modern traffic.

. . . If one thing is clear from the legislative history of this 1970 Act, it is that Congress has resolved that it will not allow federal agencies or federal funds to be used in a predatory manner so far as the environment is concerned. Congress has, indeed, gone further and said that the Department of Transportation, like other federal agencies, may no longer act as engineers alone and design and construct freeways solely by engineering standards. Congress has said that ecology has become paramount and that nothing must be done by federal agencies which does ecological harm where there are alternative, albeit more expensive, ways of achieving the result.[18]

Another recent case was an effort by the state of Ohio to invoke the Court's original jurisdiction[19] in a suit against a Michigan and a Delaware corporation and the Canadian subsidiary of one of them to enjoin them from dumping mercury into streams flowing into Lake Erie and thus polluting the lake. The Court declined to exercise its jurisdiction

18. Douglas did not participate in a later similar decision which remanded the case for an inquiry by the trial court into whether the secretary of transportation had complied with other statutes providing that highways are not to be constructed through parks unless the secretary determines that there "is no feasible and prudent alternative" and then only if the project "includes all possible planning to minimize harm" to the park. Citizens to Preserve Overton Park v. Volpe, 401 U.S. 402 (1971).

19. Under U.S. Const., Art. III, §2, Cl. 1, the federal judicial power extends to controversies between a state and citizens of another state or foreign citizens. And by Art. III, §2, Cl. 2, in all cases in which a state is a party the Supreme Court has original jurisdiction.

because many issues of local law were involved. Other state, federal, and international agencies were dealing with this and larger pollution problems, and the case presented complicated problems of taking evidence with which the Court was ill-equipped to deal. Douglas dissented:[20]

This litigation, as it unfolds, will of course implicate much federal law. The case will deal with an important portion of the federal domain—the navigable streams and the navigable inland waters which are under the sovereignty of the Federal Government . . .

Congress has enacted numerous laws reaching that domain. One of the most pervasive is the Rivers and Harbors Act of 1899 [which, among other things,] forbids discharge of "any refuse matter of any kind or description whatever other than that flowing from streets and sewers and passing therefrom in a liquid state" . . .

In the 1930's fish and wildlife legislation was enacted granting the Secretary of the Interior various heads of jurisdiction over the effects on fish and wildlife of "domestic sewage, mine, petroleum, and industrial wastes, erosion, silt, and other polluting substances" . . .

Since that time other changes have been made in the design of the federal system of water control. The Federal Water Pollution Control Act [of 1948] gives broad powers to the Secretary to take action respecting water pollution on complaints of states and other procedures to secure federal abatement of the pollution . . . The National Environmental Policy Act of . . . 1970 . . . gives elaborate ecological directions to federal agencies and supplies procedures for their enforcement . . .

There is much complaint that in spite of the arsenal of federal power little is being done. That of course is not our problem. But it is our concern that state action is not prempted by federal law . . . There is not a word in federal law that bars state action . . .

If in these original actions we sat with a jury . . . there would be powerful arguments for abstention in many cases. But the practice has been to appoint a Special Master which we certainly would do in this case. We could also appoint—or authorize the Special Master to retain—a panel of scientific advisers. The problems in this case are simple compared with those [in other cases brought as original actions in the Supreme Court involving apportionment of waters of inland waterways among various states]. It is now known that metallic mercury deposited

20. Ohio v. Wyandotte Chemicals Corp., 401 U.S. 493 (1971) (dissenting opinion).

in water is often transformed into a dangerous chemical. This law suit would determine primarily the extent, if any, to which the defendants are contributing to that contamination at the present time. It would determine, secondarily, the remedies within reach—the importance of mercury in the particular manufacturing processes, the alternative processes available, the need for a remedy against a specific polluter as contrasted to a basin-wide regulation and the like.

The problem, though clothed in chemical secrecies, can be exposed by the experts. It would indeed be one of the simplest problems yet posed in the category of cases under the head of our original jurisdiction.

30 PRIVATE PROPERTY

The Fifth Amendment provides that "private property" shall not "be taken for public use, without just compensation," a limitation long ago held applicable to the states under the Fourteenth Amendment.[1] This has raised for the Court questions, among others, as to what is "private property," when is it "taken" by government, and what is a "public purpose?"[2]

Douglas first wrote for the Court on one of these issues in a case where the TVA had condemned 12,000 of 22,000 acres of land privately owned by one who had also been given powers of eminent domain by the state, which would entitle him to condemn lands for a power site, and who had plans to exercise that power to acquire another 22,000 acres and then to construct a private power system. There was no question that he was entitled to compensation for the 12,000 acres taken, and the owner did not assert that those acres alone had value as a power site. But he contended that, in view of his powers and expectations, the award should include the water power value of those acres when combined with acreage not yet acquired. Douglas rejected that conclusion:[3]

1. Chicago, Burlington & Quincy R. Co. v. Chicago, 166 U.S. 226 (1897).

2. On the additional question of what is "just compensation," see Douglas' concurring opinion in United States v. General Motors Corp., 323 U.S. 373 (1945).

3. United States v. Powelson, 319 U.S. 266 (1943).

It is "private property" which the Fifth Amendment declares shall not be taken for public use without just compensation. The power of eminent domain can hardly be said to fall in that category. It is not a personal privilege; it is a special authority impressed with a public character and to be utilized for a public end. An award based on the value of that privilege would be an appropriation of public authority to a wholly private end. The denial of such an award to the landowner does no injustice. It is true that respondent's possession of the power of eminent domain was in part the basis of an opportunity to unite the present lands with others into a power project. But he is not being deprived of values which result from his expenditures or activities.

Douglas has also voted with the Court to hold that a riparian owner has no "private property" rights in the water power of a navigable stream which entitle him to compensation under the Fifth Amendment when his lands are condemned by the federal government,[4] and he has dissented when he thought the majority was disregarding that principle.[5] He also dissented when he thought the Court failed to apply the same principle where the condemnation was by a state.[6]

On the question of the "taking" of property, Douglas wrote for the Court to hold that the United States had taken property of a chicken farmer where the glide path of planes taking off and landing at a military base brought them within 83 feet of the surface of his property, causing many of his chickens to kill themselves by flying into the walls from fright and curtailing the egg production of the survivors. Although he agreed that the United States had, in the Civil Aeronautics Act, properly asserted complete and exclusive national sovereignty in the air space, that was not the end of the matter:[7]

4. United States v. Twin City Power Co., 350 U.S. 222 (1956).

5. United States v. Kansas City Life Ins. Co., 339 U.S. 799 (1950) (dissenting opinion); FPC v. Niagara Mohawk Power Co., 347 U.S. 239 (1954) (dissenting opinion). *See also* United States v. Gerlack Live Stock Co., 339 U.S. 725 (1950) (concurring opinion).

6. Grand River Dam Authority v. Grand Hydro, 335 U.S. 359 (1948) (dissenting opinion).

7. United States v. Causby, 328 U.S. 256 (1946). Douglas wrote for the Court again in a similar case finding a taking by a county where planes taking off and landing at its airport rendered adjoining property completely uninhabitable. Griggs v. Allegheny County, 369 U.S. 85 (1962).

It is ancient doctrine that at common law ownership of the land extended to the periphery of the universe. But that doctrine has no place in the modern world. The air is a public highway, as Congress has declared. Were that not true, every transcontinental flight would subject the operator to countless trespass suits . . .

But that general principle does not control the present case. For the United States conceded on oral argument that if the flights over respondents' property rendered it uninhabitable, there would be a taking compensable under the Fifth Amendment . . .

We agree that in those circumstances there would be a taking . . . [There would] be a definite exercise of complete dominion and control over the surface of the land. The fact that the planes never touched the surface would be irrelevant. The owner's right to possess and exploit the land—that is to say, his beneficial ownership of it—would be destoryed . . .

There is no material difference between the supposed case and the present one, except that here enjoyment and use of land are not completely destroyed. But that does not seem to us to be controlling. The path of glide for airplanes might reduce a valuable factory site to grazing land, an orchard to a vegetable patch, a residential section to a wheat field. Some value would remain. But the use of the airspace immediately above the land would limit the utility of the land and cause a diminution in its value . . .

We have said that the airspace is a public highway. Yet it is obvious that if the landowner is to have full enjoyment of the land, he must have exclusive control of the immediate reaches of the enveloping atmosphere. Otherwise buildings could not be erected, trees could not be planted, and even fences could not be run . . . The landowner owns at least as much of the space above the ground as he can occupy or use in connection with the land.

Douglas has also voted with the Court to hold that there is a temporary taking entitling the owner to recover operating losses attributable to government operation where the president, acting pursuant to statute during a time of declared war, takes possession of coal mines to avert a national strike.[8] And he dissented when a majority found no taking where the United States Army, during World War II, destroyed privately owned oil storage tanks in Manila in order to keep them from falling into the hands of the enemy.[9] But he wrote for the Court to

8. United States v. Peewee Coal Co., 341 U.S. 114 (1951).
9. United States v. Caltex, 344 U.S. 149 (1952) (dissenting opinion).

hold that there was no compensable taking where the United States built a multiple-purpose dam on the tributary of a navigable stream and thus frustrated the plans of a state to expand a state project further upstream on the tributary, distinguishing between a taking of property and "the frustration of an enterprise by reason of the exercise of a superior governmental power."[10]

The question of public use was raised in an action challenging a federal slum clearance project for the District of Columbia, which contemplated condemnation of an entire area and the leasing or selling of it to private parties who would clear it and construct housing, business, and public buildings according to a federal plan. The owners of a department store in the area sought to enjoin condemnation of their property, contending that, since it was commercial property rather than slum housing, and since the new project was to be developed by private parties, the condemnation would not be for a public use. Writing for the Court, Douglas rejected this argument:[11]

The power of Congress over the District of Columbia includes all the legislative powers which a state may exercise over its affairs. We deal, in other words, with what traditionally has been known as the police power . . .

Public safety, public health, morality, peace and quiet, law and order—these are some of the more conspicuous examples of the traditional application of the police power to municipal affairs. Yet they merely illustrate the scope of the power and do not delimit it. Miserable and disreputable housing conditions may do more than spread disease and crime and immorality. They may also suffocate the spirit by reducing the people who live there to the status of cattle. They may indeed make living an almost insufferable burden. They may also be an ugly sore, a blight on the community, which robs it of charm, which makes it a place from which men turn. The misery of housing may despoil a community as an open sewer may ruin a river.

We do not sit to determine whether a particular housing project is or is not desirable. The concept of the public welfare is broad and inclusive. The values it represents are spiritual as well as physical, aesthetic as well as monetary. It is within the power of the legislature to

10. United States v. Grand River Dam Authority, 363 U.S. 229 (1960).
11. Berman v. Parker, 348 U.S. 26 (1954).

determine that the community should be beautiful as well as healthy, spacious as well as clean, well-balanced as well as carefully patrolled . . . If those who govern the District of Columbia decide that the Nation's Capital should be beautiful as well as sanitary, there is nothing in the Fifth Amendment that stands in the way.

. . . Appellants argue that [the plan contemplates] a taking from one business man for the benefit of another business man. But the means of executing the project are for Congress and Congress alone to determine, once the public purpose has been established. The public end may be as well or better served through an agency of private enterprise than through a department of government—or so the Congress might conclude. We cannot say that public ownership is the sole method of promoting the public purposes of community redevelopment projects . . .

The rights of these property owners are satisfied when they receive that just compensation which the Fifth Amendment exacts as the price of the taking.

Although Douglas has been willing to give a generous reading to Congress' power to condemn private property for a public purpose, he has also insisted that those carrying out congressional enactments confine themselves to the purposes authorized by Congress. Thus, he dissented from the Court's refusal to review the action of the Army Corps of Engineers, which had obtained authority from Congress to condemn approximately 6,200 acres of land near Fort Worth, Texas, to build a dam 702 feet high with a storage capacity of 208,850 acre-feet of water, and had then proceeded to condemn more than 13,000 acres of land to build a 747-foot dam with a storage capacity of more than 410,000 acre feet. The trial court had found that much of the land had been taken for recreational purposes and that such taking was not authorized by Congress, which had authorized the taking "for navigation, flood control, and allied purposes." The court of appeals concluded that recreational development was an "allied purpose" and hence authorized and that the enlarging modifications of the original project were proper. Douglas thought that the latter decision should be reviewed:[12]

12. 2,606.84 Acres of Land v. United States, 402 U.S. 916 (1971) (dissenting opinion).

Justification for the excess land was necessary. The District Court found that to accomplish this, the Corps created the Great Storm and used their Great Storm as a basis for their spillway design on the dam as built. It is said that the storm will indeed be great, if it ever comes, dumping some 28.2 inches of rain in the area within a 60-hour period. The likelihood of this happening is said not to be high. Average annual rainfall in the area is 31.3 inches. The greatest storm ever recorded there dropped 12.57 inches in a 57-hour period . . .

But even with the Great Storm, record breaking though it would be, the District Court found that the Corps could not justify the height of the spillway necessary to obtain the land it wanted for recreational purposes. But one Great Storm deserves another and that, it is said, is what the Corps postulated. The Great Storm was assumed to come right after another big storm had dropped large amounts of rain in the area, thus preventing any opening of the dam gates. Furthermore, none of the spillway design criteria made any allowance for the well-established reservoir management practice of lowering the level of water during potential flood months. And large floods have occurred during only three months of the year in the Fort Worth area . . .

Finally, we do not know to what use the [excess] land has been put. If there is no development yet, what are the current plans? The National Environment Policy Act . . . requires environmental impact statements for proposed projects. So far as we are advised, no such statement has been filed.[13]

13. See also Douglas' dissent from the Court's refusal to review a case where it was alleged that the United States had approved, and provided federal assistance for, a highway through Charleston, West Virginia, without requiring the state to provide relocation assistance to displaced persons as mandated by the Federal Aid Highway Act of 1968. Triangle Improvement Council v. Ritchie, 402 U.S. 497 (1971) (dissenting opinion).

EPILOGUE: ON JUDGING A JUDGE

How does one judge the performance of a judge or, more specifically, of a justice of the Supreme Court? Much nonsense has been uttered on this question and much of it originated from those who ought to know better. Most of this nonsense has focused on one or both of two misleading formulations.

The better Supreme Court Justice, we are told by some including President Nixon, is the "strict constructionist" of the Constitution. But who are the strict constructionists of the First Amendment—Justice Douglas, who reads "no law" to mean *no* law abridging freedom of speech or press, or those justices who read it to mean no law except a law which they find permissible after "balancing" public against private interests? Are the strict constructionists Justice Douglas and those with him who read the Fourteenth Amendment to incorporate all of the guarantees of the Bill of Rights, or those justices who read it as incorporating only those Bill of Rights guarantees "implicit in the concept of ordered liberty"? Or had all of the strict constructionists departed before 1897 when the Court held, without dissent on this point, that the Fourteenth Amendment incorporated the Fifth Amendment's guarantee that private property would not be taken for public use without just compensation? Obviously, "strict constructionist" is not a useful concept for evaluating, or even comparing, judicial performance.

A second formulation for distinguishing the bad justices from the good is to differentiate the "activists" from those who practice that noblest of virtues, "judicial self-restraint." But here again, perplexities abound as one attempts to apply the test. Is judicial self-restraint being practiced by Justice Douglas when he protests that the Court should stay out of the business of carving exceptions in the First Amendment to permit the suppression of obscenity, or by those justices who forged ahead with a bewildering variety of tests on which no majority could agree? Were the "activists" those Justices who created the doctrine of licensee estoppel to prevent a patent licensee from challenging the validity of his licensor's patent, or Justice Douglas and those with him who objected that the way should be left open for the person usually most interested and qualified to protect the public against invalid patent grants? This test, like the "strict constructionist" test, leads nowhere for the very good reason that it describes no working principle for judging. It is doubtful that there was ever in the history of the Court a single justice who consistently approached the cases before him with a view to adhering to, or rejecting, a policy of strict construction or of judicial self-restraint.

How, then, are we to evaluate a justice's performance? What are we entitled to expect and by what standards are we to measure performance against our expectations? At a minimum we are entitled to expect—of a justice and of the president who appoints him—that the justice possess a high degree of technical competence. This test Justice Douglas passes with surpassing ease, as many of those with whom he is in frequent disagreement would freely concede—including the late Justice Harlan, himself a superbly skilled lawyer.

True, a small quibble would be entered by some of the more fastidious students of the Court who do not like Douglas' judicial style. His opinions lay bare the issues, come quickly to the point, and dispose of the case in language that is frequently blunt and bold. Those who favor the elaborate formulation and the elegant phrase are offended when Justice Douglas writes that the purpose of the Bill of Rights is to "keep the government off the backs of the people." At an earlier time, some of these critics were inclined to the view that Justice Douglas' approach led him frequently into error. Today, many of them would complain only that he has reached the right conclusion by the wrong route.

Beyond the question of technical ability, we are entitled to expect—of the justice and of the president who appoints him—that the justice not be a captive of any narrow interest group, that he be capable of approaching his task of interpreting the Constitution and laws of the United States in the spirit of the Preamble of the Constitution: "in Order to form a more perfect Union, establish Justice, insure domestic Tranquility, provide for the common defence, promote the general Welfare, and share the Blessings of Liberty" for the people of the United States and their posterity. No responsible critic would fault Justice Douglas on this score.

We are also entitled to expect of any justice that he apply himself diligently and conscientiously to his duties. Here again, Justice Douglas passes the test with flying colors. He has always done more than his share of the Court's work.

If these expectations are met, our judgment of the performance of a justice will vary according to our own predelictions. Just as we differ in our views on the sort of society we want and on the role we want the government to play, so will the justices differ in their views as to how they should resolve the issues that come before them.

In this respect, Justice Douglas has built a record on which he may be judged. He reads the Constitution to confer broad powers on government to regulate the economy. That view would be challenged by few today, but Douglas is more consistent and persistent than most in also reading government's economic regulation broadly to limit private power to control the economy.

But, while he is willing to read governmental powers, and the exercise of those powers, broadly, he also reads broadly those constitutional guarantees that require the government to proceed fairly—whether the one against whom the government is proceeding is an accused in the criminal dock, a suspected "subversive" before a loyalty board or a legislative committee, a government contractor, or a voting registrar suspected by the Civil Rights Commission of depriving blacks of the franchise.

He is equally vigorous in giving full scope to the Constitution's substantive limits on governmental power, particularly those provisions of the Bill of Rights designed to protect the franchise and political and religious freedom and to insure equal protection of the laws.

Indeed, if we hazard the quite plausible guess that President Nixon had in mind Justice Douglas and those who were voting with him when Nixon announced his intention to staff the Supreme Court with "strict constructionists," it may fairly be concluded that what Nixon was seeking was "niggardly constructionists" of the Bill of Rights. Although Nixon has now had four of his six nominees to the Court confirmed, he has not fully succeeded in his objective, however it may be expressed. Confirmed strict or niggardly constructionists are not easy to come by and some men's prior records provide a poor basis for reliable prediction of their performance after elevation to the Supreme Court, as President Theodore Roosevelt learned with Justice Holmes and President Eisenhower learned with Chief Justice Warren.

But Nixon has succeeded to the point that Justice Douglas' views will not in the near future prevail in many of the important cases which will come before the Court. Many will rate Justice Douglas among the great Supreme Court Justices on the basis of his record to date. Others not now willing to do so may change their minds after more experience with the new regime.

TABLE OF CASES AND INDEX

TABLE OF CASES

INDEX